GALLANT LADY

GALLANT

Ken Henry and Don Keith

A TOM DOHERTY ASSOCIATES BOOK
NEW YORK

LADY

A Biography of the USS *Archerfish*

Book design by Milenda Nan Ok Lee

A Forge Book
Published by Tom Doherty Associates, LLC
175 Fifth Avenue
New York, NY 10010

www.tor.com

Forge® is a registered trademark of Tom Doherty Associates, LLC.

Library of Congress Cataloging-in-Publication Data

Keith, Don, 1947–
    Gallant lady / Don Keith and Ken Henry.—1st ed.
        p. cm.
    ISBN 0-765-30568-2
    EAN 978-0765-30568-8
    1. Archerfish (Submarine)—History. I. Henry, Ken. II. Title.

VA65.A57K45 2004
359.9'33'0973—dc22

                                                                    2003069460

First Edition: June 2004

Printed in the United States of America

0 9 8 7 6 5 4 3 2 1

For every man who has pinned on the dolphins,
and for their families,
whose sacrifice also deserves notice

CONTENTS

CONTENTS

I remember once as we sailed down Tokyo Bay with the homeward-bound pennant flying, I involuntarily patted her on the side and I swear she responded with a shudder from within. *Archerfish*, as I know her—and I know her well—is a fine woman. But I know her to be a great and gallant lady, and I shall always remember her just that way, the way she was.

—Former *Archerfish* Commanding Officer,
Commander Robert B. (Scotty) McComb,
at her decommissioning ceremony in
San Diego, May 1, 1968

PREFACE

THE archerfish, found in the islands between Australia and India, does not appear to be all that different from any other fish. Once you learn more about it, though, you find it is quite a unique critter. This adept predator has the ability to hover just beneath the surface of the water as it watches its prey sitting on a stem or branch above. It waits patiently for just the right moment. When it's ready, it spits a jet of high-pressure water, stunning its victim, knocking it from its perch. It then devours it and moves on in search of other quarry.

Archerfish was an apt name for a submarine. A sub also has the ability to lurk beneath the ocean's surface, patiently stalk its prey, then sneak up and shoot. But it's an especially appropriate name for one particular sub.

The USS *Archerfish* (SS-311) didn't look any different than many of the other diesel-powered, *Balao*-class submarines that were being hastily assembled and launched in the Portsmouth Naval Shipyard during World War II. She was about the same size, had the same engines, and was equipped with the same weapons as most of her class. She carried the same complement of crew and, at least in her first commissioning, had similar missions assigned to her as did her sisters that were being constructed in Portsmouth at that same time.

Once you learn more about this rather unusual boat, though, you'll see that the comparison to other submarines ends there.

Like Forrest Gump or Woody Allen's Zelig, *Archerfish* had a knack for edging herself into the frame whenever history was being photographed. Her war record was not that remarkable, yet she had the distinction of sinking the largest ship ever sent to the bottom by a submarine. When the Japanese surrendered, there was *Archerfish*, proudly sitting in Tokyo Harbor, her crew sipping "Tokyo Bay joy juice" (a mixture of grapefruit juice and medical alcohol) in celebration. She sat out most of the Korean War and, so far as we know, never played a single game of "blind man's bluff" with the Russians during the cold war. Still, her supersecret mission during that period probably contributed as much to the end of the stare-down with the Soviet Union as anything else did. It was some of the members of *Archerfish*'s crew who had a close encounter with Fidel Castro's guerrillas when the revolutionaries came down from the mountains of Cuba near Guantánamo Bay. Then several other *Archerfish* sailors were there to party with Castro's men when they claimed Havana on New Year's Day, 1959. When a pair of divers set the record for the longest buoyant free ascent from the ocean's bottom, it was *Archerfish* who regurgitated those two brave men and sent them on their impossibly long float to the surface. And with her role in the successful experiment, she gave new hope to submariners everywhere that they might survive a catastrophic accident aboard their boats. One day, while routinely doing her job, it was *Archerfish* who glided over and documented the deepest trench yet found in the Atlantic Ocean.

Like their boat, *Archerfish*'s crew was a reasonably good metaphor for all the others who rode in diesel submarines. At first glance, they were no different from any of the brave men who have become submariners down through history, who have chosen to serve their country in the cramped, claustrophobic confines of a boat that's actually designed to sink. They were sons of fishermen and sailors, but they were also sons of steelworkers and dirt farmers and big-city cops. They came from cities near the ocean, where they grew up breathing the sea air, and from the nation's heartland, where the only waves came when the prairie wind blew across vast fields of grain.

But if you will take a closer look, you'll see that these men were as unique as their beloved boat and its namesake fish.

They were the ones who broke the standard rules of engagement and, in the process, broke the back of the Japanese navy. Against all odds, they sent the aircraft carrier *Shinano* to the ocean floor, the vessel's Japanese captain voluntarily going down with his ship, dying in disgrace. They were members of the navy's only all-bachelor crew, whose antics rivaled anything on the television show *McHale's Navy*, and who were later dubbed the "Playboys of the Pacific." It was a moniker they richly deserved. They were the ones who steered their boat into exotic ports all around the world, many of which had never seen a submarine before. The people in those ports had certainly never seen the likes of the *Archerfish* crew. With equal hospitality, the submarine and her crew welcomed on board dignitaries, B-girls, royalty, surviving members of the *Shinano*, schoolkids, a goat, members of the press, and Playboy Bunnies, among others. They shot skeet off the bow, barbecued on the cigarette deck, and drew a tongue-lashing from John Wayne for not showing him proper respect. They outlasted Japanese destroyers and survived a treacherous fire. They worked hard and lived even harder.

The men who became crew members of *Archerfish* were the lucky ones. At one point in the 1960s, there were over 300 names on the waiting list of those seeking a billet among the 60 or so who were fortunate enough to crew *Archerfish* then. And also in the '60s, they were the ones whose home port was movable, a mere formality to keep the paperwork straight as they steamed off for over a year at a time, dodging icebergs and tropical atolls along the way.

Follow along as we track *Archerfish* from her birth in New Hampshire in 1943 until she died an explosive but noble death in 1968, still characteristically serving her country by doing whatever she was asked to do. Look at her more closely and you'll see how exceptional this "typical" submarine was. You may well come to know and respect her as her crews did. As many of them still do.

Biannual reunions draw scores of former shipmates and their families. Her alumni, most of whom also served on other subs or ships, choose to attend the *Archerfish* gathering, even if they pass up get-togethers for their other ships. Somehow they still manage to dredge up new stories each time that no one has yet heard and produce the photos and documents and corroborating testimony to prove them true. Their well-maintained and extensive Internet site attracts thousands of visitors. The shipmates who are still around keep in touch with each other as if their service together were only last year or a decade ago, not most of a lifetime past.

One other thing. If you listen to them talk, they speak of *Archerfish* as if she were as much a living entity as they. That's why this is a biography. Her memory is still as alive with them as that of their departed shipmates. She may have been made of steel and aluminum, wires and pipe, but she lived and she died, just as so many of her crew have.

They are determined that neither she nor they will ever be forgotten. But just like those submarine sailors whose remains are forever lost in the deep, there is no solid ground above *Archerfish*'s head for a granite marker, no grave where wreaths can be reverently laid in remembrance.

No matter. Those who knew her well believe the best way to remember her is to make certain her story is told. Told for the *Archerfish* crew members still alive as well as for those on eternal patrol. Told for the thousands of submarine sailors who preceded them and for those who still ply the planet's seas on the "boomers" and "fast attacks," the nuclear boats. Told for those who admire and appreciate the skill and bravery of those who choose the all-voluntary Silent Service, even as they wonder about the manner of man who would do so.

And told for anyone who loves a damn good story populated by remarkable characters.

We agree. This is the biography of a gallant lady, a diesel boat, a gloriously unique submarine, and of her exceptional crew.

This is the biography of *Archerfish*.

FIRST COMMISSION
4 September 1943–12 June 1946

The sea, washing the equator and the poles, offers its perilous aid, and the power and empire that follow it. "Beware of me," it says, "but if you can hold me, I am the key to all the lands."

—Ralph Waldo Emerson

I

GOOD SCOTCH
AND CIGARETTES

M ALVINA Thompson laughed out loud when she read the invitation
that had just arrived from Rear Admiral Thomas Withers. The admiral had
addressed the letter to "*Mrs.* Malvina Thompson." He had also felt the
need to instruct her to keep in a "restricted status" the rather vague launch
date of the submarine she was being invited to sponsor.

Thompson took a long draw on her cigarette, downed another swig of
Scotch, and once again let loose that distinctive cackle of hers.

Not only was she most assuredly not a "Mrs.," but the letter had also
given very skimpy information. It only told her that this submarine . . .
what was it called? USS *Archerfish*? . . . was to be launched "sometime in
the middle of June 1943." Even if she happened to be sharing tea with
some Nazi or Japanese spy, she seriously doubted that such vague details
would be of much use to him. She knew from the idle conversation she
overheard around the White House that they were launching submarines
up there at Portsmouth, New Hampshire, all the time and floating them off
to the Pacific. Almost one a month by now. She figured the enemy was
adept enough at espionage to already know far more about the schedule
than "sometime in the middle of June."

Still, she was quite pleased to be asked. It was an honor to be selected
to sponsor a new submarine, and she appreciated the invitation. As the first

lady's personal secretary, Malvina Thompson usually remained in the background, behind her decidedly "foreground" boss. She had the thankless tasks of keeping up with Mrs. Roosevelt's daunting daily schedule and then reading it out loud to the press before each day's news conference. She had been Eleanor Roosevelt's right hand since being picked out of a Red Cross secretarial pool way back in 1917. The first lady appreciated her secretary's hard work and efficiency, but Mrs. Roosevelt was quick to point out that Thompson's openheartedness and sense of humor were equally valued.

Actually, Thompson was quite happy about sponsoring this submarine and was sure "ER" would not mind her taking a couple of days to go up to New Hampshire for the event. After all, Mrs. Roosevelt had experience sponsoring ships. The first lady had christened the aircraft carrier USS *Yorktown* (CV-5) in Newport News in 1936. There was another benefit, too. Malvina Thompson could invite her sister to serve as matron of honor and have her niece come along as well. That would give them some time to visit during the train ride up to Boston and back.

"Terrible waste of good champagne, though," she said out loud, and laughed some more.

"Tommy, what's so funny?" ER called from next door. The first lady always called her "Tommy."

Malvina hopped up and went to show her the letter. She knew the first lady would also get a chuckle over the admiral trying to marry her off.

Meanwhile, in the U.S. Navy Yard in Portsmouth, New Hampshire, C. M. Elder, a retired navy captain who was serving as the treasurer of the New Hampshire Auxiliary Navy Relief Society, had inadvertently made another error. Elder was charged with selecting the final design for launch tags to be distributed to attendees during the ceremonies for all the submarines that were being built in the yard. When he corresponded with the people at the Fraser Label Company in Chicago, he selected scarlet red on golden yellow as the colors for the *Archerfish*'s tag. However, in the correspondence, he omitted the hyphen in the submarine's official name. All 8,500 tags should have had the boat's name spelled "*Archer-Fish.*"

To this day, those who served on the submarine's first commission, during World War II, still spell the name with the hyphen, as it was originally intended. Those who came after have dropped it and call their boat *Archerfish*.

Such trivial mistakes were easily made in the rush of early 1943. There were far more important details to worry about. The United States was involved in a two-ocean war, one in Europe and another in Asia. The construction facility in Portsmouth was bustling, working night and day to turn out submarines for the war. At the height of production, 24,000 people worked there. Five *Balao*-class diesel submarines were under construction at the end of 1942 and in the first half of 1943. In addition to *Archerfish*, *Apogon* (SS-308), *Aspro* (SS-309), *Batfish* (SS-310), and *Burrfish* (SS-312) were either already undergoing sea trials or were well on the way to completion.

Scheduling was crucial. The boat builders made do as best they could. For example, construction on *Archerfish* was not far enough along to permit installation of her torpedo tubes when they arrived at the yard. The workmen simply installed the tubes in *Batfish*. *Batfish*, the only one of the five sisters still around today, is on display in a grassy park in Muskogee, Oklahoma. She still has the *Archerfish* designation SS-311 stenciled on her torpedo tubes. It's interesting to note that she made good use of her borrowed tubes. She was officially credited with sinking nine Japanese vessels, though the crew was certain of at least fifteen.

The keel of the *Archerfish* was laid down on January 22, 1943, and she was far enough along to float, ready to launch, on May 28. That was no small feat. Even as late as the day before she was to be officially launched, workers were still installing mooring lines, flashlights, fire extinguishers, and life preservers. Chippers and caulkers still hung from her sides, removing the last temporary clips. Painters were assigned to touch up the hull with anticorrosive and antifouling paint as the blocks, shores, and cribbing were removed. Welding ground wires and the lightning ground were not taken away until the night before launch.

Still, she was finished and presentable enough to launch on time. On Friday night, May 28, 1943, she rested in Slip 1 at the yard, ready to get the 8:20 PM ceremony over with so she could have her controls installed, begin sea trials, and get to her assigned port. The seemingly odd time of 8:20 PM was chosen for the launch because that was when the rather capricious tide would be most favorable. The Piscataqua River's high and low tides could vary by as much as seven feet, and an ebb current of twelve knots was not uncommon.

Navy Commander J. H. Spiller, the launching officer, and Captain S. E. Dudley, the production officer, were too busy getting ready for another send-off to ponder this latest boat's future. It was routine for them now, these launching ceremonies, with all their detailed paperwork and onslaught of memos that covered every possible contingency, right down to who was responsible for pulling up the christening bottle and to whom he delivered it. The men whose job it was to send these boats out to sea doted on minutiae. It likely kept them from thinking about where their charges might end up once they had left their care. They knew the odds. Many of the boats they saw launched down the Piscataqua toward the Atlantic Ocean would eventually rest on the bottom of the sea for eternity. So would many of the brave submariners who manned them.

Thirty-five riggers and laborers from Shop 72 stood by to help get her out of the slip and over to Berth 2 after the festivities, along with men from various other shops and the tugs sent over by the captain of the yard. A hospital corpsman was assigned to the submarine's deck beginning an hour before the ceremony. Divers were scheduled to inspect the slip and skids from beneath at two o'clock that afternoon, and another crew would do a thorough inspection an hour later to make sure everything was tied down for the launch.

Those yard workmen who would be busy on other projects in the area around the new submarine would be allowed to cease their work for the twenty-five minutes that the launching festivities would take. But that was all the rest they would get. They would have to resume their regular tasks immediately after the ceremony.

Commander H. Ambrose would be aboard *Archerfish*, in charge of riding her out of the slip and supervising the trip from there to her berth. Though he was the first "skipper" of *Archerfish*, his tenure would only last a few minutes, until the tugs had eased the submarine into Berth 2, port side to, and tied her off. Someone else would eventually guide her toward the Pacific Ocean and the war.

Before, during, and after the launch, the Coast Guard patrolled the fairway, making certain no one was in the area who shouldn't be, either accidentally or on purpose. Such a ceremonious occasion was hardly a good time to have a spanking new submarine collide with some errant tug. A special marine contingent kept watch, both at the launch slip and at Berth 2. There had been no incident of sabotage at Portsmouth. The commandant intended to keep it so.

Miss Thompson rode the train up from Washington that day, traveling with her sister and niece. They arrived in Portsmouth at about 6:30 PM. She enjoyed dinner prior to the launching with Rear Admiral Withers and his wife. Withers had a special place in submarine history. He was considered the father of long-range submarines, the man who had convinced the navy that subs could do more than defensively patrol our own coasts and harbors. New generation submarines like the *Archerfish* were built to carry more men, go farther, dive deeper, and run faster than their predecessors. For the first time in U.S. Navy history, these "plunging boats" were being designed to be aggressors.

During dinner, Miss Thompson refrained from mentioning the marital mix-up in Admiral Withers's first letter to her, though she still chuckled when she thought of it.

There was reason for celebration that evening. *Archerfish* was the sixth submarine to be launched from Portsmouth in the first five months of 1943. That was a matter of considerable pride to everyone involved. Still, it was to be a muted event. Gala receptions for guests had traditionally been held either before or after launch ceremonies in Portsmouth, where such events had been held for various type vessels for over 150 years. However, the parties had been discontinued during wartime. It was necessary to get the area cleared and everyone back to work as quickly as possible. Only a limited number of guests, officers, and shipyard workers were allowed to take part. That was both for security and scheduling reasons. Anyone wishing to attend had to have an invitation or direct orders or get special permission from the commandant of the yard to be there. A newly completed warship would be a juicy target for saboteurs. But, more practically, the space around *Archerfish*'s slip was quite cramped. It would be embarrassing to have some distinguished member of the sponsor's party bumped into the drink.

This would be one of the few parties *Archerfish* missed in her colorful life.

Miss Thompson's sister, Mrs. Charles Lund of Washington, D.C., who served as matron of honor, and her niece, Cynthia, were among those on the platform that night. So were Leon W. Gridmore and his wife. Gridmore was a toolmaker from the navy yard's central tool shop. He had been designated to present the employees' gift to the sponsor. It was a silver bowl with her name engraved on it. Thompson subtly checked to make certain it was engraved to "*Miss* Malvina C. Thompson," as she had specifically requested. It was.

The band began playing naval favorites promptly at 7:50 PM. The official party marched up onto the sponsor's platform, and Gridmore presented the employees' gift at 8:05. Lieutenant Ralph Curtis, a navy chaplain, offered a prayer at 8:07. After a few short speeches, a bright red warning flag flew at 8:15, followed three minutes later by one long blast on the warning klaxon and a single bell to alert Miss Thompson that it was time for her to go to work.

As she posed for the photographer, the first lady's secretary carried in her left arm a dozen roses, purchased for the occasion by the taxpayers of the United States for $24, and held the christening bottle in her right hand. When the bell sounded, she laid aside the flowers, seized the bottle in her left hand, and sang out, "I christen thee *Archerfish*!" Then she whacked the bow of the new submarine hard. Everyone who had gathered in the area of the slip and on the deck of the new boat applauded heartily as the bottle shattered and its contents spewed all over.

Immediately, the triggers were released, and *Archerfish* eased down the carefully greased skids, out of the berth and into the water. After all the frenzied work, the detailed preparations for the ceremony, the launch was over in less than half an hour.

Archerfish had been conceived on January 22. Now, on May 28, she had been birthed. It was a gestation of just over four months.

The message went out the next day to the Bureau of Ships:

THIS IS RESTRICTED X ARCHER FISH SUCCESSFULLY LAUNCHED AT 2020 QUEEN 28 MAY

There was no way any of those gathered there at Slip 1 that gentle New England spring evening could have suspected what lay ahead for the boat they had set afloat. Nor could they ever have fathomed the role she would play in her country's history over the next quarter century.

In retrospect, though, it seems especially appropriate that her sponsor was a woman who was respected for her hard work and efficiency, yet well known for her sense of humor and her fondness for cigarettes and good Scotch.

2

DOWN THE PISCATAQUA

THE U.S. Navy wasted no time after the devastating attack on Pearl Harbor on December 7, 1941. Stunned by the surprise attack, angered by its sneakiness and ferocity, the navy immediately took stock of which of its vessels in the Pacific would still float and then went to work with them. Within six hours after the dawn attack, the navy issued orders to begin "unrestricted submarine warfare" against Japan. In a sharp departure from previous naval tactics, targets included commercial shipping as well as military vessels. Within days of the assault, U.S. submarines were on station, hunting near the Japanese home islands. After a stuttering start, they would eventually be gloriously, devastatingly effective. They would also suffer awful losses, more than any other naval force in the Pacific Theater.

At no time during World War II did submarine sailors comprise more than 2 percent of the navy's total personnel. Still, they sent to the bottom more than 55 percent of all Japanese shipping, both military and merchant, that was sunk by all the agencies that were involved in the war.

No doubt *Archerfish* and her prospective new skipper, a handsome Texan, Lieutenant Commander George W. Kehl, were anxious to join the fray as they awaited completion of the boat. After the ceremonial launch at the end of May, the new boat sat patiently in Berth 2 at Portsmouth, getting herself ready, being fitted for final inspection and shakedown training. She was scheduled to be completed on September 10 and everyone hoped to be under way for the Panama Canal and on to Pearl Harbor by Thanksgiving.

There was no way to know what lay in store for this new boat, but it was built to fight, its crew was trained to fight, and it was, by God, ready to fight.

There were the usual delays. The East Pittsburgh plant of Westinghouse Electric was building the boat's electrical controls, and they notified the navy yard in July that the controls would ship eight days late. *Batfish*'s completion had already been delayed as well, from August 27 to September 6. *Burrfish* was still on schedule for September 30.

Of course, the submarine's elaborate electrical control system was crucial. Like most of the diesel boats, when she was submerged, the electric motors that were responsible for turning *Archerfish*'s screws received their juice from two banks of storage batteries. When on the surface, the motors were usually powered by generators that were directly attached to each of the four main diesel engines. The engines and generator sets also kept the batteries charged.

Though she could be gobbled up like a minnow by today's gargantuan nuclear boats, *Archerfish* was still an imposing sight when she was eased into Dry Dock No. 2 on Saturday, July 24, for more work. She was 311 feet 8 inches long from stem to stern, about the length of a football field and one end zone. Her beam was 27 feet, and she displaced 1,840 tons on the surface and 2,405 tons submerged.

In the dry dock, the yard crew found that some of the antifouling paint had failed to stick to the hull and had to be reapplied. Workers also changed some troublesome shaft bearings and painted the propellers with black varnish.

The electrical controls finally showed up from Westinghouse on July 29. It now appeared that the new completion date of September 18 could be met and that transit through the Panama Canal would come in mid-November. *Archerfish* could be at war by Christmas. The inspection and survey team from the Bureau of Ships in Washington set September 18 as a firm date for them to come up to Portsmouth and do the final run-through. The commandant of the navy yard considered the progress reports and schedule and picked Saturday, September 4, ten-thirty in the morning, as the date and time for the commissioning ceremony for "Sugar Sugar Three Eleven."

When he wasn't dealing with the incessant paperwork, Lieutenant Commander Kehl could stand on his boat's cigarette deck, the area behind

the sail, and watch the workmen put the finishing touches on her. He wondered if there had been similar holdups when they built John Paul Jones's
famous square-rigger warship, the *Ranger*, in 1777, near this very spot but
across the river.

By early September, the winds off the Atlantic were already carrying a
chill in the early mornings and evenings. It would be good to be heading
south before they got too deep into the New England winter. Kehl was
ready to go someplace where the weather was warmer, where the war was
just plain hot.

Progress was definitely being made. Barring any other delays, and subject to the inspection, they should be ready to begin shakedown and training by the third week of September. Kehl had seen the paperwork from the
disbursing officer transferring his and his officers' pay accounts to the new
boat. If they were now being paid by the navy to be billeted on *Archerfish*,
the boat might soon be headed toward the canal and on to Pearl Harbor.

Kehl had already been joined by Lieutenant Commander James Clark,
Lieutenants Sigmund Bobczynski and Clark Sprinkle, Lieutenant Junior
Grade William Crawford, Ensigns John Andrews and Romolo Cousins,
and Machinist Harold Brantner. The crew was coming together and continued to report right up until they were ready for their sea trials. Some
were experienced and qualified submarine sailors. Others were novice
sailors, NQPs, nonqualified personnel (known to experienced crewmen as
nonqualified pukes), with plenty to learn.

Officers and sailors in the U.S. Submarine Force have always been volunteers. No one has ever been forced to accept such duty. They were (and
still are) carefully selected for service in the rather unique environment in
which they are required to live and fight. During *Archerfish*'s time, before
being assigned to a submarine, most enlisted personnel spent two months
and officers six months at the Basic Submarine School at the navy facility in
Groton, Connecticut. Enlisted men then spent more time in specialty
schools such as the ones for enginemen, electricians, and torpedomen.

Once assigned to a submarine, officers served a probationary period of
one year in which they had to learn all about their boat, her machinery, pip-
ing, weapons. The theory was that any man aboard should be able to step
into any duty station and be proficient at what needed to be done. After the
probation period, the officers faced written, oral, and practical examinations administered by commanding officers from three other submarines.
If they passed, they were then entitled to wear the gold dolphin insignia
that confirmed they were qualified submarine officers.

Enlisted men had a six-month training program in which they, too, had to learn everything about their boats. After vigorous examinations by qualified petty officers, in which they had to show knowledge of all systems and expertise in all compartments, they were reexamined by a qualified officer. This was followed by a one-on-one question-and-answer walk-through of the entire boat with the executive officer (XO). If he was satisfied, the man was awarded silver dolphins and designated as being qualified in submarines.

This rigorous qualification scenario is only one reason submarine sailors have always been so proud of their dolphins. They also signify their membership in a strong, select brotherhood.

George Kehl started his navy career as an enlisted man. He used a year of prep school to help get into the Naval Academy at Annapolis, Maryland, and graduated in 1932. He was a practical joker and a good athlete. His most prized possession at the academy was a set of dumbbells. According to his class yearbook, he liked to casually toss the weights to an unsuspecting bystander while whispering a warning to "Catch!" He married his wife, Laura, in 1932 as well. He was commander of USS *R-14* (SS-91), based in Key West, when he got orders as the prospective commanding officer of a new submarine that was then being built in Portsmouth. Kehl moved his growing family into a rented house on Cutts Island, Kittery Point, Maine, not far from the navy yard. From there, he got up and went to work, just as if he were going down to the office each day, until his new sub was ready to steam away to sea.

He had the usual ups and downs of any commanding officer. As will happen, some of the wild young crew straggled in late for muster and had to be punished. Some showed up "drunk and disorderly." One crew member even got bread and water for five days for some more serious transgression. There were the usual minor injuries and illnesses and even a few cases of "gonococcus infection of the urethra" serious enough to require treatment at the naval hospital. They were sailors, after all, and it was hard for some of them to stay focused while they waited for their orders to go to where the action really was.

But there were hopeful signs that they would soon be at sea. The boat took on fuel for the first time on September 15, receiving 90,112 gallons of diesel fuel.

Archerfish was officially delivered and accepted on September 21, 1943, with only a few items still missing from her inventory: a portable hydrogen indicator, Momsen Lungs for emergency escape, and a torpedo charging valve test set among them. Kehl reported on September 23 that the "detail and assembly" of his full crew of seventy enlisted men and seven officers was "satisfactory."

She and they were about ready for their first dive.

The shakedown and testing had to be rigorous. Any faults in the boat's complicated systems were better discovered in the waters off New England than beneath a Japanese destroyer somewhere in the China Sea.

Archerfish eased out of the navy yard into the Piscataqua River for the first time on September 25, 1943, steaming down to open water, heading out for sea trials. It was a beautiful day—the seas at "state one," the wind never exceeding "force three," the temperature in the high sixties and visibility better than thirty miles. They dived to sixty-seven feet on their first attempt, taking only ninety seconds to do so, and completed a total of eight dives on her first day. All went well except for a minor injury to one of the crewmen. Fireman Second Class Charles Wells got a nasty cut over his left eye while shutting a hatch. Fred "Doc" Smith, the pharmacist's mate, took care of it, though, and Wells learned to duck when he closed a hatch from then on.

Unlike when she was in dry dock, anyone watching *Archerfish* make her way in or out of the narrow channel for her first trip to sea that day would not have been impressed by her size. That's because, like an iceberg, most of the boat was underwater. Only the superstructure, fairwater, and shears were visible when the boat was surfaced. Almost completely beneath the water was the pressure hull, a steel cylinder built to withstand the tremendous force of seawater when she went deep. Water pressure increases by one atmosphere with every thirty-three feet of depth. The pressure hull was tested to withstand the force of the sea at 412 feet. A series of tanks were installed around the pressure hull in the shape of an inverted saddle with the space between forming the boat's ballast and fuel tanks. Inside the hull were all the machinery, weapons, and working and living spaces for the crew.

If any observers on the shore that day could have toured the inside of the boat, they would have marveled at how compact and utilitarian the vessel's design was. There was no wasted space. As sub sailors like to say, "There's room for everything aboard a submarine except a mistake." For the uninitiated, though, it was difficult to imagine where all those men slept or ate or relieved themselves, or how they lived so close to one another for such long periods of time without killing each other. This, too, was a reason for such a strong bond among submariners.

A submarine is, by size and definition, a ship. Down through the years, they've been called "eel boats," "plunging boats," "pig boats," and "sewer pipes." Submariners, though, almost always refer to their vessels simply as "boats."

The "business end" of the sub was her forward torpedo room, the compartment in the boat's bow. As with most other compartments, this one served multiple purposes. There were six torpedo tubes protruding through the forward bulkhead of the compartment. Sixteen crewmen could sleep, live, and stow their worldly goods there. Fourteen torpedoes were usually stored in this area and it was also where the "fish" were maintained and repaired. Hydraulic oil, torpedo alcohol, and emergency freshwater tanks were located in *Archerfish*'s forward torpedo room. There were also a toilet and a shower for use by the officers. The sleeping berths were fitted in wherever possible among the ordnance. Many of those berths had to be taken out when the torpedoes were being moved or worked on. That was always quite a job. The torpedoes weighed over 3,000 pounds, more than a ton and a half each, and had to be moved about by a series of chain falls, ropes, and pulleys, using mostly human muscle. And, there were approximately 600 pounds of high explosive in the warhead attached to each torpedo.

An "escape trunk" allowed entry to or exit from the boat from this room. It had a hatch at both the top and bottom and an escape door on one side that allowed up to four men at a time to leave the submarine, using Momsen Lungs, in case an emergency occurred while she was submerged. The Momsen Lung was a rubber bag that recycled exhaled air. Each lung held a canister of soda lime to remove carbon dioxide from exhaled air and replenish it with oxygen. By the 1950s, submariners could also employ the "buoyant ascent" method if they were stranded 300 feet deep or less. Wearing only a Mae West life jacket and relying on their own strong lungs filled with pressurized air, they could leave the sub and rise to the surface, vigorously exhaling all the way. *Archerfish* would one day play a key role in the development of that method of rescue.

Behind *Archerfish*'s forward torpedo room was the forward battery area, where the boat's officers ate, slept, worked, and relaxed. Also located here were the wardroom and a pantry, the ship's office, berths for the chief petty officers, and three "staterooms" for the officers. In reality, there was one stateroom for the captain, and all the other officers shared the other two. Stateroom, by the way, was very much a misnomer. The rooms were hardly comparable to cruise ship staterooms. Most would consider them little more than closets, but they did provide the officers with some small measure of privacy.

Underneath these rooms was the forward battery well. It was filled with 126 tons of potentially explosive but essential storage battery cells. Along with the other bank of cells that were located in the after battery compartment, they provided the electricity to propel the boat when she was underwater. *Archerfish* could typically travel on battery power for up to eight hours, depending on her speed.

Farther back and beneath the conning tower was the control room, where the radio shack and most of the controls for diving, surfacing, and driving the submarine were located. The pump room was below the control room. This space housed the high-pressure air compressors, air conditioning and refrigeration systems, trim and drain pumps, low-pressure blower, and hydraulic accumulator. Above the control room was the conning tower, where the periscopes could be found. The torpedo data computer (or TDC), an amazing but totally mechanical computing machine, was also located there.

Behind the control room was the after battery compartment, the location of the crew's berthing space, mess, and galley. *Archerfish* carried a large chill box (refrigerator), a cold room for frozen foods, and an ammunition storage locker, all located below the crew's mess and galley. The after battery, located in the battery well beneath the crew's berthing space, was the same size as the forward battery.

One real benefit of submarine service was the food. Since crew members were required to live in a confined space, often without the benefit of sunlight or fresh air, the navy attempted to make up for their sacrifice with home-cooked meals. Officers ate the same food as enlisted men because there was only one galley. Since storage space was limited, the crew literally walked and lived on top of their stores when they left port on patrol and until they had used them up.

The only washroom for the enlisted men was located in the after battery. Here the crewmen shared two toilets, two showers, and two washbasins. One of the showers was usually used to store potatoes and the other to store garbage until it could be dumped overboard. In reality, showers were a rare luxury while at sea.

Four noisy Fairbanks-Morse diesel engines filled the forward and after engine rooms. The girls who frequented the bars at ports of call all over the world claimed they could always tell sailors from the diesel boats by the distinctive odor that clung to their hair, skin, and clothing. Whether it's true or not, old sub sailors fondly remember the unique smell of their boats, one that they never forgot, and one you can still get a whiff of if you visit those boats that have been restored and are open to visitors.

Also located in the forward engine room were two distilling plants, used to make freshwater from seawater for drinking, bathing, and the like. Most important, the stills also made battery water for the storage cells. Battery water had to be extremely pure, so it was usually distilled first. If it wasn't clean enough for the batteries, it was used for drinking instead. Another purer batch of water had to be cooked up for the battery cells.

There was an auxiliary engine in addition to the two main engines in the after engine room.

The diesel boats had a unique method of propulsion. Contrary to what most might think, the boat's diesel engines did not directly drive *Archerfish*'s screws. Instead, there were generators connected to the main engines. They produced electrical power. That electricity coursed through big switchboxes that made up the main propulsion cubicle. The cubicle filled up the forward three-quarters of the upper level of the maneuvering room. In the lower level, four main electric motors were connected to the two main shafts (two motors per shaft) through reduction gears. The shafts passed through the pressure hull in the after end of the motor room, and that's where the screws were attached.

In the maneuvering room, a strange and fascinating operation took place anytime the boat was under way. The electrician's mates who worked there used a complicated array of levers and rheostats to send the power to the batteries or to the main motors that turned the shafts and screws, thus controlling the direction and speed of the submarine. The men played the rheostats and levers like virtuosos, slapping them, twisting them, working them, clicking their release buttons. It was as if they were playing an odd musical instrument in an intricate, coordinated concert. Their performance was vital, though, to where the boat went and how fast she got there. Because of all the electrical equipment contained inside it, the cubicle was also susceptible to electrical fires.

Finally, at the stern of the boat was the after torpedo room. It was smaller than the forward room because it only had four torpedo tubes. Fifteen crewmen shared living space here with ten heavy, deadly torpedoes.

Archerfish test-fired her four-inch gun for the first time on September 27, and dived to a depth of one hundred feet for the first time that day as well. *Balao*-class subs, like *Archerfish*, were called "thick-skinned boats" and were designed to dive to a test depth of 412 feet, as opposed to the previous

Gato-class boats that were limited to 300 feet. As you will see, there were times when *Archerfish* went deeper than her test depth despite the possibly dire consequences of doing so. On the twenty-seventh, they also used the boat's condensation stills for the first time, making 450 gallons of potable water. Once they returned to Portsmouth that day, one of the crew, Ship's Cook Joseph Baroody, was sent to the hospital with a possible tapeworm.

In mid-October, *Archerfish* steamed away from Portsmouth and down the coast to the U.S. Navy Torpedo Station, located on Goat Island in Narragansett Bay, just out of Newport, Rhode Island. There they test-fired torpedoes for two days. Commander Kehl reported good results. That was a great relief to everyone.

The big disappointment in the submarine war effort in the first years of World War II had been the inaccuracy and lack of reliability of the torpedoes. Torpedoes had been deadly weapons ever since Robert Fulton, the inventor of the steamboat, had designed the first one that could be used as an offensive weapon. Even then it was little more than two floating mines held together by a chain that could be used against ships at anchor. Britain's Robert Whitehead designed the first self-propelled torpedo in the 1860s. Before that, the word "torpedo" meant any underwater explosive and usually applied to a mine or some other device, most often delivered by a surface ship or on the end of a spar. But by the beginning of World War I, the German U-boats were using a steam-turbine-driven fish that could travel very fast to the intended target. Those U-boats enjoyed considerable success.

However, the newer torpedoes being fired by American subs at the beginning of World War II had not been adequately tested. Only two test shots had been made at Goat Island, both aimed at a submarine hulk. One missed. The other struck its target and exploded. Thus, the torpedoes that America went to war with in the Pacific had a 50 percent failure rate.

When a submarine at the Battle of Midway fired the first eight torpedoes of the engagement, seven of them ran much deeper than they were supposed to and missed their easy target completely. The eighth torpedo struck the Japanese ship but did not explode. It was a dud. Thank goodness for Admiral Chester Nimitz and his aircraft carriers and dive-bombers!

Submariners all over the Pacific reported having their fish whoosh harmlessly past targets, running too deep. Or they clearly heard the duds strike their targets without going off.

The navy brass blamed everybody else—the sub captains for poor shooting, the civilian contractors who built the weapons for bad workmanship.

Many submarine commanders left their boats in frustration. Some were replaced for "lack of aggressiveness" or for ineffectiveness, but many of the skippers blamed the torpedoes. It took almost two years before the flaws in the Mark-14 torpedoes were discovered and fixed. By the time *Archerfish* was ready to head for the Pacific, the accuracy and reliability of the torpedoes had greatly improved, and they were already having a deadly effect on Japanese shipping in addition to the warships of the Imperial Navy. Kehl had to be pleased that his own tests with his new boat were, for the most part, successful.

There was one minor torpedo misfire that resulted in its own bit of irony. *Archerfish* would one day sink the biggest vessel ever sunk by a submarine. While in Newport, she may well have sunk the smallest. One of the test torpedoes fired from the boat's number-four tube had a sticky steering engine and missed its target. Instead, it traveled all the way across Narragansett Bay and struck a small yard boat that was tied up there. There was no explosion because the torpedo was not armed. The weapon did punch a hole in the little boat, and it sank quickly after impact. Nobody was hurt.

The November wind blew cold the day *Archerfish* pulled away from her berth at Portsmouth, bound for the Panama Canal and eventually Hawaii, then on to the first of her seven war patrols. As she eased past the riverbanks where grew the wild strawberries that had attracted the first settlers to this place in 1623, the crew had no way of knowing whether they would ever see these shores again. They certainly could not anticipate steaming 75,000 miles, making 908 dives, and being officially credited with sinking or damaging over 92,000 tons of enemy shipping over the next two years. Or know that they would earn the Presidential Unit Citation and the Navy Occupation Service Medal. Or that they and their boat would be sitting alongside the submarine tender USS *Proteus* (AS-19) and in company with other units of the U.S. Fleet in Tokyo Bay when the surrender papers were signed aboard the USS *Missouri* (BB-63).

No, all that would have been too immense to ponder, even if they had been so inclined. Each man concentrated instead on what he was supposed to be doing as they pointed their boat toward the open sea. If he had any concerns, they were more likely no weightier than when he would next be paid or if there would be cold beer in the next port.

Laura Kehl came down to watch the submarine depart that day, along with other family members and friends of the crew. She had been busy packing the house, getting ready to go with the children to stay with her parents in Watertown, New York. That was the usual routine when George steamed away and until he could find quarters for his growing brood at their new home port. She, as well, tried not to think about where and to what fate her husband and his boat and crew were headed. Laura, of course, had no way of knowing what the future held, whether or not her husband would ever come back, how long this war would go on, who would eventually prevail.

Nor could she have ever guessed that her family would one day be reunited and return to this area, to live in the same rented house in Kittery Point where they had spent the last few months. That they would eventually buy the home when her husband was assigned shore duty in Portsmouth and Boston. Or that one of her sons, Stephen, would one day be a member of the class of '62 at Annapolis and would live in that same house on Cutts Island into the twenty-first century.

Even now, nearly six decades later, Stephen Kehl remembers that day, watching his father's boat ease down the narrow channel and out to sea. The submarine seemed so close that he could reach out and touch it, but he knew better than to try. He was only three years old, but he wondered why all the women and older children were waving and crying. And why the men on the bridge and the lookouts were so furiously waving back. There had been none of that on the days when his father's new boat went to sea for her trials.

None of those gathered on the point that day could see the men down below, those on watch in the engine rooms and in maneuvering and at their other duty stations. And those men could only picture in their minds the scene on the shore, their wives or family or girlfriends out there, waving goodbye.

Laura, Stephen and the rest watched until *Archerfish* eased out through the entrance to the harbor, made the turn to the right, and disappeared from view. Little Stephen had seen his father's boat sail away before, and he always came back home soon after. He still couldn't imagine what was different about this day.

As the submarine squeezed out of the narrow harbor between New Hampshire and Maine, and as the coast of Massachusetts and the hook of Cape Cod reeled off to their starboard, the collective pulses of the crew of *Archerfish* quickened. They were finally under way, going halfway around the world on a righteous mission, to fight an enemy that threatened everything they and their country held dear.

As they settled in and steamed southward, the crew of *Archerfish* also knew they were off on a grand adventure. This was only the beginning, though, the first sailing of a much grander adventure than they could have ever imagined. This could well be a mission from which they would never return. No matter. They were bound to do what their country had called on them to do.

Bound to do their duty or die trying.

3

CROAKING FISH AND
THE FORMOSA STRAITS

No American submarines were damaged in the Japanese attack on Pearl Harbor on December 7, 1941. The submarine piers were totally ignored by the Japanese attack pilots that morning. They homed in on the larger ships along battleship row instead. It wasn't long before the Japanese realized this had been a major blunder. These submarines were the first and primary resource the U.S. Navy had available to throw at the enemy when war was immediately declared following President Roosevelt's rallying "day of infamy" speech.

By the end of the war, fifty-two American submarines had been lost, only three of them in the Atlantic. So were more than 3,500 submarine sailors. The last submarine sunk by the Japanese, the USS *Bullhead* (SS-332), went down with eighty-four men aboard on the day the atomic bomb was dropped on Hiroshima.

Today in Pearl Harbor there is a special memorial park with fifty-two separate plaques, one dedicated to each of those lost boats. The death toll represents about 20 percent of all men who served on subs in the Pacific.

It is a stunning statistic when you consider that one of every five submarine sailors who served in the Pacific died.

The men on *Archerfish* certainly knew the odds on November 29, 1943, as she steamed into Pearl Harbor for the first time. They were still more than ready to get on with it, to get to work. Some of the signs of the sneak attack were still visible around the base as they pulled into port, even after almost two years, but the place was bustling with activity. Everyone there was primed to keep the country's naval power focused on a victory that finally seemed to be in sight. Despite a slow start, progress was being made. Thanks in large part to the American submarine force, Japan was slowly being starved, and a tremendous toll had been taken of both military and civilian shipping.

Still it was a dangerous ocean out there. A desperate, cornered enemy had plenty of weapons of his own and a powerful incentive to use them. The Japanese Empire was fighting for its life and still taking seriously its motto: "Death before dishonor."

Captain George Kehl had already taken stock of the mettle of his officers and crew by the time they arrived in Pearl. They had worked together in the sea trials back in Portsmouth, then during the transit south, through the Panama Canal, and on the run across the Pacific to Hawaii. The boat had done well, too, except for a problem with her bow buoyancy tank vent. That proved to be a lingering hindrance.

The trip had been uneventful except for losing two things along the way. One was a sailor who turned up missing while they were tied up at Balboa in the Canal Zone. He was reported as a "straggler," and they had to wait until Henry Bristow came aboard to replace him the next day. They also accidentally left a pair of Bausch and Lomb 7 × 50 binoculars up on the bridge when they did a practice dive before entering the canal. They were lost, of course, at a cost to the taxpayers of $103.19.

Commander Kehl knew one thing for certain. After spending the better part of five months with these men, he was ready to go to war with them. As he later wrote in his summary of *Archerfish*'s first war patrol: "All hands answered every call made upon them with a will which was gratifying and which was strictly in keeping with United States naval tradition and the spirit of America."

It was important that a captain be confident in the ability of his crew, officers and enlisted men alike. On a surface ship, if a man makes a mistake during an evolution, it can get people hurt or killed. On a submarine, one man's error can cause the entire boat and its crew to be lost.

And that may well be the biggest reason for the remarkable camaraderie among submariners. Each man depends on every other for his very life. That doesn't just apply in wartime, either. Boats can be and have been lost in routine, everyday maneuvers.

Amazingly, until just after the beginning of the twentieth century, submarine duty had been considered by navy brass to be the equivalent of shore duty for sailors. Sub sailors received 25 percent less pay than their brothers on destroyers, cruisers, and other surface ships. That all began to change one blustery, rainy morning in 1905 when President Theodore Roosevelt took an impromptu ride on the USS *Plunger* (SS-2), America's second commissioned submarine. Not only was he impressed with the easy ride of the boat once she dived away from the weather on Long Island Sound, but he also took note of the pluck of her crew.

After a two-hour trip around Oyster Bay, Roosevelt declared that "submariners have to be trained to the highest possible point as well as to show iron nerve in order to be of any use in their positions." He backed up his words by issuing an executive order giving those who served on submarines an immediate ten-dollar-a-month raise. They also received an additional dollar per man for each time their boats submerged.

Of course, it wasn't the hazardous duty pay that made men like Wes Mayhew and John Potanovic and Charlie Wells and "Cactus" Yotter and the rest of the *Archerfish* crew volunteer for submarines. The money was a plus all right, and certainly patriotism was a big factor. It was obvious the submarines were making a difference in the war, and especially in the Pacific. When a submarine sank a warship, it had an immediate and visible effect on the enemy's war effort, far more so than capturing a hill on some island or holding a line on a battlefield. For men who really wanted to have an impact, submarines gave them a way.

If you asked them, though, all the men aboard *Archerfish* the day they arrived in Pearl Harbor would likely have given the same reasons men give today for choosing the Silent Service. The challenge, the excitement, the quest for the unknown, the desire to be a part of an elite, close-knit group, the same attractions that have led men to volunteer for duty with the airborne, the marines, the Green Berets, the SEALs and other select military groups down through history.

But submariners have always been a different breed, for certain. In his *Tales of the South Pacific*, James Michener noticed the way the sailors from the subs "stood aloof and silent," the way they "gazed at their 'pig boat' with loving eyes." He was struck by the manner in which the sub sailors stood apart from all the other navy men he saw. They've always been unique, and they've always been damn proud of it.

Upon their arrival in Hawaii, there were still a few more things that had to be taken care of before *Archerfish* was ready for her first war patrol. There were minor repairs needed after the trip from the States. Additionally, radar had to be installed, as did four .50 caliber gun mounts on the deck along with lockers for the guns themselves and for their ammunition. She also got a fresh new coat of gray camouflage paint. One very important addition was a food mixer, which Kehl enthusiastically described as "a great aid in making good bread and cake."

Finally, there was yet another training period from December 4 through December 20 in which she test-fired a total of thirteen torpedoes and experienced an "indoctrinational depth charging" from the USS *Wyman* (DE-1038). It wasn't the real thing, but it came as close as possible.

After loading stores and equipment on December 21 and 22, she was finally ready to depart. She first steamed toward the isolated Pacific island of Midway, 1,200 miles to the west for refueling, then headed on to her first patrol area. Their station was a broad swatch of the North Pacific Ocean and East China Sea that included the northern part of Formosa to a portion of the Chinese coast all the way up to the southern tip of the Japanese home islands. That put them over 4,000 miles away from Pearl Harbor. They burned over 36,000 gallons of diesel fuel just getting there.

Archerfish spent Christmas Day, 1943, fighting rough seas and had to put three engines on "propulsion" to "make required good speed." At the submarine base on Midway on December 27, they topped off their tanks, taking on 15,000 gallons of fuel, loaded more fresh provisions, did some minor repairs on the deck plating, calibrated the conning tower depth gauge, and touched up some of the brand-new gray paint that had been washed off by the heavy seas. All this took only four hours.

Archerfish was under way again by midafternoon. The lookouts and those on the bridge waved goodbye to their air escort at 1725 hours.

She was now finally at war, on her way across the broad, open Pacific, transiting hostile waters where every contact could be the enemy. This first patrol would not end until February 15, back in Midway, and *Archerfish*'s experiences would be relatively typical for a World War II diesel boat. There were successes and disappointments. The crew learned with each. But unlike many of her sisters, the *Archerfish* lived to return to the fight another day.

While on patrol, the crew assembled in the forward torpedo room about once a week to watch movies. It was something everyone looked forward to. The screen was placed between the tubes and the mine tables so that about fifteen to twenty crew members at a time could watch the flicks. There was also a relatively good but informal communal library aboard. Favorite reading material on the *Archerfish*, according to John Potanovic, included *Of Mice and Men*, *God's Little Acre*, and *Lady Chatterley's Lover.* For the less literary, comic books featuring Captain Marvel, Green Hornet, and Superman were also popular.

A special point was made to celebrate birthdays and holidays while on patrol. The cooks and bakers went all out, preparing special meals and birthday cakes decorated with personal messages.

In port or at sea, the boat's mess was the general gathering area for the enlisted personnel. One of the benefits of riding submarines was that the galley and the chill box were always open. In port, when there was no cook on duty after the evening meal secured, anyone was welcome to get whatever he had a craving for out of the chill box and fix it himself. There was one rule, though. The galley had to be cleaned up before 0500 when the cooks came on duty. Anyone leaving a mess had his "open ice box" privileges revoked. Still, despite the constant availability of food, most of the crew squirreled away sardines, crackers, canned peaches, and other snacks throughout the boat.

Archerfish crossed the international date line for the first time at 1:10 in the morning on December 29, 1943, making the twenty-ninth one very short day. As they drove on, they dived routinely each day, more often if contacts were sighted, and continued their ongoing drills.

Continual training is a fact of life on submarines, even today. Many of the boat's crew included seasoned submariners. However, this was the first war patrol for not only the *Archerfish*, but also for her captain and half of her officers and crew. Many of them needed all the training they could get. For example, Kehl wrote in his summary of the first patrol: "In general, sound conditions [listening to onboard sound gear to try to detect enemy ships] seemed good. Much fish noises were heard and at one time an inexperienced operator reported screws and got a turn count on what proved to be croaking fish." This wasn't the first young sailor to make such a mistake, but, where they were going, it could prove fatal.

They pulled to a stop on December 30 when they spotted an object floating in the water and determined it to be a mine. Everyone had a good time, firing two drums of 20-mm rounds and two clips from a tommy gun, but they couldn't make the thing explode. They left it bobbing and drove on.

On January 5, 1944, *Archerfish* felt the first rattle of enemy bombs aimed for her. Earlier in the day, they had sighted by radar a sampan and an apparent enemy aircraft. They either evaded on the surface or dived for the depths well before the targets got close enough for them to be seen. At 1411, radar showed an airplane at eight miles, and it was closing quickly. Commander Kehl once again gave the command to dive. Three minutes later, they all heard what appeared to be two distant explosions. Either that or they were only small bombs the plane had dropped. Still, from all indications, someone up there was trying to blow them up. They stayed underwater until 1713. There was no sign of the plane or anyone else when they surfaced.

When *Archerfish* arrived in her patrol area on January 7, a problem had developed with the boat. A gasket in the hull flange of the after engine room air induction was leaking appreciably, especially in deep dives. Captain Kehl cryptically noted in the log: "If we have to stay deep for any period of time in quiet running, this may prove embarrassing." Three men went into the submarine's superstructure to tighten up a loose bolt that was in the way of the gasket. That seemed to help the situation enough to keep them on patrol, but it remained a problem. They also made a note to recommend a different type of material besides soft rubber for that particular gasket.

By the time they were near the east coast of the island of Formosa, *Archerfish* had begun her routine of staying submerged during most of the daylight hours and running on top during the evenings. That's when they recharged batteries and hunted for quarry. Using a boat's radar, low profile, and speed, submariners had found that running on the surface was the better way to find prey. Then they had the option of diving or staying topside when they ultimately made the attack.

There were continuing problems with the relatively new boat's radar and gyro systems, but the weather was the one real hindrance to performing their mission. It seemed to never let up. It was rainy, windy, and nasty during most of their twenty-eight days in the area. Most nights they couldn't even see the stars well enough to use them for navigation. Because of the rough seas, repair work was hard to accomplish when they were on the surface. There was even worry that, if they spotted a worthwhile target off Formosa, the sea was so violent that the torpedoes would have to be set to run at least fifteen feet deep to have any chance of reaching their targets. Set at that depth, the fish would, in most cases, run right under whatever they were aimed at. That lowered the number of potential targets considerably.

As the run of bad luck continued, it was inevitable that the boat was about to have her first "close but no cigar."

Captain Kehl greatly wanted to move around to the west of Formosa, toward the northern end of the Formosa Strait and nearer the Chinese coast. He felt strongly that the hunting would be better there than in the near-empty ocean east of the big island. There were problems with stalking that area, though. The heavy seas and poor visibility made it a very risky proposition. The waters were shallower and more confined in the strait, too, and the weather had made periscope observation more and more difficult. They were relying mostly on radar to detect enemy shipping, but the heavy rain sometimes made even that problematic.

Kehl reluctantly decided to head farther away from Formosa instead. He ordered them back toward Myakojima, the biggest island at the tail end of the spine of small Japanese-held islands that stretched southwest from Kyushu and the Japanese homeland. Just after midnight on January 18, radar finally showed a ship contact at 7,000 yards. The seas were still rolling, the sky was overcast, and the rain was coming down hard, but Kehl and his crew began tracking the ship anyway as it steamed southward at seven knots. Just as they had been drilled to do over and over, they kept their distance from the ship while they worked their way ahead of it.

The entire crew went to battle stations at 0240 as they inched closer to the target. They needed to try to get a visual sighting but visibility in the storm was less than 2,000 yards. Still, the radar pip was so strong, Kehl decided to go ahead and shoot four torpedoes. He desperately wanted to set the fish to run at six feet but was afraid the heavy seas would not allow them to reach the target before exploding. He had his torpedomen set them at ten feet and fired from the stern tubes. Four Mark-14-3A torpedoes zoomed away at eight-second intervals, their exploders set to detonate on contact.

Moments later, they heard two explosions. Then, a minute and a half after that, there were two more. However, without visual contact, they couldn't confirm that the blasts they heard were actually their torpedoes hitting the target.

Kehl did not want to give up on this chance to claim credit for his first kill. He maneuvered around to run in front of where the Japanese ship was assumed to be headed. As they turned, he reloaded the stern tubes so they were ready to shoot again. This time, when they drew within 9,000 yards of the spot where the target should have been, they heard the ominous pinging of sonar. Thankfully, the noise was getting weaker. Kehl quickly surmised that they had been shooting at some sort of shallow-draft escort craft and missed it. The vessel's captain was now furiously looking for *Archerfish* as the ship moved farther away.

Sure enough, the torpedoes had underrun the target and exploded on their own when they got well past it. Ten-foot running settings had been too deep. Eventually, they completely lost the distinctive screw sounds of the target as it moved off. They were still unable to see him with the periscope in the rotten weather.

Archerfish reluctantly gave up the chase. There was general disappointment throughout the boat. They would get another chance at a target, with much better luck, four days later.

The weather had improved slightly by January 22. With the brighter skies, Kehl and his executive officer, James Clark, had decided the day before to backtrack after all. They turned back to patrol the Formosa Strait, even if it should prove to be more dangerous. That decision paid immediate dividends.

At just after 2130 on the twenty-second, as the sub steamed along on the surface, their radar showed a promising contact on a bearing of 011 degrees and a range of 24,000 yards, about thirteen-and-a-half miles away. As the submarine drew closer, they found they were approaching not a single vessel but four large ships and three smaller ones, running in a convoy. The crew knew at once that these targets were worth pursuing. For one thing, they were following a pronounced zigzag evasion course. The convoy was also attempting to hug the western Formosan coastline to avoid detection. They were prime targets!

"Let's determine his zig," Kehl ordered his executive officer. "See if you can figure out what kind of pattern he's running."

"Will do, Skipper."

In order to line up for the best shot, they needed to determine if the ships were following a regular course with their zigzagging or moving more at less at random. But in the process of trying to determine the nature of the maneuvering of her contacts, *Archerfish* almost let the whole column slip past them in the rain and darkness.

"Jim, let's go ahead and come in for a one-two-zero track before they drive off and leave us," Kehl announced.

"I've got it now, Skipper," Clark reported. "They're moving from one-nine-zero to two-four-zero, constant helm. Running three to four minute legs. Recommend we shoot the second ship in the column. She's the closest large one."

Still on the surface, Kehl pointed *Archerfish* directly toward the ship they had been watching. Visually, they could only see the target as a dim outline, but it was the only one of the bunch they could see at all. The others were only radar contacts. Still, they could tell the target was almost surrounded by the three smaller boats, one patrolling ahead, one on her starboard side, and another astern, doing all they could do to protect the larger vessel. Again, all signs pointed to this being a worthwhile use of *Archerfish*'s limited supply of torpedoes.

Kehl decided to fire four torpedoes from the forward tubes, then swing around quickly and fire four more from the aft. If he was going to raise the ire of the destroyer escorts, he was going to make certain he did not let this prize get away.

Archerfish waited patiently until the target reached the left limit of its zig and was about to start back on the zag, just as Clark had determined.

"Fire three!" Kehl barked, and then, in quick succession, sent the other three torpedos spinning out from tubes four, five, and six.

Only a minute later, a terrific explosion shook *Archerfish*. Everyone on the bridge grabbed something solid and held on. The lookout on the small platform in the shears above the bridge reported that the target disappeared only a few minutes after the hit or hits by the submarine's torpedoes. He also described a massive pall of black smoke. Because of the intensity of the explosion and the almost immediate sinking, Kehl assumed they had struck either the magazine of a warship loaded with ordnance or a large ship full of explosives.

Whatever it was, *Archerfish* did not have time to celebrate the killing of her first prey. They were still in the process of swinging around 180 degrees to fire her stern tubes when they realized someone was now shooting back at them. Kehl gave the dive order and they headed for the depths to hide. They had an anxious moment when they shifted to hand power on the bow and stern planes too soon and broached the boat. That meant her mast and fairwater popped back to the surface, making them visible to anyone looking . . . or shooting . . . their way. They quickly got that straightened out and finally slipped beneath the surface of the sea.

Then they had another problem to worry about. They had to flood in an extra 6,000 pounds of seawater to make the boat heavy enough to get through a negative temperature gradient, a dividing point where water temperature is considerably different above and below. Such a gradient can act like a "wall" in the water, and it takes more flooding to drop below it, or more pumping to climb above it. But the gradient also bends sonar pinging as well, making it more difficult for surface vessels to detect a submarine below it or for the sub to see ships on the surface above.

About ten minutes after diving, they settled at 250 feet. That was as deep as they dared go in the shallow water of the Formosa Strait. Soon they felt the first of a series of six quick depth charges boom nearby. The first three explosions did little more than rattle the sub and the nerves of the men inside her. The fourth one shook their dental fillings.

Every man held his breath. The Japanese patrol boats could be getting closer to them. Maybe the gradient wasn't making them as invisible as they had hoped. Or maybe the Japanese were just getting lucky as they blindly dropped the charges much too close to the right place.

It didn't matter. The result would be the same either way. A close blast could do enough damage to send *Archerfish* to the bottom of the sea on her very first outing. As they awaited that explosion, several men on board thought about what an inglorious turn of events that would be, getting sunk on their maiden voyage. No new vessel should have to suffer such ignominy.

The fifth blast was more distant. So was the sixth. Five more explosions rocked them over the next two hours, but none was close enough to cause damage.

Because of the way subs have to operate, claiming credit for sinking an enemy ship has always been an iffy proposition unless there are other allied units in the area to confirm the kill. Quite often, they are shooting from a considerable distance in less than ideal weather. They can hardly afford to stick around or move in for a closer view after shooting their torpedoes either. And if they are successful, their prey ends up in the mud at the bottom. In the case of *Archerfish*'s first sinking, documentation had to be forwarded after the patrol to Admiral Charles Lockwood, Commander Submarine Force, Pacific Fleet, and a determination was made, based mostly on the captain's report and best description of the vessel they sank. Admiral Lockwood's office eventually granted to *Archerfish* a confirmation of the sinking of "1—Passenger-Freighter (class unknown)—9,000 tons."

Early on the morning of January 23, the fireworks finally ceased, and the sub eased farther away from the site of its initial triumph. Spirits were high throughout the boat. Not only had they sunk their first enemy vessel (though they would not receive official credit for it), but they had also survived a rather intense round of depth charges. Each man had done his job well throughout the entire operation, and the boat remained solid.

"We got our first one, men!" Kehl finally proclaimed with a broad smile and a tip of his coffee cup to those in the control room.

"Good a way as any to celebrate a birthday," one of the crew members proudly noted.

"Birthday? Who's got a birthday?" But then the skipper remembered. "Oh, birthday!"

In his log entry for January 22, 1944, Lieutenant Commander George Kehl wrote: "We had celebrated the first anniversary of our keel laying in right smart fashion."

4

AGGRESSIVE SPIRIT

Morale is good notwithstanding disappointment over a fruitless patrol."

That was how George Kehl summed up his crew's state of mind after their second war patrol. They had begun the trip on March 16, 1944, after a month in Midway. That time had been spent fixing the lingering leak in the hull flange gasket, painting topside, and renewing brushes in the number-one main motor after it developed "severe sparking" during torpedo firing exercises. The safety tank, which was normally full of seawater, was filled with approximately 5,400 gallons of diesel fuel prior to departure. It was hoped that this extra fuel would extend the time they could remain in their patrol area.

There was also a sad note in connection with this stay in Midway. One of the torpedomen from the after torpedo room, George Hepfler, didn't show up for muster on the morning of March 2. Hepfler was known as a nice guy who mostly kept to himself. He was last seen the night before, leaving the "Gooney Bird Hotel," the submarine rest camp on Midway, headed back to *Archerfish*. There was a general fear that he might have fallen off the narrow wooden dock and into the sea. Sure enough, his body was found in the small boat basin on March 5. He had drowned.

Hepfler was buried at sea in a moving ceremony held aboard one of the harbor vessels. An honor guard from *Archerfish* served as pallbearers, but none of the men who worked side-by-side with him in the after torpedo room could attend the service. They were too busy getting ready to depart for the patrol. The base chaplain performed standard navy burial-at-sea rites. The sub had suffered its first casualty, but not at the hands of the enemy.

Once under way again, they had a "small epidemic of common colds." They also had more problems with their radar and spent a great deal of time tuning it, replacing tubes, and testing.

Despite *Archerfish*'s continuing troubles with their set, radar had proved to be one of the American submariners' biggest advantages over the Japanese. Few of the Japanese ships or submarines were yet equipped with radar. The technology allowed the Americans to detect enemy targets well before the Japanese were aware they were being stalked. Along with the torpedo data computer (TDC), another major innovation, American skippers could now draw precise coordinates to potential targets from a great distance and then shadow those targets until they had the best possible shots. Success rates were soaring. Properly working and fully tested radar, along with operators who were trained in its use, gave U.S. submarines a tremendous leg up in the battle for the Pacific.

On March 25, *Archerfish* received special instructions from ComSub-Pac to head for an area near Palau, a group of islands north of New Guinea and east of the Philippines. It was a long way to steam, and Kehl doubted there was any chance of getting there by the designated time. The trip was complicated by the appearances of occasional Japanese aircraft that sent them into hasty dives. They also had trouble with the flood valve in negative tank, which was used to provide negative buoyancy for quick diving. That made it take longer than usual to go under. There was a possible case of appendicitis with one of the crew, too. All the while, as they steamed toward their assigned area, they continually looked for possible targets.

There were none.

Kehl assumed that the major operation on Palau that they were supposed to be supporting was the reason for a dearth of Japanese shipping in the area. Whatever it was, there was nothing for them to shoot at, and dodging all the aircraft contacts was beginning to wear on everyone's nerves.

Finally, with the sub low on fuel, ComSubPac told *Archerfish* to leave the area and head for Johnston Island for refueling, then to go on to Pearl Harbor for refitting. Kehl noted, "Headed accordingly. Warned to look out for Jap subs. Plan to run submerged during daylight while in this area in hopes of knocking one off and to keep from getting knocked off."

Kehl and his crew still had hopes of bagging some kind of kill on this patrol. It was not to be. They did not encounter any Japanese ships, but *Archerfish*'s hard luck continued. After taking on 14,900 gallons of fuel at Johnston Island and setting out for Pearl Harbor farther to the east on April 23, Kehl attempted to make a dive at 0535 on the twenty-fifth.

She simply would not go under.

The lights on the indicator panel in the control room, the Christmas tree, were showing everything working normally. That was clearly an error. The boat would not submerge.

They discovered that the vent on the bow buoyancy tank, the one that had given them trouble before going through the Panama Canal, was not opening to allow seawater to flood in and take the bow down. The crew could not even force the vent open by shifting to "hand operation" and placing a long "cheater bar" on the operating arm.

That meant *Archerfish* was stuck on the surface with the sun already up, a clear target for any enemy aircraft or ships. Fortunately, they were not in what was considered enemy waters. Still, it was a tense time until the manhole cover to the bow buoyancy tank could be removed and the linkage to the vent unstuck with "bar and hammer."

They were finally able to dive again at 0720.

During the refit back at Pearl, *Archerfish* said goodbye to her first skipper. Lieutenant Commander George Kehl was replaced by Lieutenant Commander William Harry Wright.

Kehl went on to a long and distinguished naval career. He later had occasion to witness some of the most awesome firepower ever exhibited on this planet while assigned to Bikini Atoll during Operation Crossroads, the atomic bomb tests there in 1946. He also commanded the USS *Libra* (AKA-12), served as superintendent of planning and estimating at the Portsmouth Naval Shipyard, and was the senior naval representative at the meetings of the Korean Armistice Commission in 1956 and 1957. He also helped negotiate the release of a commercial airliner with twenty-six passengers and crew aboard that had been abducted by the North Koreans in 1958. Kehl eventually retired from the navy in 1961 and then taught mathematics at Portsmouth High School for six years. *Archerfish*'s first skipper died in 1973.

Commander Wright guided *Archerfish* away on her third war patrol, leaving Pearl Harbor on May 28, 1944. They were headed once again for Midway and a refueling and replenishing stop there. She was then on her way to a station near the Bonin Islands, a string of tiny Japanese-held islands in the Pacific Ocean north of the Marianas. One of the Bonins is a rocky piece of land most folks heard of later, a place named Iwo Jima, the site of the famous photo of the Marines raising the Stars and Stripes.

Sure enough, *Archerfish* suddenly found herself in the middle of the operation designed to soften up Iwo Jima for the invasion that would come the following year. Her primary mission there was to serve lifeguard duty, picking up downed pilots during the intense, carrier-based attacks that were being thrown at the Japanese on Iwo Jima. At the same time, she was still charged with watching for any possible targets.

There would be plenty.

On June 23 and 24, Wright and his crew watched all the enemy activity on Iwo Jima from a distance, but were amazed at what they saw through their periscope. They counted seventy-six enemy planes on the ground at one point and observed a fighter umbrella in the air and a constant flow of bombers taking off and landing from there. There was also plenty of ship activity into and out of the "beach."

On the second morning there, they surfaced and watched a vicious dogfight that was taking place in the sky west of the island. At least four planes went down in flames. They moved closer to try to help but had to dive when enemy fighters buzzed them. One bomb exploded nearby, and they went to 150 feet to hide for a while.

Over the next few days, they tracked and stalked a number of potential targets, but the ships they chased usually proved unworthy of torpedoes. In some cases, Wright believed shooting at them in their present position so near the island would bring down a rain of hellfire on his boat. Also, many of the ships rode too high in the water for the torpedoes *Archerfish* and the other submarines carried. Even if set to run at their most shallow, the fish would simply zoom right beneath the targets, missing them altogether. At the same time, *Archerfish* still had a primary mission of rescuing downed aviators, and unless they had their sights on an especially fine target, it was best to remain undetected.

Then, on June 29, about midmorning, they spied a target they could not resist. It was a Japanese destroyer at 4,000 yards, running alone after escorting another ship into the anchorage at Iwo Jima. Despite being close to the beach and underneath tremendous air cover, *Archerfish* boldly squared around and, in a submerged attack, fired four torpedoes from her bow tubes at a range of 1,160 yards.

The commander of Submarine Division 201 would later sum up this attack in his report to ComSubPac with something of an understatement: "The aggressive spirit displayed in pressing home this attack is noteworthy."

Commander Wright watched through the periscope as the first fish hit the target forty-two seconds later, slamming into the destroyer just forward of the mainmast. The ship was immediately enveloped in steam and smoke. The second torpedo struck beneath the ship's bridge. Wright later noted in the log that "flame, smoke, debris, and people shot out of the field of the scope. The bow was observed to break upward at about a thirty degree angle." The Japanese destroyer was a goner. "On last observation," Wright reported, "only settling steam and smoke were visible at the target."

Still, Wright saw that the sky remained filled with airplanes and that watercraft were already swinging in their direction from near the beach. They cleared the area, rigged the boat for depth-charging, and went down to 400 feet as they withdrew.

The first two nearby explosions, from either aerial depth bombs or depth charges, apparently damaged the sub's sound heads. They were effectively deaf. There were more detonations, but, thankfully, they came from much farther away. Still, they stayed below for over eleven hours before daring to come up again.

Archerfish had sunk her second ship, and there was no doubt about what this one was—a Japanese *Hatsuhara*-class destroyer, 1,400 tons. She got her next chance at a target only a few days later, on July 2.

They had spotted another enemy ship that resembled an American LST ("landing ship tank," though men who rode on them preferred to call them "large slow targets"). They had to pass on taking a shot for a familiar reason: they did not have torpedoes that could be set to run at less than six feet deep, and the LST only drew four to five feet of water. Wright noted in the log the "crying need for a torpedo that will run at a depth from surface to four feet in smooth seas" so targets such as this one and the many small escort crafts they had seen could be hit.

At 10:40 in the morning, they noticed a smudge of dark smoke on the horizon. Despite all the newfangled radar *Archerfish* carried, seeing the smoke from their stacks was still a primary way of detecting approaching vessels, just as warships had done since the first steamships began traversing the world's oceans. Sure enough, a convoy was being formed and was already zigzagging on a general southerly course away from Iwo Jima. It consisted of one large ship and four smaller ones, escorted by two destroyers.

Wright peered through his 'scope from a range of 3,000 yards.

"XO, I can see troops and equipment all over the topside of the big one," he reported. "That'll be our target. Let's fire a full nest forward. I don't want to leave any cripples."

They continued to track until they had a good angle on the big ship. Then they fired six torpedoes, set to run at six to ten feet deep. One of the destroyers spotted the bubbles that the steam-powered torpedoes emitted as they ran beneath the surface. Wright watched as the destroyer turned with the tracks but away from the submarine.

Good. Maybe they wouldn't come after *Archerfish* after all.

Meanwhile, Wright ordered the sub turned around by 180 degrees. As soon as she had her butt turned to the target, two minutes after the initial fish were away, she fired two more torpedoes from her after tubes. These torpedoes were aimed at one of the destroyers. *Archerfish* maneuvered slightly, aiming all the time as coordinates were called down and entered into the TDC. The order was given to fire the two Mark-18s that were loaded in the remaining after tubes.

At the same time, Commander Wright saw something frightening in the periscope sweep he was conducting. The first destroyer had turned abruptly and was "giving our scope a zero angle and was coming in with some speed, range 1,200 yards." The Japanese were going to give chase after all.

Wright assumed that all torpedoes were away by now and gave the command to rig for depth charge. The outer doors to the torpedo tubes were immediately slammed shut. However, the tenth torpedo had not yet been fired and still rested in one of the after tubes. Only nine torpedoes had been sent toward targets. Wright later apologized for the error, but at that moment, failure to fire one fish was the least concern on everyone's mind.

All hell was about to break loose.

The crew of the *Archerfish* heard four explosions that coincided with the estimated run times of their first batch of torpedoes. Then, the men in the conning tower heard another blast that correlated to the fish that were fired from the after tubes. The men in the after torpedo room said they clearly heard two explosions, that two of their fish had found a target. At any rate, they had certainly hit something. They were later credited with inflicting damage on the large transport and on one of the destroyers, a total of 12,000 tons, but despite all the mayhem they had set loose, the boat did not receive credit for sinking any of the ships they had shot at.

There was no time for confirming sinkings or celebrating just then. They were diving fast and deep, passing four hundred feet and drawing off to the westward, trying to evade the destroyer that was now chasing them. They picked up the sound of the ship's screws directly overhead, and then heard the ominous splashes of its powerful depth charges as they hit the water and sank toward them. Moments later, the sub was rocked by a thunderous series of nearby explosions. Over the next hour or so, a total of 107 charges were dropped. Radar Technician Richard M. Cousins, who manned the JP sonar, counted them all as he listened, his body braced as best he could against the violent concussions.

Commander Wright later wrote, "Although the effect [of the brutal depth charging] was sobering, the lads that day learned to love a boat that could take such punishment."

And she did take the punishment. Despite the fierce barrage, *Archerfish* held together just fine, and all compartments reported no damage.

Archerfish picked up her first downed aviator on Independence Day, 1944, within sight of the island of Iwo Jima. He was a young pilot named John B. Johnson, flying off "Big Ben," USS *Franklin* (CV-13). His Gruman F6F had been struck by Japanese fire. He parachuted into the blue Pacific and then floated there in his bright yellow raft.

When the crew pulled the grateful pilot aboard, he asked if he could keep his raft as a souvenir. The captain was hesitant but finally agreed. There wasn't time to deflate it and bring it down a hatch so they secured the raft to the cigarette deck. They realized by the nearby splashes in the water that shore batteries had opened up on them. They were being shot at! There was also a blip on radar that indicated a plane was ten miles out but heading their way quickly.

"Executed well-known maneuver commonly known as 'getting the hell out of there,' " Wright recorded in the log.

Captain Wright told Johnson he would have to work for his keep and sent him to the lookout platform in the shears (the area above the bridge where the scopes and masts are housed) to keep an eye on the approaching aircraft. As it grew nearer, the rescued pilot kept reassuring the captain that the plane was "one of ours." When it was only a mile away, Wright suddenly called out, "Clear the bridge! Clear the bridge! Dive! Dive!" As the skipper sounded the diving alarm, the lookouts were already scrambling from the shears to jump down the upper conning tower hatch.

They immediately headed for the depths, but by "decks awash," just as the ocean was beginning to cover the sub, they were wickedly strafed by the Japanese fighter. Captain Wright turned to Johnson and pointedly said, "No wonder you were shot down. You can't tell one of theirs from one of ours! I could plainly see the 'rising sun' and you had the binoculars."

A damage report was requested, and all compartments reported a "tight boat." They later found an antenna shot away and 20-mm fragments in the shears, but there was no other serious damage.

They also took a wicked depth-charging. The captain was puzzled about how the Japanese planes circling overhead were able to pinpoint their position so closely while they were underwater. Then he realized they were likely using the pilot's yellow raft, which was still lashed to the cigarette deck, as a convenient bull's-eye. Even at several hundred feet deep, the bright colored object was visible from the air. As soon as it was safe, they surfaced and deep-sixed Johnson's souvenir.

John B. Johnson went on to become a rear admiral and assistant chief of naval personnel for the Naval Reserve. During the course of the war, submarines rescued over five hundred airmen, including one of our future presidents. George H. W. Bush was rescued by USS *Finback* (SS-230) after his torpedo bomber was brought down by antiaircraft fire over Chichi Jima.

On July 6, *Archerfish* picked up another downed pilot, but this one was an oil-covered Japanese aviator who had been shot down in all the furious action above Iwo Jima. Although there were other enemy survivors in the water, he was the only one of them willing to be rescued by an American boat. The prisoner was manacled to a bunk in the after torpedo room, and the electricians were assigned to guard him. He was delivered to Midway at patrol's end. Naval police took him off the boat with a pillowcase covering his head.

Later that night, after picking up the prisoner, they surfaced into an eerie scene. They popped up in the midst of oil and other flotsam, the obvious remains of a wreck or crash. They passed three people floating in the water. However, when they called to them, there was no response. There were other instances of passing through wreckage as they headed back east, of seeing cadavers floating in the water, but they could no longer do anything for these men.

Archerfish returned to Midway on July 15. Three weeks later, after an excellent refit accomplished by the tender *Proteus*, they were off again, on their fourth war patrol, to an area east of Kyushu and south of Shikoku, the southern islands of Japan's homeland.

Among the crew members were Vinny Brundage, the chief cook, Ed Keast, his assistant, and John Healey, a seaman striker who later became a great baker. Joe Baroody was another cook, but he had a rather severe problem, one much worse than the tapeworm he had suffered from before the boat completed sea trials in Portsmouth. It seemed that he was susceptible to seasickness and allegedly turned green, even when the boat was moored at the pier, just from the harbor swell. Willie Baird was an electrician's mate who loved to play "The Wabash Cannonball" on the record player in the crew's mess, much to the chagrin of his shipmates who were not from the South and didn't appreciate the "hillbilly" music. But tears rolled down Baird's cheeks as Roy Acuff sang the old standard. Another character aboard at the time was a throttleman named Bill Sherman, who was observed during a depth-charging, leaning back nonchalantly on a big toolbox, enjoying sardines and biscuits while all those around him were saying their Hail Marys.

Less than a week into the trip to the assigned station, not far out of Midway, Wright and his crew ran up on an enemy diesel trawler, armed with two 20-mm or 40-mm deck guns and with depth charges prominently loaded in the after rack, ready to drop on an American submarine. Wright hesitated. If any of his men should be wounded in an attack, they would have to be treated on board the sub for the next thirty days, until the patrol was over.

After consideration, he decided they were five hundred miles from the nearest land, so the enemy ship would not be able to summon any help. Besides, the target was simply too good to pass up. They stayed outside the trawler's likely effective range of 3,000 yards and did a surface attack, using *Archerfish*'s four-inch deck gun instead of torpedoes. It was early in the patrol, so Captain Wright wanted to save those for bigger, less maneuverable targets.

Once they surfaced, the Japanese patrol boat spotted them immediately and began firing at them, but its shots were falling a good thousand yards short. *Archerfish*'s crew fired five rounds at the trawler with their four-inch deck gun, and the enemy boat was suddenly lost in a cloud of smoke.

Wright squinted through his binoculars.

"You see what they're doing?" he asked Bob Bobczynski, who was now his executive officer.

"Looks like they lighted a smoke canister and now they're hiding in all the smoke," the exec answered.

"Right! They want us to think they're on fire."

Then, as the smoke suddenly cleared, Wright and the rest of the men on the bridge watched as the ship jettisoned its depth charges and headed directly for them. They could now see the damage they had inflicted. The trawler's upper works were heavily damaged, and its mast was gone. *Archerfish* continued to fire away. Though there were no signs they had inflicted any damage on the engineering plant or below the patrol boat's waterline, they felt they had almost certainly caused casualties. Also, the damage to the ship's topside ensured it would have to leave its station and return to port, no matter what.

Wanting to err on the side of caution so early in the patrol, Wright decided not to move in for the kill. The Japanese patrol boat still had the ability to shoot back, even if it was afire and heavily damaged.

They drove on. They were later credited with damaging a patrol boat, 250 tons.

The enemy patrol boat would turn out to be their only target for the entire patrol. They returned to Midway on September 24 without firing another shot or launching a single torpedo. The disappointment is obvious in the commander's personnel report in the final patrol summation: "Although contacts and action with the enemy were at a disheartening minimum, the officers and men retained their sharp spirit of aggressiveness throughout the patrol. Their state of training and morale remain high as all hands look forward to better luck next time."

As they picked up the pilot boat and obediently tailed the vessel back into Midway once again, several men noted that it had been just over a year since their boat's formal commissioning and they had four war patrols under their belt. They had nothing to be ashamed of. They had struck blows against the enemy. Still, as their captain noted, they all looked forward to better luck next time out.

But now, as they eased back into Midway, as they prepared for their next assignment and picked up yet another new skipper, no one aboard *Archerfish* could have imagined the "better luck next time" that they were about to have.

Nor could they have ever comprehended the size of the prize they were about to bag.

5

"O-BOAT JOE" AND *SHINANO*

OUT of war there inevitably emerge stories of victory and defeat, and we are sometimes reminded how narrow the boundary can be between each. The sinking of the Imperial Japanese Navy's most prized, supersecret vessel, the aircraft carrier *Shinano*, by a U.S. diesel boat named *Archerfish* is a perfect example. It shows how luck, skill, and tenacity can all come together, resulting in a glorious, history-altering success. Or how those same attributes can spell tragic defeat, depending on one's perspective.

The story of that historic, fateful encounter includes so many unique aspects, so many fascinating subplots, it almost reads like well-crafted fiction or plays like a Hollywood movie. But it is all true, and its characters are real. There's a Japanese captain, soon to receive his stars as a rear admiral. This captain had once watched as two of his comrades deliberately and ingloriously went down with their doomed ship after a fiery defeat at the hands of the Americans.

Another primary character in this scenario is a massive new vessel, newly constructed, an "unsinkable" supership that is almost certainly the last great hope the Japanese navy has if it is to regain the upper hand in the battle for the Pacific. But this spectacular vessel is jinxed from the very beginning.

Add in another interesting character, a promising but discouraged submarine commander, a self-doubting man who finds himself reborn, primarily as the result of a late-night poker game.

Even the sign of the zodiac figures into this fascinating story, one that is now recognized as a classic of submarine warfare. Those are only some of the elements of this story. And never mind that it also includes a dramatic six-and-a-half-hour encounter on the high seas that may well have turned the course of the war. And that most assuredly changed history as well.

Certainly, as with any historical battle, there are the elements of tactics, of decisions made under intense pressure, of guesses, right and wrong, that will be studied, dissected, analyzed for generations to come. But it is mostly a story of two men, two crews, two vessels, brought together one night on a moonlit sea. It is a story that begins in North Dakota and in the highest reaches of the Imperial Japanese Navy, starts to come together at a poker game on the South Pacific island of Midway and in Drydock No. 6 at Yokosuka Naval Shipyard on Tokyo Bay, and culminates off the south shore of the Japanese home island of Honshu two days before Thanksgiving in 1944.

Captain Joseph F. Enright seemed to have an unlikely heritage for a man who would become captain of a submarine. He was born in 1910, about as far from the sea as a man can be. He was a North Dakotan, the son of an Irish father and Norwegian mother. It was his uncle Frank, his dad's brother, a World War I navy veteran, who lit the spark. Frank Enright had regularly mailed his nephew postcards from the many exotic ports he visited, urging him to consider Annapolis when he was old enough. There was some appeal in those postcards to a young man who was growing up, working odd jobs, and going to school in Bismarck, on the cold prairies of the upper Midwest, so Joe decided to follow his uncle's advice. Thanks to his father's urging, U.S. Senator Gerald P. Nye gave young Joe an appointment to the U.S. Naval Academy in 1929.

He did his family proud. Joe graduated from Annapolis in the top half of his class in 1933. As a raw ensign, he served for three years on the USS *Maryland* (BB-46) before entering submarine school. His first duty as a submarine officer was aboard USS *S-38* (SS-143) stationed at one of those glamorous places pictured on his uncle's postcards, Pearl Harbor in Hawaii. In 1939 he was transferred to USS *S-22* (SS-127) based in New London, Connecticut. He was serving as that boat's executive officer and the vessel was in Argentia Bay, Newfoundland, when word came of the Japanese attack on Pearl Harbor.

Enright's boat was quickly dispatched to Panama. Their mission there was to guard the Pacific entrance to the canal from the Japanese. Six months later, *S-22* was sent to Great Britain, but Joe Enright was not to make the trip. The navy had bigger plans for the boat's promising young exec. He stopped off in New London to assume command in June 1942 of USS *O-10* (SS-71). The *O-10* was a school and teaching submarine that was used to take Submarine School students out for practice dives in Long Island Sound. Enright enjoyed this duty and was quite popular with everyone stationed in New London. He quickly became known to his friends as "O-Boat Joe of the Oh One Oh."

Less than five months later, Enright became part of a new navy initiative designed to get the service's best and brightest young submarine officers ready for the unique, brutal undersea war that was already being fought in the Pacific. He was assigned to Prospective Commanding Officers School at New London. The school was really little more than a cram course in how to run submarine war patrols. Its first class was made up of ten experienced sub commanders who were on a fast track to captain new boats that were bound for the Pacific. Joe Enright was one of them.

They had no textbooks. They used actual war patrol summaries from battle action, reports so recent that they often showed up by airmail, fresh off the duplicating machines in San Francisco. Much of their class time was spent aboard two submarines, the USS *Mackerel* (SS-204) and USS *Marlin* (SS-205). While these were new, well-equipped boats, they did not have the size or range to be used against the Japanese. Still, they gave the students great experience in stalking and "shooting" at targets provided for them out on Long Island Sound. This also gave them the opportunity to practice the practical tactics that sub skippers were finding most useful against the Japanese. They could experience real-life situations only a few weeks after they had actually occurred halfway around the world.

In March 1943, two months before a new boat named *Archerfish* was christened up the coast in Portsmouth, New Hampshire, Joe Enright was designated Prospective Commanding Officer of a brand-new *Gato*-class submarine, USS *Dace* (SS-247). This was the first sub constructed in Electric Boat Company's Victory Yard in Groton, Connecticut. A great many of the workers who helped build her were women. As Enright noted, " 'Rosie the Riveter' had been replaced by 'Wendy the Welder.' "

Joe Enright was a lanky, round-faced man, with pale blue eyes, a quick wit, and a broad, easy smile. He was well liked by his crew on *O-10* and by the other officers with whom he attended the Prospective Commanding Officers' School, just as he had been at the academy. He was also clearly on the verge of becoming the promising submarine commander that the 1933

Lucky Bag, the Annapolis yearbook, had predicted. Both he and his new boat were on a fast track for action. He had been promoted to lieutenant commander in October 1942. He reported to the supervisor of shipbuilding at Electric Boat Company to take over the *Dace* in March 1943. The boat was launched on Easter Sunday, April 25. She was commissioned in July, did torpedo testing in Newport, Rhode Island, in August, and left for the Panama Canal on September 6, two-and-a-half months ahead of *Archerfish*'s trip through "the Big Ditch."

Like many sub commanders, Joe Enright was his own man. He insisted on having a few comforts in his cabin that were not exactly regulation. He had a two-foot-by-four-foot patch of carpet on the floor because he didn't like the feel of the cold deck on his bare feet. The North Dakota winters had given him more than enough of that. He also made sure the polished metal mirror was replaced by one made of real glass. He told anyone who asked, "I'll take full responsibility if I get hit with flying glass while I'm shaving during a depth-charging."

With his glass mirror and carpeted stateroom and brand-new boat, the young commander was more than ready to take on the Japanese. Enright later wrote, "I was elated. [Getting the *Dace* command] was another of my lucky breaks. I was one of the first of my class to get command of a new sub right from the building yard." He was also delighted to find that his crew included an executive officer, Bill Holman, and a number of other officers and crewmen who had already served on war patrols in the Pacific. Even as confident as he was, the skipper knew how valuable the war experience of his shipmates would be for a rookie captain.

Lieutenant Commander Enright's elation was to be short-lived.

Dace steamed into Pearl Harbor on October 10 and was off on her first war patrol seventeen days later. When Enright and his officers opened their orders, they were quite pleased. They had been assigned to patrol area number 5, a busy box in what had been termed the "Hit Parade," south of the major Japanese home island of Honshu. There would be targets aplenty, and the young commander was sure he could quickly prove that the faith his superiors had placed in him was justified.

However, for one reason or another, they never seemed to be able to get into position to shoot at anything. At one point, they received solid intelligence that gave them the location, speed, and course of a Japanese aircraft carrier steaming nearby. It was the *Shokaku*, one of the carriers from which the attack planes bound for Pearl Harbor had been launched. The Japanese carrier had also participated in the Battle of the Coral Sea. It would be sweet revenge and quite a coup for its promising young commander if Enright and *Dace* could send that flattop to the bottom on her very first patrol.

Later, Enright admitted that he made one crucial mistake. He worked the attack "by the book" instead of following his gut instincts. Whatever the reason, in the process of shadowing *Shokaku*, *Dace* allowed the carrier to slip past, and she was gone. They never even got a chance to fire a torpedo at her.

Joe Enright had failed miserably on his first big opportunity.

It was a bitter pill for the confident young commander to swallow. As they pointed *Dace* back toward Midway, he doubted he would ever again have such a perfect target presented to him. By the time he stood on the bridge on December 11, watching their tiny destination island come into view, Enright had already convinced himself it was all his fault, that he was the weak link that had let *Shokaku* slip away.

There was no denying the facts. He had a fine, experienced crew and a new boat. They had been presented with an ideal shooting gallery for a patrol area. A textbook target had floated right before their eyes. Now here they were, the patrol over, disappointedly returning to Midway with nothing to show for it all.

The next day, after a sleepless night, an embarrassed Enright asked Captain J. B. Longstaff, the senior submarine officer on Midway, to relieve him of his command of the *Dace*. He told Longstaff that a skipper who could do a better job should replace him.

Such a request was unheard of. Sub commanders tended to be an ego-driven bunch. They rarely admitted mistakes, let alone asked outright to be replaced. Such a move would certainly damage an officer's career beyond repair. Still, Longstaff passed along Enright's request and the navy granted it, even though no one ever blamed him for failing to mount an attack on the *Shokaku*. No one but Joe Enright himself. Most of the brass, and especially the commander of the Pacific Fleet Submarine Force, Admiral Charles A. Lockwood, knew how difficult it was out there. They rarely engaged in second-guessing their sub commanders. And Lockwood pointedly forbade it.

The command of *Dace* went to one of Enright's best friends, Lieutenant Commander B. D. Claggett. The *Dace* played a major role in the battle for Leyte Gulf in the Philippines and eventually ended up in the Italian navy in the 1950s, renamed *Leonardo da Vinci*, before being scrapped in 1975.

Soon, despite giving up his command, Enright found himself serving in another important and useful position. He was named executive officer of the submarine base at Midway, which had become known as "Gooneyville" after the awkward-looking gooney birds that lived there. But in the grand scheme of things, Enright knew he was now "on the bench," out of the game. He certainly wasn't doing the one thing he had trained all those years to do.

One of the hardest things had been to tell his parents what had happened. They had come out from North Dakota by train the previous July to proudly watch as their son's new boat was commissioned. The letters from his mother almost always mentioned how pleased she and his father were of what he had accomplished. When he gave up his command, it was heartbreaking for the disillusioned young man to write to his mother and tell her about it. His parents knew better than anyone how hard he had trained, how proud he had been of his submarine and crew. Now, when they read this letter, they would also know how disappointing his failure was.

As he watched from his office window the constant coming and going of the submarines, as they hastily refueled and restocked and then drove back out for more battles, Joe Enright felt more than ever that the war was passing him by. He lay awake at night and considered asking for another command, but he always dismissed the thought. He had been given his chance and he had blown it. There was a vicious war to be won. Somebody who was a better skipper than he was required out there, manning that conning tower or bridge, running the attacks, firing the deadly complement of fish at enemy ships.

It eventually took a sudden death and a fortuitous poker game to get Captain Joseph F. Enright back on the bridge of a submarine where he belonged. To get him back on the way to bagging *Shinano*.

THOUSANDS of miles to the west of Gooneyville, a mammoth form was finally taking shape in Dry Dock 6 at the Yokosuka Navy Yard, just down the bay from Tokyo. The *Shinano* had been under construction for four years. In the beginning, she was intended to be a superbattleship, a sister to *Yamato* and *Musashi*, two of the biggest warships ever constructed. However, the Japanese had learned a bitter lesson at the Battle of Midway. They realized that any hope of victory depended on the use of fighter aircraft launched from carriers. The decision was made to complete this behemoth as an aircraft carrier instead of as a battleship.

The ship was so massive it had to be assembled in the dry dock instead of the usual slipway. Her statistics boggled the mind. She had a displacement of 72,000 tons, a hull that was almost 840 feet long, and a flight deck that was forty-eight feet above her waterline and the size of two football fields. Powered by steam turbines, she was designed to run at a top speed of twenty-seven knots and have a range of ten thousand miles without refueling. Her hangar deck and flight deck were built of steel almost four inches thick, backed with three feet of concrete sandwiched between steel plates, all to repel dive-bombers such as had wreaked such havoc on the Japanese fleet at Midway.

Traditionally, the Empire's battleships were named for the provinces of Japan. *Shinano* was originally named for an ancient prefecture now a part of Nagano. The prefecture bore the name of the country's longest river, which flowed north to the Sea of Japan. The decision was made to keep the battleship name, though, even when she was completed as an aircraft carrier. That was more for superstitious reasons than practical ones. It was considered bad luck to change a ship's name once it had been written down.

Shinano was built behind an unbelievably thick veil of secrecy, even for those treacherous times. U.S. Naval Intelligence was aware that at least two of the massive battleships were under construction, and they were also aware when they were eventually launched. They had no idea whatsoever that there was a third vessel being built, that it was being converted to a carrier, or that it would be the largest warship in the world. Neither did the Japanese people, until well after the war was over.

The yard workers who were assigned to her construction were required to live in Yokosuka so the Kempeitai, the Japanese secret police, could better watch them. A thick, galvanized steel fence surrounded the dry dock on three sides. A tall, steep cliff effectively blocked the view of the other side. No curious eyes could see the ship at rest as she was being completed. No one was allowed to have a camera anywhere in the shipyard. *Shinano* was the only major warship built in the twentieth century that was not photographed during its construction. The ship could not even be mentioned, much less named, in any radio transmission. Security was so complete that there was no image or description of *Shinano* or anything similar in the U.S. Navy's *Recognition Manual,* the book carried by all submarines to aid in identifying targets.

Security was not perfect. The United States did unwittingly snap one photo of the ship. An American B-29 bomber named *Tokyo Rose,* flying a reconnaissance mission more than 30,000 feet over Tokyo in early November

1944, took a picture of the bay at the same time *Shinano* was out of her "barn" for builders' trials. It was a bright day, the sky free of clouds. The monstrous carrier left a huge V-shaped wake behind her as she steamed at twenty-four knots to practice recovering aircraft on her deck. She showed up clearly on the photo the airplane took that day. The irony is that the picture never made it to the U.S. Submarine Command, and due to a shortage of photointerpreters, no one knew what a prize they had until well after the war was over. The secret of *Shinano*'s existence was still safe.

One person on board the *Shinano* that November day noticed the lone B-29 high overhead, though. And he correctly assumed a photo had been taken. However, he had no way of knowing that the picture the reconnaissance plane had snapped would never directly cause him or his new ship any harm.

Captain Toshio Abe was shocked and alarmed when he spied the plane high in the sky. Now, after all their precautions and secrecy, the Americans knew of the existence of his new supercarrier. They would almost certainly be waiting for her when she was finally launched. They would arrange to target her with a wolf pack of submarines from their bases in the Marianas. There was no doubt about it.

Every decision the new vessel's captain made in the next few fateful weeks was tinged with the belief that the enemy now knew of his top-secret carrier and that they were poised to destroy her as soon as she left Tokyo Bay.

Abe was an experienced officer. He was a graduate of the Japanese Naval Academy, commander of Destroyer Division 10, and an experienced torpedo officer. He was slated to receive his stars, making him a rear admiral, as soon as they took *Shinano* into the Inland Sea on her maiden voyage, on the way to the Philippines.

Abe had seen his share of war. He was captain of the destroyer *Kazagumo* at the ferocious Battle of Midway in June 1942. American dive-bombers had mortally wounded four proud Japanese aircraft carriers, including *Hiryu*, the flagship vessel of Admiral Tamon Yamaguchi. Even though it was clear *Hiryu* could not survive her wounds, Abe eased his destroyer alongside to offer help in fighting the inferno and to give water to the men who were still trying to save the ship. Finally, early in the morning, Admiral Yamaguchi gave the order to the ship's captain, Tomeo Kaku, to abandon ship.

With eight hundred hands assembled on the deck of the doomed carrier, and with Toshio Abe watching from the bridge of his destroyer,

Yamaguchi made an emotional speech in which he accepted blame for the loss of the carrier and vowed to ride the ship down to his death. Captain Kaku expressed his own desire to go down with his ship in disgrace as well. The two men then ordered Abe and the other nearby destroyer skippers to torpedo the damaged ship once the crew was off, assuring that the Americans would not capture her hulk.

Toshio Abe could not believe the two officers were really going to die with their ship. It was an ancient tradition, but one frowned upon by modern commanders. Abe went aboard *Hiryu* in a last attempt to persuade Yamaguchi and Kaku to save themselves, to live on to fight another day. He knew that Admiral Yamamoto, the commander of the Combined Fleet, had expressly ordered that no more of his officers die in such ritualistic sacrifice. Their experience and skill were far too valuable in a war that was quickly turning against them. Still, despite Abe's best efforts, he was unable to change the officers' minds. They thanked him and ordered him back to his ship.

Just as the sun rose that morning, its rays mockingly resembling the Japanese navy flag, Captain Abe gave the command to fire their torpedoes, sending the carrier, her admiral, and her captain to a deep, watery grave.

Still, Abe never forgot the bravery, the dedication of Admiral Yamaguchi and Captain Kaku. He could not stop thinking about the two men riding *Hiryu* to their deaths. As he returned to Tokyo with what was left of the fleet, he had to wonder how he would act should a similar situation ever present itself to him. Would he strap himself to the bridge and die with his ship? Or would he choose to live to fight another day?

The war took a sharp downturn for Japan after Midway. Now, more than ever, they needed the supercarrier completed and headed for the Philippines where the Americans were already advancing on the Japanese garrison at Leyte. There was no one else to send. Two other carriers, including the *Shokaku*, the target Joe Enright had missed on his first patrol, had recently been lost to American subs off the Marianas. In addition, the superbattleship *Musashi*, originally one of *Shinano*'s sisters, had been sunk at the Battle of Leyte Gulf. The colossal carrier was their last and best hope.

Japanese naval headquarters rushed *Shinano* to completion, and, though hardly finished, she was shipshape enough to be launched four months early, on October 5, 1944. A small crowd gathered for the formal event at eight o'clock that morning. But when the dry dock valves were opened and the water rushed in, a portion of the gate that had been keeping out the waters of Tokyo Bay suddenly gave way. The force of tons of sea-water ripped off and snapped the mooring lines, lifted the giant ship violently upward, and slammed *Shinano* viciously against a concrete wall. Then, on the recoil, she crashed hard into the wall once again. Scores of sailors and dockworkers were hurt, and the ship's bow and sonar compartment were heavily damaged.

Repairs were accomplished in only three weeks, but *Shinano* already had gained the reputation of being a jinxed ship. Many sailors vowed quietly among themselves that they would never serve aboard such a cursed vessel.

Once she was seaworthy and her sea trials completed in the confines of Tokyo Bay, Toshio Abe was ordered to take the carrier to a rendezvous with what was left of the rest of the fleet near Kure, in the Inland Sea, a protected body of water almost completely surrounded by the main Japanese islands. He was to leave his covered berth on November 28. In order to get to the rendezvous, though, he would have to take the ship out of the bay for the first time and steer her through open ocean, where he was certain American subs were lurking sneakily, waiting to attack.

Still, he was confident of his chances of successfully making the run. He was convinced that his new ship's twenty-seven-knot speed was enough to easily outrun any submarine the Americans had. The ship was heavily fortified, especially against dive-bombers. And she was also protected against torpedoes. She was equipped with large metal bulges below the waterline, called "blisters." These were designed to cause any torpedoes to explode well before they could reach the ship's main hull. That limited them to only minor damage. However, because of all the weight from the other armament she carried, *Shinano* only had half the number of blisters *Yamato* and *Musashi* had, and they were installed farther below the waterline, at the depth where the American submarine captains seemed to prefer shooting their torpedoes when the targets were larger. Even with his concerns about the existence of an American wolf pack, Abe was still certain his ship was unsinkable, that they could run to the Inland Sea and he could claim his admiral rank.

A week before he was to sortie, intelligence officers seemed to confirm Abe's suspicions. A wolf pack of American submarines had left the Marianas, bound for the waters off Honshu, the main Japanese island, on which Tokyo was located. Another pack had left Saipan and Guam, likely on their way to hunt the same waters. Abe was more convinced than ever that the Americans knew of his new ship once the airplane had caught them in the bay. Now they were coming to get ready for him when he steamed out of Yokosuka.

There was still more confirming intelligence. There had been at least seven submarines already operating in the waters near Honshu in the last few weeks, sinking picket boats and generally wreaking havoc. Abe had a chart on the wall on the bridge of *Shinano* with X's marking the spots where the American submarines had struck. There was no doubt they were all forming up out there, that they were waiting for him to steam out into the open sea with the Empire's brand-new warship.

Of course, Abe could not have known that those seven subs he was hearing about, called "Burt's Brooms," had no inkling of his existence. They had been sweeping the area of Japanese picket boats so they would not be able to warn the defense forces of a planned attack on the mainland by the U.S. Third Fleet. Now the Americans had determined that the subs were attracting far too much attention and would hinder more than help the planned approach. That attack was later postponed, and, by the time *Shinano* left Tokyo Bay, the submarines had already been dispersed and sent to other areas. Abe never learned, either, that the submarines coming his way from the Marianas would never make it to the waters off Honshu. They were forced back by stronger than expected resistance, bad weather, and bad luck.

But then the captain was faced with a greater and more immediate threat to *Shinano* than the American submarine wolf packs. A threat that would ensure the carrier must leave the harbor as soon as possible. The same intelligence briefing that told of the submarines also warned Abe that there would almost certainly be heavy bombing in the next few days by the American B-29 Superfortresses. It was no longer safe to leave the massive carrier in the shipyard. Even if the Americans did not suspect that she was there, the bombers could unknowingly damage the carrier with the pounding they would inflict on the construction facility. The Yokosuka Navy Yard would certainly soon be a primary target for those American bombs.

Still, even with that knowledge, Captain Abe wanted to wait a few more days before leaving. Flooding tests on the ship's various compartments had not been completed. There were many other portions of the massive ship that remained unfinished.

His request was denied without comment after American bombers struck hard at the Nakajima aircraft factory near Tokyo on November 24 and then again on the twenty-seventh. It was no longer prudent to keep *Shinano* in her berth where she might be destroyed without ever launching a plane in battle. She would make her maiden voyage as planned.

Right on schedule, *Shinano* eased out of the yard on November 28 and passed the sea buoy at the entrance to Tokyo Bay at about six in the evening. Because parts had not arrived on time, only eight of her twelve boilers were operating. That meant she could not run at full speed, but everyone agreed the twenty-four knots she could make if pressed would be more than enough to outrun any American submarines. The ship's 1,100 compartments had still not been fully tested to Abe's liking, but his bosses were satisfied with her seaworthiness. About 300 shipyard workers were still aboard as they pulled away, finishing up as much as they could as *Shinano* steamed toward the Inland Sea. In all, the carrier had over 2,500 officers, sailors, and workers riding her out of the bay that evening. Additionally, she carried fifty *Okah* "special attack" (suicide) airplanes and six *Shinyo* suicide boats. She was delivering them to the other ships she was slated to meet up with in the Inland Sea for transit on to the Philippines. *Shinano* was to get her own complement of aircraft when she finally got to the safety she hoped to find in those guarded waters.

Anyone watching her departure that day would have noticed, in addition to her stunning size, two other striking things about *Shinano's* appearance. One was her unusual rounded bow, a special design to allow her to better cut through the water while cruising. Some said it made the carrier look as if she wore a clown nose. Others said, quietly, that it made the ship downright ugly.

The other oddity was the way her tall smokestacks were canted twenty-seven degrees from the vertical to her starboard side instead of standing straight up or leaning to the stern as they do on most ships. This was a concession made when the decision came to build her as an aircraft carrier with its elevated flight deck instead of as a battleship. The pronounced tilt was necessary to vent the stack gases away from the ship's superstructure, but the effect was to make *Shinano* look as if she were continually listing drunkenly to port.

Captain Abe had learned a week before that he would have no air cover for the transit. That made a night run even more necessary, even if that was prime hunting time for submarines. Now, as they steamed out of Tokyo Bay and toward the open ocean, he had every man aboard busy completing inspection. They were to especially make certain that no lights showed at all. They still weren't using their radio. Throughout the entire four and a half years of construction, for security reasons, the ship had never been mentioned on any radio transmissions. Now, he could make out the dim shapes of his three escort destroyers, each one captained by experienced men who had lived through much in these last three years of war.

As they entered open waters, Abe scanned the horizon, wondering where the wolf pack was by now. He knew there were at least seven of them out there, waiting, looking for his massive shape. But so far, things had gone well.

As he and his escorts passed the island of Inamba Shima, he felt a strong renewal of confidence. They would make the Inland Sea by tomorrow morning. They would then steam on with the fleet to the Philippines. And there, with the help of the new supercarrier, they would win a great naval battle that would once again redirect the course of this war in favor of the emperor and the ancestors.

He gazed at the gilt-framed picture of Hirohito mounted in its assigned place on the bridge. He mentally renewed that solemn vow to his supreme leader. Then he turned and watched the bulbous bow of his wonderful new ship as she plowed ahead into the darkening Pacific, steaming toward glory.

BACK on Midway, Lieutenant Joseph Enright had had a change of heart. While doing his duty as executive officer of the Midway sub base, he had gotten word that his mother had died suddenly from a brain aneurysm. Again, he recalled how proud she and his father had been when he graduated from the academy, when he got his dolphins, when he received his command on the *Dace*. She had never said a word in her letters, but he knew she was disappointed that he no longer commanded a submarine after he had worked so hard to get there. She was not disappointed *in* him. She was disappointed *for* him. That made it even worse.

Shortly after his mother's death, he wrote a letter to Admiral Lockwood requesting another chance as a submarine skipper. He imagined his chances were small but he owed it to his mother's memory to try.

He was still awaiting a response when he found himself involved in a red-hot poker game one night at the Brass Hat Club in Gooneyville. He knew immediately he was in over his head. These guys were serious, and the money in the middle of the table looked like a small fortune to him. Then, late in the game, with lots of luck and a daring bluff, he won a sizable pot from one of the other players, a submarine squadron commander named Leo L. Pace. Joe had held his ground, staring at two pairs in his own hand while Captain Pace showed a couple of jacks on the table. And as he swallowed hard but tried to look calm and cool, Joe drew the perfect card, giving himself a full house, and claimed the pot.

Pace just sat there, looking at the cards on the table in front of him, watching Enright pull the money his way. The squadron commander finally looked up and grinned.

"Joe, if you had the chance, would you run a submarine the way you play poker?" Pace asked, looking Enright straight in the eye.

"Yes, sir!" Enright answered quickly and emphatically.

Pace rubbed his chin thoughtfully. He knew Enright was a good officer. They had first met at the Naval Academy where Pace was a duty officer while Joe was a student there. Unbeknownst to Enright, his letter to Admiral Lockwood seeking reinstatement had been routed through Pace as well. And now the commander had observed the skill and daring with which the young man played cards.

"Tell you what," Pace said. "You can have *Archerfish* when she comes in."

The commander was as good as his word. Enright got his new orders within ten days after the fateful card game. He rode *Archerfish* from Midway back to Pearl Harbor with then-captain William Wright. He assumed command once they got to Pearl. Captain Wright immediately went back to the States where he had a new construction command awaiting him, a submarine still being built that he would skipper.

Enright was well pleased with his boat and crew, and it was clear his reassignment was a popular choice. When *Archerfish* left Midway, a big crowd of Joe's friends was on the dock to wish him well. They even had music, provided by big-band leader Ray Anthony and his group, who happened to be in Gooneyville at the time. The trip to Pearl gave him a good opportunity to get to know the men he would be working with.

"They were the finest band of brothers I ever had the privilege of working with in the navy," he later wrote.

There was the inevitable paperwork to complete, the inspections to carry out, an eight-day training exercise to perform, and all the other work necessary in order to get ready to go back out on patrol, but *Archerfish* and her eager new skipper finally left Pearl Harbor on October 30, 1944. They were rushing to get to their assigned area off the main Japanese island of Honshu, going by way of Saipan in the northern Marianas north of Guam. Then they got word on November 2 that the operation they were to support had been delayed, so they slowed down. That gave them time for test dives and other drills, and they took advantage of the opportunity.

They were moored in Saipan for two days while still more repairs were made to the boat. While work was done on *Archerfish*, the officers were driven around the tiny mountainous island on a much appreciated sightseeing tour. Meanwhile, the enlisted crew members went ashore in walking parties, escorted by officers who were stationed there. They were urged to stay close to each other. The marines had only captured the island from the enemy four months before. There was a real danger from some of the booby traps that were still being discovered. Some Japanese troops remained on the island as well, hiding to avoid capture.

Inevitably, four of the *Archerfish* sailors got separated from the rest. They went off looking for adventure and cold beer, not necessarily in that order. The men decided to take a shortcut through a cane field. One of them pulled up short when he heard something rustling in the thick canebrake ahead of them.

"Halt!" he called out in a voice that he hoped sounded like an angry, mean, rifle-toting marine.

Just then, three Japanese soldiers burst from the cover directly in front of them and ran wildly in the other direction. The fleeing troops left behind a loaded rifle, a bayonet, a medical kit, K rations, and other items, plus four wide-eyed submarine sailors.

"It is very fortunate that we don't have four casualties," Enright later wrote.

Some of the crew also decided to take a swim, against the advice of the marines. Sure enough, for the next several days, there was a high incidence of "furuncles, sties, and other various infections" that kept Chief Pharmacist's Mate Bill Hughes busy dispensing ointment and lancing boils.

With repairs completed and a new story to tell, *Archerfish* left Saipan headed for her patrol area. Once on station south of Tokyo Bay, the boat had two primary assignments: serve lifeguard duty for downed B-29 pilots who were supposed to resume pounding the Tokyo area over the next few days, and report weather conditions to the 73rd Bomber Wing so they could better plan their raids. The boat arrived at her lifeguard station November 11, the day *Shinano* came out of her shed and conducted her builders' trials. The same day *Tokyo Rose* shot her portrait and put fear into Toshio Abe. And the same day the portrait of Emperor Hirohito was hung on the bridge of the colossal carrier.

Over the next two weeks, *Archerfish* dived and surfaced over and over, dodging air and ship contacts. Occasionally they saw bombers headed for the Japanese mainland, but, so far, they had no pilots to pull from the Pacific. They sometimes saw Japanese trawlers or other ships not worthy of torpedoes, but no other potential targets presented themselves. The fact was, with the lifeguard assignment, they were not free to range very far to look for anything to shoot at.

Joe Enright was beginning to wonder if his bad luck still held sway. Maybe he had been right the first time. Maybe he wasn't cut out to be a sub skipper after all.

Then, on November 27, a blustery Monday, he received a radio message that additional bombing raids on the Tokyo-Yokosuka industrial area were being delayed. For the next couple of days, he and *Archerfish* were relieved of their lifeguard duties and could roam at will, looking for anything they could find to sink. The transmission also alerted him to the fact that there were no other submarines anywhere in the area. The ocean was all theirs.

This was wonderful news. Theirs was a promising triangle of ocean, prime for any shipping into and out of Tokyo Bay. Once again, Joe Enright had been blessed with a fine boat, an experienced crew, and a teeming patrol area.

The radio message concluded with "Good hunting!"

As he stood on *Archerfish*'s bridge, the cold sea spray in his face as he guided the boat closer to the Japanese mainland, Commander Enright fingered the rosary beads in his pocket as he thought of his wife, Virginia, and his young son, seven-year-old Joe Jr. He also thought of Minnie, his mother, and of how proud she would have been that he was back doing what he so desperately wanted to do. He hoped he could make them all proud this time, that he could live up to the faith so many people had placed in him, the confidence this bright, determined crew had in him. He also hoped that he would do the right thing when the time came.

Somewhere along the way, someone mentioned to Enright that they were now in late November and that the message that they were free to hunt this crowded stretch of ocean had come just as the sun entered the zodiacal sign of Sagittarius. That, he knew, was the sign of the Archer. Such astrological stuff wasn't such a big deal to a devout Catholic like Joe Enright, but considering his luck so far as a sub commander, he looked for positive omens wherever he could find them.

Just before they were to dive at dawn on the twenty-eighth, the skipper's thoughts were interrupted by his radar officer, Lieutenant Joe Bosza, who had come to the bridge.

"Captain, request permission to take the SJ radar out of service for repairs," he said.

"We got a problem?" Enright asked.

"Just some minor ones, Skipper, and we need to adjust for better performance," Bosza reported. "We'll have it back up by 1700."

Enright thought long and hard before he gave permission to go ahead. Once night fell, they would be blind without the radar. He wanted to be ready for a good night of hunting once they came to the surface at dark. Bosza assured him they would have everything working by then. Enright reluctantly gave his permission.

Still, he stopped by the radar area several times during the day to check on the progress of the repairs. Seventeen hundred hours came and went. Everything was going fine, he was told. They would be back up and sweeping well before dark.

Now, they were close enough to the Japanese mainland to see, and even photograph, Mount Fuji through the periscope. They surfaced just before nightfall, still without radar. There had been no contacts during the day, but with darkness quickly blanketing them, it was time to become more aggressive, to go in search of targets. That's what these fleet boats were designed to do, and *Archerfish* and her crew were ready to finally make a name for themselves.

At 1930, Enright heard from his radar crew that the system was now working but they needed to do some testing and tuning. The skipper groaned when he heard the report. Japanese vessels carried radar detection systems. Once Bosza and his team turned on the radar, the enemy would know that they were there. That took away the sub's best weapon, surprise.

There was no choice. They had to have a working, calibrated radar if they hoped to be as effective as they so desperately wanted to be this night.

Enright told the lieutenant to go ahead and do what he had to do.

Finally, about 2030, Bosza reported everything was working properly. The watch standers on the bridge had already sighted Inamba Shima and called the report down the hatch to the radar team.

"We don't see the island on the radar" came Bosza's response after a short, telling silence.

Joe Enright groaned again. If the radar they had worked on all day couldn't see a damned island, how in hell would it find a destroyer or battleship?

"Radar contact zero-three-zero degrees," Joe Bosza suddenly sang out.

Enright slapped the bridge railing in anger.

"Joe, no matter what your radar shows, Inamba Shima is at zero-six-zero degrees," he growled back. "Fix it!"

"Aye, aye, sir," came the meek reply from below.

But only a few seconds later, the young radar officer reported something new. The excitement was obvious in his voice when he called up to those on the bridge.

"Captain, your island is moving!

CAPTAIN Toshio Abe allowed himself the slightest of smiles when he heard the report his officer of the deck was giving him.

"Sir, we have detected enemy radar. It is the proper frequency for an American submarine."

It was a little after 2030 and the Americans were already bathing them with their radar. Abe knew he had been correct all along. There was a wolf pack of submarines out there beyond the small islands, waiting for *Shinano* to steam out to the open waters. He also snorted at the arrogance of the Americans, daring to use their radar so blatantly, knowing they would certainly be detected.

But then something dawned on him. It was only one of the submarines in the pack that was using her radar. They were intent on misleading anyone who detected the signals into believing there was a lone hunter out there. That boat would then act as a decoy while her mates circled, while they swam into position for the mass killing.

Abe immediately ordered his topside watch standers to be on the lookout for the submarines. The moon was almost full, shining brightly through occasional clouds, and the Americans were likely running on the surface, as was their practice after night had fallen. The ship and her escorts had already assumed the predetermined zigzag evasion course, moving at a quick twenty knots, faster than any American submarine could go. Abe had also once again reminded the destroyer escorts that they were not to venture out from their assigned positions, that they were not to try to sink any of the subs that might be out there watching them, no matter how tempting they might be. Instead, their job was to stay close to *Shinano*, forming a protective screen. They were not to go off chasing some obvious decoy that might be attempting an enticing ruse, luring them away from the carrier they were supposed to be guarding.

A nervous ripple spread throughout the ship as the public address system alerted everyone to the submarines' presence. Captain Abe, though, was still not worried. He could see the nearby dark shapes of the three protective destroyers, diligently guarding his ship. Each carried thirty-six depth charges, more than enough to deal with the Americans. He also knew from watching the construction that *Shinano* was truly as well armored as any ship that had ever been built. She was deceptively fast, too. It would take far more than a swarm of slow American pig boats with their inferior Mark-14 torpedoes to cripple such a floating fortress.

Abe checked the bridge clock, right next to the unsmiling face of his emperor: 2245. They would be safely in the Inland Sea by 1000 the next day, less than twelve hours away.

Just then one of the lookouts reported seeing something, an unidentified vessel about nine miles away. Without the brightness of the moon, no one would ever have been able to see it, but sure enough, several others squinting through their binoculars spied something that appeared to be the sail of a submarine. Abe ordered the signalman to flash a coded recognition message toward the vessel. He did. There was no reply. Whoever and whatever it was, it was certainly not an Imperial Navy vessel.

Suddenly, one of *Shinano*'s escort destroyers broke ranks, abruptly left its screening position, and began a thirty-five-knot dash toward the interloper. The destroyer's lookouts had spotted the dim smudge on the moonlit horizon as well. Her captain knew without a doubt that he could quickly and easily take it down. The mystery vessel was already within range of the destroyer's powerful deck guns, and even if it was a submarine and should dive for the deep, this deadly ship would be on top of the shadowy vessel in minutes. They would be dropping depth charges well before the Americans could go anywhere deep enough to save themselves.

If those were Americans in that submarine out there, they had only about five more minutes to live.

ENSIGN Justin "Judd" Dygert was serving as officer of the deck aboard *Archerfish*. When he heard the radar report of a moving contact at just over fourteen miles away, he swung his binoculars in that direction. He couldn't see anything but moonlight on the water and blackness on the horizon. Above him, a young torpedoman, Marteen W. "Bob" Fuller, was stationed on the lookout platform that was attached to the periscope shears. Captain Enright later noted that Fuller had the superior eyesight of a younger man or he might never have spotted the dark shape so quickly. The contact might well have gotten away in the lost time.

"Contact two points off the starboard bow!" Fuller shouted with conviction.

Now, with that information, Enright and several others could just make out the "bump" on the horizon that Fuller had somehow picked out of the darkness. The captain ordered the sub's bow swung around so they could "track from ahead" and called for full power from the sailors in the maneuvering room. At the same time, every man in the fire control tracking party rushed to his station. Lieutenant John Andrews climbed quickly to the bridge to relieve Ensign Dygert as the officer of the deck. Over the coming hours, Andrews proved just as effective a cheerleader as he was an OOD. Dygert went below to help plot their course in relation to the contact. In the conning tower below, Lieutenant Davis Bunting had the TDC up and running and was already entering the coordinates as they were being reported.

The first tasks were to try to determine what kind of course the contact was following, how fast it was traveling, and, of course, what kind of vessel it was. The blip on the radar screen indicated it was something sizable. If it could be seen from fourteen miles away at night, even as a distant, dim bump on the horizon, then it was definitely something worth pursuing for a bit.

Even though they were still quite a distance from the contact, Torpedoman Edward Zielinski was already on station, making sure his fish were ready to swim. At the command of "Man the tracking party," Lieutenant Rom Cousins became diving officer. Cousins was one of the original crew members, aboard since the commissioning of *Archerfish*, and one of the first in a rather long line of characters who made up the ship's company over the years she was in service. He was an orphan from San Francisco who went on to a career as a bootlegger in San Diego during Prohibition even though he was only sixteen years old at the time. A judge gave him the option of jail or the navy. He made the obvious choice, and had developed into a skilled submariner. He was also a renowned storyteller.

Finally, when they had gained some distance on the contact, Enright ordered "All stop" so they could plot and use the TDC to get a feel for the course and speed of the "moving island."

Southwesterly, two-one-zero degrees. Twenty knots.

It was big all right, but whatever it was, the thing was moving extremely fast for its size. Captain Enright ordered a course to match the contact's, 210 degrees, and for flank speed, about eighteen or nineteen knots while the boat was on the surface. He wanted to keep the target in the "moon streak" on the water, not his submarine.

Now O-Boat Joe had his first crucial decision to make. Textbook tactics demanded that they drive to a position in line with the contact's course, dive, and wait for him to come their way. Then when he was within prime torpedo range, a thousand to two thousand yards, they would shoot.

That's the way a cautious cardplayer would do it. But this was no time to play it wary, not even if he was holding two pairs and the other guy had a jack showing. No, it was time to draw a card and hope for a full house.

"John, let's stay on top and see if we can figure out what that thing is," Enright told Andrews. "Maintain flank speed and let's see if we can get ahead of him and figure out if he's zigzagging and what kind of escorts he's got."

"Aye, sir!"

The dance was on.

Finally, in the light of the moon, Enright could see his gigantic new contact better. He had hoped for a warship of some kind. Now, his hopes fell as he turned to his executive officer, "Mr. Bob" Bobczynski, who had joined him on the bridge.

"Looks like an oil tanker. I can't think of anything else that might be that shape," the skipper said.

"Agreed, Captain. At least for now."

If it was a tanker leaving Tokyo Bay, it was likely empty, headed back to the Philippines for a refill. Not the juiciest of targets, not the warship that he craved, bristling with guns and loaded with ordnance or troops, but still something worth pursuing.

The radar operator reported a small blip now showing up to the left of the target. That made the diagnosis even more likely. It was a lone tanker with a single escort. With that information, Enright decided on a daring surface attack. Whatever it was, he and his boat needed to sink it. They would have to be within 3,000 yards of their target to be effective, but, with the moon behind the tanker and with *Archerfish's* bow always pointed toward the target, they should be able to sneak up and shoot.

"Turn right to a course of two-seven-zero. Stop when we are five miles from the target's track," Enright ordered. Then he gave the command that every man on board had been waiting for. "Man battle stations."

"Man battle stations torpedo!" Andrews sang out.

The sub's gong resounded throughout the boat. All compartments reported in order and immediately that they were ready. From the "snipes" back in the engine rooms to the lookouts on the bridge, every man aboard *Archerfish* did his job quietly and efficiently.

Enright alternated between his spot on the bridge, peering through his binoculars at the dark hulk, and popping down the hatch to the conning tower to see the contacts on the radar screen. He still worried about continuing to use the radar as if they were the only vessel on the ocean tonight. He knew the enemy had detection equipment and had certainly picked up their signal already. The "book" said to keep the scan to a minimum. But in his gut Enright knew he needed to keep a close eye on this target until he could answer all the questions he had about its identity and course. Besides, neither the contact nor its escort had yet shown any interest at all in him and his submarine.

There was no doubt the enemy knew by now that *Archerfish* was out there stalking. They apparently didn't care.

Meanwhile, the boat was racing at top speed across the ocean's surface, trying to take a position ahead of the prey, ready to fire torpedoes when they had the best shot at the empty tanker. Then they could turn tail and run.

About 2140, everything changed. Several of the lookouts reported the contact didn't look like a tanker at all but appeared to be some kind of aircraft carrier. Bobczynski and Andrews concurred. There were also at least three destroyers running interference for the immense ship. Excitement ran through the boat as the word was spread. They were no longer stalking a 5,000-ton tanker but a prime warship contact. Enright and his exec studied the *Recognition Manual*, looking at the classes of carriers they knew the Japanese had. Nothing in the book looked anything like the target they were watching out there in the moonlight.

A surface attack was out. Their only hope was to try to run on the surface as fast as they could, hoping to get far enough ahead of the swift-moving giant to give them time to dive and get set up for a shot. And even then they needed the leviathan to be running some kind of zigzag that might bring it closer to them. Already, with *Archerfish* straining to run at nineteen knots, the Japanese ships were going faster, about twenty knots, and that one-knot difference was enough to cause the sub to steadily drop behind.

As he squinted through his binoculars, Joe Enright felt a hint of déjà vu. He had had the *Shokaku* in his sights, too, and she had slipped away.

Then, as if to confirm his earlier thought that the mystery vessel probably knew of *Archerfish*'s existence because of their radar signal, the ship flashed a challenge light in their direction. Enright ignored it.

He told Andrews to keep the lookouts sharp and report any change in the course or condition of the targets. Then he went below to the conning tower. The radar scan confirmed what he was seeing visually up there on the bridge. The massive ship they were tailing was definitely pulling away from them.

Just then, one of the lookouts yelled a chilling report down the hatch.

"One of the escort destroyers is headed our way! He's coming fast!"

Enright quickly ordered everyone below except for the officer of the deck, then the captain climbed back up to stand beside Andrews. As En right watched the destroyer grow larger in the lenses of his binoculars, he heard the radar report called up. The menacing ship was less than five miles away and closing at thirty-five knots.

Again, the skipper was faced with a quandary and not much time to resolve it.

He could dive now and he would definitely lose the contact of his dreams. If he stayed on the surface, he knew the destroyer coming at them had enough weapons to blow *Archerfish* out of the water. Or he could turn his stern to the onrushing warship and shoot torpedoes at him. That would be a tough shot, and it would take a ton of luck to have any hope of hitting him. Launching torpedoes would also let the destroyer know for certain that there was a submarine out here, if she didn't already.

The Japanese navy had drawn the second jack. They now had a pair of them showing. Should Joe Enright stay in the game and take his chances in the highest stakes poker he had ever been involved in?

Enright decided not to do a thing; to continue paralleling the carrier's course while ignoring the destroyer. He could picture the faces of his crew below, anxiously awaiting his command to dive.

The warship was now on what looked like a collision course with *Archerfish*. There was no doubt they would soon both arrive at the same point in the Pacific Ocean at the same time. Still, the Japanese destroyer captain had not fired a shot or even challenged them with a light. Enright could not imagine why.

"One more minute, John," he said calmly. Cold spray was hitting him in the face, and he could feel his heart racing with the excitement of the moment. This run was the most exhilarating thing the young commander had ever experienced in his life. "Stand by to get below if we have to pull the plug."

One more minute and they would dive, hoping the destroyer was running at them blindly, seeking the source of the radar beam they had doubtlessly intercepted. Even in the semidarkness, they could easily see the unlighted destroyer, even without their binoculars.

Thirty seconds passed. In half a minute, the destroyer would be right on top of them.

But then the two officers on the submarine's bridge distinctly saw a bright red light flash on, coming from the aircraft carrier. It shone vividly from the topmost point on the giant ship and stayed lit for a full ten seconds. Went out. Flashed on for ten more seconds. Went out again.

Enright's first thought was that it was an order for the destroyer to open fire. He fully expected to hear the booms and see the flashes from the warship's decks any second. He made ready to order the dive.

But Andrews had his binoculars to his eyes once again, and there was an odd expression on his moonlit face.

"She's turning, Skipper. She's going back toward the carrier."

Amazingly, she was doing so without firing a single shot.

It seemed like no time before Andrews reported that the destroyer had resumed its screening position next to the carrier. Radar confirmed his assessment. Then, moments later, they called up the word that all four ships had changed course and were running in a direction that would take them farther away from the *Archerfish*, almost due south.

Enright went back below to poll his officers on what they thought about the encounter with the destroyer and the new course. Everyone was baffled about the sudden pullback and the strange red light on the carrier's mast. Bob Bobczynski had a thought on the sudden veer to the south, though.

"I'll bet her true course is two-one-zero, like she was doing when we first spotted her," he said. Everyone, including Captain Enright, listened. Bobczynski had grown up a few miles from the navy yard in Portsmouth. He, like Rom Cousins, was one of the original crew members of *Archerfish*, and he had great wartime experience prior to coming aboard before her commissioning. He had been aboard one of the first submarines to patrol the waters within sight of Mount Fuji only days after the debacle at Pearl Harbor. His opinions carried great weight aboard *Archerfish*. "Something also tells me if we just head on down, we'll intersect when he makes the turn and zigs back this way."

"So we stay on a course of two-one-zero at flank speed, gain ground on him, and pick him up when he comes back toward us?" Enright confirmed.

"Right. And if we lose sight of him, we can keep him on radar. He doesn't seem to give much of a damn about it."

So that became the new tactic. Once again they had thrown the standard rules of engagement out the window and followed their educated hunches.

At about 2330, Captain Enright ordered his radioman to wake up Pearl Harbor, where it was 0430, with a message to Admiral Lockwood that they were stalking big game off Honshu. Then he went back up to the bridge.

The black "bump" was now almost out of sight on the horizon, even when they used their binoculars. Joe Enright rubbed the bridge of his nose and gritted his teeth. If they had guessed wrong, that aircraft carrier would not only be out of sight. It would soon be out of radar range as well, gone for good, lost. Just like *Shokaku*.

He could only hope that devilish Japanese skipper had not just called his bluff.

CAPTAIN Toshio Abe was livid. The captain of the destroyer must have lost his mind! He was clearly disobeying orders, dashing off to chase what was looking more and more like a decoy, intent on drawing away the screeners so the rest of the pack could shoot at *Shinano* like a very large fish in a very small barrel. Even as the disobedient destroyer bore down on the unidentified American ship, the brazen enemy continued beaming his radar as if he didn't care whether the whole world knew he was out there. Even more proof the contact was a blatant chunk of delectable bait.

"Must I remind everyone again that our mission is not to go chasing rogue submarines?" Abe snapped. "We are to deliver *Shinano*, intact, to Kure in the Inland Sea tomorrow morning!"

He quickly ordered a course correction, to the south, and then, in the same breath, told his second in command to light the big, red light on the carrier's mast, calling the destroyer back from his foolish run. From his vantage point on the bridge, he could imagine the warship's captain's anger as his ship heeled over sharply, turning back toward *Shinano*, just as he was about to run up on his target at point-blank range. Abe vowed he would later see to it that the man faced disciplinary proceedings for his reckless disregard of orders.

Now, with the course change, Abe was more certain than ever that they could outrun the pack of American submarines. Once the subs had been left far behind, *Shinano* and her screeners could swing back around and eventually resume the course for Kure and the sanctuary the Inland Sea would offer.

Just when it appeared all was going well, Abe received word from the engine room that one of the shaft bearings was running dangerously hot. If they did not slow the screws, they ran the danger of warping the shaft and causing damage that would take weeks to repair. Again, Abe felt his temper soar, but he knew there was no choice. After giving the reporter of the bad news a tongue-lashing, as if he was totally responsible for the misbehaving bearing assembly, he okayed slowing the boat to the eighteen knots his engineers recommended. It was not lost on the captain that eighteen knots was also about the top surface speed for most American submarines. Anyone chasing them would be able to at least match speed with his carrier.

There was also news from the radio room that a strong, nearby signal had been heard, on a frequency used by the American subs. It was encoded, of course, and the operator had no idea of the message's contents. Abe had a clear suspicion, though. The American boat they had been dodging was likely giving the carrier's position and course to his pack members and bragging to his headquarters about the large quarry he had been shadowing. Well, would the American submarine captain be bragging after Abe and his little convoy had driven off and left the surreptitious hunters far behind?

Just before 0300, Abe ordered that their course be adjusted once again, to 270 degrees, due west. This invalidated the information the decoy submarine had transmitted to his friends. Besides, they needed to head back toward the home islands, toward the entrance to the Kii Suido Strait, the narrow passageway into the Inland Sea. This would allow them to make the transit from open sea to strait as soon after sunrise as possible.

Admiral-to-be Toshio Abe had no idea that when he ordered the change to a westward tack, he had just put his colossal new ship on a virtual collision course with the *Archerfish*.

ALMOST immediately after Shinano's initial zag to the south, Chief Yeoman Gene Carnahan on the *Archerfish* reported the course change to Joe Enright and the rest.

"Range is 13,000 yards," he added.

Enright felt his heart race. If the big vessel was zigging and zagging as he and Bobczynski had guessed, they had to be careful. *Archerfish* did not want to be spotted if the quarry abruptly turned back her way. If the Japanese commander and his screener captains were convinced the American sub had given up the chase, all the better. At the same time, they certainly didn't want to lose contact with the convoy, even for a short while.

If the big ship's course was supposed to be 210 degrees, toward the Philippines, it would make yet another turn soon, more to the southwest. *Archerfish* had to race ahead, paralleling the carrier, matching her speed as closely as she could, and be ready when that turn came so she would have a shot. The target still had to turn or slow down if she were going to bag it. Otherwise it would be difficult for the sub to have an optimal chance to fire any torpedoes.

At about 0200, Enright and his exec finally noticed a slight change in the speed of the ship they had been shadowing. She had slowed. Not a lot, but enough to make a difference. At least, after all the long, tense hours, something had changed. They could not imagine what the Japanese commander was up to, but it was an interesting development. Enright knew dawn was not that far away. They would become visible to the lookouts on the warships well before the sun appeared.

At about 0230, Joe Enright ordered his radioman to give Admiral Lockwood and his staff back at Pearl Harbor a quick update on their progress. Or the lack thereof. The message was receipted at 0241. By that time, Lockwood and his staff were up and fully awake, anxious to get word on what the submarine was stalking and whether or not they had attacked yet. Lockwood radioed back, "Good luck, Joe. Keep after him. Your picture is on the piano." It was good to have an admiral with a sense of humor.

The same message was broadcast on the submarine-to-submarine frequency, just in case some friendly boats might be coming to offer assistance. Enright knew the Japanese would likely hear these transmissions, but he doubted it would have any effect on the carrier or on their plan of action. The enemy knew *Archerfish* was still out there somewhere, and it had not seemed to bother them one whit so far.

About then, Joe Enright realized for the first time how tired he was. The strain of the full night of stalking was pulling heavily on him. He ignored his aching muscles, his stinging eyes, as he stared at the contact, steaming along complacently. The bastard had still made no move to turn in their direction as they had expected, as they had been wishing she would do for the past four or five hours.

Then, at 0256, as if Joe Enright had willed it to happen, the huge carrier began to change course, almost imperceptibly at first. Something that big did not turn on a dime. But then it was clear. He watched, disbelieving, and heard the excited shouts from the men in the conning tower below as they called out the new course information.

"Ship contact number 4" on *Archerfish* war patrol number 5 had just turned. It was headed directly at the submarine, and it was coming her way at what looked like full speed.

TOSHIO Abe knew at once what the nearby coded radio transmissions on the American submarine-to-submarine frequency meant. The leader of the pack of submarines that swarmed around his ship had relayed *Shinano*'s position, course, and speed to all the others. Now, they would get into position to attack from all sides. Even with the reduced speed, he still had advantages, though. Submarines had to be on the surface to match speed with the carrier. Yet they would likely have to dive to shoot their torpedoes and still escape the destroyers. He knew at least one of the stalkers was on the surface because they were still seeing his radar on the carrier's detectors.

He quickly considered his chances against the pack of submarines.

If they were so damned determined to shoot him, then let them go ahead. They would not sink his vessel. They would have trouble enough hitting a target as quick as his ship. Because of the carrier's blisters and heavy armament, it would take many torpedoes making direct hits to damage *Shinano*. Even then, she would not be likely to go down. Of course, the Americans still had no idea of the course she might take, so the run was still on. Daylight was not far away, and if he could dodge them until then, the Americans would have to slink off and hide once again. He and his ship would be safe.

Now, another turn was necessary. The wolf pack was likely arrayed west of them, along the routes favored by merchant captains steering their ships from Tokyo Bay to the Inland Sea. The submarines would be lying in wait there, lined up, ready for them to steam right into their hornets' nest.

"Come to course two-one-zero," Abe ordered abruptly.

The helmsman steered the ship to the new direction. He and the rest of the crew could feel the gargantuan vessel heel only slightly as she responded to the course change. All the while, Abe stared at the chart on the wall with its nest of *X*'s marking the recent reported observations of American submarines, mostly north and east of where they now ran. On the new course, they were moving farther away from those ominous *X*'s, leaving them behind.

The admiral-to-be felt better already, but he knew another zig would be necessary soon, before the submarines could determine his course and line up again for an attack.

At 0305, he was informed that the incessant radar transmissions from the mystery vessel had abruptly ceased.

"He has finally dived," Abe said, as much to himself as to anyone else. He raised his voice when he ordered, "Inform the screeners. We are at greatest peril now."

At 0310, Toshio Abe gave the command to again change direction to run due south. That should confuse the American vultures!

Abe knew some of his officers and crew disagreed with his decision to remain passive, to not send the destroyers after the submarine whose radar they had been intercepting all night. Of course, they never questioned his tactics out loud, but he could see it on their faces. He was more convinced than ever that his was the proper action. When they finally floated the Empire's wonderful new carrier through the strait and into the safety of secure waters, the doubters would then believe.

Daylight was only a few hours away and the Americans would cease their hunt before then. All they had to do was avoid a fight a little longer. Abe was certain they could zigzag and run fast enough to accomplish that. And that his ship, the savior of the Empire, would be delivered whole.

A few minutes after 0300, Joe Enright gave the command to dive. *Archerfish* was now less than seven miles from the target and they needed to maneuver to be able to get anything close to a broadside shot. Six torpedoes were ready forward and four more rested in the after tubes. The skipper took his position at the boat's twin periscopes.

"Bring her level at sixty feet," he ordered. That would leave the scopes just above the surface of the ocean.

One minute after the first yodel of the diving alarm, *Archerfish* was at depth and waiting. Quartermaster Bill Sykes began calling out the range and bearing of the target from the calibrated wheels on the night scope as Enright focused on their contact. Lieutenant Davis Bunting entered the information into the TDC, keeping it updated. The skipper had already decided to set the torpedoes to run at a depth of ten feet. The "book" didn't say to do it that way. It recommended a running depth of twenty-five to thirty feet when attacking a carrier. Enright had no idea that the target's blisters would be ineffective at that depth. He was once again relying on gut instinct, assuming that punching a hole higher up on the side of a target that massive would tend to help capsize the vessel. He also knew the torpedoes he was using had a history of running deeper than their settings called for them to do. He figured that he could score a hit, even if they ran deeper than they were supposed to. They certainly wouldn't underrun her.

Because the night scope was larger and more likely to be spotted by lookouts on the target ship and her escorts, Enright used it sparingly, raising it, taking a look, and lowering it. On one of the quick looks, he noticed the carrier seemed to be leaning sharply, as if she were in the midst of a huge turn so sharp she was banking like an airplane.

Bunting and the TDC said differently. The carrier was still on its original course. It would be much later, when Enright learned of the unusual canted stacks on *Shinano*, that he realized why the vessel looked to be turning even when she was plowing straight ahead.

Now, with the range only a couple of miles, everyone on *Archerfish* knew he had to be ready. As the carrier drew to within range and ran past them, they would have only a brief opportunity to see a glimpse of her beam and to shoot all six forward torpedoes. They were now at an angle sharp on her bow, making the target appear much shorter than they knew she was. It was hardly a perfect shot but it was likely the best they could get considering her speed.

The next time Enright raised the scope and took a look, the words "Fire one!" were already forming on his lips. But when he spotted the carrier again, he couldn't believe his eyes. This time there was no mistaking the fact that the target had made a pronounced zig. That unexpected turn had given *Archerfish* a perfect setup. In another two minutes, the massive vessel would be in the absolute best part of the ocean for the sub's fish to find her.

With his ideal view, the commander described to those nearby what he could see of the vessel. As he later wrote, "Never before or since have I seen such an apparition!" They were still trying to figure out which of the remaining Japanese carriers this mammoth could be. Enright even grabbed a piece of paper and a pencil and quickly sketched out a rough picture of the odd-looking giant that now filled his scope lens.

"She looks like this," the captain said. Everyone who looked at the drawing stared blankly. It looked like nothing any of them had ever seen, and it certainly didn't resemble anything they were looking at in the identification manuals.

"Skipper, the Japs don't have anything like that," one of the men finally said.

"The hell they don't!" Enright snorted. "I'm looking right at it!"

Just then, there was something new to worry about. As Enright stared intently at the target, he noticed that one of the screening destroyers had pulled close to the carrier, apparently to receive a message. But then it eased away and started back toward its station. It didn't take long for Enright to realize that the warship, in returning to its screen, would pass very near *Archerfish*'s periscope.

Close enough to see it if it didn't run right over it!

Enright's eyes grew wide when he saw the ship so near, and he dropped the scope quickly. He asked that the boat be lowered another few feet, just to make certain the destroyer could pass over without striking any part of the sub. Every man aboard held his breath, listening to the awful groan of the warship's engines as it passed directly overhead, and likely less than twenty feet from the highest point on *Archerfish*.

The destroyer moved on, unaware of how close it had come to running into the enemy.

Finally, Enright could raise the scope again and call out the coordinates for the TDC. His stomach churned when he located the huge vessel again. The delay while they dodged the destroyer had allowed the carrier to get past the prime shooting point. He heard Sykes call out the new information for Bunting and the TDC while he held the scope's crosshairs on the middle of the carrier's beam.

She was no longer a perfect target, but she was still wide enough to blow sky-high if they did their jobs correctly.

Coolly, calmly, Joe Enright gave the command to fire the torpedoes. The sub bucked slightly as the first weapon whooshed away. Then, eight seconds later, she shuddered again as the next one left its flooded tube. In short order, all six fish were headed toward the target.

Enright held his breath as he stared through the scope at the huge target. It seemed to take forever for the torpedoes to make their run. Just as he was sure all six had somehow improbably missed the island-sized objective, he saw a beautiful sight. A stunningly bright fireball exploded near the target's stern and climbed up her clifflike side. An instant later, everyone aboard *Archerfish* heard the muted boom, then felt the pronounced shock wave rock the sub, even from a mile away.

Next, fifty yards forward of the first blast, another explosion ripped up the towering side of the carrier.

As much as Enright wanted to wait and see the other torpedoes strike home, to watch the carrier sink, he noticed the destroyers were already turning and heading for his position. Amazingly, as they prepared to go deep, they distinctly heard a total of six explosions. All *Archerfish*'s weapons had apparently struck home.

The jubilation didn't last long. Everyone was busy as they dived toward four hundred feet. Those three destroyers would be dropping their ash cans within moments, and it would almost certainly get very rough very quick.

Still, Joe Enright could not get that last view he had out of his head. Two fish had hit hard, and the carrier was already listing. Even now, the sonarman was reporting the unmistakable noises of water rushing into a ship, of a huge structure breaking up under the forces of the sea.

When the boom of the depth charges finally came, they were distant. The destroyers had no idea where their attacker was hiding. The explosions soon stopped. The screeners had returned to the carrier, likely to pick up survivors.

Now, the crew of the *Archerfish* could finally celebrate. It didn't last long. Joe Enright and some of the others soon headed for their bunks for some much needed sleep. It had been a long night. There was a regular day of duty ahead for most of them, a day of patrolling along the Japanese coast looking for more targets.

Even though he was exhausted, Joe Enright had trouble going to sleep that morning. Adrenaline still rushed through his veins, and he couldn't help reliving each step of the chase and attack. He had relied on his gut, on his well-honed instincts, and he had won. He couldn't wait for Captain Pace and Admiral Lockwood and the others who had given him this chance to learn what had happened. He only wished his mother was still alive back in North Dakota so he could tell her about what he and his shipmates had accomplished this night.

Archerfish and her crew had bagged their biggest quarry. But they still had no idea just how big it really was.

COMMANDER Toshio Abe's initial thought was to try to get his wounded carrier to shallow water and ground her. However, the explosions had already cost them fresh water for the boilers, so they were dead in the water.

Next, he ordered two of the destroyers to stop looking for their attackers and tie up to *Shinano* in an attempt to tow her to shallow water. There was no way they could pull anything so massive. The lines snapped and the attempt was abandoned.

The SOS transmitted from the carrier's radio room that morning was the first time the name of *Shinano* was ever mentioned in any radio transmission. When American codebreakers heard the SOS and translated the name, they assumed the distressed ship was a cruiser. They were typically named for rivers. The Shinano River was Japan's best-known stream.

When it became clear that the carrier was going down, when Abe was finally willing to concede that *Shinano* could possibly be sunk by enemy torpedoes after all, he reluctantly called his officers to a meeting on the bridge. He ordered them to abandon the ship but closed the meeting with the words, "I shall remain aboard."

Out of respect, they did not try to talk him out of his wish to die with his ship.

One of his young officers retrieved the Japanese flag, wrapped it around himself, and returned to stand beside his captain on the bow of their colossal, "unsinkable" vessel. As the survivors paddled frantically away or watched from rescue boats, the ship's stern slipped deeper beneath the water while the odd-looking bow rose high in the air. Seawater rushed into the fire rooms, forcing air out the tilted stacks in a painful, deep-throated scream.

Archerfish's first torpedo struck the side of *Shinano* at 0317 on November 29, 1944. The last great hope of the Imperial Japanese Navy dropped beneath the waters of the Pacific Ocean at about eleven AM, less than one full day into her maiden voyage. She took down with her over 1,400 sailors and civilian workers, many of them sucked to their deaths by the violent force of the sea rushing into the elevators and lower compartments as the gargantuan ship sank. Ocean depths in that area are typically near 4,000 meters, so it is unlikely her remains will ever be visited.

The Japanese people were not told of the loss until after the war was over.

NOVEMBER 30 was Thanksgiving Day. The cooks aboard *Archerfish* prepared an especially sumptuous meal for the crew that day, featuring dressing, yams, creamed onions, peas, freshly made cakes and pies, and strawberry shortcake with whipped cream. Captain Enright carved the turkey and said a special prayer of thanks.

The boat's fifth war patrol ended at Guam on December 15. That's where Joe Enright and his crew received some very disappointing news. The navy brass could not credit them with sinking an aircraft carrier. Intelligence maintained there were no carriers in Tokyo Bay, so how could they have sunk one coming out? Enright was asked if he would settle for credit for sending a cruiser to the bottom since the SOS from their victim had appeared to refer to a ship named after a river.

"Not just 'no,' but 'hell, no!' " was Enright's answer. It had been a bright, moonlit night, and he had had a perfect view. He knew what he had shot, and he felt strongly that his boat and her crew deserved credit for it.

His immediate superior agreed to attach to the report Joe Enright's rough sketch of the target, the one he scratched out just before shooting his torpedoes. He had thrown it away, but one of the officers retrieved it from the trash and saved it. Even then, *Archerfish* was only credited initially with sinking a "CV (carrier) *Hayataka*-type or possibly larger, 28,000 tons." That was nothing to be ashamed of, but it certainly wasn't what Enright wanted or felt his guys deserved. Still, there was no way to swim down four thousand feet beneath the Pacific and take a look at what they had sunk so they could prove their claim.

After the war, Japanese records confirmed that the vessel that *Archerfish* had sunk was, indeed, a brand spanking new supercarrier on her maiden voyage. This information also showed *Shinano* to have a full-load displacement of 72,000 tons. Still, the navy would only give official credit for 59,000 tons. That was more than enough to finally give *Archerfish* recognition for sinking the largest vessel ever sent to the bottom by a submarine. It was also the shortest-lived warship ever destroyed by any means. Of the almost 1,700 war patrols conducted by U.S. submarines in World War II, *Archerfish*'s fifth patrol was the most productive, based on tonnage, thanks to *Shinano* and her awesome bulk.

Incidentally, Japanese accounts also showed that only four of the six torpedoes Enright and his crew fired that night actually hit the target. The other explosions heard by *Archerfish*'s crew were run-bys. They had sunk the giant with four well-placed hits, making the feat even more remarkable.

Captain Joseph F. Enright was awarded the Navy Cross by Secretary of the Navy James Forrestal. The *Archerfish* received a Presidential Unit Citation.

The crew of the sub, or at least the ones who remained aboard for the sixth patrol and the new men coming to the boat, were able to spend the Christmas and New Year's holidays at Camp Dealey, the rest and recuperation camp on Guam.

The text of the Presidential Unit Citation they received summed up nicely what *Archerfish* and her crew had accomplished:

"For extraordinary heroism in action during the Fifth War Patrol . . . relentless in tracking an alert and powerful hostile force which constituted a potential threat to our vital operations in the Philippine area, the USS ARCHERFISH culminated a dogged six and one-half hour pursuit by closing her high speed target, daringly penetrated the strong destroyer escort screen, and struck fiercely at a large Japanese aircraft carrier . . . to sink this extremely vital ship. Handled with superb seamanship, she responded gallantly . . . toward the ultimate destruction of a crafty and fanatic enemy."

When Enright and his crew "struck fiercely" that full-moon night off Honshu, they struck what was certainly one of the most damaging blows of the war against that "crafty and fanatic enemy."

History had been unalterably redirected by a diesel boat named *Archerfish*.

6

"TOKYO BAY JOY JUICE"

JOE Enright never liked the term "wolf pack." It reminded him too much of the German U-boats that had preyed on Allied shipping during World War I and in the current conflict, employing that very tactic. Now, here he was, commander of a wolf pack himself. *Archerfish*, along with her sister boat, *Batfish*, and the USS *Blackfish* (SS-221), left Guam January 10, 1945. Enright didn't care much for the name assigned his wolf pack either. Dubbed "Joe's Jugheads," the three-boat group headed for the South China Sea and the Luzon Straits.

After a month of numerous aircraft contacts and small, unworthy targets, on February 14, *Archerfish* fired eight torpedoes, four from the bow tubes, followed by four more from the stern tubes when no hits were heard, all aimed at a target they believed to be a Japanese submarine. The crew heard the explosion of one of the Mark-18 torpedoes fired from the stern tubes and then the distinct sounds of a vessel breaking apart. They initially received credit for sinking a submarine of 1,100 tons. Later, though, this target was removed from the sub's list of victims. To this day, crew members who were aboard *Archerfish* that Valentine's night maintain vociferously that they sent one of Hirohito's submarines to the bottom. Those eight fish turned out to be the only torpedoes fired on the sixth patrol.

Batfish had better luck. She and her crew sank three subs in three nights. After experiencing trouble with the bow planes that made quick, evasive dives impossible, Enright took his boat back to Saipan for voyage repairs on February 19. They departed there for San Francisco by way of Pearl Harbor on the twenty-second. They were due for a major overhaul and dry-docking at Hunters Point Naval Shipyard in the Bay Area.

As usual, all along the way, they continued to practice various maneuvers, including diving and surfacing. Not far out of Saipan, one of the new officers on board was acting as diving officer for a trim dive. As soon as the boat's bow went beneath the waves, the sub suddenly pitched to a dangerously sharp angle and began a mad drop toward the sea bottom.

"Mister, can't you control the dive?" Enright yelled down from the conning tower.

"No, sir!" the young officer quickly confessed.

Captain Joe immediately had him relieved by one of the more experienced officers so he could get the boat back under control. He was able to do so, but not before *Archerfish* had bulleted to over six hundred feet deep.

It didn't take long to figure out what had caused the uncontrolled dive. The submarine was carrying a huge load of mail from Saipan back to Pearl Harbor. It had all been placed in the forward torpedo room, and the young officer had not taken that added weight into account as he calculated the compensation prior to diving.

The boat arrived on March 13 at Hunters Point, a spit of land that juts out into San Francisco Bay south and east of the city. Among other things to be accomplished while they were there, someone had to do an inventory of the wardroom. They found the following items missing: 2 table forks, 1 table knife, 1 pepper shaker, 2 salt shakers, 2 sugar spoons, and 4 teaspoons, all "misplaced" during six war patrols. The yard also attempted to fix the lingering air-conditioning problem. Their attempts didn't help the situation. Temperatures on the next war patrol averaged above ninety degrees in the control room and in the forward and after battery compartments when they were in warm waters. That led to "loss of sleep and 'prickly heat,'" according to Enright's summation.

Life could be tough enough aboard a submarine, even if the air-conditioning worked properly. There was one particular chief electrician's mate who bunked in the chief petty officer's quarters in the after battery compartment on the fifth and sixth patrols. Though he was recognized as being one fine electrician and an all-around good fellow, he was a perfect example of another colorful *Archerfish* character. He proudly wore the same pair of dungarees for an entire patrol and didn't change his mattress cover once during the whole trip, even when a full can of talcum powder was spilled in his bunk. He also bragged that he would not shower until they were back in home port. He was still a likable sort, with a lazy eye and a ragged old chief petty officer hat he wore tilted to one side of his head. He most resembled Popeye and loved to go about the boat singing the cartoon character's theme song.

One day after returning to Pearl Harbor and before leaving on her next patrol, *Archerfish* was conducting exercises with a destroyer, diving and surfacing, making trial torpedo runs and radar checks. She was running submerged when a rather heated discussion began in the after torpedo room between one of the new officers who had just come aboard and Gunner's Mate First-Class John Pryor, an experienced submarine sailor. They had a difference of opinion about the proper way to load and fire the signal ejector, a device that allowed the submarine to send a flare to the surface to signal the units there with which she was operating. As usual, the officer won, even though Pryor had far more expertise in the use of the signal gun.

Leo "Doc" Carter was in the after battery crews' mess when the IMC announcing system blared out, "Doc to the after torpedo room!" Carter grabbed the first-aid shoulder kit that was always kept in the control room and ran aft as fast as he could. He found a terrible scene when he got there. There was smoke, blood, and smoldering clothes everywhere and dazed men trying to deal with the emergency. He found Pryor, the most seriously hurt, lying on the deck, bleeding badly, the flesh ripped away from one side of his head. Carter did the best he could, giving him a shot of morphine and dressing the wounds. He managed to control the worst of the bleeding with the limited gear he had aboard, but he could only hope that his work had somehow saved "Gunner's" life. Looking at all the blood he had lost and at the severe injuries the man had suffered, he knew it would be touch and go.

Captain Enright surfaced at once and raced at four-engine flank speed toward Pearl Harbor, talking along the way on the radio with the medical staff back at the base. The doctor who met them in a motor launch at the entrance to the harbor quickly examined the injured man and assured Carter that he had done all the right things. Pryor was transferred to the naval hospital and would survive.

It was during *Archerfish's* sixth war patrol that "Doc" Carter found himself having to perform first aid on a most unusual casualty . . . himself. Carter was on lookout watch when a dive was ordered. He scrambled down from the shears and was coming through the conning tower hatch just ahead of the other lookout. He wore his binoculars around his neck, and on the way down the ladder, they struck a rung and bounced back up, striking him hard above the eyes. The resulting lacerations were bleeding profusely. He was relieved of duty and allowed to go aft to his medical locker. There he stood before a mirror in the crew's washroom and stitched up his wounds. Afterward, he returned directly to lookout watch.

Back in the Pacific for her seventh war patrol, *Archerfish* was once again in familiar waters, off Honshu and Hokkaido, serving lifeguard duty for Admiral Halsey's carrier-based aircraft while they continued to pound the home islands. That onslaught was about to be taken to an awful new level, but one that hastened the end of the war. *Archerfish* was on station just off the Japanese coast on August 6 and August 9, 1945, the days on which the atomic bombs were dropped on Hiroshima and Nagasaki, less than a thousand miles away. That was too far away for them to see the mushroom clouds or hear the otherworldly roar of their impact, but they soon learned of them and what they had done.

On August 11, at about 0230, in the morning, Enright heard sonar pinging and assumed it was from a Japanese submarine. He and his officers figured its captain was closing in, looking to get in one last shot before the war was finally over.

"Boys, I don't want to take the offensive or the defensive," he bluntly announced to the crew in the conning tower. He had made the decision not to engage. He ordered them to dive and avoid the Japanese boat.

The log entries for August 15 are subdued with no hint of the elation that was sweeping the boat at the time:

1451	Surfaced. Heard over RBo that President Truman had announced that the Japs surrendered.
1545	Submerged.
2001	Surfaced.
2145	Received ComSubPac serial 32 ordering the end of offensive action.

On August 16, as Captain Joe Enright later wrote, "Enthusiastically complied with Admiral Halsey's message to 'Splice the main brace.'" That was an old nautical term meaning, "Let's have a drink!"

The skipper met each of the three watch sections as they completed their watches and offered them a toast "to peace." That day, when they attempted to meet their regular radio schedules with Guam on 4235 kilocycles and 8470 kilocycles, the circuits were unusually busy, backed up with traffic from all the vessels trying to communicate at the same time about the end of the war.

On August 19, only four days after they received official word that the war was over, things were so relaxed that *Archerfish* swapped movies with USS *Gato* (SS-212), but in a most unusual way. While still in their patrol area, off the approach to the Tsugaru Strait between Hokkaido and Honshu, *Gato* sent over the movies they wanted to swap in a rubber raft. The trade was made and the sailors paddled back to their boat. All this took place in broad daylight in the middle of the afternoon with both boats lounging on the surface of the Pacific Ocean.

Soon they learned they were to be one of a dozen submarines that would be a part of the flotilla that entered Tokyo Bay. Technically, they were part of an "invasion force" and would be in the bay for the surrender ceremony. The subs were immediately named "Benny's Peacekeepers" after Captain Benny Bass of the USS *Runner* (SS-476). He was the senior commander among the skippers. They rendezvoused with the short-hull destroyer USS *Maddox* (DD-731) on August 30 to begin the trip toward Tokyo. A kamikaze pilot had heavily damaged the *Maddox* off Okinawa the previous year but she had come back to play a big part in the last major battle of the war. Her captain, Selby Santmyers, was an old classmate of Joe Enright.

Santmyers set a fast pace. When he noticed the subs were having a tough time keeping up, he radioed back and asked when they would come up to position. One of "Benny's Peacekeepers" called back, "At this speed it will be sometime Tuesday!" The destroyer captain slowed down by one knot.

The American ships passed Sagami Nada and entered into Tokyo Bay just after first light on August 31. The aircraft carriers remained at the mouth of the bay. There was still a real fear that the Japanese might attempt to pull one last bit of treachery or that radicals might stage some sort of suicide attack. The aircraft on the U.S. carriers were ready to fly at a moment's notice should that happen. Three destroyers proudly led a long single-file column of warships followed by the submarines as they steamed up the bay. Enright noted that the formation was so exact that only the last warship in the column could be seen from *Archerfish*'s bridge, and the line of ships stretched from horizon to horizon. The *Missouri*, the submarine tender *Proteus*, and a hospital ship were already there waiting. *Archerfish* moored port side to *Proteus*'s starboard side.

It was an odd feeling. Here they were, in the harbor of the main city of the enemy they had fought so viciously for almost four years. But at least the dying was over. The mood on all the American ships tied up in Tokyo Bay was festive, like Christmas and New Year's Day rolled up into one.

The next day, Joe Enright and a couple of his officers went ashore and took a walking tour of the massive Yokosuka Naval Yard, where many of their contacts had been constructed. They noticed that caves had been carved out of the limestone hills around the yard and that's where many of the shops were housed. They saw a huge dry dock, labeled "6," and they speculated that this was likely where their victim of November 29, 1944, had been built. They later learned that they were correct in their guess.

They also noticed a number of small submarines under construction. These subs ranged in size from two-man to eight-man boats, and there were hundreds of them in various stages of readiness. Clearly they were being built to help repel Allied amphibious ships and their loads of troops when the inevitable D Day–like storming of the Japanese homeland beaches finally occurred. All the other yards in the Empire likely had similar mini sub projects underway. The officers could only imagine what these boats would have done if an invasion had actually been necessary. The loss of life on both sides would have been tremendous.

Enright later wrote, "When anyone has asked me the question, 'Was it necessary for the United States to use the A-bomb?' I think of the subs they were building and the tremendous loss of our troops, even before reaching the beaches, had invasion been necessary. My answer is always, 'Yes. There is no question in my mind that the loss of life on both sides would have been many times larger if we had not used it.'"

The atmosphere was even more electric on September 2. Most of the *Archerfish* officers moved over to the tender to listen to the ceremony on loudspeakers that had been set up there. The actual signing of the peace treaty took place on the teakwood deck of the *Missouri*, which was sitting almost a mile from where *Archerfish* rested. Among those taking part were General of the Army Douglas MacArthur, Fleet Admiral Chester W. Nimitz, and Admiral William F. Halsey Jr., who was aboard *Missouri* already. The only representative from the Silent Service was Vice Admiral Charles Lockwood. There were also representatives from Great Britain, China, the Soviet Union, Australia, Canada, the Netherlands, New

Zealand, and France. Mr. Mamoru Shigemitsu signed for the emperor of Japan. General Yoshijiro Umezu inked the treaty on behalf of Hirohito's armed forces.

Back on *Archerfish*, Doc Carter brought up topside a half gallon of pure medical alcohol, several cans of grapefruit juice, and a bucket of ice. Beneath the overhang of the cigarette deck, he began dispensing a concoction that was quickly hailed as "Tokyo Bay joy juice." The recipe was a bit strong to begin with, and a few of the celebrants of the armistice got sick. After they got the mixture right, several more trips below for ice and grapefruit juice were necessary.

Once the peace accord was signed, the sky was filled with aircraft from the carriers anchored at the entrance to the bay. They swept overhead with a deafening roar, a din matched only by the cheers from the decks of all the ships that were tied up in the harbor.

Admiral Lockwood hosted his submarine skippers at a party that afternoon in a building at Yokosuka that was already named "U.S. Submarine Officers' Club." Somehow he had managed to arrange for the nicely lettered sign as well as full bar service and a nice array of snacks. Lockwood told the twelve commanders that he was finally making good on his frequent promise over the last several years to buy them drinks once they had whipped the Japanese. As always, Lockwood was loyal to "his guys."

Still, the *Archerfish*'s seventh war patrol was not yet completed. She left Tokyo Bay the day after the treaty-signing ceremony, accompanied by ten other subs and bound again for Pearl Harbor. Enright noted that the boat's navigational lights were now turned on at sunset for the first time since she had put to sea. There was no enemy to hide from anymore.

They arrived in Pearl on September 12, 1945. In his summation paperwork for this final patrol, where the document asked for "Limiting factors this patrol," Enright cryptically entered "Surrender of enemy."

A month after *Archerfish* arrived at Pearl Harbor Captain Joe Enright was relieved of his command and assigned to teach engineering to the plebes at the U.S. Naval Academy. He later served as a submarine squadron commander in San Diego and New London, in the Military-Political Division at the Pentagon during the Korean War, as commanding officer of the sub tender USS *Fulton* (AS-11), as a member of the NATO Defense College in France and England, and as chief of staff to Rear Admiral Frederick B. Warder, Commander Submarines, U.S. Atlantic Fleet. This last assignment came in 1957, just as the first nuclear submarines were being deployed. He later commanded USS *Boston* (CAG-1), a heavy cruiser that had been modified to carry Terrier surface-to-air missiles. That made her the world's first guided-missile cruiser, and O-Boat Joe was her captain. When he left the navy in 1963, Enright went to work for the Northrop Corporation, helping design long-range radio navigation systems. He died in Fairfax, Virginia, in July 2000, two months short of his ninetieth birthday and only two weeks after Jerry Cornelison, Mike Klein, and Kim Gebhardt, a contingent of former *Archerfish* crewmen from the sixties, had stopped by for a visit. During that visit, they presented him with a scrapbook filled with memorabilia and a baseball cap with the sub's name embroidered on it. They asked him how he felt about sinking the *Shinano*, not sure if his memory was good enough to recall even that monumental event. But the old sub commander smiled broadly and answered heartily, "Good! I feel good! We sunk the bastard!" He also seemed to have an amazing grasp of other events and details of his command on *Archerfish*. The visitors' last memory of O-Boat Joe as they left that day was of him sitting there in the retirement home dining room, smiling, proudly wearing his *Archerfish* cap.

Commander W. S. Finn took command of *Archerfish*. The boat was now assigned to Submarine Squadron 1 in Pearl and was to be used mostly for training purposes. The truth was that she didn't really have much to do. Captain Finn's biggest challenge was to ride herd on seventy or so young and vigorous sailors who were now free of the stresses of patrolling enemy waters and had too much time on their hands. There were also ample opportunities for them to find mischief in Hawaii once that war was over.

On New Year's Day, 1946, the day before *Archerfish* was scheduled to leave Pearl Harbor and head for Tiburón Bay, San Francisco, one of the crew members pulled off maybe the most daring bit of larceny in naval history. He stole a submarine. A very special submarine.

Late that evening, Torpedoman Wilbur Wesley "Wes" Mayhew came back to the boat after what appeared to be a hard night in Honolulu, celebrating the arrival of the new year. The deck watch merely grinned and waved his shipmate aboard so he could go below, sleep it off, and be ready to work the next day. Mayhew did go below, but he returned topside only a few minutes later, carrying bolt cutters, a couple of burlap bags, and an assortment of hand tools. The sailor seemed to be on his way somewhere in a purposeful hurry. The deck watch could only shake his head and shrug his shoulders. He had long since given up wondering about sub sailors. He watched the torpedoman disappear down the dock and then went aft to check the mooring lines.

The deck watch might have been more diligent had he known where

Mayhew was off to. He had designs on liberating "Uncle Charlie's submarine." "Uncle Charlie" was Vice Admiral Charles A. Lockwood, Commander, Submarine Force, U.S. Pacific Fleet. His submarine was a beautiful five-foot brass replica of a fleet-type submarine that rose from the decorative pond in front of the submarine base's administration building. It was truly the admiral's pride and joy. He stood at his window and watched it, its bow positioned out of the water at a ten-degree-up angle, water pouring from its limber holes as if it were proudly surfacing from the deep.

A few hours later, the deck watch saw Mayhew staggering back down the dock, his arms full of tools and something wrapped in the burlap bags that appeared to be quite heavy. He pitched right in, though, and helped Mayhew get the load across the sub's brow and down into the forward superstructure. Wes wired his prize in place just forward of the forward torpedo room escape trunk so it wouldn't roll around once they were under way. Meanwhile, the deck watch hurried back topside to make sure Mayhew had not been followed. Now that he knew what Mayhew had done, he knew he would be labeled an accomplice if the larcenous torpedoman were found out.

The next morning, they were under way for San Francisco, and Mayhew, now quite sober, saw the whole situation in an entirely different light. He had no idea how he was going to get that heavy thing ashore once they got to Tiburón Bay, nor how he was going to avoid brig time when he inevitably got caught.

He came up with the perfect solution. He sold the purloined brass submarine to Torpedoman Third Class Jim Steward, who worked with him in the forward torpedo room, for $10. Now it was Steward's problem.

As they drew closer to the California coast, the one-week passage almost over, Steward had his own second thoughts. No problem. He sold the sub to a torpedoman's mate named J. W. "Squarepeg" Roundtree. Steward got $20, doubling his money, and was quite proud of the deal he had made.

Now it was Roundtree's problem getting the sixty-pound brass sub off the boat without getting caught. He arrived at his own perfect solution. His ex-brother-in-law ran the "honey barge," which took the trash and garbage from all the vessels anchored at Tiburón Bay. The barge pulled alongside *Archerfish*, apparently doing its dirty but necessary duty. Roundtree, with his purchase and a couple of his buddies to help, climbed aboard the honey barge and rode across to the wharfs of San Francisco.

To this day, nobody knows the whereabouts of "Uncle Charlie's brass submarine." Or at least, despite the fact that the statute of limitations has expired by now, nobody admits they know where it is.

On March 13, 1946, *Archerfish* went to San Francisco Naval Shipyard for an inactivation overhaul. Two months later, an army tug towed her around Pinola Point and up to Mare Island Naval Shipyard. That was also on San Francisco Bay, up north near Vallejo. The final stages of inactivation were performed there. Commander Finn was relieved of his duties as commanding officer, and Lieutenant Commander C. J. Beers took over. It was his job to see her through her final days as an active vessel.

After less than three years of service, *Archerfish* was decommissioned and placed in an "out of commission in reserve" status on June 12, 1946. She was turned over to the 19th Fleet to be berthed indefinitely at Mare Island.

Some of the vessels from World War II found a second life with the navies of other countries. Others were sold to private companies and used as merchant ships. Some of them were modified for future duty with the U.S. Navy. Still others were cut up for scrap, used for target practice, or ingloriously junked.

No one knew it in June 1946 as they sadly towed the *Archerfish* to her new berth at the northern reaches of San Francisco Bay, but this boat they were putting to bed had only begun her glorious and gallant history. She still had plenty of parties to crash. She had many more photo opportunities to nudge her way into. There were still many more hazards for her to bravely overcome.

The old girl was far from ready to go to peaceful sleep.

SECOND COMMISSION
7 March 1952–21 October 1955

Oh! thou clear spirit of clear fire, whom on these seas I as
Persian once did worship, till in the sacramental act so burned
by thee, that to this hour I bear the scar.

—Captain Ahab, in Herman Melville's *Moby-Dick*

THE DOOR TO HADES

EXPLOSION, flooding, and fire are three of the things submariners fear most. Many people assume that anyone who is confined to one of those steel cylinders while it is running deep beneath the ocean would be most afraid of drowning. Not so. An explosion, fire, or inrushing seawater could lead to drowning, of course, but even if the casualty is not initially catastrophic and even if everyone aboard does his job and shuts off the damaged compartments, the problem can still send a boat to the bottom. If the vessel is not crushed by the pressure of the sea before it reaches the bottom, that can leave its surviving crewmembers to die a slow, agonizing death before they have any hope of being rescued.

Fire is quicker, for certain, and there is no place to run away from it on a submarine the size of *Archerfish*. If the flames aren't contained quickly or if they are not confined to a single compartment, then the fire and choking smoke can come and get them, seek them out and claim them as surely as flooding seawater can.

Archerfish, like her sister submarines, was prone to flooding, explosion, and fire. She carried 126 tons of lead acid storage batteries in each of the two separate battery compartments. Charging batteries gave off potentially explosive hydrogen. Since she was an electric propulsion boat, there was more than ample opportunity for a spark to start a conflagration.

Components wore out. Contacts got corroded. Insulation frayed. The danger was constant.

None of these hazards was on the minds of the men reporting aboard the about-to-be-activated *Archerfish* in December 1951. After all, prior to decommissioning, their boat had been inspected, repaired, overhauled, and inspected again. She was in good shape. Since then, *Archerfish* had been resting peacefully for five-and-a-half years at Mare Island, California, near Vallejo, awaiting either the scrap heap or further service to her country. No one knew for sure which it would be for most of that time.

Then the Korean conflict continued to rage on. The undeclared war lasted into the new decade. *Archerfish* was once again needed.

The decision was made to reactivate the boat, along with her sister, *Batfish*, and many of the others that had been stored away. After refurbishing, sea trials, testing, and training, *Archerfish* was slated to be sent to Key West, Florida, by way of San Diego and the Panama Canal. There she had a variety of duties, including helping to train other navy vessels and fighting units in the use of sonar and other antisubmarine warfare techniques.

The crew that began assembling on December 15 was an all-new group of men. So was their attitude toward life in general. Despite what was going on in Korea, there was no real feeling of eminent danger, no zeal to get under way in order to strike an immediate blow against a clearly identifiable enemy as there had been during World War II. Now there were the Russians, rattling sabers and turning down the thermostat on the Cold War. The Red Chinese were flexing their muscles over North Korea. But there was nothing like the palpable threat of Imperial Japan.

These submariners were all professional in their duties, still proud of the jobs they did each day, still cognizant of the dangers that were present anytime they went out to sea in their boat. But these men did tend to display a wild streak, one that was off the scale, even for sailors. During this period of her life, both while still in San Francisco and once they arrived in Key West, *Archerfish* mostly was involved in single-day missions. The exercises allowed the ship to return to port each evening. That gave the men ample time to find trouble in the Georgia Street bars in San Francisco and the Duval Street bars in Key West.

During the war years, it was not uncommon to see notes in the boat's logs mentioning men being overdue from liberty by a few hours. Typically, a captain's mast was held, and the offending party was found guilty. Unless the crime was especially egregious, the punishment was confinement to the boat for one or two weeks. The sentence usually began on the same day

Archerfish left for patrol, when they were confined to the boat for weeks anyway. Almost from the beginning of the boat's new life, the crew seemed considerably more aggressive in their failure to return to the boat prior to the expiration of their liberty. Captain's masts were more common. The unauthorized absences were for increasingly longer periods of time. Accordingly, the punishment was usually harsher.

One of the first crew members to report aboard the soon-to-be-reborn *Archerfish*, on December 23, was a submarine veteran named Donato "Donny" Persico. He was the chief of the boat, the highest-ranking enlisted man on board. As a twenty-year-old kid, Persico had survived one of the worst submarine accidents in American history. He had been aboard the USS *Squalus* (SS-192), a brand-new sub that went down in 243 feet of water off Portsmouth, Maine, while doing dive tests in May 1939. When a valve failed, the boat was suddenly jerked deep at a sharp angle. Persico and two other men, working in the forward torpedo room, were in the process of loading a dummy torpedo when the accident happened. With almost superhuman strength, he and the others were able to wrestle the heavy weapon into place and secure it before it crushed all three of them.

Twenty-six men died immediately. Thirty-three, including Persico, were rescued by a new and previously untested method, an experimental diving bell developed by renowned navy deep-sea diving and salvage expert Lieutenant Commander Charles B. "Swede" Momsen. He was also the namesake for the rescue breathing apparatus carried aboard all submarines.

Momsen rushed to the scene of *Squalus*'s sinking to oversee the rescue of the crew and then the salvage of the boat. Four navy divers won the Medal of Honor for their efforts in the rescue of the crew of the *Squalus*. Persico was among the eight crew members to be brought up on the bell's final trip. On the way to the surface, the line to the bell became entangled and they were almost lost again. They sank back to the sea bottom while divers struggled to get them clear.

But Persico lived to dive again. So did his sunken boat.

The *Squalus* was raised and towed back to Portsmouth with help from several other vessels. One of them was another submarine, the USS *Sculpin* (SS-191), who located the sunken sub on the sea bottom in the first place. Back in Portsmouth, *Squalus* was not only refitted, she was renamed USS *Sailfish* (SS-192). The recycled submarine went on to conduct twelve war patrols during World War II.

On one of those patrols, one of the cruelest ironies of the war occurred. *Sailfish*, the old *Squalus*, sank a Japanese ship one night in near-typhoon conditions. Her captain was proud of their significant accomplishment, which had occurred under less than ideal circumstances. He had no way of knowing at the time that aboard the enemy vessel they torpedoed were twenty-one survivors from an American submarine that had recently been sent to the bottom by the enemy. All but one of the American survivors aboard the ship died in the attack by *Sailfish*.

The name of the sunken sub from which the Japanese had rescued those Americans? The *Sculpin*, the same boat that had found *Squalus* and helped in her rescue and salvaging.

Preactivation of *Archerfish* began on January 7, 1952. On March 7, Captain W. A. Lent, Commander, Mare Island Group, Pacific Reserve Fleet, officially placed her in commission. Lieutenant Commander Maino des Granges assumed command as her skipper. He was formerly the executive officer, then the skipper, of USS *Bowfin* (SS-287) until that submarine was decommissioned in February 1947.

During the several months while she was being reactivated, the crew took the *Archerfish* out of her slip at Mare Island, eased down San Francisco Bay, drove beneath the Golden Gate Bridge, and headed out to the Pacific for drills. She got her official insignia during this time, too. Yeoman Second Class William Weathered, from New Jersey, had joined the crew of *Archerfish* in Mare Island. He had taken some art classes back at Dumont High School, and when he heard the boat's new softball team needed an insignia for their uniforms, he drew one up. It featured a fish, wearing a "Robin Hood" cap, using a bow to shoot a torpedo. A copy was sent to the Pacific Fleet commander, and it was approved as the official unit emblem. It had taken Weathered only one night to create the design. He knew it was a hit when it began showing up on the boat's official stationery. But he really knew it was accepted when he learned that at least one of the crew members had already had the insignia tattooed on his forearm.

Finally, on March 27, *Archerfish* left Mare Island, headed for San Diego for a three-week shakedown cruise. The feelings of one of her crews, a young submariner named Les Brown, might have been typical.

"I was sad when it was time to leave the yards at Vallejo. I had just started making it with Bobby Robison's girlfriend [Robison was another sailor aboard *Archerfish*] the week before. This was with Rob's approval. We shared everything. Once we were underway, my sadness soon turned to anticipation and I started looking forward to getting back to San Diego and my old girlfriend there. I hadn't seen her since I left *Aspro* to recommission *Archerfish*."

On the way out of the bay, they passed beneath the Golden Gate for what they assumed was the last time for a while. It was about noon. That evening, they encountered one of the typical fog banks along the northern California coast. With visibility down to a thousand yards, they sounded fog signals for most of the next hour, until conditions improved.

After that, the transit seemed to be going well for the newly refurbished boat. By six the next morning, they were almost halfway to San Diego, about a hundred miles west of Lompoc and Point Conception and northwest of the Channel Islands, proceeding normally on the surface. The four-to-eight watch was better than half finished, though there was considerable complaining because some of the men were having to stand extra watches, four on and four off, due to a short crew.

At about 6:20 in the morning, an awful explosion rocked *Archerfish*. The boat was immediately in serious trouble.

Three electricians were on watch that morning. Electrician's Mate First Class Charles Brock, a submarine veteran of World War II, was the senior controllerman, Electrician's Mate Second Class Kenneth W. "Kilowatt" McCarter was junior controllerman, both in the maneuvering room, and Electrician's Mate Third Class Jim Monte was the auxiliary electrician, stationed in the control room. At the time of the explosion, a battery charge was in progress, and Monte had gone forward to take gravity readings on the cells in the forward battery compartment. The boat was making standard speed on two main engines and one main engine was on the finishing rate of the battery charge. The bridge had ordered that all four main engines be placed "on propulsion" as soon as the charge was completed and that a "zero float" be maintained with the "dinky" engine.

This meant that the oiler in the after engine room had started the auxiliary engine (the dinky) so it would be up to operating temperature when the electricians were ready to use it. The generator attached to the auxiliary engine would provide current for the auxiliary motors. That current would be fed from the batteries through the forward and after auxiliary distribution switchboards. When on line, the auxiliary generator would provide voltage to the batteries to match the amount of juice required to meet the auxiliary power needs throughout the boat. That would make the drain on the main storage battery zero. Moments after setting up the after auxiliary distribution switchboard for the changeover, Brock and McCarter sat back to await the completion of the battery charge.

Suddenly, the auxiliary distribution switchboard began spitting hot sparks and boiling smoke poured out. Brock acted instantly, springing to kill the field circuit and remove the auxiliary generator voltage. Before he could get there, though, the switchboard exploded in his face. Stunned but still conscious, he reached for the emergency engine shutdown lever over his head. He couldn't believe what he saw when he looked up to try to find it.

A thick wall of liquid flames that looked exactly like some kind of living monster had already followed the curvature of the pressure hull and now licked at the overhead. He would have had to reach through a two-foot-thick stream of fire to find the shutdown lever. Instantly he knew he had only one chance if he didn't want to be incinerated—and if he didn't want the hungry flames to spread to another part of the boat.

He leaped as hard as he could for the watertight door that led to the after torpedo room. He had no idea if he could beat the flames to it or not, but he knew it was his only chance to survive.

Kilowatt McCarter was on the other side of the maneuvering room when all hell broke loose. By the time things had quit flying around the room and he had his bearings, he looked over to where his shipmate had been only seconds before.

Charlie Brock was no longer there. His seat was completely lost in the smoke and flames. He was certainly a goner.

McCarter's first thought was the same as Brock's, to try to get to the doorway to the torpedo room. He dismissed that at once. There was no way he could get through that seething mass of fire now. The only other way out was past the ship's lathe, where it was installed almost right up against the starboard side of the solid cubicle. He would have to try to squeeze through the narrow opening between the starboard side of the cubicle and the pressure hull. Then he could get out the doorway into the engine room.

But when he tried to get around the cubicle, his heart fell. Through the smoke, he could see that the space, like every nook and cranny on the boat at the beginning of a trip, was full of provisions and spare parts. Since there wasn't really enough room for anyone to comfortably squeeze past there and no one used it as a route through the maneuvering room, it was typically used for storage. Now, it was crammed full with dozens of large, square twenty-pound coffee cans and a big stack of film canisters, the movies for the trip.

McCarter began digging wildly, frantically, trying to make enough room to ease past and escape. It didn't look good. His only way out of this hellish firestorm seemed hopelessly blocked.

Jim Monte was still forward, checking the readings on the batteries, when he heard the deafening explosion. He suspected immediately that it came from either the maneuvering room or the after torpedo room. Either one was bad news.

He dashed wildly that way, worried about his shipmates back there, many of whom were likely still in their bunks. As he rushed through the after battery sleeping compartment, he found the rest of the crew was already reacting, bailing out of bunks, following the emergency procedures they had drilled on so many times already. He had to fight his way past the mob of men until he finally reached the after engine room. A firefighting party had already been organized. Someone put an RBA (rescue breathing apparatus) on him. Smoke was thick in the engine room, and it was hard to find air to breathe.

Someone touched him on the shoulder.

"Charlie Brock's still in there, Jim," the sailor said. "I don't think he made it out."

He didn't mention Kilowatt McCarter. Monte didn't hesitate. He grabbed a battle lantern and went through the watertight door, stepping into the blinding smoke of the maneuvering room, determined to try to find his shipmates.

Les Brown was the oiler on watch in the forward engine room. He was tired, half asleep, worn out by the first night of double watches and all the celebrating they had done the previous few nights before getting underway. He was almost knocked sprawling by the thunderous explosion.

His first thought was that a torpedo had exploded in the after torpedo room. Just then, as he turned to look that way, several giant fireballs came rolling his way along the deck of the after engine room. He tried to dodge them the best he could.

The concussion had knocked his throttleman, Will McBryde, off his feet. He scrambled up and climbed on to one of the engines to try to get away from the Roman candle shots hurtling his way.

When they could, both men moved to try to get the watertight door to the after engine room closed. If it was a torpedo that blew up, it would have breeched the hull and seawater would be pouring in already, sinking the boat by the stern. They had to seal off that compartment. Of course, closing that door also meant shutting off anyone back there from rescue.

Soon, they learned that the fire was in the maneuvering room, that it was confined to that compartment, and that it was being fought from back there already. They tried not to think about the men who had been working in maneuvering—McCarter and Brock—and what kind of shape they might be in. They began to attack the blazes from their side.

Bobby Robison was in the galley, helping the cook work up a good breakfast after their first night at sea. He, too, heard and felt the horrible explosion, as the whole boat seemed to shudder with the concussion. He, too, thought of a torpedo somehow detonating by accident and of the damage it could do to the boat. Smoke soon worked its way to his compartment.

A few minutes later, he glanced at the hydrogen indicator on the bulkhead. Robison swallowed hard. The needle was pegged to the right.

The hydrogen level in the boat was dangerously high. Another explosion was very much a possibility, but there was no place to go to get away from it. If the hydrogen ignited, they were all likely goners.

When Charlie Brock fell backward through the doorway into the after torpedo room, his first notion was to get back up and try to shut and dog the door. He didn't want those teeming tongues of flame to reach out into this compartment and find something else to consume, to feed on, to keep going. The heavy smoke was already pouring through the doorway into the after torpedo room. But try as he might, he couldn't find the strength to reach back into the maneuvering room and grab hold of the door. Something seemed to be holding him back. And that something was now screaming at him.

"Don't go back in there! Dammit, Charlie, don't go back in there! You'll get burned up!"

It was the boat's chief electrician, John Shewell.

"John, I'm just trying to shut the door!" Brock yelled.

"I thought—"

Shewell was certain Brock was trying to get back into the inferno, trying to go back in to attempt to save his shipmates. He had a firm grip on Brock's belt and wasn't going to let him commit suicide. He finally let go and helped Brock secure the door.

Charlie Glasberg was asleep in the after torpedo room when something woke him. It sounded like a blast furnace. He jumped up in time to see Charlie Brock fall through the doorway. He could see brilliant hot fire blazing everywhere on the other side of the door until Brock and Shewell closed it. He and several others grabbed all the CO_2 fire extinguishers in the compartment, reopened the door, pinned the extinguisher handles open, and threw them into the hellish inferno, then pulled the door shut again.

By now the torpedo room was almost filled with thick, black, heavy smoke, and there was no ventilation. The men crouched down near the deck to find the only breathable air.

Lieutenant Jack Venable, the officer of the deck, was on the bridge that morning. As soon as he could breathe, Charlie Brock called him on the 7MC and reported the fire, then told him that three engines were still running; two of them were on propulsion, and one engine was still on battery charge. Then, in a halting voice, he told the OOD that McCarter was still in maneuvering, still in the midst of that hell. Though it seemed like hours, that report to the bridge came only a minute or so after the explosion of the switchboard.

Venable gave the men in the after torpedo room permission to open the topside hatch onto the main deck so they could proceed forward, away from the choking smoke. He also ordered all engines shut down from the engine rooms and asked Brock to come to the bridge as soon as he could manage so he could give him a full report.

A minute later, Les Brown and the others in the engine room reported to Venable that they had formed a firefighting party and that a man with an RBA was entering the maneuvering room to check on the extent of the emergency. That man was Jim Monte.

Monte found the going impossible once he was inside amid the smoke and fire of the maneuvering room and looking for Charlie and Kilowatt. The smoke was so thick he couldn't tell if the battle lantern was working or not, even when he held it right next to the RBA's faceplate. The place was hellish, like the inside of a kiln. CO_2 fire extinguishers were spewing all around him but he could see that they were, thankfully, helping knock down the fire. As he tried to squeeze his way through the narrow space around the port side of the cubicle, he spotted someone working his way forward toward him.

"I was looking for you and Kilowatt!" the man yelled.

"I'm looking for Charlie and him, too!" Monte responded.

"Charlie got out into the torpedo room. He's okay. If Kilowatt's in here, he's a goner."

The heat and smoke were unbearable, and it was clear there was nothing else they could do in there. They went back out the way they came in.

Meanwhile, everyone who could was continuing to rig the fire extinguishers and throw them into the maneuvering room. A rough brigade was formed. One man strapped on an RBA, opened a door, threw in an extinguisher, then turned and walked back before the fire blistered him. The next man took the RBA off the first man's face, put it on himself, grabbed an extinguisher, and went to toss it into the inferno.

Finally, because of the CO_2 and the fact that most anything in the compartment that would burn had already been consumed, the blaze seemed to be dying out.

As he made his way to the bridge, Charlie Brock couldn't stop thinking about Kilowatt McCarter. Before the blast, he had been showing him some of the intricacies of making an old boat like *Archerfish* behave herself. During his submarine career, McCarter had so far served only on the more modern boats, but he had been eager to learn, interested in doing the best job he could do now that he was on *Archerfish*. He was most likely still down there in the midst of all that smoke and fire, and he was almost certainly dead.

Brock couldn't get out of his mind the fact that he had bailed out of the room and closed the door behind himself when he did. He had closed and dogged the only way out of the fiery hell that was the maneuvering room.

That had been the right thing to do. Absolutely the right thing to do. Save the boat. Save the other men and the boat, even if it cost the life of a shipmate. He knew it was the right thing to do, but it didn't make it any easier for him to take.

Once on the bridge, Brock repeated what he had told the OOD before on the 7MC, including his belief that Electrician's Mate Kenneth McCarter was dead in the maneuvering room. As he talked to Venable, Brock noticed the OOD kept staring oddly at him. Finally, Venable said, "Find Doc McDonald, Charlie. Get those burns taken care of."

For the first time, Brock realized that his face and neck were stinging mightily. His hair and eyebrows were singed, his head and neck badly scorched, and his right ear painfully blistered and oozing. He went below, looking for Jim McDonald, the hospital corpsman, but when he got to the control room, Brock made a truly frightening discovery.

The hydrogen detector was pegged. Not just in the red danger zone. Pegged.

The amount of the explosive gas in the air inside the sub was well above safe levels. In all the excitement and chaos during the fire, the main battery disconnects had not been pulled. They had been charging right up until Venable ordered all engines stopped.

Brock felt faint. With the air as saturated with hydrogen as it seemed to be, even the slightest spark could trigger a catastrophic explosion. It had happened to the USS *Cochino* (SS-345), up near the Arctic Circle, back in 1949. A series of fiery hydrogen explosions would have led to the loss of her entire crew had another submarine, USS *Tusk* (SS-426), not been nearby to rescue them. Even then, the boat was lost, one civilian engineer from the *Cochino* died, many crew members were seriously burned, and six men aboard the *Tusk* drowned in the brave rescue that played out that day on heavy, arctic seas.

Now Brock knew that there was only one thing left to do. He had to pull the disconnects and take the batteries off-line or there would certainly be an explosion. He quickly asked Venable for permission, and it was granted. He didn't tell the OOD of the imminent danger. Likely, Venable knew it only too well. He also likely knew that there was no other choice.

If there should be any kind of spark when he pulled the disconnects, and if the hydrogen concentration was any greater than 3 percent, the fire in the maneuvering room would be nothing in comparison to the conflagration that would be set off.

Brock didn't hesitate. His hands trembling, he reached up, grabbed the disconnects, and broke the circuit.

All was well. There was no spark, no flaming blast.

Now, he finally could go aft to the galley to find Doc. As he rounded the coffee pot, he saw a familiar face. It took him a moment to realize who it was, calmly sitting there, getting ointment applied to burns on his face and arms.

Kilowatt!

Brock grabbed his friend and hugged him, ignoring the stinging pain and Doc McDonald's fussing.

He couldn't believe it. The guy was alive!

McCarter was just beginning to tell about how he had somehow clawed his way through all those coffee cans and film canisters and squeezed impossibly between the lathe and the cubicle, where there was not enough room for a man his size to pass, and how he got out of there into the engine room. He had just started to tell him how bad he had been feeling because he believed he had left Brock behind to die. That's when a couple of officers separated them, taking Brock to the wardroom and keeping McCarter in the crew's mess. They wanted both men's versions of what had happened, but they wanted them separately, without collaboration.

It was the navy way.

Now there was another problem. *Archerfish* was dead in the water, bobbing on the Pacific at least thirty miles from land. Fortunately, the seas were relatively calm, but they needed to go somewhere soon.

The fire had destroyed all the cables feeding the auxiliary power board. There was more damage, of course, and it was obvious that it would take days to find and fix it all.

Captain des Granges called a meeting in the wardroom as soon as the emergency was past. Clearly, they would need to return to Mare Island to assess the damage and get it repaired.

According to the scuttlebutt that swept the boat afterward, the skipper pulled no punches at that hastily called meeting.

"Boys, my father-in-law owns a marine towing company . . . the one that would most likely be sent to come get us." He scratched his chin, then set his jaw stubbornly as he went on. "My worst fear is that one of his tugs would be sent out here to give us a tow. I'd rather hang off the turtleback and kick my feet in the water and paddle us all the way back to Mare Island than have him come get me!"

With that, he told them they had no choice but to find a way.

The chief electrician, John Shewell, was the one who came up with the jury rig that got them back. He removed enough shore power cable from the after engine room to splice the burned cables back into the auxiliary power distribution board. This allowed them to run the lighting motor generators, main motor cooling pumps, bilge pump, and other necessary equipment. After a couple of hours, they were able to get under way at reduced speed, using the main engines.

Not everything worked. Bobby Robison remembers that only one of the two grills in the galley and the coffee pot were functioning. No one complained about having to wait for a cup of joe. They were just happy to be alive.

Only two men suffered burns serious enough to be noted: Charlie Brock and a torpedoman named Santo H. Formolo, who was likely the man Jim Monte encountered in the smoke and fire of the maneuvering room while looking for his shipmates. Neither man missed any duty time because of his injuries.

It was later determined that the original explosion was caused by a dead short across the after battery auxiliary power circuit breaker. The fire was officially listed as having started at 6:20 AM. It was reported out at 6:28.

At 10:00, while thirty miles west of the Point Conception light, *Archerfish* reported to ComSubFlot One about the fire and the extent of the damage and, near the end of the transmission, that there were "no serious personnel injuries." By then the boat was already moving under her own power. Captain des Granges's father-in-law was never called.

Though it was never confirmed, several reports by crew members said that all but one of the fire extinguishers on board were used to control the fire.

The first endorsement to the official report to the Judge Advocate General concerning the potentially disastrous fire on *Archerfish* did not blame anyone for the accident. It did say, "While the casualty which occurred is not attributable to any violation of existing instructions on the part of personnel aboard the USS *Archerfish*, nevertheless, its seriousness must not be minimized. Information as to the probable cause of this electrical casualty and the methods by which the possibility of such a casualty can be minimized will be disseminated to the force."

It was so disseminated. The boat's close call may well have prevented a more tragic occurrence on another boat somewhere. Battery circuit breakers, designed to prevent such a fire, were soon installed on all active submarines. The Bureau of Ships also decided that using a less flammable material in the switchboards would likely prevent an accident like *Archerfish*'s. However, when it was learned that such a change would cost a whopping $15,000 per submarine, the plan was tabled.

Incidentally, the endorsement to the report to the Judge Advocate General was authored by Charles B. "Swede" Momsen, the man who made possible the rescue of Donny Persico and the thirty-two other men from the *Squalus* back in 1939.

Les Brown, the oiler on watch in the forward engine room when the front door to Hades opened, put the event in perspective.

"What an experience! What a crew! I think it helped us bond faster."

But Brown did have one lingering concern. Now that they were returning to San Francisco, what would happen with the girlfriend he and Bobby Robison had been sharing?

No need to worry. When they got back to Mare Island, he and Robison discovered their mutual love had already found herself another sailor. They had to find romance elsewhere until *Archerfish* was once again ready to head for the Caribbean and her next great adventure.

8

THE BIG DITCH

ARCHERFISH'S first trip through the Panama Canal, on her way to Pearl Harbor and the Pacific war back in 1943, had been relatively uneventful. There was the incident with the binoculars, and the one straggler who simply didn't come back to the boat when she was scheduled to leave. This time, in the middle of 1952, the crew members seemed intent on leaving their mark on the Big Ditch during her four-day passage.

Archerfish moored port side to at the north side of Pier 2, Berth 6, at Rodman Naval Station, Balboa, Canal Zone, on the Pacific side of the isthmus on June 30. There was trouble almost immediately, and it is no surprise it involved sailors who had gone ashore or that it was aggravated by demon rum.

The narrative from the boat's log said:

> July 1 1845—The below named men were placed under arrest by the Duty Officer and were directed to remain below decks for alleged violations of the Uniform Code of Military Justice (U.C.M.J.):
>
> EMFA(SS) Jay D. Kelly, violation of U.C.M.J. Article 134, Disorders to the prejudice of good order and discipline (unauthorized diving overboard while under the influence of intoxicating liquors);
>
> EMFN(SS) Joseph V. Patterson, violation of U.C.M.J. Article 134, Disorders to the prejudice of good order and discipline (unauthorized

diving overboard while under the influence of intoxicating liquors), and U.C.M.J. Article 109, Wasting or spoiling property other than military property of the United States (diving overboard with the Executive Officer's laundry and losing it).

1900—Kelly broke arrest and departed from the ship in direct disobedience of orders from the topside deck watch.

1909—Kelly was apprehended by duty personnel, returned under guard to the ship and sent below.

1930—Kelly again broke arrest and attempted to depart from the ship. Apprehended by duty personnel and sent below.

1950—Patterson broke arrest and departed from the ship in direct disobedience of orders from topside watch.

1952—Patterson was apprehended by duty personnel, returned to the ship under guard, and sent below.

Kelly and Patterson had been part of a big group who left the boat to play in a "beer ball" game, which is typically little more than an excuse to get off the boat early and drink beer. In beer ball, each team can have as many players as it wants, but only nine (including pitcher and catcher) can be on the field at any one time. Most of those nine would take their beers with them. One version of the game places a beer at each base, and a runner must chug a beer before advancing to the next base. A fielder must chug a beer before throwing the ball. The batter must do so before advancing to first base. Usually, no one bothers to keep score, and the game lasts until the brew is gone or nobody bothers to take the field. As was typical, there was more beer than baseball at the game Kelly and Patterson and the rest attended that day.

Afterward, as the group approached the boat, Kelly decided to jump off the wharf into the harbor and swim across to *Archerfish* rather than walk all the way around the basin to the pier. Charlie Brock, Jim Monte, and some of the others who were along talked him out of it, but the idea of taking a swim had been implanted.

When they stepped on board the boat, Kelly spied a big pile of brown paper packages of clean laundry on the deck. It had been recently delivered and was neatly stacked there, waiting for the owners to pick it up. He grabbed a package and headed for the side, intent on throwing it over. Again, cooler heads prevailed, and he was dragged back before he sent somebody's fresh, clean clothes into the drink.

Suddenly, Joe Patterson saw his chance. He grabbed a bundle and jumped over the side, clutching the package to his chest like a life preserver. When he hit the water, he began ripping open the paper and tossing the nice, clean, freshly pressed uniforms into the air. With the distraction, Kelly jumped over the side as well.

The others looked on in horror. The uniforms were khaki. Officer's clothes. The two "well-oiled" sailors were making a mess of the laundry belonging to the boat's executive officer, Lieutenant Vance R. Wanner.

Once they were corralled and sober, the men knew that they had picked the wrong bundles of laundry to toss into Balboa Harbor. Four days later, when they were through the Canal and under way for Key West, Captain des Granges held mast for the two mischievous sailors. Patterson got fourteen hours of extra duty and "verbal warning and admonition." Kelly got one week's confinement in the brig, beginning when they arrived at Key West, and received his own tongue-lashing. Most of those who were witness to the crime thought they got off lightly, but it was still comical, seeing the two men cavorting in the water with the exec's clothes floating all around them.

While making the trip through the Panama Canal, *Archerfish* caught up with and passed a big Swedish freighter while crossing Gatun Lake. They sped up and got some distance ahead of the ship, running at full speed through the freshwater lake that makes up a part of the canal. They wanted to flush out the main motor and main engine coolers. When they reached the approach to Gatun Locks, there were several ships ahead of them in the queue, and the canal pilot ordered "All stop." He notified the skipper that they would have to lay to until the traffic jam ahead cleared. A tropical rain shower was passing over, and the skipper figured it would be a good time to hold a short swim call. The officer of the deck passed the word.

"All hands not actually on watch may lay topside for swim call."

Most of the crew was happy to oblige. A few tugged on their swim trunks. Those who didn't have trunks handy stripped naked and stood around on the submarine's forward deck, allowing the rain to rinse them off. Some dived into the murky water and enjoyed a good swim.

They paid little attention to the big Swedish transport they had passed as it eased alongside. The ship was close enough for those on her deck to get a good view of the American submarine crew, many of them naked as the day they were born, dancing around on the deck in the warm rain and splashing in the lake.

The ship was directly alongside when the *Archerfish* crew heard laughter. Female laughter.

Sure enough, a sizable contingent of women had gathered on the transport's railing, and they were laughing and pointing at the naked sailors. The crew had no idea it was customary for Scandinavian merchant ship crews to carry their wives with them.

On July 3, they were through the Canal and under way for their new home as part of Submarine Squadron 12 at Key West. They were now officially transferred from the operational control of ComSubPac and were part of ComSubLant.

At the same time, the boat had now left a significant part of her past behind. She was no longer the World War II diesel boat plying the waters of the Pacific in search of the enemy. She was in new waters and had new priorities.

Archerfish had now, truly, begun her second life.

9

GITMO AND GUERRILLAS

ARCHERFISH pulled into Key West, at the very end of the Florida Keys, on July 7, 1952. There was no rest for the weary. They started exercises the very next day. Their primary job was to be the "mechanical rabbit" for the Fleet Sonar School, which was located at Key West, teaching young navy sonarmen how to find submarines with their ears. They also ran extensive torpedo exercises with the other subs, which involved firing practice torpedos at each other. It was, for the most part, fun duty, even though they had occasionally to dodge lobster pots and nonchalant fishermen. Then, their duty done, they were back in port almost every night.

There was another fire, this one in the boat's control room, on July 12. This occurred while the commander of Submarine Squadron 12 and his staff were aboard conducting a "personnel, material, and administrative inspection." Fuses had blown in the number-two motor generator as a result of "personnel error." With no injuries and little damage done, it was no more than a reminder of what had happened off the California coast a little over three months before.

On July 14, *Archerfish*'s home yard was changed from Mare Island to Portsmouth. In a manner of speaking, she had come home.

In addition to performing its tasks in Key West, the boat also spent a great deal of time in Guantánamo Bay, "Gitmo," an arid outpost on the southeastern tip of Cuba. The mountains north of the base are covered with junglelike rain forest, but they prevent much rain from falling on the city and naval station there. There are hurricanes, mostly in late summer and fall, and even occasionally earthquakes. One especially strong one in 1947 cracked the pavement on Wharf Baker and littered Sherman Avenue, the base's main street, with boulders. Except for the drier than normal weather, the climate is tropical. Those who were stationed there at the time still laugh about a Defense Department memorandum that came down in 1950, ordering the base to begin keeping track of ice buildup in the harbor. Of course, there has never been any. The area is known for its diving spots, but otherwise, it is not an especially hospitable place.

Nowadays, its location in Castro's Cuba makes it an especially dangerous place to be. Since Castro cut off all water and other utilities in the early sixties, the base is totally self-sufficient. It even maintains its own desalinization plant.

When *Archerfish* tied up there for the first time on August 6, 1952, Castro and his rebels were already active in the nearby Sierra Maestra, just beginning their civil war against the government of Cuba. It would be seven more years before he prevailed.

There were usually two or more Key West–based submarines in Gitmo, providing services to the fleet training activities there. All surface craft in the navy on the East Coast were required to go to Guantánamo regularly to be tested for operational readiness. The submarines' job was simple: prove the other navy craft were *not* ready. They often did just that.

There was yet another close call for *Archerfish* during this time. A deck log entry calmly recounts the incident without even hinting at its potential deadliness: "1105—Submerged. 1105.15—Main induction failed to shut in normal power. Made unsuccessful attempt to shut main induction by hand. 1106—Surfaced."

This was the exact same malfunction that had sent the *Squalus* to the bottom of the Atlantic Ocean thirteen years earlier. The only difference here was that the *Archerfish* Christmas tree correctly indicated that the valve had not shut properly. The crew was able to surface the boat before potentially mortal flooding began, or *Archerfish* could have met the same fate as *Squalus*.

Ironically, Donny Persico, the last sailor out of *Squalus* alive, was still serving aboard *Archerfish* the day the main induction valve failed to shut. It's not clear if he was chief of the watch at the time or not. As chief of the boat, he well could have been. It's easy to imagine the thoughts that coursed through his mind in that quick minute or so, remembering the tragedy of his old boat even as he took steps to prevent its happening again on this one.

Shooting to the surface likely saved their lives. There's no indication of what caused the problem in the first place. All we know is that the log indicates "conditions normal" only a minute after the failure.

As you might have assumed, life in Key West and the area was not all work and no play for the *A-fish* crew. In August, after a week of exercises in the Guantánamo Bay operating area, they steamed about a hundred miles west to Santiago for a few days' liberty. A couple of young *Archerfish* sailors, one an officer, got introduced quickly to the ways of the world when they wandered into a large bar in the town. They were enjoying one of the island's signature drinks, rum and Coca-Cola, when a very friendly and attractive young lady joined them, without invitation, at their table. They were savvy enough to realize she was likely a prostitute, but they were not ready for what she did after talking with them for a bit. Before they could even realize what was happening, she suddenly removed a breast from her bra and, without comment, squeezed milk into each of their drinks.

"*Rum y Coca-Cola con leche,*" she announced with a flirtatious grin. "Rum and Coca-Cola with milk. Welcome to Santiago de Cuba."

The two wide-eyed navy men thanked her politely, then promptly got up and left the bar.

A potentially dangerous encounter took place a few days later, back in Gitmo. A group from an aircraft carrier challenged the *Archerfish* crew to a beer ball game. Of course, the *311*-boat could not allow any challenge to go unanswered. After the game, one of the sub sailors was not able to find his baseball glove. He asked the carrier guys if he could look in their equipment bags to see if they had picked it up by mistake. They quickly became surly, accusing the sub sailor of calling them thieves. That didn't stop the search. He dumped four bags of equipment on the ground and started rummaging through it all. Sure enough, he found his mitt.

By then, the carrier boys' mood had turned very ugly, and three chief petty officers started toward him. The sub sailor picked up a bat and suggested strongly that everyone should calm down and go about his business. One of the men took a run at him anyway, and, with perhaps the best swing of the day, the sub sailor laid the CPO out cold.

Before anyone else became brave enough to try something else, the *Archerfish* guys made a quick retreat. One seaman from the submarine, Jack Andrews, remembers that it appeared they were outnumbered about forty to one, so that was likely a prudent retreat. It turned out that the "skimmer"

CPO was okay, except for a sizable knot on his head to go along with his wounded pride. The *Archerfish* crewman of the lost glove and quick bat was busted down a rank when official word of the altercation got back to the skipper.

Beginning with her second commission, *Archerfish* typically had a different photo taken each year for its Christmas card, the one the crew members sent home to their families, to their girlfriends, and to their favorite barmaids. The picture that was used for Christmas, 1952, showed the boat passing majestically between Windward and Leeward Points at the entrance to Guantánamo Bay.

One day in January 1953, the frogmen assigned to Guantánamo announced to all vessels in the harbor that they would be holding a drill that night. Their intent was to simulate blowing up every ship in port. In preparation, all ships beefed up their security that evening in an attempt to foil the announced plan. There was a battleship, a couple of cruisers, some destroyers, several auxiliary ships, and, of course, *Archerfish*. When night fell, all the surface ships illuminated their huge spotlights and continuously swept around their ships, looking for the "enemy." *Archerfish* maintained three topside watches armed with flashlights with fresh batteries.

Still, despite the warning and all the vigilance, the frogmen did, indeed, manage to "sink" every ship in the harbor that night without getting caught. Even though the watch standers on *Archerfish* claimed to have spotted one of them and threw their coffee cups at his bubbles, the frogmen managed to set off a flare in the area of the boat's bow planes, simulating an explosion.

The next day, the frogmen showed up at each vessel with a letter, asking that the skippers sign it to verify the "sinking" the night before. Captain des Granges refused to sign.

"That charge would never have sunk us," he maintained. "We would have sealed off the forward torpedo room to stop the flooding, and we would have remained afloat."

The frogmen were angry and told des Granges that they would certainly be back to prove their point.

Despite an even bigger watch than the previous evening, the frogmen somehow managed to get on board the boat, set off a flare over the conning tower, and get back off the boat again without anyone seeing them. This time, they had thoroughly "blown up" *Archerfish*. Des Granges then had to admit that the guys were good. He willingly signed their letter when they showed up again the next morning.

Whether they were in Key West or Guantánamo Bay, the *Archerfish* crew was always mindful of the civil war that was just beginning in Cuba, but they never felt any closer to the struggle than when in Gitmo. Fidel Castro and his band of guerrillas were in the early stages of their attempt to overthrow Fulgencio Batista, the Cuban dictator. They operated out of the mountains north and west of Guantánamo City in Oriente Province. Later, in July 1953, Castro led his most ambitious assault yet, an attack on the Moncada army barracks in Santiago, which was not that far away. That assault resulted in Castro's capture by Batista's troops and his incarceration, but it also gave the young revolutionary the national prominence he needed to continue his revolution.

As part of the navy's public relations efforts, the *Archerfish* held a Visit Ship Day in mid-January. Locals who worked on the base along with military personnel assigned to the base and their families were invited to come aboard and tour a real, live submarine and talk with her crew. No one was surprised when some of the Cuban visitors arrived carrying rifles. It was not uncommon to see young, rifle-toting men in Guantánamo in those days, and everyone assumed they were part of Fidel's revolutionary forces. These armed visitors were told they would have to leave their guns topside, and they complied. Still, several of the crew noticed that these men were very young, and seemed truly menacing. It was clear then that Castro's fight was getting more and more serious.

A few days later, on a day when there were no operations under way, a group of men from *Archerfish* decided a fishing trip and picnic would be a good way to beat the boredom. Everyone was broke, and there was nothing else much to do on the base in Gitmo. Among the band of happy fishermen were Les Brown, J. D. Kelly (he of the exec's laundry fiasco), Bobby Robison, Kelly Elkins, and John "Poopsie" Welsko.

They managed to scrape together enough money to buy a case of beer for every man on the trip and several bottles of rum. It was hot, after all, and they kept reminding each other that it was a bad idea to drink the water in that place. They also swiped lunch meats, cheese, bread, and condiments from the galley. The fishermen checked out a twenty-foot navy motor launch and some fishing tackle from base Special Services and then they were all set for a fine afternoon of angling.

The plan was to venture up the Guantánamo River. A decent-sized stream that ran swiftly down from the mountains, it was hardly a lazy river. Its water was green, dirty, and filled with debris. Still, the fishing was supposed to be good up that way, or so somebody said, and off they went in that direction. Never mind that no one had thought to bring bait for the fishing tackle they had checked out. If they had to, they decided, they'd just use bologna and cheese.

As soon as they were out of sight of the dock, they broke out the beer. That's when they realized that they had also forgotten to bring ice, but warm beer was better than no beer at all. It was a hot, clear day, and they were all dressed in dungaree shorts and sandals. No one had thought of suntan lotion either.

Once across the bay and on the river, their progress slowed considerably. The current was swift. Nobody seemed to mind. The beer was good, the scenery magnificent, and they were all having a wonderful time, each man trying to outlie the rest. The riverbank looked like a jungle, with vines and trees overhanging the river, like pictures of the Amazon. Some of the men even jumped into the muddy water for a swim, further slowing their quest for a good fishing spot. Eventually, though, they were well up the river. Nobody had bothered to wet a hook yet.

None of them noticed the small gunboat until it was almost on top of them. It appeared out of nowhere, grumbling downriver toward them. Its occupants were all armed and wearing camouflage uniforms. The vessel had what appeared to be a 20-mm deck gun on the bow. Whoever they were, they were serious.

Several of the men on the navy launch thought at first that it must be the MPs. They busily tried to hide the beer and to look sober while doing it.

Then it was obvious these were not true military types at all. They had to be some of Castro's young guerrillas. They had the same hard look in their eyes as the rifle-toting men who had toured the submarine.

Now, though, the *Archerfish* guys had invaded their territory. They could not ask them to abandon their rifles this time.

The coxswain of the navy launch idled down and the guerrilla gunboat pulled up alongside and tied the two vessels together. No one on the gunboat said a word. They just stared across at the Americans, their faces grim.

With as much beer as had been consumed, it was inevitable that someone on the navy boat would say something smart. Several did. More than a few desperately needed to pee and were about to make the request.

They hushed quickly when the guerrillas waved their rifles in their direction and said something back in rapid Spanish. Whatever their words were, they were not a friendly welcome to Cuba.

Bobby Robison knew a little Spanish and tried to communicate.

"Qué es el problema?" he asked, the words skewed by his Missouri bootheel drawl.

Then one of the guerrillas, one who appeared to be a bit older than the others, at least twenty years old, said something in half English, half Spanish. Robison couldn't believe his ears. It sounded as if they were being accused of coming up the river to try to get to a convent farther upstream. That they had designs on raping the nuns there. And they were serious!

It didn't take much knowledge of the Spanish language to deny the accusation.

"No! No!" Robison told them, as emphatically as he could. He told them they were just looking for fish. That they didn't even know about any convent or nuns.

All the while, the two boats, still lashed together, floated back down the swift stream. The guerrillas on the gunboat continued to nervously wave their rifles at the wide-eyed sailors, glaring at them angrily, menacingly.

Eventually, they must have believed Robison's denials. Or decided this launch full of drunken sailors posed no threat to the revolution. At least not to anyone else but themselves.

The guerrillas slowly turned the launch around. As they unhooked their lines, they emphatically pointed downstream, the way the submariners had come. There was no mistaking the message now. They were to leave, do so immediately, and not come back this way again.

That's exactly what they did, and much quicker than they had made the trip upriver.

Along the way, someone pointed out a big sign on the riverbank that had somehow escaped their attention earlier. It warned that no one was to go any farther upriver than this point.

Back in Guantánamo Bay, with most of them severely sunburned, the beer and rum mostly gone, and not a single fish to show for their adventure, they returned the launch. They were thankful for two things: the menacing young rebels had not seen fit to shoot them all to death, and they now had one hell of a story to tell the guys back at the boat.

Les Brown left the navy not long after that to take advantage of the GI Bill and get an education. He later wrote: "Oh, the good times and the stories that crew provided. I shall never forget. I would never have left if I had known what was up for that wonderful boat."

It's a safe assumption few others would have either.

10

THE PROJECTOR

THE challenges of a submarine command are many. Some of the seemingly more trivial ones are actually the ones that try a skipper's patience most.

On March 13 1953, Captain Maino des Granges sat down and wrote the following memo, using his best military style, to the supply officer at the U.S. Naval Supply Center in Mechanicsburg, Pennsylvania.

Subject: 16 MM Sound Motion Picture Equipment, Type IC/QEM-1A, Serial 206, Mfg by Ampro Corporation, request for instructions on repair to.
Ref:

a) BSSO 212069, and NSD Mechanicsburg Inv. 275936/0 of 1-26-53

b) Instruction Book for 16 MM Sound Motion Picture Equipment Type IC/QEM-1A, (NavShips 385-0217), (Preliminary I.C. Instr. Book 646)

1. Subject equipment was received on 18 February 1953, pursuant to reference (a). After approximately twenty five hours of operation, the projector, stock No. SO 18 P 0247070493, became inoperative due to failure of piece number 24 D of fig. 72 (Intermittent Assembly) of reference (b).

2. Inasmuch as the failure occurred well within the one year equipment guarantee, as stated on page ii of reference (b), instructions as to proper action to repair subject projector are requested.

A copy of the memo was sent to the Bureau of Ships as well. *Archerfish's* movie projector was on the fritz, and that was serious business. Captain des Granges hoped to quickly get the part they needed and get the projector going again.

That, as you may have guessed, would not happen.

LIFE is tough enough on a submarine without having someone screw up in a most disgusting fashion. Barry Buckley was standing in the boat's mess one day, just inside the door that led to the adjacent berthing space. All the seats were taken, filled with hungry submariners enjoying their meal, and he was waiting for someone to finish eating so he could get his own food.

Suddenly a powerful jet of the most foul-smelling, disgusting mess imaginable shot from the drain under the drinking fountain next to the sink. The stuff rained down on everyone in the mess hall. There was no doubt from the very beginning of the noxious explosion about what it was. It was pure, raw sewage from the boat's number-two sanitary tank. Sailors scattered everywhere, cursing, yelling, running for doors and hatches, trying to escape the nasty fallout that was raining off the overhead and turning the atmosphere in the compartment into a moist, stomach-churning mist.

Buckley managed to duck back through the door and dodge the revolting shower, but others weren't so lucky. It is an unwritten rule on submarines that the unfortunate person who forgets to shut a drain valve before blowing sanitary tanks has to clean up the revolting mess. The belowdecks watch was the one who had to mop up the nauseating result of his inattention. He had been blowing the sanitary tank and forgot to shut off the valve to the drain, blasting the men in the crew's mess with . . . well, a true mess.

ON March 23, 1953, the commanding officer of the Ships Parts Control Center at the Naval Supply Depot in Mechanicsburg, Pennsylvania, forwarded Captain Maino des Granges's memo about the malfunctioning movie projector to the Chief, Bureau of Ships, in Washington, D.C., for "appropriate action."

JACK Peach admits he was out all night having a good time and that he showed up back at the boat just in time to go on duty as the "stew burner" for the day. He managed to make it through the noon meal okay, despite a strong hangover and a weak stomach. By midafternoon though, he was quickly fading.

Then he noticed the menu called for liver and onions for the evening meal. His stomach did a flip-flop. Still, duty was duty. He had to get it done.

Somehow, in a feat of superhuman effort, Peach managed to get the liver and onions cut up and fried without losing the battle with his digestive system, though he almost fell asleep several times as he stood there, wavering dizzily over the grill next to the hot deep fryer. He poured the cooked liver into a pan and put it in the oven to keep it warm until mealtime. Then, his body finally at the point of shutting down, he told the mess cook he was going to grab a nap and asked him to wake him up in time to put out dinner.

Of course, the mess cook forgot to wake him until just before dinnertime. The warmed-up liver had the consistency of shoe leather, and the onions could have been shoestrings. The first men to sit down to Peach's disastrous meal let their feelings be known in no uncertain terms. The duty officer, Lieutenant Chuck Cushman, put it a little more succinctly when he jumped on the 1MC announcing system.

"Anyone in the duty section not actually on watch may go to the boat next door to get a respectable meal," he told the entire boat.

That was when Peach made the decision to change his rate to sonarman. He knew his cooking days were numbered.

ON April 16, 1953, J. R. Tucker, "by direction," sent a memo from Chief, Bureau of Ships, in Washington, D.C., prepared by J. P. Daly and typed by B. Goldstein, to Commanding Officer, USS *Archerfish* (SS-311), c/o Fleet Post Office in New York. It said, "Your ltr SS-311;RDZ;wew L8 ser 102 of 13 Mar 1953 and SPCC Mech endorsement 748;ECP;vc ser 3047D of 23 March 1953. Damaged part should be returned to Ampro Corporation 2835 North Western Avenue, Chicago 18, Illinois, under the guarantee clause of contract AF33(038) 11493 for repair or replacement and return."

Now Captain des Granges was getting some action, and right from BuShips itself. He had been told what he needed to do to get his motion picture projector fixed. He had someone box up the part and off it went to Chicago.

They would be watching movies again in no time.

DESPITE all the hijinks and good times, *Archerfish* was involved in serious work during her days in Key West. At one point, the inner door on the number-four torpedo tube was removed and replaced by a new and special type. This new door was designed to allow the firing of the brand-new wire-guided torpedoes that the navy was experimenting with. *Archerfish* may not have been the first sub to try the new torpedoes, but she was certainly in the forefront.

With the new fish, a wire actually spools out behind the torpedo and stays attached to electronics inside the submarine. The weapon can receive continual updates from the boat's fire control computer, giving it much more accuracy. The wire is eventually cut after detonation or when the torpedo runs past its target. The wire-guided weapons are still commonly used on today's nuclear submarines, but the wire is finer, it spools out from both the submarine and the torpedo, and the torpedoes are much faster.

George Nuckols remembers another exercise in which the *Archerfish* was involved, one that seems harrowing to the uninitiated but was commonplace for submarine crews at that time. They were ordered to go out of Key West a ways, into the area of the Gulf Stream. Then they were to dive and sit on the bottom of the ocean, simulating a distressed submarine. Submarine rescue vessels (ASRs), like the USS *Penguin* (ASR-12) and USS *Petrel* (ASR-14), then lowered their diving bells and attached air hoses to the boat in an attempt to rescue the crew.

On this day they were down for what Nuckols was sure was at least seventeen hours, a long time for a boat like *Archerfish*. He remembers that, after thirteen hours, the air inside the boat was so foul it was impossible to light a match.

Things did not go well. The Gulf Stream was so strong at that spot that they had not accomplished much at all. Finally, the exercise was declared over, and it was time to head for the surface. But when they began blowing the tanks, the bow was stuck in the sandy bottom. The stern was coming up just fine, but the sub was standing on her nose.

Nuckols was on watch in the after engine room. He recalls a desk drawer coming open and spilling its contents everywhere, and a rain of loose objects, anything not tied down, went rattling past him as the stern assumed a sharp up angle.

To everyone's relief, the bow was finally torn away from the bottom, and they quickly corrected the angle. Nobody was hurt, but the inside of the boat was littered with stuff that had flown around. Everyone breathed easier once they were sure the drill would not turn into the real thing.

AS he had been told to do, Captain des Granges had sent the bad part from *Archerfish*'s movie projector back to the manufacturer on May 7, 1953. Almost three months passed. He heard nothing. On July 31, he sent the following memo on *Archerfish* stationery to the Ampro Corporation in Chicago:

> Subj: 16 MM Sound Motion Picture Equipment Part; repair of
> Ref: (a) C. O. U.S.S. ARCHERFISH ltr SS311;VRW;cgc, serial 199 dtd 7 May 1953
>
>   1. In accordance with instructions received from the Bureau of Ships, Washington, D.C., the intermittent assembly from subject motion picture equipment was forwarded to you for repair or replacement under the guarantee clause of contract AF33 (038) 11493 on 7 May 1953.
>   2. It is requested that information concerning the repair or replacement of subject part be furnished this command.
>   3. It would be desirable to have an operable part furnished this command as soon as practicable in order to make use of the equipment. This equipment is the only motion picture equipment on board this vessel.

As always, a copy of the memo went to the folks at the Bureau of Ships in Washington. After better than four months without a movie projector, the skipper of the *Archerfish* was getting steamed.

ARCHERFISH was on her way back to Key West from another trip to Guantánamo. The boat was running low on provisions, and for breakfast one morning, the cooks served up a thin, watery gravy poured over grits. There was the usual grousing, but no one thought any more about it.

Back at the Key West Naval Station, the boat proceeded to the marine railway where she was dragged from the water and serviced. She had been in the water for 359 days since her last docking, 166 underway and 193 in port, so she was in need of some work. About a third of the hull was sandblasted. The rest of her had to be cleaned by crew members using wire brushes. It was hard, dirty work and nobody liked doing it, but it was an "all hands" operation.

Apparently, as the hot tropical sun beamed down and the torturously slow work went on, one of the sailors remembered the grits-and-gravy breakfast of a few days before. Now was the time to get some revenge. As he scraped away at the corrosion and barnacles, he neatly scoured out USS GRITFISH in large letters on the boat's bottom. Everyone admired the handiwork, had a good laugh, and went on about his work.

The skipper was not pleased when he saw it, though. Everyone available worked that section of the hull until the boat's new nickname was cleaned off.

Soon after she was back in the water, *Archerfish* was also converted to a children's day-care center. At least, she was for a little while.

Jim Petralba's wife, Betty, had to be hospitalized at the naval hospital in Key West for several days. Petralba received four days' emergency leave so he could care for his three small children. He was due back aboard *Archerfish* before she left port the next Monday morning for a week's worth of operations. Monday came and Betty was still in the hospital. Petralba requested an extension of his leave, but it was denied. He couldn't find a babysitter anywhere who would be able to keep the kids for up to a week.

There was only one thing to do. Petralba packed up the kids, put them into the car, and drove to the base. Without hesitation, he brought them aboard *Archerfish*, ignoring the curious stares of his shipmates. He sat all three down on his bunk in the after battery while he changed into his dungarees and got ready for his assigned duty once the boat pulled away from her mooring for a full week at sea.

Somehow word of the young stowaways got to the wardroom. The chief of the boat was summoned, and he soon hustled on back to the after battery berthing space, heard Petralba's story, looked into the eyes of the contented young submariners on the bunk, and made a quick command decision.

"Get these kids and your butt ashore," he said. "I'll take care of getting your leave extension granted."

CAPTAIN des Granges never received a reply to his letter to the Ampro Corporation in which he politely but emphatically asked for help replacing the bad part to his boat's movie projector. A notice did show up on September 7 indicating a replacement part had been shipped twelve days before. The shipment was never received. Finally, by the end of September, the skipper wrote the following letter and dutifully, as always, copied the Bureau of Ships:

Dear Sirs:

Piece Number 24D of figure 72 (Intermittent Assembly) of Instruction Book for 16 MM Sound Motion Picture Equipment Type IC/QEM-1A, (NavShips 385-0217), (Preliminary IC Instructor Book 646) was forwarded to you for repair or replacement on 7 May 1953. A request to you for information dated 31 July 1953 was not answered. On 7 September a copy of your form No. 8291 serial number 48327 was received indicating that a parcel post shipping date of August 26, 1953 was scheduled. The repaired piece has not been received to date, and more important, the projector which has been out of commission since March 1953 is still out of commission. That is a period of seven months.

It is considered that the above resume of service would be unsatisfactory to any customer, including a naval vessel. The Bureau of Ships is requested to review the strength of its contracts and contractors.

It is requested that this correspondence be considered a tracer on shipped material, a fervent plea for better service, or whatever else that might assist in placing the projector back in commission.

A submarine can be hazardous to a man's health if he is not constantly aware of his surroundings. Because of the close quarters, bumped heads, lacerations, and the like were common aboard *Archerfish*, and such casualties kept busy whatever Doc was serving on board at the time. If a man watched his feet to keep from stepping into an open hatch, he might well crack his head on something overhead. If he was watching for obstructions protruding from the overhead, he could easily step into an open hatch.

Lieutenant Bill Chipman had been checking "Rig for dive" one day when he stepped from the galley into the control room at a particularly inopportune time. Someone had opened the deck hatch outside the radio shack to go below to the dry storeroom and had left the hatch open. Chipman disappeared down the hole in the boat's deck.

He fractured his arm in the fall.

ON October 19, 1953, the Department of the Navy, in response to Captain Maino des Granges's letter of September 29, instructed the commanding officer of the Naval Supply Depot in Mechanicsburg, Pennsylvania, to send "One (1) Projector 16 MM Motion Picture Sound Type AG 2-(1) S18-P-2-707-7" to the USS *Archerfish* (SS-311) at the Naval Station, Key West, Florida. The estimated cost was $650.

The saga of the broken movie projector was finally over. It had taken only eight months to get it resolved.

ON July 21, 1954, Commander Maino des Granges was relieved of his command of *Archerfish* by Lieutenant Commander Stanley R. McCord. Not much else changed.

Chuck Micele remembers that they still did daily operations, mostly out of Key West for the sonar school, and that they spent their evenings in the Brown Derby, "or other watering holes of choice. But the 'Tan Sombrero' was particularly popular with the crew at that time."

Captain McCord recalls August 2 as a typical Monday morning in Gitmo, one in which his old boat showed she could still hold her own. As usual, two submarines opposed the fleet's sortie out to the training area. The two subs on this particular morning were *Archerfish* and USS *Odax* (SS-484), a Guppy conversion. "Guppy" meant that the boat had received the "greater underwater propulsion power" modification to make her faster and more maneuverable. *Odax* had been the first boat to undergo this transformation, back in 1946, and as a result, she had been the navy's fastest submarine for a while.

The two subs left Guantánamo Bay before dawn with each boat taking up a patrol area outside the bay, *Odax* to the west and *Archerfish* to the east.

Soon the fleet came steaming out of the bay, one carrier and two cruisers escorted by four destroyers, intent on detecting the submarines and "sinking" them should they "attack." *Archerfish* was angling, working to get into firing position, when the crew heard on the underwater telephone that *Odax* had been detected and was being worked over by the destroyers.

McCord and his crew decided to take advantage of the situation. They managed to penetrate the screen of the destroyers while they were occupied with *Odax* and "fired" salvos at the carrier and a cruiser. Then, to show everyone that they had company in their midst, they fired off two green flares. Finally, to further demonstrate to everyone how completely their convoy had been penetrated, McCord ordered an immediate surfacing, right in the middle of the fleet.

McCord remembers signal lights flashing all over the place when the surface ships saw the "attacking" submarine pop to the surface. The exercise ended right there.

"We received all kinds of congratulations when we returned to port that night," Captain McCord recalls. "The point had been made that the old fleet boats were still a threat."

Still, things were changing rapidly for the navy's submarine fleet. On January 17, 1955, the historic words, "Under way on nuclear power," were transmitted from aboard a brand-new boat, just leaving Groton, Connecticut. The USS *Nautilus* (SSN-571) had become the world's first nuclear-powered submarine, capable of running submerged for months instead of hours.

But most of the old fleet boats found a new life, another way to contribute. It was also in 1955 that *Archerfish* took on one of these new challenges. They were ordered to head for Ascension Island and to perform a most unusual mission while she was on the way there and back.

That sent many of them to their atlases.

Ascension Island is a rocky, thirty-five-square-mile volcanic peak, resting south of the equator, due east of Recife, Brazil, in the middle of the South Atlantic Ocean between South America and Africa. The island was used extensively as an air base by the United States in World War II. It remains a strategic U.S. Air Force and Royal Air Force base today. Because of its handy location in the middle of the ocean, it also is used by various communications companies and is still valuable as a tracking station for NASA.

In 1955, the lonely outpost figured heavily in a top-secret effort by the United States military. On a regular basis, rockets were being fired toward Ascension Island from Cape Canaveral, testing their ability to deliver warheads to an enemy country such as the Soviet Union. And regularly, those rockets were missing their targets by a discouragingly wide margin. Finally, someone figured out a possible cause: the variation in the earth's gravitational pull. It is simply not the same everywhere on the planet's surface, and those differences were enough to cause the rockets' courses to vary.

Archerfish's job that January was to ride down to Ascension Island and back and do measurements the whole way to verify the hypothesis. They had two hitchhikers, Dr. Lamar Worzel and another scientist from the Lamont Geological Observatory at Columbia University. With them they brought an odd-looking contraption called a gravity meter. It looked like an old-fashioned icebox, but it contained a complicated series of calibrated pendulums. The meter was designed to measure the earth's gravitational pull from a relatively stable platform, like the one offered by a submerged submarine. Someone had realized that submarines were actually more stable than ships, since they could go beneath the surface to calmer waters. *Archerfish* was the submarine chosen for this mission.

While there is no verification that this was the first gravity meter on a submarine, there is documentation that the first such use took place in 1955. Once again, *Archerfish* was outfront.

The trip to Ascension Island was monotonous, since the boat had to stop and dive to a depth of one hundred feet at regular intervals, then remain as motionless as possible . . . while attempting to gain a "stop trim" (maintaining a neutral buoyancy) and "zero bubble" . . . as the scientists took their readings. Still, even though most of the men aboard were a bit gray about the nature of the stopping-and-starting mission they were on, they were glad to be doing something different, and something that everyone assured them was worthwhile.

Once they got to Ascension Island, Lieutenant Stan McCord and some of his officers did take a quick trip ashore while they were anchored in Clarence Bay. They borrowed a car from the resident British magistrate and drove over to evaluate the condition of the old World War II airstrip. They had learned that the island was mostly known for the green sea turtles that nest there and for the several hundred air force and RAF guys who called it home. There really wasn't much to see, but they counted potholes in the old runway so the CO had something to enter into his report.

After a brief stay at the island, they followed the same routine—dive, hover as best they could, measure, surface—day in and day out for the next four weeks, all the way back to the Keys. A future incarnation of *Archerfish* would find her involved in similar work, but much more thoroughly performed, and that vital job would give the old boat a continued reason for existence.

It was early 1955, and though the crew didn't realize it at the time, *Archerfish* soon began a long, slow voyage to another term in the Reserve Fleet. She spent part of February in Trinidad in the British West Indies. Back in Key West, Lieutenant Commander George Now replaced McCord. There was a change-of-command ceremony on the afterdeck at 0900 on April 2, 1955. *Archerfish* ended April anchored off Front Gable, White Hall, in the Severn River at Annapolis, Maryland. For the next week, Reserve officers and sailors from Houston, Texas, spent time on the submarine, marveling at the continual stories of the boat's history.

On May 8, she was moored to the Ammunition Pier, Fort Mifflin, Pennsylvania, near Philadelphia, where she off-loaded "miscellaneous lots of small arms and pyrotechnics." Later that day, she moved over to Pier C at the Philadelphia Naval Shipyard for a major overhaul as part of the decommissioning process.

She was getting herself ready for bed once again.

Archerfish had one more brush with fire before she went back to sleep. On June 27, a welder was working with a cutting torch in the chain locker. The sparks ignited the pitch coating in the forward superstructure. Nobody was hurt and there was no serious damage, but it took an hour to get the fire out and to make sure it stayed out.

At the end of August, the boat was hitched to a civilian tug named *McAllister Brothers* and pulled out of the Philadelphia navy yard. *YTB-149*, a navy tug, was moored to the port quarter of *Archerfish* to provide steering for the tow. Four hours later, *McAllister Brothers* transferred her charge to the navy tug USS *Accokeek* (ATA-181) for the trip up the coast past New Jersey and Long Island to New London, Connecticut. Once there, the crew had another rash of captain's masts for violations of the Uniform Code of Military Justice, Article 86, "absent without leave," and a bout with a hurricane toward the middle of September. There were no casualties from either.

On October 21, 1955, Rear Admiral F. T. Watkins, Commander Submarine Atlantic Fleet, came on board, "broke his flag," and placed the vessel "out of commission in reserve."

The last entry in that day's log reads: "Final diary entry. No personnel remain on board. Activity decommissioned."

Archerfish was asleep again, enjoying a well-earned rest. None of the people who were there that day, not Rear Admiral Watkins, Commander Now, Chief Gordon Larson, Steward's Mate Third Class James Whitten, nor any of the others, could have dreamed how much she was going to need a nice, long nap.

THIRD COMMISSION
THE KEY WEST YEARS
1 July 1957–22 January 1960

The man who knows it can't be done counts the risk,

not the reward.

—Elbert Hubbard

11

PINK SUBMARINE

THE submarine's next life, a period of about two-and-a-half years from mid-1957 to just inside 1960, found the old diesel boat in familiar territory, doing customary work. But *Archerfish* still found an opportunity to get herself into the record books, see her picture in *Time* magazine, and make her motion picture debut.

Toward the end of the period, there appeared a very dark cloud on the horizon. It was clear the navy had every intention of finally putting *Archerfish* to sleep for good.

In late November 1956, though, the navy still had use for the old girl. The chief of naval operations issued Notice 04770 directing the activation of *Archerfish* from the Reserve Fleet in New London. After six months of refitting and repairs at the Thames Shipyard in New London, Connecticut, she was placed back into commission at 0821 on the morning of August 1, 1957. Lieutenant Charles E. Beck was named her new skipper. A month later, he was promoted to lieutenant commander, retroactive to the day of his boat's commissioning and just in time for him to take her back south.

Once again, there was scurrying activity all around the freshly painted submarine, everyone working hard to get the boat back in service and ready for sea. Most of the new crew reporting for duty came from other boats and were already "qualified in submarines." However, they now had to re-qualify in *Archerfish*. Once again each man had to learn the location and purpose of every valve and switch in the boat. In addition to their primary duties as electricians, cooks, enginemen, torpedomen, and the like, they had to became involved in the seemingly never ending "school of the boat." That included the officers, too. "Learning *Archerfish*" became each man's priority. They knew that not only their own lives but the lives of their shipmates and that of *Archerfish* herself depended on their being able to react instinctively to any emergency in any part of the submarine.

Soon underway training began, and it wasn't long before the crew was beginning to function as a team. Simulated drills for fire, flooding, collusion, chlorine gas, and any other conceivable emergency were practiced all hours of the day and night. Then, just when the crew thought they were getting good at it, they were practiced again.

During this training period, there was an incident that reminded everyone anew how dangerous duty on a submarine could be, even when she was still in a training mode. *Archerfish* was routinely tying up to her mooring when a freak accident almost ended tragically. Whoever had the conn at the time tried to pull the stern into the pier by using the after capstan. The eye splice in number-four mooring line was secure to the cleat on the pier. The line handlers had taken about four turns of line around the drum of the after capstan and were holding the line taut to prevent slippage as the capstan head slowly rotated to tighten the line. As they waited for the strain to drag the sub's stern toward the pier, the tension on the three-inch nylon line became more than it could take, and it snapped like a broken rubber band. The end of the line whipped around viciously and struck the chief of the boat, Sidney Burke, a brutal blow to his back, near his kidneys. Burke never fully recovered from the injury, but it could have been worse had it struck him in the neck or head.

Archerfish was officially transferred back into the active fleet in a ceremony at 0930 on September 14, 1957. The next day, members of the United States Submarine Veterans of World War II came aboard and held a memorial service on the main deck aft. It was obvious to all in attendance that this boat, the one that had sunk the *Shinano*, still held special meaning for these old submarine sailors.

It was also obvious that each man who attended that day had a personal commitment to "perpetuate the memory of those shipmates who gave their lives in submarine warfare." Today, there are over 3,500 men still at their battle stations aboard the fifty-two U.S. submarines that were sunk during World War II. They are not considered to be lost but are, instead, "still on patrol." James Haywood, president of the United States Submarine

Veterans of World War II in 1985-1986, wrote: "It is our belief that no shipmates shall ever be lost to the nation or to history as long as any living person has knowledge of their sacrifices or remembrance of them." One of the ways that commitment continues to this day is through ceremonies such as the one held aboard *Archerfish* that September day in 1957.

At last it was time to get under way, assume a heading of 180 degrees, due south, and once again return to the familiar waters of the Caribbean. After stops in Charleston (to work) and Savannah (to play), *Archerfish* was once more back in her old haunts, Key West and Gitmo, once again part of Submarine Squadron 12, and once again moored "starboard side to" Pier 3 at the U.S. naval station. Most of the next two years were spent the same as before, helping the fleet train sonarmen in detecting submerged submarines, practicing firing torpedoes, and doing it all mostly on daily operations. The bars in Key West and Guantánamo once more became a home away from home for the crewmen of *Archerfish*.

In early 1958, the scientists in the Navy Hydrographic Office again needed a stable platform that only a submerged submarine could provide. They requested the services of *Archerfish* for a special mission. The boat left Key West on January 13, steamed by way of San Juan, Puerto Rico, and crossed the equator on February 8. They stopped long enough to welcome aboard King Neptune and his Royal Court and to go through the obligatory Pollywog-Shellback crossing ceremony. Steve Ramos was aboard at the time, and he described the traditional ritual as "gruesome," and says, "We were all happy to get that ordeal over with." Pollywogs are sailors who have never crossed the equator before. Those who have, the Shellbacks, devise all sorts of disgusting initiation rites for the ceremony. Once the torture is over, the new Shellbacks receive a certificate, signed by Davy Jones himself, and then have the right to be the ones to dish out the punishment to a new group of Pollywogs in future crossings of the equator.

Though not an official part of naval regulations, this traditional rite of passage is taken seriously enough by the navy to generate an entry in each man's official service record, indicating the date, the longitude when crossed, where the vessel was bound, and the proclamation that the man be recognized as a Shellback. Without this proof, a man could be required to submit to the entire ritual all over again the next time he crossed the equator.

On February 15, *Archerfish* moored at Berth 12, Broadway Square, Recife, Brazil. They had chosen a most opportune time to visit Brazil. It was Carnival, the annual pre-Lenten party, and the whole town was swirling in a festival that put Mardi Gras in New Orleans to shame. Steve Ramos was a young lieutenant junior grade when they visited Recife, but he remembers that the captain, Charlie Beck, and the exec, Pete Poteet, made certain *Archerfish* arrived in port on Saturday, the day before the festival began. They knew all the shops would be closed when Carnival kicked off on Sunday and wouldn't reopen until after Ash Wednesday, four days later. The skipper wanted the crew to be able to take advantage of the tremendous bargains on gemstones that were to be found in the town's famous markets.

The primary thing crew member Sam Houston remembers about the visit to Recife was the unusual way the townspeople toasted the festival. He and his shipmates went ashore and were fascinated by the wild parades that wound their way through the streets. He noticed that the marchers mostly consisted of Indians who had come in from the nearby jungles, and that even the townspeople lined the streets to look at the revelers' wild, colorful costumes and primal dances.

When the sailors went into one of the nearby clubs for a nightcap, they were puzzled to see that almost everyone in the joint was walking around with a handkerchief held to his or her nose. There was an odd smell in the place, unlike anything they had encountered in other aromatic port bars. Someone finally saw that the club's patrons occasionally squirted some sort of pressurized gas from little cans they carried, containers that looked like ether cans, saturating their handkerchiefs, and then deeply inhaled the fumes. Houston and his shipmates decided to stick to alcohol, though they felt dizzy already from all the fumes in the air inside the club.

One sailor, J. J. Kronzer, had another nagging problem. He had met a young girl while ashore, a local beauty with no front teeth. He really had no interest in the girl but she apparently fell in love with him at first sight. She spent the next four days trying to lure him off the boat, much to the embarrassment of Kronzer and to the amusement of his shipmates.

After a stop in Port-of-Spain, Trinidad, *Archerfish* returned to Key West on February 28 with another raft of stories to tell. In April, she took a run up the east coast of Florida to Jacksonville. They were not at all prepared for the rousing welcome they got as they entered the mouth of the Saint Johns River.

NBC Television had just begun running the documentary series *The Silent Service* on the network. One of the early episodes had included the story of *Archerfish* and her showdown with *Shinano* that night back in November 1944. The crew was surprised to see local television news crews out filming them as they eased into Jacksonville. The boat moored at the Naval

Reserve Training Center and held open house all day Saturday and Sunday. The publicity brought them plenty of customers. Tom Salisbury, one of the crew members aboard that weekend, remembers crowds so large that visitors often had to stand in line for three hours to go down the after torpedo room hatch, the point where the tour began. This enthusiastic reception foreshadowed the boat's popularity when she visited ports of call around the world over the next few years and invited the locals to come aboard.

Archerfish stopped by Kingston, Jamaica, in June 1958 and spent a couple of days in Havana Harbor in September, a mere three-and-a-half months ahead of Fidel Castro's New Year's Day takeover in 1959. That's also about the time the boat got official word that she was to be deactivated once again, beginning in March 1959. Then, only a few days later, an odd letter from the chief of naval operations arrived, saying the inactivation had been deferred, pending a decision that "would be made prior to 1 February 1959." No one knew what to make of it, but it was still clear that *Archerfish* had only a short time left before going back into mothballs.

Since there was no accounting for the rationale of the navy brass, *Archerfish* and her crew carried on, conducting their exercises, with all aboard working hard and having a good time in the process, especially during a visit to New Orleans in the middle of December 1958.

Later that month, several *Archerfish* crew members decided to spend their Christmas leave in a brothel in Havana, Cuba. They were scheduled to fly back to Key West on New Year's Day, 1959, and return to the boat the next day. Their plans were unexpectedly changed when they walked out of the Hotel Packard on New Year's morning. Cars were wildly racing up and down Prado Boulevard in front of the hotel, blowing their horns, waving Cuban flags, and tossing firecrackers. Or at least the sailors thought they were firecrackers. They soon realized they were hearing gunshots.

Fidel Castro's revolution had arrived in Havana. The city was under siege by an army of rebels. For the next several days it was touch and go trying to get back to Key West. All flights had been canceled, no public transportation was operating, and there wasn't a taxicab in sight.

The sailors figured they would be able to think better over a couple of beers, so they started the long walk to the waterfront bars where they had been spending most of their time the last few days. The first one they found open was New Henry's, about halfway between New Chico's and the Miami Bar. Once inside, they found the bar lined with other submarine sailors out of Key West who had found themselves in like circumstances. There were three men off USS *Trutta* (SS-421), two from USS *Chivo* (SS-341), and several off *Odax*.

Soon after the sailors had settled down to some serious drinking, a group of well-armed rebels burst through the front door and lined them up against a wall. The rebels were getting ready to kill them when the bartender somehow convinced the rebel leader that these were merely American submarine sailors, there on leave and without their boats. After checking the sailors' military ID cards, Castro's men finally lowered their weapons and demanded drinks for everybody. Using the bartender to interpret, the rebels explained that the sailors would be placed in protective custody. They were escorted upstairs to the "rooms-by-the-hour" hotel and locked in, then advised not to attempt to leave the hotel until the rebels got full control of the waterfront district. Then they would be back to release them.

It wasn't such a bad deal. The sailors were given a couple of cases of Hutey beer (144 bottles to a case) and a case of rum from the bar just in case they got thirsty. Several hours later, the rebels returned, but not to free them. Instead, they brought some "companions" to keep the submarine sailors company while they mopped up those still loyal to Batista. Apparently the armed resistance in the area was stronger than they expected as they fought to gain control of the waterfront.

It was about midnight when they finally came back again, and this time they let the sub sailors go. At the same time, they were invited to the victory party the rebel group was getting started at the Miami Bar. It was one hell of a party, and the deposed Cuban leader, Fulgencio Batista, indirectly paid for everything for the next couple of days.

The sailors finally started getting nervous about being over leave and, as a group, decided they had better walk to the American embassy and turn themselves in. The place was packed with American civilians trying to flee the country. There was nothing to eat and only water to drink, kids were crying, and the air-conditioning was on the fritz. It didn't take long for the sailors to proclaim that they had had enough of the embassy and that the party they had left would be a far better spot to await their ride. They told the marines guarding the door that they were returning to the waterfront and would be back in a couple of days when things were a little quieter.

The marines told them in no uncertain terms that they weren't going anywhere. It was late in the day when the sailors were finally herded into a stake-body truck and taken to the airport. There a plane provided by the State Department was waiting to take them to Key West.

It was back to Gitmo and weekend liberty in Montego Bay, Jamaica, in mid-January. During this time, the boat was conveniently allowed to pick a southerly operating area on Fridays and for the following Mondays. This allowed them to surface after the end of the week's exercises, head south on all four engines, and spend the weekend in Jamaica. Ocho Rios was a crew favorite. There were two new tourist hotels there, and it was far from Kingston's depressing slums. The hotels seemed eager to have young sailors around to socialize with unaccompanied female tourists, and the crew members of *Archerfish* were more than happy to oblige. They also spent time in Port Antonio, a favorite haunt of movie star Errol Flynn.

In February, the *Archerfish* narrowly missed her opportunity to become the navy's first pink submarine, but she still managed to get some camera time in a classic motion picture.

Director Blake Edwards, who later did the *Pink Panther* features, was shooting a movie, a comedy titled *Operation Petticoat*. It starred Cary Grant, who played a harried submarine skipper, and Tony Curtis, who portrayed the fictitious boat's conniving supply officer. Ironically, Curtis had actually been a submarine sailor in the final days of World War II. He had been inspired to join the navy and volunteer for the submarine service when, back home in New York City, he watched Grant playing a sub captain in a 1943 movie called *Destination Tokyo*.

Edwards needed the services of several World War II–era submarines, including one that was to be painted a brilliant pink color as part of the madcap movie's plot. The director asked for and got the navy's cooperation and brought his crew to Key West to shoot.

Lieutenant Albert "Sam" Houston remembers that *Archerfish* had all but been selected to be the pink submarine and the star of the film. She would have played a big part in the movie, but the captain of the USS *Balao* (SS-285) was apparently a better politician. His boat ended up getting the leading role instead of *Archerfish*. Scuttlebutt was that the boat's seaman gang was paid $40 each, a considerable sum in those days, to do the pink paint job on *Balao*.

Still, *Archerfish* showed up in several of the scenes and was involved in shooting much of the underwater footage for the movie. The log entry for February 20 revealed the official name of the Hollywood-oriented operation:

> *0745—Balao* under way from alongside.

> 0950—Set speed 10 knots, commenced "Operation MoPix" with YTB-543.

The log entry for February 27 was more explicit:

1015—Commenced steering various courses at various speeds while shooting various scenes for the movie "Operation Petticoat." In company with YTB-543.

YTB-543, a navy tug named *Etawina*, was used as the platform to film the underway scenes.

Mike Klein remembers a morning in Key West when a group of old World War II fighters, dressed up to look like Japanese Zeroes, zoomed overhead, so low one of them clipped the whip antenna of another submarine. They were part of whatever scene was being shot that day, but Klein saw several of *Archerfish*'s crew members do double takes. They had actually been in the war and the Zeroes looked all too real to them. Word was the producers had hired crop dusters to fly the planes because they were the only ones crazy enough to do the stunts.

Part of the fun of the movie being shot in Key West was spotting the stars as they traveled to and from the set. Curtis and Grant passed by in their convertibles at the end of each day's filming, but it was difficult to get close enough to the set to actually see anything that was going on. *Balao* was tied up most of the time she was in port, way down near the coast guard station. Still, some of the sailors ventured down there and tried to attract the attention of the starlets. They had no luck.

A few weeks later, *Archerfish* was involved in much more serious operations. Once again they were diving to the bottom, resting in the sand, mimicking a distressed submarine. The *Petrel* lowered a diving bell from the surface to the sub to effect a simulated rescue attempt. On this day, Captain J. M. Hyde, commander of Submarine Refresher Training in Key West, elected to ride down in the bell. Once the bell had sealed itself against the boat at the forward torpedo room escape hatch, Hyde opened the hatch and entered the submarine. A few minutes later, he went back out the hatch and entered the bell again, then ascended to the surface.

Drills such as this one continued for most of the rest of the year. They eventually culminated in a truly amazing feat that put *Archerfish* right back in the news once again.

The boat was scheduled to spend some time in the marine railway in March 1959. That's where one of the junior officers, Michele Giambattista, and some of the sailors gained a new appreciation of the character of the submarine on which they were serving. They learned one day that they had a stowaway aboard. There was a small alligator living in the bilge below the maneuvering room. No one knew, or admitted that they knew, where the critter had come from. Some of the sailors wanted to keep it around as a pet, but, of course, they couldn't. The ill-tempered critter had to be removed so chipping could get under way in preparation for painting.

Later that day, a couple of the men were working away, chipping paint in the after motor room bilges when one of them yelped in surprise. His buddy thought he might have found another gator, maybe the sweetheart of the one they had kicked out of the bilge.

Not so. The sailor had spotted daylight!

They could look out through a hole in the hull and see the dry dock. For who knew how long, there had been little more than layers of paint between the crew of *Archerfish* and the sea.

Holes in her hull or not, *Archerfish* soon found herself involved in yet another cutting-edge operation. The navy had devised a hybrid weapon that was half torpedo, half rocket. They had dubbed the ordnance Subroc, or "submarine rocket." These odd fish were designed to be launched from a submarine's torpedo tubes, then, once away from the boat, they ignited their rocket motors and roared away, breaking the surface of the ocean and heading for their objectives. They were designed to hit targets up to thirty-five miles away, usually on land, or they could be used against other ships or submarines. Since they were designed to carry nuclear warheads, a direct hit was not necessary. They were intended from the outset to pack quite a wallop.

In 1959, though, the Subrocs were not yet reliable. *Archerfish*, operating out of Port Everglades, Florida, had to sit on the sea bottom in order to give a stable enough platform for the rockets' launch out of the boat's torpedo tubes. Mike Lintner remembers that there was a high abort rate. The strange fish were quite temperamental. The work *Archerfish* was doing proved eminently valuable, though.

The sad word they had all awaited finally came in June 1959. *Archerfish* would likely be decommissioned in February of the next year. As if she were showing her opinion on the subject, the boat's number-two sanitary tank overboard discharge line ruptured on the same day the notification came down, causing one smelly mess.

A complete shipyard overhaul was already scheduled for the first few weeks of the following year, but if she was to be deactivated only a month later, that made no sense at all. Captain Beck told his superiors that he thought, with just a little loving care and some dry dock time, the boat could meet all her commitments until the first of the year and serve her country right to the end. He was of the opinion that a full yard overhaul so close to decommissioning was a waste, but that it would be a good idea to do some upkeep in August or September to take care of the deteriorated areas they had discovered in the superstructure. F. J. Harlfinger II, Commander Submarine Squadron 12, concurred.

So that was the plan. They would nurse the old girl along until she could be laid down to rest, likely for the last time, early in 1960.

She had done her job well. Hell, she was still doing her job well every day.

Despite that, it appeared once again that *Archerfish*'s days of service were numbered.

12

FROM THE BOTTOM

As a young officer fresh out of Annapolis, Michele Giambattista found himself spending a long, cold winter as a student in sub school at New London, Connecticut. The harsh, biting wind off Long Island Sound seemed to find its way easily up the Thames River to the submarine base. Or one wicked nor' easter after another lined up to smack them with cold rain, sleet, or stinging snow. That made it most imperative that he request warm weather duty when he put in for his first service aboard a submarine. The possibilities he preferred were Charleston, San Diego, Pearl Harbor, or Key West, where he had lived for a while as a child. However, assignments were based on academic standing in the sub school, and Giambattista had admittedly done less than his best while in New London. He just knew he would end up someplace with winters as bitter as they were there in New England, and he wished a thousand times he had studied a bit harder.

Still, he managed to land an assignment to Key West after all. It wasn't necessarily his first choice, but it would certainly be warmer there than up north. Besides, his childhood memories of the place were pleasant enough.

He chose *Archerfish* for the same reasons most of the other wardroom officers did: She mostly operated only on weekdays, in and out of Key West. It was perfect for those who wanted a relatively normal family life, or, on the opposite end of the scale, those who enjoyed the island's notorious nightlife.

Giambattista reported to *Archerfish* for duty the same day as one of his classmates, Jim McNerney, known to his friends as "Nummy." Though they had been at the Naval Academy at the same time, Giambattista had not known McNerney while they were there. That soon changed when they reported to sub school and became housemates in the same "snake ranch." All the occupants of the house had a good time, but Jim's seemingly continuous partying was coupled with an indifference to studies that made Giambattista look like a scholar.

"I had concerns that having Nummy here with me on our first submarine might not be to my benefit," Giambattista remembers.

They usually got under way early from the submarine basin and proceeded out the South Channel, a route used only by *Archerfish* and the fleet of shrimp boats. They were on station in that day's operating area by 0800 and proceeded to dive to one hundred feet or so while turning into the Gulf Stream. They assumed a forward speed of three knots and most resembled a salmon that was attempting to swim upstream but mostly remained in the same spot. After diving, they hovered there, conducting their drills, spending the rest of the day bucking the ocean current, until four or five in the afternoon, when they surfaced. The atmosphere inside the boat was stifling, humid, and by the time they reached the surface, the air was so foul it was hardly fit to breathe. They usually found that they were in about the same spot where they had dived that morning.

Giambattista's concerns about Nummy and his escapades soon proved to be well founded. Only a few days after he reported aboard *Archerfish*, they had to hold up getting under way so McNerney could dash down the pier and race up the brow to report for duty. Giambattista also got into his only serious trouble, thanks to Nummy. The exec put Giambattista in charge of making sure his fellow Annapolis alum showed up in time for duty. Of course, that was an impossible task, and Mike had to pay the price.

Later, Nummy had an opportunity to make it up to his old sub school classmate. *Archerfish* was in transit, heading back to Key West down the Florida Strait between the mainland peninsula and the Bahamas, when they encountered unusual sea conditions. A twenty-five-knot wind was opposing a brutally strong tide that night, and the waves were crashing on top of the resulting chop. That meant Giambattista, who was on watch on the bridge, was getting doused. The sky was black, moonless, and the eerie bioluminescence of the water washing over the bridge was almost hypnotic. The young officer was getting a good bouncing around, and that, along with the breaking waves, the swirling phosphorescence, and the lack of a horizon for reference, eventually had him totally disoriented.

Just when Giambattista realized that he was in trouble, that he didn't know up from down, his old buddy Nummy showed up fifteen minutes early to relieve him. For once, Giambattista was more than glad to turn over the watch to him.

The atmosphere in Guantánamo Bay was certainly different when they returned there for operations in mid-January 1959. Because of Castro's revolution, Guantánamo City was no longer available to them for an evening's recreation. From that point on, there was a fierce stare-down going on between the marines at Gitmo and Castro's troops just across the fence that marked the perimeter of the base. Sailors visiting Guantánamo had to settle for whatever recreation they could find on the naval base itself.

The world was most definitely changing, and *Archerfish* was admittedly getting tired. One malfunction caused the old boat's crew to rely on truly ancient navigational methods. They had made one of their weekend runs down to Jamaica and were on the way back on Sunday night so they could be ready for operations on Monday morning. As they left Ocho Rios behind, the boat's gyrocompass quit working. The "armored car" magnetic compass had long since given up the ghost due to neglect. They had no reliable way to tell which direction they were going. When Mike Giambattista took the watch at midnight, navigator Bill Willis advised the young officer to simply steer by the North Star. He instructed Giambattista to keep Polaris "two points on the starboard bow" and they would eventually make landfall on the south coast of Cuba, hopefully close to their assigned operating area.

It worked. They did.

Charlie Beck was relieved of his duty as skipper of *Archerfish* on September 5, 1959. He was reassigned to the Naval War College in Newport, Rhode Island, for duty on the staff there. Lieutenant Commander William Evans assumed command of the boat in a change-of-command ceremony at 0830 that morning. One month later, he and the crew were involved in one of the most amazing human feats ever accomplished, and one that only added to *Archerfish*'s already storied history.

In late September, a quartet of brave divers had begun riding out into the open sea with *Archerfish*. They were Medical Corps Commander George Bond, Chief Engineman Cyril J. Tuckfield, Commander W. F. Mazzone, and Lieutenant L. S. Van Orden. The submarine slid to the bottom of the ocean, to a depth of around two hundred feet. Once there, resting in the sand, a pair of the divers slipped into the forward torpedo room escape trunk, went through an elaborate rapid-pressurization routine, and then opened the door to the outside. From there, using nothing more than their swim fins and Mae West life jackets, they floated to the surface. It was all in an effort to prove the possibility of relying on such a buoyant free ascent to save the lives of sailors who might find themselves trapped aboard an imperiled submarine.

In addition to wartime sinkings, there is a long list of peacetime submarine accidents that have claimed the lives of most or all of the crew of those unfortunate boats. The navy had noticed that many peacetime submarine accidents occurred in depths of three hundred feet or less. However, in many such accidents, those who had survived the initial trauma that caused the sinking still died before they could be rescued. They were unable to escape the sunken submarines and get to the surface. While successful rescues had been mounted over the years using everything from cranes to diving bells, many sub sailors died on the ocean floor awaiting help. There were those in the navy who believed strongly that a "buoyant ascent," a long float to the surface after quick pressurization, was possible from depths as far down as three hundred feet. That's what *Archerfish*'s brave passengers were intent on proving in the early fall of 1959, despite the naysayers who maintained that the whole thing was impossible, and would almost certainly be suicidal for those who tried it.

The boat's operation on October 1, 1959, did not look promising in the beginning. Hurricane Gracie had passed to the north over the last few days and then worked her way up the Atlantic coast of the United States. Hurricane Hannah had been heading for the Atlantic coast as well, following closely in the footsteps of her destructive sister. But then, in a hopeful development, Hannah made a sudden veer to the north and was not likely to strike land or interfere with *Archerfish*'s mission.

Indeed, when the submarine arrived in her operations area that morning, fifteen miles southwest of Key West near Vestal Shoal, the seas were almost glassy calm and the sky had only a milky overcast. Just as he had been doing for the past several weeks, Captain Bill Evans ordered the boat to go to the bottom. This day, though, the seafloor was a good hundred feet deeper than where they had been operating most recently. That was by design. They finally settled into the sand at a depth of 320 feet.

Remember, the pressure of water increases by one atmosphere every 33 feet. And *Archerfish* was designed to operate no deeper than 412 feet.

Remember, too, that conventional wisdom prior to that time was that a human could not survive if he tried to float to the surface from any great depth without a breathing apparatus. The pressure of the air he had in his lungs would have to be equal to the awful squashing pressure of the seawater around him. He would have to somehow let that pressurized air out as the water grew less dense. Even if he managed to breathe out, the pressurization process would compress nitrogen in his blood, causing nitrogen narcosis or the notorious "rapture of the deep" in which the diver would behave irrationally and possibly in a suicidal manner. Those same nitrogen bubbles in the blood would also cause the "bends," an agonizingly painful condition that could lead to serious injury or death.

With the help of *Archerfish*, the divers had already proven that, if the proper procedure was followed, the buoyant ascent could be accomplished with few side effects from depths down to two hundred feet. Today, they were going for the record. They were determined to prove that their fellow submarine sailors could have a fighting chance for survival even if they became stranded at what had previously been thought to be deadly ocean depths.

The submarine rescue ship *Penguin* hovered overhead, letting *Archerfish* know by underwater telephone when she was in place. Next, she dropped her diving bell into the green waters. Three scuba divers rode the bell down, holding on outside as it plunged deeper and deeper. Another man was riding inside the bell. All four men were there to observe and photograph the experiment as well as to try to rescue the researchers if something went wrong.

Meanwhile, in *Archerfish*'s forward torpedo room, Commander George Bond, a navy doctor from Bat Cave, North Carolina, and Cyril Tuckfield, a gregarious chief petty officer from Miami, were getting ready to go to work. They wore only swim trunks, face masks, a Mae West life vest, and, on their wrists, pressure gauges. They looked as if they might be getting ready to take a dip at the beach back in Key West instead of earning themselves a place in navy history and the *Guinness Book of World Records*.

When word came that the bell was on the way down from *Penguin*, the two men climbed up into *Archerfish*'s forward escape trunk and dogged the hatch beneath them. Now there was no way to communicate verbally with the crew of the sub, the men with the diving bell, or the men on the rescue ship that floated just over three hundred feet above them.

Bond and Tuckfield began to quickly run down their checklist. Satisfied all was in order, Tuckfield opened a valve, and seawater began gushing into the escape trunk. It was surprisingly cold, considering they were off the southernmost tip of Florida, but they were also on the murky sea bottom. The sunny surface was a football field's length above them.

In no time, the cold water was up to their chins.

Next, just as they had done at more reasonable depths and on less historic days, they cracked another valve that allowed highly pressurized air to hiss into the cramped compartment. They breathed it in deeply.

When the air pressure around the two men reached the equivalent of about 240 feet of ocean pressure, the gauge on Dr. Bond's wrist cracked. It was of no more use to him. As the atmosphere in the constricted compartment grew heavier and heavier, Bond held his nose while keeping his mouth closed tightly and tried to equalize the pressure in his head to keep his ears from rupturing.

The entire pressurization process took less than half a minute. It had to go quickly. Taking longer would have dire consequences.

All the while, Bond held his feet against the door that led outside the submarine, out into the unbelievably harsh surroundings of the ocean depths. He would not have to kick the door open. When the pressure inside the escape trunk was equal to the tons of seawater outside, the door would ease open on its own. That would be their signal that it was time to go.

When Bond felt the doorway move slightly, he yelled, "Bottom!"

Tuckfield quickly shut the air valve.

The sixty-eight-degree water was still up to their necks, and they were breathing air that was pressurized to ten atmospheres, about 134 pounds per square inch higher than the pressure of air on the surface of the ocean, where they were headed. The two men were thankful for one thing. The scientists had warned them that air under such intense pressure would likely be painfully hot. Instead, this stuff was only pleasantly warm compared to the frigid water that had them shivering and their teeth chattering.

Now, with the pressure inside the escape trunk equal to that of the seawater outside, they had to move in a hurry. They would begin to feel "rapture of the deep" if they tarried too long.

Quickly, Commander Bond used an air hose to inflate Tuckfield's Mae West jacket to 140 pounds of pressure and the chief returned the favor. Then they each slipped through the door and outside the submarine.

Even a big, barrel-chested man can normally hold only about seven quarts of air in his lungs. Bond and Tuckfield had the equivalent of eighteen *gallons* of air compressed into theirs when they eased out the door in the side of *Archerfish*'s escape trunk at just after eleven o'clock that morning.

Cameraman John Light, one of the divers who had ridden the diving bell down, saw the bubbles of air already escaping from the mouths of Bond and Tuckfield as the two men began to ascend. He quickly snapped a photo that showed up in *Time* magazine two weeks later. The two researchers, in swim trunks and face masks, are visible in the photo, rising upward amid the bubbles with the dark bulk of *Archerfish* in the background.

All the way up, Bond and Tuckfield forced the compressed air to escape out their mouths as the water pressure around them lessened with every foot they rose. The air in their Mae Wests leaked out through automatic valves as well, or they would have exploded.

From the escape trunk door in *Archerfish*'s forward superstructure to the surface of the sea above was a distance of 302 feet. The two men made the ascent in only fifty-three seconds. From the time they first entered the escape hatch until they reached the surface, only seven minutes had passed.

When they grabbed the life ring and were pulled aboard the *Penguin*, both men reported feeling fine. There was no evidence of nitrogen poisoning or of the bends.

The crews of *Archerfish* and *Penguin* and the two brave divers had shown the world. The risk was certainly worth the reward. They had just given new hope to generations of submarine sailors to come.

There were several interesting side notes to the story.

In one of their ascents, Bond and Tuckfield were able to equalize the air pressure in the escape trunk to the water pressure outside in only thirteen seconds. In a real emergency, with five or six dozen men in need of rescue, it was good to know escape could be done that quickly.

Archerfish loaned a life raft to the submarine rescue vessel to be used by the naval photographers and their support personnel who were documenting the events of October 1. When they got it back, the morphine that was part of the raft's emergency supplies was missing.

There was also Chief Tuckfield's infamous retort before one of their departures from the escape trunk door. Dr. Bond politely asked the CPO if he would like to be the first one out of the submarine this time. Without hesitation, Tuckfield responded, "Screw you, oh glorious leader!"

Bond, as had been customary in their previous ascents, led the way out into the ocean depths that day as well.

13

SS TO AGSS

Between her recommissioning in 1957 and the middle of November 1959, *Archerfish* had steamed almost fifty thousand miles, enough to circle the world twice, with a little left over. By that time, all indications were that she was about to be decommissioned for the third time, and the general understanding was that she would end up like so many of her sisters: sent to the navy of some foreign government, scrapped, or used for target practice.

Then, around Thanksgiving, the boat received some odd news. They were being sent back to the Philadelphia Naval Shipyard in January, as anticipated, but not to get her ready for mothballs. *Archerfish*, despite her glorious past, no longer had any modern military capability. The new nuke boats were assuming more and more of the operational roles. No one could imagine what the navy had in mind for the old girl this time.

To further confuse the issue, a call for volunteers was sent throughout the submarine force. Only single men were eligible to apply. No married men need bother to try. Personnel selected would report to *Archerfish* and prepare for a "two-year special mission."

In early December, the boat steamed up the east coast of Florida once again, bound for Jacksonville. She was to help with target practice for the "Airedales," the navy pilots who were based there. As usual after a day's work, a sizable contingent of crew members went ashore to quench their thirst. Despite its being December, most of them decided it was time as well to take a swim in the ocean. They stripped down to various stages of undress and dived into the surf off Jacksonville Beach just as the Shore Patrol rolled up and started yelling at them.

When ordered out of the water, the swimmers ignored the command. They told the Shore Patrol, "If you want us, you'll have to come in and get us!" They had no plans to cut their swim short. The Shore Patrol had no intention of getting soaked trying to pull a bunch of drunken submarine sailors out of the surf either. They could only hope none of them drowned as they climbed back into the vehicle and drove on.

When they got good and ready, the *Archerfish* sailors, now refreshed and ready to finish their tour of the local establishments, waded out of the Atlantic, got dressed, and continued on to the next bar.

Just before Christmas, 1959, the commander of the Atlantic submarine fleet notified the Philadelphia Naval Shipyard that *Archerfish* would be there beginning the first of February for docking and repairs. It was estimated that the work would cost $10,000, and that's all that was allotted for her refitting.

Somehow, they had to get it done.

December 22, 1959

Dear Mom and Dad:

I won't be coming home as planned. Today I shipped over for four more years. I'm now on the USS *Archerfish* (SS-311). We are leaving Key West for the yards in Philadelphia on the 26th of January for about ten weeks and from there we are off on a two-year world cruise. This is the reason I shipped over. I think that a chance to go around the world for two years is worth another four years in the navy.

Kenny

Kenneth "Pig" Henry first heard about *Archerfish*'s new assignment while he was still serving aboard *Trutta*. Word was they were looking for volunteers who were unmarried. The navy wanted an all-bachelor crew because the boat would be gone for so long at a time and it would not be convenient for crew members to go home for any family emergencies. It was all still something of a mystery, but it certainly sounded intriguing. Trouble

USS *Archerfish* (SS-311) is launched, May 8, 1943,
Portsmouth Naval Shipyard. *(U.S. Navy)*

The original name of the submarine, *Archer-fish*, was misspelled when the ship-yard ordered 8,500 launch tags. *(Jerry Cornelison)*

On September 4, 1943, Captain C. H. Roper, U.S. Navy, reading orders of commissioning at the Naval Shipyard, Portsmouth, New Hampshire. *(U.S. Navy)*

Moored port side to USS *Proteus* in Tokyo Bay, September 1, 1945, for the Japanese surrender ending World War II. USS *Cavalla* (SS-244) is moored to starboard. *(Leo Carter)*

Archerfish is placed back into commission, March 7, 1952, by Captain W. A. Lent, Commander, *(front and center)*, Mare Island Group, Pacific Reserve Fleet. *(Bob Robison)*

Standing out of San Francisco Bay, May 1952. *(U.S. Navy)*

Transiting the Panama Canal heading for Key West, July 2, 1952. *Left to right:* Les Brown, John Welsko, and Bob Robison. *(Bob Robison)*

Archerfish sailors, *(back to front)*, Lieutenant Junior Grade Clifford P. Barnes, Torpedoman First Class Santo H. Formolo, and Torpedoman Second Class Earl R. Woike, manhandle a torpedo into Tube 4 in the forward torpedo room during the second commission. *(U.S. Navy)*

Standing in to Santiago, Cuba, August 8, 1952. *Left to right:* Vince Salerno, Danny Persico, Don Guthrie, and Don Erdman. Chief Persico, the chief of the boat at the time of this photo, was one of the thirty-three survivors rescued from the sunken USS *Squalus* (SS-192) in May 1939. *(Bob Robison)*

Record buoyant ascent performed from USS *Archerfish* on October 2, 1959, by Medical Corps Commander George F. Bond and Chief Engineman Cyril J. Tuckfield. This same photo appeared in *Time* magazine on October 19, 1959, accompanying its account of the feat. *(U.S. Navy)*

J. P. Cunningham in the after torpedo room reading the machinery-history log. The chair in which he is relaxing is the captain's bridge wing chair that was "borrowed" from the USS *Tarawa* (CV-40). *(Joe Osier)*

Standing inspection, October 12, 1960, in Halifax, Nova Scotia. The original Sixty Thieves of Operation Sea Scan. *(David Dimmick)*

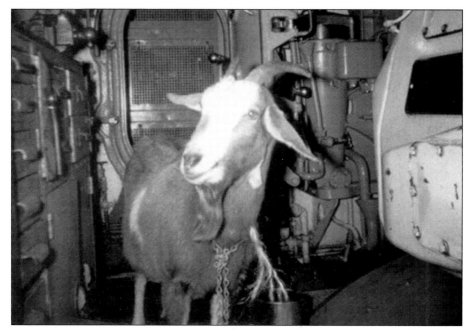

The goat in the after engine room, January 19, 1961, New London, Connecticut. *(Don Englert)*

Lieutenant David K. Dimmick, Executive Officer, *(left)*, and Lieutenant Commander Kenneth Woods, Commanding Officer, *(right)*. The boat was at U.S. Naval Station, Balboa, Canal Zone, at the time of this photo. *(Ted Armstrong)*

His Royal Highness Crown Prince Vajiralongkorn visits *Archerfish* in Bangkok, Thailand, August 14, 1961. Executive Officer David Dimmick and topside watch Fred Yentz salute while Joe Cummings, the duty officer, and a Thai Navy lieutenant steady the brow. *(Bill Roberts)*

In March 1962, *Archerfish* crewmembers Garrett Kelly, Jim Blackburn, John Reilly, Sam Liller, and Larry Dachenhausen enjoy a ride in a *carramotos*, a popular form of transportation in Cebu City in the Philippines. *(Jim Blackburn)*

Archerfish operating off Kaena Point, Hawaii, on November 19, 1965. *(Gordon Engquist)*

The *Archerfish* in dry dock 4 at the U.S. Navy ship-repair facility in Yokosuka, Japan, in April 1966, not far from where the aircraft carrier *Shinano* was constructed and launched over twenty years earlier. *(U.S. Navy)*

The crew of *Archerfish*, Pearl Harbor, May 24, 1967. That day the boat was awarded Commander Submarine Force Pacific Commendation for Operation Sea Scan. The sailor holding the plaque is Chief Engineman Benjamin F. Chadwick, chief of the boat. *(U.S. Navy)*

September 1967. Surrounded by a bevy of *Playboy* Bunnies, *Archerfish* Captain
John Wood presents the manager of the San Francisco Playboy Club with a
"Playboys of the Pacific" plaque. *(Mike Burkholder)*

On October 17, 1968, a Mark 14-5 torpedo fired from the USS *Snook* (SS-592) hit *Archerfish* amidships and the explosion lifted her out of the water. Her screws were still turning. *(U.S. Navy)*

Periscope view from the USS *Snook* as the torpedo struck *Archerfish* amidships. A sad ending for a gallant lady! *(U.S. Navy)*

Archerfish jacket patch from World War II, designed by crew member Yeoman Second Class William Weathered. *(Ken Henry)*

Co-authors Don Keith, *(left)*, and Ken Henry, *(right)*, aboard the USS *Drum* (SS-228) in Mobile, Alabama, June 2002. *(Charlene Keith)*

was, Henry also heard that over 300 submarine sailors had volunteered for the 61 enlisted positions on the boat. There were also plenty of commanders and executive officers in Key West who were taking advantage of the opportunity to transfer over their worst troublemakers, making sure they were out of their hair for at least two years. Henry had concluded there was little chance he could get a billet aboard *Archerfish*.

Besides that, Henry was tired of the navy. He had fulfilled his military obligation and was counting the days until he could get out.

Finally, his time came. He was transferred to the Receiving Barracks at the Key West Naval Station to await discharge. He had purchased a bus ticket to Miami and a plane ticket home to Baltimore. With help from some shipmates, two cases of sea-store cigarettes (fifty cartons) had been smuggled off the base and were safely secured in the baggage room at the Greyhound bus station. He had already written his folks, letting them know he would be home by Christmas. Now all he had to do was sit in the legendary Gate Bar, so named because it was just outside the main gate to the base, and wait for his discharge date. One afternoon, he struck up a conversation with a second class personnelman from the Receiving Barracks who was also drinking lunch that day.

"Pig, what would it take to get you to ship over?" the personnelman suddenly asked, out of the blue.

Henry had not even considered staying in the navy. He figured it was time to go home and get started on a career that would keep him out of bars and on solid ground. But a quick thought hit him, and he spoke before he realized it.

"Get me a set of orders to *Archerfish* for that world cruise and I'll stay," he answered.

The personnelman told him to sit right there until he got back. Henry told him he had no intentions of going anywhere until it was time to catch that Greyhound and ride it to Miami, then fly home to Baltimore.

Three hours later, the man was back with orders in hand. Henry had not moved.

"Here you go, Pig. The boat's on the way in from daily operations. You can ship over after you report aboard."

Henry was speechless. Just like that, his life had taken a sharp right turn. He was about to re-up for four more years, with at least the first two aboard a diesel boat that was supposed to be leaving soon for an unheard-of two-year world cruise. He was so close. So close to going home, to not being in the navy.

"What the hell! I'll do it!" he said and motioned for Betty, the barmaid, to bring him and his new best friend another beer.

Henry reported aboard *Archerfish* that night, and to this day he maintains that it was one of the best decisions he ever made. Unwittingly, he had just become part of a crew that would be envied for years as they sailed throughout the world on what was truly to be a once-in-a-lifetime opportunity. By the way, he safely smuggled the two cases of tax-free sea-store cigarettes back onto the base.

Mike "Mother" Lintner didn't have a choice. He was one of the guys who had run afoul of his exec and soon found himself *Archerfish*-bound. He had shipped over on the USS *Atule* (SS-403) when her skipper promised him he could stay with her for at least a year. When the CO went on leave, though, the boat's XO promptly informed him he was gone. Gone for two long years. He was reassigned to *Archerfish*, the boat he had recommissioned in 1957.

"I'm really doing you a hell of a favor," the exec told him. Lintner didn't believe it for a minute. He tried to reach the captain to plead his case but it was to no avail. The squadron commander's office simply told him to "put in a letter." Meanwhile, the exec pointedly instructed him to pack his seabag and get off the boat or the chief of the boat would do it for him. And the COB would deliver sailor and seabag to the brig.

Lintner stomped across the brow and off the *Atule*. He made his way over to *Archerfish*'s berth, still trying to figure out a way to get his old billet back. It didn't take him long to realize that the exec on *Atule* had told him the truth after all. He had, indeed, done him a favor. He didn't know them all at the time, but in short order, he would serve alongside "Turkey Neck," "Nasty," "Chainfall," "Pine Tree," "Greasy Joe," "Pig Pen," "'Bacco Bill," "Squeaky," "Looney," "Dirty Hermie," "Bush," "Dinky," and a whole bunch of other colorful characters.

Mike Lintner had just become the latest to join what would truly be the grandest of adventures.

ARCHERFISH conducted her final operations as an "SS" on January 11, 1959. She fired a torpedo for the final time that day, a Mark-14-3A. Lieutenant Junior Grade Jim McDermott was the boat's first lieutenant, gun boss, and torpedo officer as well as being a "mustang" (an officer promoted up from the enlisted ranks) who had ridden submarines during World War II as an enlisted man. He made the approach and final setup and gave the order to fire. The launch was McDermott's "qualification shot" in order for him to receive his gold dolphins.

On January 22, the chief of naval operations sent out Notice 5030, re-designating *Archerfish* from an SS to an AGSS, an auxiliary submarine.

From that day forward, though she was no longer classified as a man-of-war, she would continue to be a warrior in her own right.

The boat left Key West on January 25, headed up the eastern seaboard for Philadelphia. No one aboard knew it at the time, but after all her years there, she would never return to Key West again.

Archerfish arrived at the mouth of the Delaware Bay on a foggy after-noon. The pea soup was so dense they postponed the long navigation up-river, past Wilmington to Philly, until visibility improved. Captain Evans gave the order to anchor for the night. The boat showed anchor lights and crew members were told to take turns ringing the ship's bell so no one would run over them in the fog.

There was one problem. Nobody could locate the bell.

It was later learned that Abie Snyder, one of the cooks, had thrown it over the side with the trash one night soon after the boat sailed from Key West. He wanted to make sure that the cooks would never have to polish it again.

The crew had to improvise. They found a piece of angle iron in the pump room, hung it from the shears, and beat on it all night with a hammer to keep someone from running them down in the murky fog.

Michael Klein remembers it was a mild night, and the captain gave permission to use the cigarette deck. The bay was flat calm, and the fog and darkness only added to the peacefulness of the evening. After all the tur-moil she had been through, it seemed appropriate that the boat have a rest-ful night before she started getting ready for her next escapade.

Later, Klein was on watch in the radio shack and assisted Captain Evans in placing a ship-to-shore telephone call to his mother, who lived in Chester, Pennsylvania. She was expecting her son home that night, and the fog had delayed his arrival until the next day. Such calls were much more complicated in those days, before satellite links and cell phones. They were limited to only a few hundred miles offshore. The cost of the call was determined by the vessel's precise location, and the charge had to be calcu-lated using a convoluted grid system that appeared in the boat's telecom-munication manuals.

The radioman on the vessel had to initiate the call by contacting a ship-to-shore operator. The charges were usually reversed with the party to whom the call was placed paying for it. Otherwise the radioman on the boat had to keep up with the cost, based on the complicated grids and formulae in the manuals and how long the call lasted. Then it was also his job to collect the money from all the men who made calls and mail it to the telephone company.

Once both parties were on the line, the conversation was awkward at best. It was necessary for both people to remember to say "Over," at the end of each thought so the person on the other end knew it was his or her turn to talk.

Still, in addition to the captain's call, Klein assisted several other *Archerfish* crew members in connecting with home that foggy night as they lay at anchor in Delaware Bay.

And yes, Radioman Klein did call his own mother that night. She was thrilled to hear from him.

OPERATION SEA SCAN

23 January 1960–1 May 1968

It may be that the gulfs will wash us down;

It may be we shall touch the Happy Isles

And see the great Achilles, whom we knew.

Tho' much is taken, much abides; and tho'

We are not now that strength which in old days

Moved earth and heaven, that which we are, we are—

One equal temper of heroic hearts,

Made weak by time and fate, but strong in will

To strive, to seek, to find, and not to yield.

—From *Ulysses* by Alfred, Lord Tennyson

14

A SAILOR'S DREAM CRUISE

For the next eight-and-a-half years, *Archerfish* led an existence that would have challenged the credibility of even the most creative Hollywood scriptwriter. At times, it seemed she was trying to outdo the movie *Operation Petticoat*, in which she had played a bit part. Or provide fodder for the writers who created the gambling, bootlegging, rule-flaunting crew of *McHale's Navy*, a television sitcom popular during much of *Archerfish's* Sea Scan years. The irreverence and adventures of her crew might even have topped that of the crews of other military-related sitcoms, *Hogan's Heroes*, which first aired in the mid-sixties as well, and *M*A*S*H*, which wouldn't debut until four years after *Archerfish* was gone.

It is important to note, though, that the boat and her very able crew spent those years doing far more than simply testing the limits of naval decorum and leaving a legendary legacy of unsurpassed hijinks. She was also engaged in a vital, top-secret mission that helped in no small way to maintaining U.S. nuclear superiority over the Russians and other potential enemies during the cold war. She never fired a shot or faced down a Russian vessel, but her contribution was just as valuable as anyone else's in maintaining the crucial nuclear balance that has so far kept the atomic bombs at Hiroshima and Nagasaki the only ones ever dropped in anger.

The nature of that important mission was hardly a factor, though, in how most of her crew ended up taking the ride of their lives. They wanted in on what one newspaper dubbed "a sailor's dream cruise."

Like Ken Henry before him, Dale A. "Nasty" Ness was intent on getting out of the navy and heading home to Joplin, Montana. He had been in Portsmouth Naval Shipyard as part of the commissioning crew on USS *Barbell* (SS-580) and was looking forward to putting the navy behind him. The yeoman had already begun the discharge process. They were talking one day, filling out the paperwork, when the yeoman casually mentioned something interesting that had recently crossed his desk.

"I got this notice from ComSubLant that sounds kinda crazy," he said. "They're looking for volunteers . . . single men only . . . to take a two-year cruise around the world."

"Hold on!" Ness called out. "You say a two-year around-the-world cruise?"

"That's what the notice said."

"Stop writing and listen," Ness said. "If you can get me orders on that boat, I'll ship over for two more years."

"You serious?"

"Damn right!"

"Well, go on back to the galley and I'll see what I can do."

Later that day, the yeoman looked Ness up and reported that he had made a few phone calls. His orders to *Archerfish* would show up in the mail on Monday. Sure enough, they did. Dale Ness shipped over on Monday afternoon and caught the train that night for Philadelphia to join his new boat.

William G. "Dinky" Earl had gone a step farther. He had already left the navy after making Second Class Engineman on the USS *Bream* (SS-243). He missed the life, though, and rejoined in 1959, even though he had to take a reduced rating as a fireman to get back in. When he got to Key West and reported aboard *Atule*, he met Mike Lintner and "Bacco Bill" Hiesley. They told him that they had just gotten orders to a boat that was about to leave on a two-year trip that would take them all over the world. Hiesley was excited, but Lintner was still angry about being transferred off *Atule*. Earl liked the sound of the mission and went over to *Archerfish* with his records to see if he could talk himself aboard.

The engineering officer at the time, Lieutenant Jack Willis, didn't sound very promising, though.

"I've still got one married second class engineman I've got to transfer off," he said. "But I can't swap him for a fireman."

"Wait. Look at my record and qualifications."

Willis did.

"Hmmm. You aren't nearly as bad as some of the others that are coming aboard," he said. "I'll approve the swap."

George Hughes knew all along that he wanted to be on *Archerfish*. He was serving aboard *Trutta* in Key West and shared the same wing of the barracks with the *Archerfish* crew. He remembered wading through their empty 7-Up cans each morning, the remains of their rum-and-seven parties the night before. He vowed then that he would one day serve with those guys. When the chance came, he took it.

A Kentuckian named Dewell E. "Possum" Perry was fortunate enough to get an assignment to *Archerfish* right out of Submarine School in New London. He was more than ready to get out of New London and onto his first submarine. He was packed and set to leave when he got word that he had to stick around for a while longer, for a three-week submarine electrician school on the base and that he had to wait two weeks for an opening in the class.

It seemed like forever, but Perry finally finished the class. His woes were just beginning.

When he got his orders to *Archerfish*, he grabbed the first bus that would get him close to home, Harlan, in the far southeast corner of Kentucky. It was sort of on the way to Key West and his new boat, and he wanted to spend a few days with his family. The bus got him to within thirty miles of Harlan and dropped him off there at two AM. He had to hitchhike and walk the rest of the way home. Somewhere between Connecticut and Kentucky, though, Greyhound had lost his bags. All he had was the uniform he wore, his orders, and one change of civilian clothes that he carried on a hanger.

After his leave was up, he put the few other civilian articles of clothing he had in a bag, climbed into his lone uniform, and caught a Greyhound for Key West. In his haste to get on the road, he forgot to throw his orders into the bag. By the time the bus arrived in Miami, he was dirty and tired. Dirty enough that the Shore Patrol picked him up at the bus station and threw him into a paddy wagon. They finally believed his lost-baggage story and let him go, but not before he agreed to put on his civvies instead of the grungy white uniform in which he had been traveling. They delivered him back to the bus station just in time for him to catch his ride down U.S. 1 to Key West.

The marine guard at the gate to the naval station was suspicious.

"Let me see your liberty card," he barked.

"I don't have one. I'm traveling under orders and reporting to *Archerfish* for duty."

"Then show me the orders."

"I left them at home in Kentucky."

"Where's your uniform?"

"Greyhound lost them."

"They lost all your uniforms?"

"All but one."

"Then why don't you have it on?"

"It's filthy. I rode all the way from Harlan County, Kentucky, in it, and it was dirty. The Shore Patrol in Miami made me take it off, or they were going to put me in the brig."

"You're not getting in this gate without a uniform on."

With that, "Possum" went and put on the wrinkled, filthy uniform, and the guard finally let him pass.

Lieutenant Jerry Davi, the exec on *Archerfish*, wasn't sympathetic either. He threatened to court-martial Perry for showing up for duty in such a messy uniform and with no orders. Still, when he heard the whole story, Davi calmed down and turned him over to the chief of the boat, Joe Pino. He and the crew got the young sailor cleaned up and found him some dungarees to wear.

Perry knew then that he was finally home.

William E. "Robbie" Roberts was aboard USS *Toro* (SS-422) at Portsmouth Naval Shipyard when he got word he had been "selected" to go to *Archerfish* if he wanted to. He had heard enough about the boat and her mission that he was more than ready to go. Trouble was, he was in Maine, his new boat was in New London by then, and he had less than forty-eight hours to report. He managed to make it down to New London by the next night and dropped off his records and seabag just in time to get some sleep.

There was one other complication, though. Roberts still had his car parked just outside the gate. He could hardly leave it there for two years!

"COB, can I have liberty long enough to see if I can sell my car?" he asked "Pappy" Bettis the next morning.

"You got till noon. We get under way then."

Roberts ended up giving the vehicle back to the finance company along with an extra $100.

Some of the crewmembers who joined *Archerfish* later in Operation Sea Scan had their own interesting stories to tell about how they came to be aboard.

"Lightning" Larry Meyer almost made a terrible mistake. He and a friend had decided to volunteer in 1963 for Operation Deep Freeze, the navy's aptly named mission in support of the exploration of frigid and desolate Antarctica. Two days after they put in their requests, Meyer saw a message about the need for an unmarried electrician on *Archerfish*. He, too, had heard plenty about this boat and her round-the-world escapades. He went, hat in hand, back to the exec's stateroom to request that his Operation Deep Freeze transfer chit be returned, that he had changed his mind about the frosty assignment for which he had put in.

"I see you came to your senses," the exec said with a smile as he handed the papers back to Meyer.

"No, sir. I got a better deal," Meyer proclaimed as he handed him the chit for transfer to *Archerfish*.

Kenneth R. "Andy" Anderson may hold the record for traveling the longest distance to join *Archerfish*. When he graduated from Submarine School in New London in the spring of 1963, he received orders to report to *Archerfish* in San Francisco. He flew across the country, reported to Treasure Island, and gave his orders to the yeoman there.

"Welcome aboard, but your boat is now in Japan," the yeoman happily told him. "Oh, and you have to get your shots before you leave."

Anderson went through the agony of getting all his immunizations, then caught a bus headed northeast, to Travis Air Force Base and a plane that would take him to Japan. When he got to Travis, he discovered the hospital corpsmen at Treasure Island had not added his immunization records to his orders, so he had to take the battery of shots all over again. Still, he was soon on his way, doubly inoculated, across the Pacific to Yokosuka, Japan, where *Archerfish* was supposed to be.

But when he got to the base at Yokosuka and stuck his orders through the window to be stamped, the yeoman there looked at him sideways.

"Sailor, your boat is in San Francisco," he told him.

"I just came from there," Anderson explained. "They told me it was here."

"Nope. She's in San Francisco all right," the Yeoman assured him and arranged for him to hop a flight back across the Pacific.

Back at Treasure Island, he again stuck his orders through the window to be stamped. The yeoman there looked at the paperwork for a moment.

"Hey, there was another guy here a week ago looking for *Archerfish*. She's in Japan."

"That was me. I just got back from Japan. They say she's here!"

"Naw. She's in Japan. No doubt about it."

So it was back to Travis, but no round of inoculations this time. After his second westward trip across the Pacific, Anderson again went to the submarine base at Yokosuka and shoved his papers through the window at the waiting yeoman. The yeoman considered the young sailor's orders for a minute, rubbing his chin thoughtfully the entire time. "You know, there was a guy in here a few days ago looking for *Archerfish*. That boat's in San Francisco."

With amazing calm, Anderson explained once again that he was that guy, that he had made two trips to San Francisco and two to Japan looking for *Archerfish*, and that the boat didn't seem to be in either place. The yeoman did some checking and assured him that she absolutely was still in San Francisco. Anderson had no choice. He caught another plane eastbound for San Francisco. This time, the yeoman did some more serious checking and found that *Archerfish* had been at Hunters Point all the time, just down the bay, almost within sight of Treasure Island.

Anderson caught a ride down to Hunters Point and reported aboard on Sunday night. He was just in time. *Archerfish* was under way early the next morning.

Her first scheduled stop after a brief stay in Hawaii? Yokosuka, Japan.

"I should have been awarded wings along with my dolphins for all the time I spent in the air," Anderson says.

By 1967, the boat and her exploits were near mythical throughout the navy. When Gerald L. "Corny" Cornelison was in Submarine School in January of that year in cold, snowy New London, his instructors liked to warm up their students with tales about various submarines in the fleet. Those stories were often about a legendary "all bachelor boat" that had literally sailed the Seven Seas with its "playboy crew." The boat that was the subject of all those stories was never named, and "Corny" and his classmates assumed she was an amalgam of several vessels or that the stories were mere fairy tales, little more than liberally embellished "sea stories."

After graduation, the class was assembled to receive their assignments to the various submarines in the fleet. When the chief got to Cornelison's name, he did a double take.

"Cornelison? USS *Archerfish*. Son of a bitch!" he exclaimed. "*Archerfish!* That's the boat, sailor! The all-bachelor boat. How the hell did you get on *Archerfish?* There's a two-year wait to get on that boat. Son of a bitch!"

Corny joined *Archerfish* in Hawaii as soon as she pulled in from Midway. He still doubted the veracity of the tall tales about the boat, but getting an assignment to a boat everyone seemed to admire, and to do so in Hawaii after a long, chilly New England winter, was more than he could have hoped for.

It didn't take him long, though, to learn that the stories he had heard told and retold in his Sub School classroom on those cold, snowy days were absolutely true.

Totally and absolutely true.

15

KENNY WOODS AND
HIS SIXTY THIEVES

SOMEONE had come up with the idea of meeting a commitment to the United States Air Force by providing a submarine that would have otherwise been put out of commission. *Archerfish* was an unmodernized fleet boat, with no role in the mix of nuclear and high-speed diesel-electric submarines that were being used by the navy in the 1960s. She was eighteen years old and in too poor repair to be a candidate for modernization, but she was, oddly enough, perfectly suited for the new job she was assigned.

A Fleet boat like *Archerfish* was actually a very effective surface ship that just happened to be able to dive. She was designed to handle much better on the surface than when submerged. She was, in reality, slow and clumsy underwater but an excellent vessel when operating on the surface. Her bow was flared and had a large buoyancy tank. That made her tend to ride over waves instead of trying to bore right through them the way modern submarines want to do in those rare times when they are on the surface. The bridge area of a fleet boat was designed for surface operations as well. The fairwater extended back on either side of the conning tower and periscope supports, or shears, and ended in a deck area called the cigarette deck. In addition to those on watch, other crew members could come topside and enjoy the open air and relatively generous space. *Archerfish* also had a small superstructure; her weight was concentrated low in the hull, allowing her to ride well for a ship of her size, much better, in fact, than most surface ships of the same displacement.

In short, all this made her a perfect hydrographic survey vessel. And for the delicate work she would be doing, she would be able to dive as necessary and offer a much more stable platform under water than any ship could possibly do on the surface. She would be required to take readings at least every sixty miles along a prescribed track, using an extremely sensitive device that compensated somewhat for the ship's motion. When the sea was calm, those readings could be taken on the surface, and almost any old vessel would do. However, when the ocean was too rough, the submarine could simply dive, go to a depth where sea conditions were calmer, take the essential readings, and then surface again and drive on.

From all the articles that the navy public relations guys managed to get published in the local papers and the military publications, it appeared that Operation Sea Scan was to be a relatively mundane undertaking. The releases admitted that her mission was classified but hinted that, as with most hydrographic survey operations, she was to steam over a broad area of the North Atlantic in phase one and the Pacific in phase two, measuring and recording such exciting things as wave heights, seawater temperature, the composition of the ocean bottom, and weather conditions. There were photos accompanying the articles showing the exotic racks of equipment that would be used. They weren't exactly lying. Those ocean and meteorological readings were, in fact, religiously taken, recorded on computer punch cards, and sent back for analysis by the U.S. Naval Hydrographic Office. The information they gathered contributed considerably to the updating of ocean charts and to oceanographic research.

In truth, though, *Archerfish* and her crew had a far more crucial role to perform, one that got no play whatsoever in the press because of its top-secret nature.

As with her mission to Ascension Island several years before, she would also be taking precise measurements of the earth's gravitational field, and she would do so with other equipment that was much less visible. The air force was still having trouble keeping missiles on target because of variations in gravitational pull at different places on the globe. Simply put, if it was necessary to accurately send a nuclear warhead to an enemy target by intercontinental ballistic missile, it would be difficult to do so. The scientists programming the rocket that carried it could not factor into its trajectory the correct force of gravity along the way. A nuclear force offered little deterrence if it was not accurate enough to be a real threat. There was a real fear that the Russians might eventually find out that the United States could not hit the broad side of a barn with their ICBMs. They might well decide then that they could go claim a few new countries for communism with impunity. Or launch their own first strike against the United States.

The vital information the air force needed to make their ICBMs more accurate would come from *Archerfish*, the scientists from the Naval Hydrographic Office who rode along, and their supersensitive instruments. That was the real reason for Operation Sea Scan and for prolonging the sub's life for at least two more years.

The areas they were to probe on this mission were primarily missile ranges. Parts of the globe that had been surveyed already were mostly on land, but vast areas of the earth's oceans were still a mystery. The readings *Archerfish* took in her first month alone provided more information than had been gathered up to that time.

While there was some interest by the media in her disguised oceanographic surveying job, most of the considerable news coverage focused on the unusual length of her cruise and the odd requirement for becoming a member of her crew. She would be gone for a long time and would seldom return to her home port. That's why the navy sought only unmarried crewmen. The expense of moving families and dependents from the East to the West Coast and the likelihood that married sailors would worry about their wives and children were the primary reasons for the requirement. Another reason was the way the mission was to be conducted. It would be difficult to break off the strictly regimented survey schedule to return some sailor to a port should a family emergency arise.

Some higher-up in the navy had concluded that having all bachelors would make things much less complicated. They neglected to consider the rather obvious complications that cooping up five-dozen unmarried sailors on such a long voyage might create.

The *Philadelphia Evening Bulletin*, in an article printed on April 19, 1960, made note of the two-year mission and the all-volunteer crew. That and the fact that all but two of her crew members were bachelors.

"The submarine USS *Archerfish* is being readied at the Philadelphia Naval Base for a two-year sailor's dream cruise of the world—with liberty in every port," the article began. "The navy is also providing fulfillment of its famous old enlistment slogan: 'Join the navy and see the world.'"

Dolphin, the publication of the submarine base at New London, and *Naval Base News* at Philadelphia also pointed out that Catholic priests and

Protestant ministers had recorded sermons to be played back on the boat since she was to be gone for so long. They, too, made much hay of the all-volunteer, almost-all-bachelor crew.

But even with all the hoopla, and despite the secret vital mission she was to perform, *Archerfish* arrived at Philadelphia in early 1960 to find that there was very little money available for the refitting she desperately needed. The navy didn't want to spend any money on the boat. They had turned her over to the Hydrographic Office already. The Hydrographic Office maintained they didn't have any money allotted for that purpose. They were under the impression that the navy was going to fix up *Archerfish* so she would be seaworthy. The orders were that the boat was to be made safe to dive to a depth of two hundred feet and be able to maintain a speed of ten knots. The two-hundred-foot restriction would keep them from having to find and fix problems with the boat's watertight integrity at greater depths. The only work that was approved was whatever it took to accomplish those two simple goals. Not another penny was to be spent on *Archerfish*.

The crew quickly realized the quality of the overhaul they were to receive was directly proportional to their ingenuity and the limited time they had to accomplish it. Not only that, but time was as scarce as money. The first phase of Sea Scan was to be conducted mostly in Arctic waters. If they didn't complete the overhaul quickly and get under way on schedule, the weather in the higher latitudes would quickly worsen in the fall. The mission would have to be postponed for a full year. It was far too crucial a job to be put off that long.

Despite that obvious fact, neither help nor sufficient money was forthcoming from the navy.

After off-loading the boat in Philadelphia, they moved into the submarine barracks in Building 619. It was a far cry from their digs in Key West. The berthing area was one big room, considerably larger than what they were accustomed to but with a lot more people. The entire room was filled with double bunks with only lockers separating each man from his neighbor.

They made the most of their spartan living quarters, though. The barracks craps game that had been going on here for as long as anyone could remember was still under way. There was also a poker game in the lounge that had at least as much longevity, and there was always a long line of sailors waiting to grab the next open seat. There were also the bars of Philadelphia to keep them distracted.

Much of that soon changed. When the seriousness of the job they faced was fully realized, the crew of the *Archerfish* turned to and performed miracles. Despite the continual crap games and long nights in the bars, these dedicated men performed superhuman feats of strength and endurance. They also displayed a streak of larcenous ingenuity that was beautiful to watch, unless the observer was the one having his pocket picked. Still, they did whatever was necessary to ensure that the boat was seaworthy in time to leave the yard the first week in May, bound first for New London, then the North Atlantic.

Even before their new captain assumed command, and before the new executive officer came aboard, the crew was already beginning an amazing scavenger hunt, trying to find the gear they needed to make *Archerfish* ready for her mission. Often they could not afford to go through channels or do the proper requisitioning paperwork. They simply found what they needed and did whatever they had to do to appropriate it.

The creative acquisitions began as soon as they berthed in Philadelphia. Even before leaving Key West, they had requested new sonar equipment to replace the totally outdated JP system in the after port corner of the forward torpedo room. There was no money available for such a luxury. About the same time, they learned that the sonar school in Key West was replacing some of their obsolete but far more modern JT equipment. Instead of being scrapped, that gear ended up on *Archerfish*. Since they had managed to find the sonar equipment on their own, BuShips was kind enough to okay its installation. Not pay for it, mind you. Or make sure the crew had all the accessories they needed to put it into operation.

Once they acquired the sonar gear for nothing, Ted Armstrong ordered cable for it. It was supposed to be waiting for them at Philadelphia. It wasn't, so more was ordered. Time was running short, though, so Armstrong, with the help of Tom Salisbury, scavenged up enough cable around the shipyard to get the job done. Maybe it did belong to another submarine that was to be refitted, but it was not being used at the moment, so Armstrong and Salisbury put it to immediate good use on *Archerfish*.

Speculation had been rampant since they left Key West about who their new skipper would be for Sea Scan. He would have to be a unique individual. It was highly unusual for a submarine skipper to be single. The leading contender was, ironically enough, a Philadelphian named Kenneth Woods. He had grown up at 4015 Nielson Street, not far from where *Archerfish* was tied up at the confluence of the Delaware and the Schuykill Rivers. At that time, Woods was commander of USS *Sea Lion* (APSS-315), a boat that was also overdue for decommissioning. He was actually looking

for a command that would take him back to the Pacific and had been assured he would get the next boat out of San Diego. When he was first offered *Archerfish*, he couldn't accept it, even though everyone agreed that he,
a bachelor, would be perfect for the job. Shortly before, he had called in a
marker with the detailer, Commander Eric Hopley, who had promised him
the San Diego boat. Woods had already said he would accept the Pacific
command when it became available. Now he was stuck.

Woods was the stepson of a Philly police detective and a solidly honest
man. He would not go back on his word to Hopley after the detailer had
pulled strings to grant his request, even if it meant he would miss out on a
truly remarkable command. Still, he didn't say a firm no to the all-bachelor
boat when he left for operations aboard *Sea Lion* near the Virgin Islands
over Thanksgiving, 1959. While there, he got a call from his division commander. Did he want *Archerfish* or not? After pondering the offer for a couple of days, Woods finally agreed to take the boat, but only if it was okay
with the detailer who had stuck out his neck to get him the Pacific command he had asked for.

It was. In early 1960, Woods was relieved of his command of the *Sea
Lion* and headed for Philly to take over *Archerfish* from Bill Evans. Woods
was surprised when he arrived to see stories about his new job on television
and in the papers. The navy publicity machine had made much of the
"hometown boy makes good" angle to the story.

Woods was a graduate of Frankford High School in Philadelphia and
of the Naval Academy, where he had played both football and baseball. He
had been in the Submarine Service for nine years. His stepfather was Frank
Vandergrift, a police officer in the city's North Central Detective Division.
He and Woods's mother were present for the change-of-command ceremony in early March.

Woods was a popular choice among the men who were already on
Archerfish. He had a reputation as a skipper who always watched out for his
crew. He also had the knack of good leadership. Word was that he made
each man want to carry out his duties to the best of his abilities at all times.
And best of all, no matter what time it was locally when they pulled into
port, Ken Woods always granted liberty as soon as the maneuvering watch
was secured.

It was a few days after Woods took command, a Tuesday and a cold,
snowy day. Dale Ness and Ken Henry were in good spirits because they
were going to be getting a new executive officer that day. They had had
several run-ins with the departing exec, and they looked forward to getting

off on the right foot with their boat's new second in command. They were also feeling good because they had been doing some "day drinking" as well.

The two men were running an errand but decided it was too far to walk all the way from the barracks over to the marine railway and back. They spotted an unoccupied dock mule (small tractor) with a string of trailers hooked behind it and decided to borrow it for the trip over and back. Ness took the wheel and Henry hopped on the rear trailer, acting like the brakeman on a runaway train. Soon the two sailors were having the times of their lives, speeding and weaving the "train" through the slush and icy puddles, splashing cold, dirty water on anyone who got too close to their winding route.

Suddenly, an officer wearing dress blues stepped out from nowhere directly into their path. Ness didn't slow down one bit. He figured the guy would have no idea who they were, and if he got splashed, well, he could just get his uniform cleaned.

When he saw the runaway dock mule heading his way, the officer tried to dodge to keep from getting run over or drenched. When he jumped, he slipped in the slush and dropped the papers he carried directly into the tractor's path. Ness jumped on the brake and just managed to get his train stopped before running over the officer.

The enraged officer jumped to his feet, slapping at the mud on his uniform and picking up the scattered papers he had been carrying. He was seething.

"What boat are you men from?" he demanded.

Ness gave him a semblance of a salute and a crooked grin and, in his best military manner, said, "*Archerfish*, sir!"

A slow smile broke out on the officer's angry face.

"Good! I'm Lieutenant David K. Dimmick, your new executive officer." He paused a beat for effect. "Now, what are your names?"

Dimmick was in for another shock when he first saw the boat he had inherited. *Archerfish* was literally in pieces, and the work that was being done looked like total chaos. But he also learned that Kenny Woods and Jim McDermott, the boat's first lieutenant and gun boss, had already inspired a sense of loyalty among the crew. The schedule was impossible, the funds almost nonexistent, but the crew was unbelievably devoted to getting the job done any way they could.

"If I had demanded a textbook relieving procedure, I'd still be there [in the naval yard]," Dimmick says. He quickly took his cue from the crew. Their job was to get the boat shipshape by the first week of May, whatever it took. He was willing to do his part. He learned to turn his head and ig-nore the crew's actions when appropriate and to do whatever it took to ex-pedite them when called for. If someone handed him a paper to sign, he simply signed it without reading it and told the bearer, "Now go away."

There was an ominous moment that first day on his new boat. It hap-pened as Dimmick went through one of *Archerfish's* hatches. As he grabbed hold to keep his balance, a large piece of rust came loose and fell into his hand. He promptly called his life insurance agent in New London and in-creased his policy by ten thousand dollars.

The yard period had actually gotten off to a very slow start. Then, when Woods and Dimmick came aboard and the new engineer, Miles T. Graham, showed up, things finally began to happen.

Kelsey Ray "Chain Fall" Farrell can attest to that. He was working out-board of the number-four main engine when he realized he had forgotten to bring a needed pipe plug into the cramped space with him. Rather than wiggle back out to get what he needed, he yelled, "Hey, inboard! Give me a pipe plug!" He didn't specify a size because anyone working there knew precisely what he required.

There was no response, so he yelled again, this time a bit more pro-fanely. He needed the pipe plug!

"What size?" came the reply, in an unfamiliar voice.

"About the size of my gawd-damned thumb," an irritated Farrell screamed back.

There was silence for a moment, and then a large, red face, clearly an-gry, appeared at the front end of the engine.

"I'm the new engineer," the newcomer growled. "Now, how big is your thumb?"

Like Dimmick, Miles Graham's first impression of *Archerfish* was less than stellar. When he arrived at the shipyard, he went directly to the boat to check in. No one seemed to be doing much of anything productive, and the whole situation was a mess. He was told that all four main engines needed overhauling, none of them were operational at the time, three of the four main generators were grounded, the one good generator was on an engine that had a bad blower, and there was no good blower available. Both high-pressure air compressors were in pieces, completely disassembled, as was most of the auxiliary equipment. The stills were not capable of making wa-ter. Despite all this, there was only one engineman and no auxiliarymen or electricians working on board when he got there.

Graham could not believe what he was hearing.

He spun around and promptly headed for the boat's office to see what was going on. He found the engineer he was to relieve sitting back, his feet on a desk, reading a comic book.

Graham did not bother with any pleasantries.

"I relieve you," he blurted out. "Where is the crew?"

The man told him he was not sure, so Graham gave cab fare to "Flunky" Joe Forrest, a sailor in the duty section, and told him, "Go find my people and get them back here. Now!"

The first sailors to straggle back that day were assigned to the port section. The rest went to the starboard section. Shifts for everyone in the engineering department from that point forward were twelve on and twelve off, seven days a week.

That was the point where the crew really began to come together, where they learned what they were made of, both as individuals and as a submarine crew. Those who weren't willing to do the job were quickly gone. The rest became closer than any crew since the war, developing a strong bond that still exists today. The work and pressure of the next couple of months were what tempered this ragtag group of men into hard steel.

Joe Cummings says, "Most boats were divided into three crews: the wardroom [officers], the chiefs, and the rest of the crew. On *Archerfish*, we only had one group, one crew, and we were all part of it."

After about two weeks of the punishing new schedule, Graham mustered all the members of the engineering department at shift exchange and made an announcement.

"Men, we are no longer going to do the twelve-hour shifts," he proclaimed.

Everyone looked at each other. The boat was in almost as big a mess as when they had started the impossibly torturous work hours. Time was running out, too. They were in serious danger of not being ready to depart on time. The entire mission was in jeopardy. They couldn't imagine why he was willing to let up on them now.

Graham ignored their blank stares, clenched his jaws, and went on.

"From now on, we are going to work around the clock. I expect each of you to work until you can't stay awake. When you can't stay awake, sleep where you are. When you wake up, start working again."

There was no doubt at all about how serious Graham was. All liberty was canceled. Gene "Doc" Barboza gave the men little white pills that helped them stay alert. Someone else discovered another way to keep awake. The electricians were using half-gallon cans of "gilly," 190-proof alcohol that was used to fuel torpedoes and clean electrical parts. If the sailors took the rags and dirty parts out of the liquid and allowed the bits of dirt and solder to settle to the bottom, they could then pour off the cleaner liquid from the top of the container, mix the stuff with coffee or soda, and drink the devilish mixture or use it to chase down Doc's little white pills.

The need for sleep disappeared entirely.

When David Dimmick strolled through the boat, he was pleased to see everyone now busy, working together, getting her ready. But what he saw in the engine room gave him pause.

"There were no deck plates as such, only makeshift walkways fashioned from two-by-twelve planks. One misstep and a body would crash many feet into the bilges with the probability of receiving severe injuries. The only acknowledgment of my presence was the glazed-over pairs of eyeballs. They all seemed to be focused on infinity. Those on their feet moved as if they were in a trance. They looked as if they had been drugged."

When Dimmick found out that was precisely what was going on, he took it up with Miles Graham. The exec soon learned his opinion didn't matter down there. It was Graham's engineering space, and those men were his personnel. It was his internal affair. Dimmick could only worry, hoping nobody died or went loony before they finally got under way.

Even the yard workers noticed how hard the *Archerfish* crew was working, how serious they were about getting their boat ready for sea on time. They knew too well the obstacles the men faced. Some of the yard workers began punching out at the end of their shifts, then staying on to work for free, helping the crew out for several more hours, either out of the goodness of their hearts or for the barter materials the crew members seemed to be able to come up with.

By this time, Mike Giambattista had had his duties expanded. He was no longer just the boat's SLJO ("shitty little jobs officer," the one who got the bulk of the jobs no one else wanted). He was also named supply officer. Once they were off on the mission, he quickly learned what a chore it was to feed the crew and replenish supplies and refuel outside the navy's well-established supply chain around the world. As it turned out, his training by the boat's leading cook, Commissaryman Second Class Clarence D. "Red Dog" Balthrop, and the things that happened there in the navy yard, were excellent preparation for what lay in store for *Archerfish*.

Balthrop, from Nashville, Tennessee, was a master at getting the most for his money. After each meal, he had the mess cooks put their leftover but perfectly good food into number-ten cans instead of throwing it away. Then he handed it out the backdoor of the galley to appreciative yard workers. In return, the workers did extra tasks for the boat in their shops. Tom McCormick remembers that among the extras they received in return for the food were engraved belt buckles for the entire crew.

The commissaryman in the submarine barracks took an immediate dislike to the guys from *Archerfish*. Thirty-five-pound cans of coffee and sugar seemed to suddenly begin disappearing not long after the boat first sidled up to her berth in the yard. The large tins made wonderful cumshaw, or bartering material. "Greasy Joe" Osier recalls that they managed to get all the boat's handhole covers and injector drip pans for each of the four main engines chrome-plated in exchange for the items that had been appropriated from the galley.

The enginemen, in their quest to get help for their impossible task, were constantly slinking around the galley, trying to lift the coffee and sugar cans for their own cumshaw. They were so clever and relentless that there was no way to stop them, so Red Dog came up with a partial solution. He sent Tom McCormick and another mess cook to one of the shops to bring back sheets of brown cork insulation, the material attached to the inside of the boat's pressure hull. The wily cook had a creative use for the cork. He ground the material up until it had about the right consistency and then blended it into the cans of coffee. He cut at least five pounds of cork into every thirty-five-pound tin of coffee before he "allowed" the enginemen to steal his special blend of joe.

Soon, though, the crew had moved beyond expropriating coffee and sugar. The boat was in desperate need of a left-hand blower for the number-two main engine. When Mike Giambattista called the Naval Supply Depot in Mechanicsburg, Pennsylvania, near Harrisburg, they maintained there were none available for Fairbanks-Morse diesel engines. Graham got on the phone that night, woke up a supply clerk, and explained that the things came in pairs, and the depot had already sent them a right-hand blower by mistake. The matching left-hand one, the one they really needed, had to be there somewhere in his warehouse if he would only get off his duff and go look for it.

"You're welcome to come up and take a look," the clerk told him sarcastically. He was only interested in getting back to sleep and told Graham what he wanted to hear. "I'll even let our security folks know you're coming. Help yourself when you get here. Good night."

The sleepy clerk likely never thought the *Archerfish* boys would take him up on his offer. He didn't know Miles Graham. The engineer grabbed Jim McDermott, got a car, and struck out for Mechanicsburg, which was about 120 miles to the west. They got there at two AM. It took them a while to locate the correct warehouse, but once they did, they quickly began opening crates, looking for the right blower. When they found it, they knew they had to find a way to get it back to the boat. It was too big to take in the car.

No problem. They found a navy truck with the keys in it, loaded the crate on the back, and strapped it down. Graham drove the borrowed truck, and McDermott followed in their car.

The marine on the gate at the naval yard was more than curious about the late-night delivery and the lack of paperwork. Graham merely told him that the truck's precious cargo was the one single element that would win or lose the Cold War. Its contents were top secret, highly classified, but crucial to the effort.

"I cannot tell you more," the engineer bluffed. "It is a matter of national security. I'm not at liberty to divulge any further information about our mission. For your sake, I hope you won't force me to have to call the officer of the day."

The intimidation worked. The guard allowed them to pass. They arrived at the boat just as the day shift was reporting. A big crane swung over, picked up the blower, and placed it in position. It was bolted into place before the sun was up.

There was fallout. A few days later, Captain Woods and Lieutenant Graham were summoned to the office of the commandant of the Fourth Naval District. They had to explain why they took the blower without the proper paperwork and why they had borrowed a truck to get it back to Philly. When the commandant heard the whole story, and the fact that the clerk had told them to come up and get whatever they needed, he simply commended them on their ingenuity in solving the problem and wished them well on their impending trip.

Kenny Woods was still in the process of evaluating his new crew and the work they were doing. He always carried a small green memo book in his pocket, and he used it to make notes to himself about things that urgently needed to be done. He had noticed one engineman in particular. When he asked the officers who the man was, they answered, "That's 'Pig Pen.'" He thought they were saying "Thigpen."

Woods wrote in his notebook, in bold letters, "GET RID OF THIGPEN!"

Thankfully for both, he never got around to doing it.

While they were getting some of the things they needed through normal channels, like anticorrosive and antifouling paint, it was still difficult to get smaller parts such as fuel injectors for the engines, spare valves for the compressors, and other expensive items. It was common knowledge that the other submarines in the yard for overhaul had an abundance of such parts in their cages, the fenced, locked storage areas that were assigned to each boat, but they were not willing to share.

The *Archerfish* crew happened upon a scheme that worked quite well. They sent a couple of guys to the cage area that had been assigned to one of the other boats. They went on the pretext of trying to find someone who they needed to talk with. While one sailor engaged the other boat's men in conversation, an accomplice slipped around and unlocked one of the windows to the cage. He also memorized where all the parts were stored.

All the other boats in the yard were on normal daytime working hours. Only *Archerfish*'s crew worked around the clock. That meant the other boats' cages were locked but unguarded at night. Since the weather was cold, the windows stayed closed and were rarely checked at quitting time when everyone left for the day. In the wee hours, the men from *Archerfish* sneaked back and crawled through the window that had been unlocked the previous day. They were able to "shop" at their leisure for the parts they needed.

Once inside the cage area, it was often necessary to pick locks to get at the stuff they wanted. Mike "Mother" Lintner and Galen O. "Turkey Neck" Steck became very adept at it. They fashioned burglar tools from tap extractors and hacksaw blades, and these implements became invaluable in filling the "orders" for the parts they were unable to obtain through normal channels.

It's important to note that there was a strict ethical code in place during this entire process. The *Archerfish* crew never took anything they didn't specifically need. And they *never* took anything personal. Since it was navy property in the first place and they were going to use it on a navy boat, it wasn't really stealing. They were merely enhancing the navy's distribution process, redirecting items to where they were most needed. Besides, it kept the supply petty officers from having to worry about all that paperwork, so their methods were good for the navy in the long run.

Since the *Archerfish*'s unique requisition system seemed to be working so well, the men became even bolder. Mike Lintner was determined to replace the missing ship's bell, the one that was thrown overboard on the way out of Key West by Abie Snyder so he wouldn't have to polish it anymore. One night, Mike went aboard USS *Hake* (SS-256), the reserve training submarine for the Philadelphia area, and helped himself to their bell. He also spotted a desk and a safe in the yeoman's office that he knew *Archerfish* needed worse than *Hake* did. He had to take the desk apart to get it through the torpedo-loading hatch. Lintner also managed to remove the captain's bridge-wing chair from the aircraft carrier USS *Tarawa* (CV-40). These items went into Lintner's "office" in the after torpedo room and became the home of the slush fund. Using cumshaw, he was able to Formica the fronts of all lockers on the port and starboard sides and added stainless steel trim. He gathered two years' worth of "Playmates of the Month" from *Playboy* calendars and had the beauties laminated into the Formica. The whole thing added a nice decorative touch and made life in the after torpedo room much more pleasant.

In mid-April, the commandant of the shipyard in Philadelphia notified the Hydrographic Office that there was no way to finish the requested work on *Archerfish* in time to meet the deadline. BuShips sent Hydro a succinct two-word message: "Now what?"

The crew didn't care. They were still determined to make the voyage they had signed on for, and to begin it in 1960 as planned.

David A. "Loony" Stevens recalls that a crucial part of the periscope assembly needed to be replaced. Naturally, there was no money available to buy a new one. Stevens and Joe Cronin, the chief auxiliaryman, borrowed a couple of pairs of coveralls and two hard hats from one of the shops, grabbed their tools, and went aboard one of the other boats that was in the yard for overhaul. They had long since discovered that if you act as if you belong where you are, you can usually bluff your way into any place. They proceeded to the conning tower, removed the built-in stadimeter housing assembly from the bottom of the periscope, and calmly walked off the boat, back to *Archerfish*. No one challenged them along the way.

"Speedy" Gonzales was walking through the yard one day when he spied a small water valve. It was just like the one they needed in *Archerfish*'s pump room but had not been able to get through proper channels. There was a rub, though. The valve was still attached to a copper line that supplied water to a spigot outside one of the yard buildings. Gonzales happened to have his tubing cutter with him and promptly liberated the required valve. He ignored the spray of water and the quickly forming puddle he left behind as he returned to his boat to install the much-needed part.

Then there were the aluminum deck plates from the after engine room and the angle iron framing that held them in place. The old ones somehow got misplaced during all the confusion when the boat first hit the yard and they began tearing her apart. Again, no problem. One night, the guys from the engine room found what they needed, right there on the dock on a pallet where they had been removed from USS *Angler* (SS-240). At least the deck plates were there. The framing was still rigged inside the other sub. It took them most of the midwatch (midnight to four AM), but they managed to get the framing unbolted and everything moved to *Archerfish*. Before daylight the entire deck assembly was installed, deck mats fitted, and bench lockers in place.

When the boat first arrived in Philadelphia, over five thousand gallons of lubricating oil had been pumped out of her storage tanks and main engine sumps. It, too, had disappeared by the time they needed to reload it. There certainly was no money set aside to go out and buy more oil.

Some of the riggers from Shop 72 in the yard located a railroad flatcar loaded with fifty-five-gallon drums of oil. They were only too happy to assist the *Archerfish* crew in acquiring the stuff. It was after midnight when the riggers delivered the flatcar full of oil to the pier. They had borrowed a steam pump and hose from Shop 56, then, even though their shift was over, they stayed long enough to help strike down the oil. When the job was finished, they even helped wipe the empty drums clean and returned them to the storage area.

This episode almost ended in disaster. Larry "Doc" Dachenhausen was working belowdecks that night, making sure the lube oil storage tanks were buttoned up and ready to receive the purloined petroleum. He had crawled into number-four lube oil storage tank, looking for rags or other debris before bolting down the manhole cover. It was a tight squeeze into the L-shaped tank as it turned back under the main motors, but he had wriggled back to its far reaches, away from the manhole that let him in.

Suddenly, he saw oil pouring into the tank through the fill pipe. There was no other way out except through the torrent of oil.

Dachenhausen yelled at the top of his lungs. No one could hear him over the noise of the shipyard. He held his breath and crawled through the deluge of oil until he managed to make his way to the manhole before he drowned in the stuff.

It turned out that the filling and transfer valve for the oil tank had not closed properly.

"I can think of better ways to find out a valve is not working properly," Dachenhausen says with a touch of understatement.

Next on the shopping list were new mooring lines. The old ones were seriously frayed, but, as usual, there were no funds for new ones. This time, the USS *Cutlass* (SS-478) was selected to be the latest donor to the *Archer-*

fish "refurbishing fund." They had 1,200 feet of brand-new nylon line lying right there on the pier, prime for the taking. By morning, new eyes had been spliced in the line and all the old stuff had been replaced. For a nice touch, dirt and grease had been tossed on it so it looked well used.

A lot of people were looking for the line the next day. They never noticed that *Archerfish* had already put it to good use. The boat was tied up with it!

It wasn't long after that incident that an irate executive officer from another boat showed up in Dave Dimmick's office.

"One of your thieving crew stole a watertight locker right out of our superstructure," the officer charged.

"No way," Dimmick answered. "We don't need your damn locker. We already have one."

And to prove his point, he took his fuming counterpart down to the boat to show him. Sure enough, there was the locker, welded into the forward superstructure up by the escape trunk, just as Dimmick had said.

Neither man knew that the *Archerfish* crew members had gone aboard *Cutlass* in the dark of the night, removed the locker, brought it over, welded it into place, cleaned the welds, then painted it to match the superstructure of its new home. They had accomplished all that before anyone aboard *Cutlass* even knew it was missing.

Then there was the anchor chain incident. This particular scrounging expedition was not quite so successful, however.

When it came time to house the boat's anchor and chain, they were nowhere to be found. Again, they had been lost in the confusion and disarray of the last several months. Luckily, the usual reconnoitering mission to the shipyard's outside security cage turned up a beautiful refurbished chain of the proper size and length, already sandblasted, painted, and color-coded, and a submarine anchor as well, both waiting conveniently for them on pallets, ready for the taking. The crew members borrowed a forklift, did some smooth talking to get past the security guard at the gate, and loaded it aboard *Archerfish*.

Soon they were getting the blame, as usual, for lifting the chain and anchor. With innocent faces, the crew members denied everything, assuring everyone involved that the stuff was theirs. They offered to show them the items to prove it. Who could tell any different? After all, all chain and anchors look the same.

This time, though, they were caught red-handed. Welded onto the fluke of the anchor was the designation SS-477. The USS *Conger* (SS-477) got her anchor and chain back. *Archerfish* had to go out in search of more. They eventually found them and this time made certain not to get caught.

There is one more chapter to the stolen anchor story. Dave "Dutch" Holland was serving aboard *Conger* at that time. He reports that after his boat got its anchor back from the "bunch of thieves on the *311* boat," it was installed in its proper location. Shortly afterward, *Conger* was out for sea trials. It was time to go through the routine of dropping anchor. When the chain was let go, it played out smoothly, except it kept going and going and going until the anchor and the chain rested on the bottom of Delaware Bay. A tug had to come out and drag for it until it could find and recover it.

One day when *Archerfish* had loaded aboard all of the mattresses they could find, they realized they were still short seven bunks and mattresses. Mike Lintner noticed that *Cutlass* was nearby and loading out at the same time. He casually walked over to their work barge and got in line with the guys who were moving stuff from the barge to their boat. He had already diverted four skid bunks and mattresses and was carrying another when a lieutenant junior grade from *Cutlass* noticed him.

"Hey! You're an *Archerfish* sailor. What are you doing with *Cutlass* stuff on your shoulder?" the officer called.

"I'm just helping my buddies out," Lintner answered with a straight face. "Just being a good sailor."

The officer was so impressed with Lintner's willingness to help that he ordered two of his own sailors to pitch in and give him a hand. They unknowingly helped him steal the last three bunks and mattresses they needed, carrying them right on board *Archerfish*. Lintner told them that his boat had loaned them to the *Cutlass* at the beginning of the yard period and were simply taking them back now before getting under way.

By the last few weeks of the refitting, all the other submarines in the yard set up rotating watches on both the *Archerfish*'s brows to stop any more of their stuff from finding its way to the boat. They made lists of anything coming aboard to check against items that suddenly turned up missing. Eventually, no one from *Archerfish* was allowed on any other submarine in the yard. Each boat checked yard badges and navy ID cards. If an *Archerfish* sailor needed to see someone on another boat, he had to wait on the pier until the person came out to talk to him.

No matter. The crew had somehow accomplished the impossible.

On May 5, 1960, the overhaul was pronounced complete, at a cost of $562,910. Of course, there is no way to determine what the work and equipment would have cost if a lot of it had not been creatively appropriated.

The crew was excited to finally be on their way, but there was one sad note. One of the longtime *Archerfish* sailors, Joe Snow, was transferred off the boat just before they left. Joe came aboard as part of the precommissioning crew in April 1957 and had been aboard ever since. He knew the boat as well as anyone and had worked his heart out over the last several months, just like the rest of the crew. If anyone deserved to go on the cruise, it was Joe, but he had one big strike against him. He was married. Snow had actually talked his wife into giving him a divorce with the promise to remarry her when he got back in two years, but that didn't move the brass. They were adamant about wanting only crewmembers with minimal family ties.

When the boat got under way that afternoon at 1600, they still didn't have everything they needed. For example, Roy P. "Rick the Rack" Hardin lamented that they had forgotten to get themselves a couple of chairs for the radio shack. They had to sit on apple crates en route to New London.

By the time *Archerfish* reached the mouth of the Delaware River, the boat had been "rigged for dive," and both the rigging and compensation had been double-checked in preparation for the first dive. The skipper had decided that all its dives would be green-board dives. Instead of sounding the diving alarm, commencing the dive, and shutting the openings while the ship was in the process of descending, *Archerfish* would shut the openings first, then begin to dive. All the safety indicators would be green ("Green board!") before the dive started.

When they were far enough out into the Atlantic, they made a green-board trim dive. All compartments were checked for leaks and the equipment was cycled using an extensive checklist as the boat was eased down to two hundred feet. Notes were made of the many discrepancies they found. When Captain Woods was satisfied with the results, they surfaced and headed for New London.

There was no time in their schedule for them to return to the yards. All problems had to be corrected by ship's company.

It was extremely rare for a submarine to leave the shipyard without sea trials, and just as unusual for a boat not to be able to return to correct discrepancies. No one knows of any other instance, either, in which BuShips restricted a boat's dive depth rather than fix the weak spots in the submarine's pressure hull.

Rumor has it that soon after *Archerfish*'s departure from Philadelphia, one of the boats in the shipyard sent a priority message to the submarine base in New London. Its contents were supposedly quite straightforward: "Lock up your wives and daughters and all your loose equipment. Kenny Woods and his sixty thieves are heading your way!"

LAST CHANCE

Hoyt Weathers was not sure what he had gotten himself into. He was a marine geophysicist with the U.S. Naval Hydrographic Office, and one of six civilian "hydros" assigned to ride with *Archerfish* up from Philadelphia to New London to make sure the compartment where the equipment was installed was satisfactory. One of the other scientists aboard for the cruise was Hoyt Salisbury. They were the only two Hoyts on the boat.

The day Weathers reported aboard, he noticed workmen welding a steel patch in place over a hole in the boat's hull. He learned that there had been an accident the day before. Someone had been sandblasting above the waterline, getting the hull ready for painting. When the air compressor was shut off at the end of the shift, the workman forgot to shut off the air-supply valve to his nozzle and simply laid it down and left. When the compressor was fired up again for the next shift, the nozzle blasted a hole in the hull before anyone noticed it.

Weathers had never been in a submarine during a dive before. This one, with a patched hole in her side, dived twice on her trip up the coast.

He soon learned that the patch would hold just fine and he had nothing to fear in that regard. He discovered other problems. The sensitive scientific devices were stored in a small compartment that could only be accessed through a deck hatch in the control room passageway, directly below the radio shack. The room tended to sweat when the boat was in colder waters. When not in use, the delicate, highly sophisticated equipment had to be covered with sheets of plastic to keep it from being damaged by the condensation.

Archerfish arrived at New London on Sunday morning, May 8. This became their nominal home port as long as they operated in the Atlantic, and they became part of Submarine Development Group Two. Just after 0930, they moored port side to the south of Pier 9. There was quite a greeting party waiting for them. That was very unusual. It looked as if every staff officer from the base was there.

The brow went across, and the official party came aboard. Everyone was smiling, saluting, shaking hands, doing all the things officers do when they get together in public. It wasn't long, though, before the lecture began. The crew was forewarned that the larceny that had occurred back in Philadelphia would not be tolerated here. All the shops on the base and all the vessels in port had been alerted and were keeping their eyes on anyone from *Archerfish*.

While the warnings were being delivered on the forward deck, the electricians were jumping back and forth from the after deck to the tank tops to the pier to take on shore power, as was the norm when berthing. But there were some extra sailors hopping off the boat as well, and they ventured a bit farther. They headed on across the pier, down onto the tank tops of the boat tied up on the opposite side, and up onto her after deck. The enginemen were out of rags, and their mission was to "acquire" the several bales that rested near the other boat's after engine room hatch. They quickly formed a line of "white hats" across the pier, moving the bales of rags to their new home.

The few sailors who were topside on the other boat were so intent on what was taking place on the forward deck of the *Archerfish* that they never noticed what was going on over their shoulders. The official greeting party was so busy telling the *Archerfish* crew what not to do that they didn't realize they were already doing it.

The stay in New London was expected to be ten days. No one at the base really anticipated having the boat ready for an extended cruise in that short time. There was still plenty to do. Woods and his crew also avoided telling anyone that there had been problems with one of the two working engines on the trip up from the Philadelphia Naval Shipyard.

"If they thought we were in bad shape now, they should have seen us a few weeks before, back in Philly," Miles Graham says. "We were not authorized to draw any spare parts, not even those necessary to get our engines running. It was starting to sound as if we were in a different navy than those other boats around us."

They would have to once again rely on ingenuity. The base was only willing to give them fuel, lube oil, and stores, as they knew *Archerfish* couldn't leave without those items. And the general implied sentiment was that everyone at the base wanted *Archerfish* to leave as soon as possible.

Lubricating oil was a necessity for sure. Without it, a boat was dead in the water. Finding a way to carry enough aboard for *Archerfish's* lengthy cruise had posed a knotty problem. The solution was ingenious. Someone came up with the idea of converting torpedo tubes seven and eight to bulk lube oil storage. They carried no torpedoes anymore, and the space inside the tubes was being wasted. Prior to loading, the jack nuts on each tube were jammed shut to keep the outer doors securely on their seats. Each tube held 410 gallons of oil.

There were two ways to get the oil into the tubes. The best was to use the hose that was specially made to run from the vent pipe on top of number five lube oil storage tank to the back roller connection to the torpedo tube. The enginemen intentionally overfilled number five, forcing the oil through the hose into the tube. When the tube was full, the hose was removed and stored until the oil was needed. At that time, the torpedoman put pressure into the tube, forcing the oil through the hose and back into the normal lube oil system.

The other way to fill the tubes was manually from fifty-five-gallon drums. In this method, a drum cradle was placed on deck near the after room hatch, and the hose was connected to a large funnel under the cradle. The enginemen had to manually put the drums on the cradle, and then the oil would gravity-feed into the tubes. This method took longer and was very labor intensive.

The sailors who had used those torpedo tubes to hurl weapons at the Japanese could have never dreamed they would one day be used as oil storage tanks. They would have certainly admired the ingenuity of their brother submarine sailors, though. That resourcefulness is one trait that has never changed in the Silent Service.

Shortly after their arrival in New London, William Fong from the Hydrographic Office came down to check on the placement of the equipment on *Archerfish* and meet with Captain Woods. There were only two or three pieces of this highly specialized gear in the world, and be wanted to make certain it was being loaded and installed properly. As he walked down the pier to where *Archerfish* was moored, he spotted one of the large crates he knew contained the fragile, carefully calibrated equipment. The word SENSITIVE was painted in large letters on the crate's sides along with bold arrows and the command THIS SIDE UP! Of course, the arrows pointed toward the pier, and all the words were upside down.

Everyone aboard knew New London was their last chance to get items they needed or to take care of personal business. It would be seven months before they returned to the States, so many of the men drew advanced pay and headed for town. Pig Pen Henry and Turkey Neck Steck went to Mike's Tailors on Bank Street for sets of custom-tailored dress blues. Others hurried off to Ernie's or the Dolphin, two well-known Bank Street establishments that catered to submarine sailors.

The crew spent every night in the bars on Bank Street. Since *Archerfish* was the new boat in town, they had no bar to call their own, as most of the local boats did. Abie Snyder says, "We had to try them all. The one that liked us the best was the Dolphin, and it became our home. The one that liked us the least, and soon refused to let us in the door, was Ernie's."

James G. "Bush" Blackburn remembers that the crew went "a little crazy" in New London. The workload was half what it had been in the Philly yard, and they were actually granted liberty. The enginemen were only working twelve-hour days! He remembers that during their ten days in New London, 138 men went to jail. Not bad for a crew of 60.

Doc Barboza was thinking ahead. He knew the boat would be spending quite a bit of time in cold climes north of the Arctic Circle so he began taking orders for quilted thermal underwear. He collected the money and went to a sporting goods store on Bank Street where he bought the underwear. Those who didn't invest in the thermals would be very sorry before the year was out. Ted Armstrong says he still has the bottoms he so wisely bought through Barboza and uses them to this day when he goes duck hunting.

There were other priorities as well during those ten short days. Jim Blackburn was convinced by his throttleman that he needed a tattoo before they cruised away. Blackburn was guided down a dimly lit alley in a seedy part of town and led up the rickety staircase of a dilapidated old building. A crooked sign nailed to the wall outside a door proclaimed that this was the place for TATTOOS. Blackburn had never been in a tattoo parlor before and wasn't sure what to expect. The place was a mess, with a single lightbulb hanging from the ceiling and the walls papered with brightly colored drawings of everything imaginable. And some things that weren't.

Blackburn slowly circled the room, looking for something he wouldn't be ashamed to show the folks back home in Bloomingdale, Ohio. He also wanted a design that wouldn't show, even when he had on a short-sleeve shirt. Blackburn finally settled on the cartoon character, Alley Oop.

He awoke the next morning with a bloody bandage on his right arm, totally amazed that he had actually done it. It wasn't long, though, before he realized that when he wore a short-sleeve shirt, Alley Oop's feet stuck out below the sleeve.

Meanwhile, work continued and new crew members were added.

When the boat was still in Key West, all eight of the exhaust manifolds, two on each of the four main engines, were cracked and leaking water and exhaust into the engine rooms. Getting them replaced had been a priority in Philly. However, the ship's company had not had time to replace the exhaust manifolds on number-four main engine. That was completed in New London, so that by the time they got underway, all four main engines had new exhaust manifolds, both inboard and outboard.

Lieutenant Joseph D. Cummings joined the boat during this time, and he, too, had that initial reaction of "What in hell have I gotten myself into?" He had served a tour as an instructor for the Venezuelan navy and their one-submarine fleet. When his orders to *Archerfish* came, he had less than forty-eight hours to get to New London. He drove to his mother's house in Los Angeles, left his Austin-Healey, and caught a plane for the East Coast.

He was stunned when he stepped aboard *Archerfish*.

"The Venezuelans weren't much on seamanship and tactics, but they were hell on glitter," Cummings says. "It was a real shock to come from a boat where everything was paint and chrome and the topside was Simonized to a boat that, being as kind as possible, could use a lot of work."

It got worse. He was walking through the boat with Ken Woods, the commanding officer, when his heel went right through the deck in the maneuvering room. He thought the boat and its crew looked like something out of *McHale's Navy*.

"How do you like the boat?" Woods asked after the tour.

"She needs a hell of a lot of work," Cummings answered honestly. He doesn't think Woods ever forgave him for his blunt but accurate assessment.

The very next day, Cummings was hit up for $100 for a party the *Archerfish*'s seven-man wardroom was throwing for "every submarine officer on the East Coast," in honor of their impending cruise. Before that event, he and some of the other *Archerfish* officers attended another party, and Cummings got a good idea of the sort of individuals with whom he would be spending the next little while.

They attended ComSubLant's reception at the officers' club on the base in honor of the officers from the USS *Triton* (SSRN-586). *Triton* had recently returned from a record-setting eighty-day trip around the world. The nuclear boat had stayed submerged for the entire time, except for broaching briefly to remove an ill crewman to a helicopter. Her skipper, Commander Ned Beach (who wrote the classic book on the Silent Service, *Run Silent, Run Deep*), had just come from the White House, where he had received the Legion of Merit from President Dwight D. Eisenhower. The newspapers and television were playing the amazing feat to the maximum, telling the world about the submarine that had circumnavigated the world, staying submerged all the way. Except for the one time they partially surfaced for the helicopter, of course.

The *Archerfish* officers were at the O club that night, arranging for their own party, and apparently felt the *Triton* guys were getting a little too full of themselves. During the evening, *Archerfish* executive officer David Dimmick, Joe Cummings, David "Duke" Durgin, and some of the others mingled with the guests at the *Triton* reception and proceeded to make themselves at home.

Dimmick had been walking around all evening with a very conspicuous shoebox under his arm. He changed the subject anytime anyone asked what was inside it. Finally, he boldly walked up to the front of the room, took a position behind the podium as if he belonged there, and switched on the microphone.

"Ladies and gentlemen, if I may have your attention," he began. The room quieted and looked his way. "First, let me commend the officers and crew of the *Triton*. We all honor you for your excellent display of seamanship." There was polite applause among those assembled. Dimmick went on. "It is quite a feat, putting a helicopter party on the deck of a submarine and off-loading a man, all while remaining submerged."

There was more applause but several of the attendees looked at each other, a puzzled expression on their faces. Dimmick was just getting warmed up.

"We must also salute the *Archerfish*, about to embark on an 880-day, around-the-world submerged cruise. And she will only broach to go into ports for liberty."

Now the crowd was really confused. Dimmick held up the shoebox for all to see and continued his speech.

"To insure that President Eisenhower will not have problems with getting us our awards when the time comes, and in order to spare the president the inconvenience of having to fly all of us to the White House for the ceremony, I have here enough Legion of Merit awards for every member of our crew. We can award them to ourselves as appropriate!"

The crowd did not know how to react. A livid Captain Ned Beach did. He shoved Dimmick aside and took his place behind the microphone.

"All *Archerfish* officers are to leave this party immediately," he announced.

The boat's own wardroom party went on as scheduled the night before *Archerfish* got under way. Sure enough, submarine officers had shown up from all over the East Coast, and the party was one to remember. However, about ten PM, the manager of the officers' club told David Dimmick that his men and their invited guests had already finished off all the food and drinks they had paid for in advance. The exec began circulating, telling everyone the party was over. Captain Woods intervened.

"How much will it cost to go another hour?" he asked the club manager. The man gave the skipper a figure. "Okay, just bill it to me."

He went right along behind Dimmick telling everyone that the event was still open. The party went on until at least midnight.

"New London never seemed like a home port to me," Joe Cummings says. "We were treated as if we were a pirate ship, a vessel that was only tolerated because we were needed for an important mission, that we were not wanted around nice people."

Cummings remembers that, on the day they left New London, only the four sailors who had been transferred off the boat at the last minute (Jim McDermott, Jim Hughes, Bill Pickens, and Dick Stettler) and the squadron duty officer were there to see them off on the longest continuous cruise in submarine history. The last thing the division commander told Captain Woods prior to sailing was "If you cause an international incident, don't come back!"

"Jumping Joe" Cummings went on to earn a significant honor later in his navy career. After leaving *Archerfish* in June 1962, he received the military's second-highest medal for bravery for his actions during an ugly incident at the naval base at Okinawa. An American sailor had apparently gone berserk, waving around a loaded pistol, threatening to kill a group of officers he had forced to line up against a wall. The deranged sailor had already fired at least one shot at them. Though he was unarmed, Cummings marched bravely up to the sailor to disarm him. The man pointed the gun at Cummings and pulled the trigger, but the cartridge jammed. Cummings grabbed him and subdued him before he could clear the pistol.

Cummings later served as commanding officer of the White Beach and Buckner Bay naval bases on Okinawa.

On May 18, 1960, at 1800, the *Archerfish* crew was mustered. For once, there were no unauthorized absences. Everyone was ready to get this cruise underway. When quarters were secured at 1811, Vern "Pappy" Bettis, the chief of the boat, gave the order to station the maneuvering watch. Captain Kenny Woods was on the bridge. Lieutenant David Dimmick, the executive officer and navigator was in the conning tower. Lieutenant Joe Cummings had the deck.

There was one long blast of the ship's whistle followed by three short ones, warning the world that *Archerfish* was under way on yet another great adventure. Phase one of Operation Sea Scan officially began at 1856 PM on the evening of the eighteenth.

The maneuvering watch was secured at 1934, and at 1936 the boat took her departure from New London, Connecticut, bound for Portsmouth, England, the namesake in the Old Country of *Archerfish*'s birthplace in New Hampshire. In accordance with ComSubDevGru Two Op Order 8-60, their course was 117 degrees east, and they were making standard speed (seventeen knots) on four main engines. Later, with the maneuvering watch secured and the regular underway watch set, the boat quieted down as everyone not on watch tried to catch up on the sleep they had lost, both in port at New London and while they were at the yard in Philadelphia.

Spirits were high on the boat that night. Almost to a man, they had signed up for this duty because they wanted to take the long cruise to exciting new ports, many of which had never seen a submarine before. Now, finally, after the months of backbreaking work, the continual scrounging for the things they needed just to exist, and the last-minute parties, they were under way.

Belowdecks, the boat was loaded like one going on a wartime patrol. Stores were skillfully placed so the crew could eat their way through them and still have variety. Every nook of the boat had food crammed into it, and the walking deck had at least one layer of cases of tinned goods covering it.

Never mind that the stills weren't operable yet and couldn't make fresh water, only one air compressor was limping along, and the number-four main engine should have been officially out of commission.

Miles Graham was topside that night when they passed the Montauk Point lightship. He was happy to be under way but depressed about all the work that still needed to be done. At least he could request parts be sent to Portsmouth, England, to be waiting for them when they arrived. By a quirk of navy regulations, a vessel at sea could get parts sent anywhere in the world to effect voyage repairs. A ship in port had to go through normal channels.

By the third day out of port, the crew was more or less adjusting to the world of artificial light and the ever-present smells: dirty bodies, greasy food, a poorly vented sanitary tank, and hot oil that sloshed in the bilge. Those who had been sick with hangovers were feeling better and ventured out, looking for food. Those prone to seasickness were feeling the effects of the increased sea state and vowing never to eat again.

During the first week at sea, there was always fresh fruit and vegetables, a variety of somewhat-fresh breads and pastries, eggs still in their shells, and real milk. After that, there was less fresh stuff. The bread got stale and the eggs began to smell "different" when they hit a hot grill. By then, any fruits and vegetables consumed came from the freezer or out of cans. Eggs were always scrambled and were dipped from a two-and-a-half-gallon can labeled For Baking Purposes Only. The crew actually looked forward to running out of store-bought bread and pastries that had been loaded aboard before they left. "Red Dog" was a good baker, and everyone looked forward to his fresh, hot bread. He did his baking at night and always tried to have a few loaves on the table next to the coffeepot, along with a big bowl of butter. That was his way of keeping the crew away from the pies that were cooling on another table for the next day's meals.

Along the way, Lieutenant Graham told the yet-to-be-named boat newspaper that over eight hundred gallons of water had been used the previous day. And he maintained that that was way too much.

The exec put out the word that he still needed one Roman Catholic and one Protestant lay leader to run the tape recorder in the crew's mess for church services on Sunday mornings. There were no volunteers.

The newspaper finally got a name on May 21. It would henceforth be called *The A-Fish-L-Blast*. "Speedy" Gonzales was the editor and Joe Cummings the wardroom representative (or censor, according to Gonzales). To this day, the newsletter published for former crew members of the *Archerfish* still bears that name and is on volume forty-two as of this writing.

One night during the transit, chili and rice were on the menu for the evening meal. Abie Snyder was working on preparing the dish when he dug deeply into the rice bin with a large metal scoop. He heard the unmistakable crunch of breaking glass. There was obviously something else stored in the bin besides rice.

Red Dog Balthrop, the boat's leading cook, had a strong predilection for Scotch and some ingenious places for hiding it. Chain Fall Farrell knew the cook had quality booze hidden on the boat, but he could never find it. One night, he walked past the galley and caught Balthrop taking a big swig of "vinegar." Farrell watched as he screwed the top back on the vinegar bottle and placed it on the shelf above the sink, being very careful to set it to the left of another bottle of vinegar.

So that was it! He kept his Scotch right there in plain view, the last place anyone would expect. Balthrop figured right-handed cooks would always grab the other bottle when adding vinegar to dishes. One day, though, a left-hander seasoned the spinach with the wrong bottle. That's when Balthrop began burying the bottle in the rice bin.

Red Dog had a rather thin skin for a submarine cook. If anyone complained about the food, he promptly threw it all away. If someone eating on first call said anything about lumpy mashed potatoes, Balthrop came flying out of the galley, grabbed the bowls of potatoes off the tables, and threw them in the garbage. Then he could be heard in the galley, scraping all the other potatoes out of the big mixing bowl and throwing them away as well. Second- and third-call diners got none of the lumpy potatoes unless they wanted to dig them out of the garbage.

On May 28, the word was passed: "Up all bunks; clean up ship in preparation for entering port."

Portsmouth, England, waited just over the horizon, and farther ahead were Norway, Scotland, Greenland, the Arctic Circle, Nova Scotia, Ireland, and more firsts than any other submarine in naval history. Over the next seven months, *Archerfish* crossed the Atlantic four times, made sixteen crossings of the Arctic Circle, and was the first submarine to cruise in Hudson Bay and Foxe Basin.

It should come as no surprise that she did all this in fine style, doing her crucial job all the way, and that everyone aboard had one hell of a good time in the process.

17

AVA AND ICEBERGS

WITH the approval of the wardroom, the sailors aboard *Archerfish* had their first anchor pool of Operation Sea Scan sold out well before they arrived in Portsmouth, England. Sixty chances were sold, one for each minute in the hour. The winner would be the one who held the exact minute when the first line was made fast to the pier or when the anchor was dropped. He got $40. The men who held the minutes on each side of him got $10 each.

David Dimmick admitted they almost steamed right on past the entrance to Portsmouth harbor. The quartermasters either missed the entrance or didn't recognize it. Dimmick, who was the navigator, just happened to step up into the conning tower and take a look out the scope in time to see the gateway to Portsmouth quickly sliding past. He gave the emphatic order to make a ninety-degree turn but never mentioned the desperate course change to the skipper. He simply reported the new heading to Woods as if nothing had happened.

Just after 0830 on May 29, 1960, they moored port side to Berth 3 at HMS *Dolphin*, the support and training facility for the British submarine service. Representatives of the famous men's tailors, Alexander's of London, were waiting on the dock and came aboard to take orders for custom-made clothing. Dimmick ordered a Harris tweed jacket for $22.50 and still had it in his closet when he passed away in 2000.

Miles Graham, the engineer, was pleasantly surprised to see that all the spare parts they had requested had arrived and were waiting for them. With the help of the British repair shops, they went right to work to fix the equipment that was still out of service. While the rest of the wardroom headed for the station and the train to London, Graham remained on board and made certain that the enginemen and electricians in the duty sections had what they needed to get the repairs completed before the boat sailed.

That afternoon several members of the crew, decked out in their crackerjack dress blue uniforms, were sitting in a local pub adjusting to the British preference for warm beer. They paused to look at a woman who came up to Ed "Fudd" Blackford and put her hand on the back of his jumper. She asked, "Do you mind if I touch your dickey, sailor?" Ed got up, turned toward her with a big grin, and yanked down the flap on his thirteen-button pants so she could get to it.

That is when they found out that the dickey she was referring to was the flap on the back of a sailor's jumper. In Britain, civilians considered it good luck to touch one. An embarrassed Fudd buttoned up, backed up, and drank up! The rest of his shipmates had a good laugh at his expense.

After the usual adventurous night on the town, Ken Henry and Dale Ness were running late getting to the train station in London to head back to the boat. To make matters worse, they had trouble rounding up a taxi. They happened on a trash crew that was busy emptying the dustbins in the area. The two sailors offered to help them dump the trash and to give them a few hits off their bottles of booze in exchange for a ride to the station. Their offer was accepted.

The men made quite a sight, two American sailors in dress blues hanging on to the back of a garbage truck, being delivered to the drop-off zone at the Central London–Waterloo Station.

When they got there, they soon spotted their skipper, who was attracting his own share of attention. When he had had a bit to drink, Captain Woods liked to do his patented one-legged dance. He stood on one leg and squatted down with the other leg straight out in front of him, then extended both arms to the sides for balance. Next he threw back his head and placed a highball glass filled with booze on his forehead. While singing a decent rendition of "The Muffin Man," he stood up, still using only the one leg, switched to the other foot, and crouched back down, all the while keeping the whiskey glass in place on his forehead and singing a tuneful version of the song.

The crowd loved it. Of course, Woods was in his dress blues as well, with two-and-a-half gold stripes on each sleeve, obviously a naval officer.

"That's our skipper!" Ness proudly proclaimed.

They got back to the boat just in time for Ness to get to work fixing breakfast. He hid his half-empty bottle of Johnny Walker in the rice bin and went to work. The pancake batter was a little stiff, and he had used all the milk that had been broken out. He didn't relish, in his condition, having to climb down into the chill box for more. While he pondered the predicament, he pulled his bottle from the rice bin and took a slug. That's when inspiration hit him. He poured enough whiskey into the batter to make it the right consistency, cooked the pancakes up, and sent them off to the wardroom. He later got word that Captain Woods instructed the steward, "Tell that cook these are the best damn pancakes I ever had!"

A few nights later, some of the crew were back in London and ended up in a bar called Sabrina's. During the evening, Larry Dachenhausen and Ken Henry were standing at the bar when a very attractive woman approached them. She took considerable interest in Henry's appearance.

"Why do you have a beard and an earring?" she asked him.

"None of your business," Henry replied in his usual direct manner.

The attractive woman turned and went back to her table in a huff. A barmaid came running over, a look of panic on her face.

"Don't you know who that was?" she asked.

"Don't know and don't care," she was told.

"That was Ava Gardner!"

Henry marched right over to her table to determine if the barmaid was telling the truth. He asked for identification to prove she was who she was supposed to be. After some coaxing, the woman produced her driver's license and even signed her name on a cocktail napkin. Henry mumbled something to the effect of "Okay, I guess you are." He stuffed the napkin in his jumper pocket. As he started to turn away, the woman asked, "So what's the reason for the beard and earring?"

By now the guy who had been sitting at the table with her was getting irritated. She told him to shut up, told Henry to sit down, and called for a couple of beers, one for her and one for Henry. She paid for the beer and Henry told her some sea stories.

A couple of beers and several sea stories later, she suggested they get out of Sabrina's. Henry readily agreed.

They left, abandoning the man she had come in with but impressing the hell out of the *Archerfish* sailors who remained behind. Gardner and Henry grabbed a cab and she took him to a very dark club where all the other patrons and the help were black. The music "wasn't country" and was too loud for Henry, but he stayed long enough for a couple more beers, at her expense. She wanted to stay longer and tried to convince Henry to remain with her, but he was ready to go.

Henry kept the cocktail napkin with the autograph on it for a long time as a reminder of his night on the town with one of the most famous, most glamorous motion picture stars of all time and the former wife of Mickey Rooney, Artie Shaw, and Frank Sinatra.

Repairs were completed on *Archerfish*, and they got under way from Portsmouth on the evening of June 1. Donald E. "Whitey" Englert was on lookout watch as they transited Dover Strait. Captain Woods came up on the bridge just as the famous white cliffs came into view off the port bow. The skipper immediately broke into a fair rendition of the song about bluebirds over the white cliffs of Dover. Englert had never before heard a submarine captain singing on the bridge. Kenny Woods was that kind of skipper.

They made their way out of the busy English Channel and into the chop of the North Sea. They passed through the Fair Isle Passage between the Orkney and Shetland Islands on the June 3 and things became much calmer. Once into the North Atlantic, the skies cleared and the seas were markedly smoother. They took a northwesterly tack, toward the southern tip of Greenland.

Hoyt Weathers was anxious to begin taking his measurements, but they had a way to go first. The crew seemed to him to be loose, at ease, and an all-round fun bunch. One day Weathers was strolling through the boat when he came upon two sailors sitting on the engine room deck between the bench lockers, the huge Fairbanks-Morse diesel engines pounding along around them. He couldn't believe what they were doing. The two roughneck sailors were sprawled there, cross-legged on the deck facing each other, fiercely engaged in a game of jacks, the children's game.

There were a couple of close encounters with Soviet vessels along the way to their initial survey run. With all the fun they had had in London, it was possible for the crew to forget for a moment that these were especially chilly times in the cold war. Gary Powers and his U-2 spy plane had been shot down over Russia only a month before, and international nervousness was at a peak. *Archerfish* carefully steered clear of the Russian ships and steamed on toward the point where her vital work would begin.

They crossed the Arctic Circle at longitude 7 degrees 52 minutes west. The air temperature was thirty-six degrees. Speedy Gonzales noted that there was lots of talk around the boat of warm, balmy Havana about then.

This was a tough climate for a boat and crew that had spent most of their lives in tropical waters. Someone had discovered that the bundles of rags they had "acquired" back in New London contained complete articles of clothing. It wasn't unusual to see someone walking about the boat wearing an ill-fitting old shirt or even a dress. Anything to keep warm.

About then, the enginemen and electricians began wearing foul-weather jackets when they were on watch in the engine rooms and maneuvering room. The only heat in the after torpedo room was a pair of antique navy-issue floor-standing four-kilowatt electric heaters. "Heater" was a misnomer. They put out very little heat. Almost everyone aboard was now wearing the thermal underwear bought on Bank Street in New London.

Ken Henry and Jim Blackburn were on watch one day in the after engine room when a continuous, rhythmic clanking noise coming from the forward engine room finally got the best of them. When Henry went to investigate, he found Joe Osier sitting on the bench locker next to number-two main engine. He held a two-shilling coin in one hand and a soupspoon in the other and was methodically turning the coin between his fingers as he continually struck its edge with the spoon. That was the source of the irritating, metallic "Clank! Clank! Clank!"

"What are you doing?" Henry asked.

"Making a ring," Osier answered, without breaking rhythm.

Henry rolled his eyes and went back to the book he had been reading.

Several hours later, Greasy Joe showed his project to the guys. They couldn't believe it. The coin was getting thinner and flatter on the edge, taking on the appearance of a wedding band. By halfway through the next watch, Joe had the coin beaten down to the size he wanted. He drilled out the middle and used a rat-tail file to enlarge the opening until he had a perfectly fitting ring. On one side, the words REGINA + ELIZABETH XII X DEI X - GRATIA X were clearly visible. On the other, FID : DEF : 1959 TWO SHILLINGS was readable. It was an impressive ring. Over the next few days, the guys on watch in the after engine room drove the men in the maneuvering room crazy as they clanked away, working on their own two-shilling rings.

On June 7, something new showed up on the boat's radar. It was the polar ice field, 8,000 yards ahead. Soon they could clearly see the pieces of floating ice and growlers, the small icebergs. They proceeded to steam back and forth across the Greenland Sea for the next week and a half, taking their gravity readings and marveling at the ice and the mirror-calm sea. At one point, they passed within 7,000 yards of Jan Mayen Island and got a glimpse of their first glacier.

The boat had to submerge in order to take readings for the first time on June 8. The sea had been so calm that they had completed over two thousand miles of readings on the surface. Now the decision to use a submarine as a platform for this sort of delicate survey work would really be validated.

On the dive, Thomas McCormick grabbed the lanyard to shut the upper hatch before the cold seawater could pour in. It was the first time he had ever done this job, and when he slammed the lid, it bounced back open and the dogs caught it, not allowing it to fully close.

That was serious business.

Shelby Dean "Ty Ty" Tygart was the quartermaster of the watch and was waiting at the bottom of the ladder to dog the hatch. He sprang up the ladder in one big hurry, yelling, "Open hatch!" at the top of his lungs, notifying the conning officer and control room. The command "Emergency surface!" sounded throughout the boat as "Ty Ty" tried to clear the hatch.

From below them, someone in the control room yelled, "Bye, bye, suckers!" and slammed the lower hatch shut, effectively sealing them in the conning tower.

Tygart quickly got the hatch dogs clear and the hatch seated and secured, even before the boat was back on the surface. It was a close call, but neither man was hurt. The quick warning and emergency surface even kept them from getting a cold shower of icy seawater.

On June 12, a little over a week before summer officially began for most parts of the northern hemisphere, the air temperature around *Archerfish* was twenty-seven degrees. They steamed within 877 miles of the north pole that day and within a thousand yards of the polar ice pack. Still having to submerge to take their readings every sixty miles, they next aimed southward for Hammerfest, Norway, a city that claimed to be the northernmost municipality in the world. Seas were rough along the route, so rough that George Hughes, who was on lookout watch, banged his head hard enough that he needed stitches to close the gash.

They had been out of London only two weeks, but everyone was ready for the three-day stopover in Hammerfest. They had heard about the beauty of the town and the friendliness of its people. However, they would quickly learn that the fine folks of Norway were a bit wary about the presence there of an American vessel.

The weather got worse as they drew close to the Norwegian mainland. It was clear they were going to be late arriving. A message was radioed to the harbor pilot in Hammerfest, telling him that they would be six to eight hours overdue. The message came too late. The pilot had already left port to come out to meet them. He and a helper rowed out to the mouth of Hammerfest's harbor in a tiny dory and waited there for hours in the rolling seas until *Archerfish* showed up. David Dimmick reported that the pilot never complained once about his cold, wet, and stormy wait for the overdue submarine.

They arrived from the north, entered port just before midnight on Tuesday, June 14, and moored starboard side to the north of Quay 3. *Archerfish* was the first submarine to steam into Hammerfest since *Tusk* had been there in August 1949, over a decade earlier. That visit by an American submarine had been a far from joyous occasion. *Tusk* had brought to safety the survivors of the *Cochino* after a fatal battery fire and explosion caused the loss of the boat.

Red Dog Balthrop, *Archerfish*'s leading commissaryman, had been aboard *Cochino* the day of the fire. He was awarded the Silver Lifesaving Medal for his heroic actions during the daring rescue of the seventy-six survivors.

It was already policy on Operation Sea Scan that liberty began as soon as possible after mooring. Because the sun was shining dimly through the clouds, no one seemed to notice or care that it was three AM local time when the crew of *Archerfish* ran across the brow, ready to see the sights of this far northern port of call. Of course, the streets were deserted, and all the establishments were closed for the night. Still, Hammerfest was a beautiful little town, an immaculately clean fishing village that climbed up the nearby mountains picturesquely from the harbor. Though it was summer, the mountains were covered with snow, and a clear, cold stream ran down the middle of town. Everyone was amazed at how new and freshly painted everything in Hammerfest seemed, even though the town had been around for centuries.

The sailors later learned why the place appeared to be so new. The Germans had occupied the area during World War II. When they left, they demolished the entire town, destroying every single building except one, a stone chapel that stood in the middle of a cemetery. Everything else had been rebuilt in the decade after the war ended. The quaint little town had paid a heavy toll to war.

Suffice it to say that the *Archerfish* crew located an all-night bar in the basement of a closed lounge and soon joined some of the locals and a few Russian fishermen who happened to be there. Later in the day, when the rest of the town awoke, an official welcoming party took some of the officers on a tour. They visited a hospital, municipal buildings, and the one thing the town was most proud of, its fish processing plant. There was one small problem there, though. When they entered the plant, the doorway was decorated with a Norwegian flag and a Soviet flag. One of the officers mentioned it to their hosts and when they came back out after the tour, the Stars and Stripes had replaced the Soviet flag.

"We got our days mixed up," the tour guide told them apologetically. "The Soviet delegation is coming tomorrow."

The townspeople of Hammerfest seemed abnormally curious about the submarine. Many of them hung around the pier all the time *Archerfish* was tied up there, apparently trying to get a look down the boat's hatches to see what was below. Everyone in town seemed friendly enough, but there still remained a noticeable bit of aloofness that was hard to figure. It may or may not have been the typical Scandinavian reserve. Still, *Archerfish* was only scheduled to be there a few days, so no one worried much about it. It would be near the end of their visit before the crew learned why the Norwegians were a bit standoffish and so nosy.

Hoyt Weathers, one of the hydrographic scientists aboard, secured his equipment one morning, changed into clothes that didn't smell too heavily of diesel fuel, and went into town for breakfast. He was enjoying a good meal at a pretty little café when one of the locals, a man, walked right over, asked permission to sit down at his table, and immediately started a conversation.

Maybe the folks here are friendly after all, Weathers thought.

The man volunteered that he was a toy salesman but didn't tell the American much about his work. Instead, he was quite interested in what Weathers did for a living. Of course, the scientist was not going to tell him anything at all about why he was crisscrossing the North Atlantic, and he certainly was not going to give even the slightest hint about his mission aboard *Archerfish*.

"Oh, I'm just a tourist," Weathers said. The man laughed heartily, in obvious disbelief. "What's the matter? Don't you get tourists in Hammerfest?" Weathers asked.

"Yes, but not by submarine!" the toy salesman said, and then he laughed some more.

The local fire chief later shared with Weathers that the man who enjoyed breakfast with Weathers that morning was a known Communist sympathizer.

Dale Ness and some of the sailors were sitting around a table at a bar one day, getting to know some of the local merchant seamen. One of them, noticing that his surname was Scandinavian, asked Ness if he had any relatives in the area.

"I think I have an uncle somewhere in Norway," he answered. "I have no idea where he might be, though.

"There is a 'Conrad Ness' that lives out on an island just up the way," the seaman told him.

"Seems like my uncle's name was Conrad," Ness said. But what were the odds his uncle lived just outside Hammerfest?

The seaman went to a phone and called Conrad Ness. Sure enough, it was Nasty's uncle. He came in to town, picked up Ness, and took him back to meet his aunt and cousin and served him dinner.

Conrad also shared with his nephew the reason why the townspeople had been so standoffish to the *Archerfish* crew. The rumor around Hammerfest had been that this visiting American submarine was on its way to retaliate against the Russians for shooting down Gary Powers and the U-2 spy plane. The people on the pier, trying to get a look down *Archerfish*'s hatches, were sure they would see nuclear missiles down there.

There was good reason for their concern. Powers's final flight would have landed at the once-secret base at Bodo, Norway. The Norwegians in general and the citizens of Hammerfest in particular, people who still had vivid memories of the awful consequences of armed conflict, were convinced that a shooting war was inevitable between the Russians and the United States, and they were sure the conflagration would erupt right there in their country, with the Norwegians caught in the crossfire.

Archerfish actually left Hammerfest early. A Soviet ship was due to arrive, and the Americans wanted no confrontation. They took on 24,500 gallons of fuel, even though they had not planned on refueling in Hammerfest. They had used more diesel than they had anticipated while trying to get ahead of schedule and complete the first two weeks of surveying. Thankfully, the paperwork needed to get that amount of fuel on short notice was in order, and the refueling went smoothly.

The weather was clear and calm as they left the harbor, steaming past the pastel-colored houses on the shore. Then there was nothing but bleak mountains, eerily illuminated by the perpetual sun. They headed south, crossed the Arctic Circle on June 20, surveyed points 42 though 47, and then aimed the sub's nose for Iceland.

Archerfish was doing more than its gravity studies during this time.

The stealth of a submarine is significantly compromised when it is not submerged. At the same time, the requirement for a shore-based submarine fleet commander to be able to issue orders to or communicate with his assets has always been crucial. There is a problem in reconciling those two facts.

Radio waves do not penetrate water well. When the submarine is submerged, the seawater grounds out the antennae. That renders them useless and requires the submarine to surface to receive very low frequency (VLF) transmissions.

For several weeks, *Archerfish* had been testing receipt of VLF messages using an experimental long, floating-wire antenna. In order to "string the wire," it was necessary for a couple of lookouts to uncoil the antenna from its stowed position on the cigarette deck and toss it over the side. Then the boat submerged and tried to receive radio messages at various depths. The floating wire was buoyed up by a rubber fishing float that caused it to stream in a more vertical direction, with the end of the antenna on the surface. When the test was complete, the boat surfaced and the lookouts had to haul the wire out of the icy water and back aboard using the time-honored method of hand-over-hand retrieval. Next, the one-inch-diameter coaxial cable was coiled on the cigarette deck and secured in place with marline. Only then could the lookouts mount the shears to man their assigned positions.

It was difficult for the lookouts and the quartermasters who helped them secure the wire to the deck to convince themselves that what they were doing was a proving ground for the future mainstay of communications for the Submarine Service. It was even harder for them to see the value of their testing when the weather was lousy.

However, from these experiments conducted by *Archerfish* and other boats came the successful floating wire antenna. It consists of a radio antenna encapsulated in a watertight, rubberlike material that floats on water. The theory sounds simple enough. A submarine hovers at a given depth, allows the antenna to float to the surface, and is able to communicate. However, this device remains a nemesis to this day. If the submarine builds up too much speed while the antenna is deployed, the wire is dragged below the surface and can even "sing" like a banjo string. That makes it easy for an enemy submarine to detect the boat's presence on their sonar. There is also the worry about turning the boat too sharply and cutting the wire with the submarine's propeller. The oceans are resplendent with such "seagull perches" provided by submarines of many nations.

On this leg of the boat's cruise, a close brush with a friendly nation would almost set off a major international incident, the kind Kenny Woods and his crew had been specifically warned about when they left the States. While taking measurements, *Archerfish* ventured too close to what appeared to be a deserted corner of Iceland. They were getting especially good readings on their current heading and did not want to change course, even though they were getting extremely close to the coast of Iceland. Suddenly a couple of patrol boats appeared from an undetected harbor. They were bow-on with a rapidly decreasing range when they began ominously flashing a challenge message. The patrol boats were clearly nervous about this submarine and what it was doing so close to their island nation. The international situation at the time had everyone on edge. That included even those nations that were historically allied with the United States.

Captain Woods did not want to tarry and have to explain his mission to these guys. Or risk that the approaching warships might shoot and ask questions later.

"Clearly we're outgunned," he announced to those on the bridge with him. They carried only a few M-1 rifles, some .45-caliber pistols, and several Thompson submachine guns. Nothing else. "Let's leave."

That's exactly what they did.

The folks in the Hydrographic Office were delighted with the measurements the close encounter with Iceland produced. However, the duty officer at the State Department back in Washington was not quite so pleased. He was awakened from a sound nap to be told that a U.S. submarine had violated Icelandic territorial waters.

Nothing came of the incident, but the next harrowing encounter *Archerfish* had with a friendly power gave some of the crew members a much worse fright.

It was still dark on the morning of June 30 when *Archerfish* surfaced after taking a series of readings north of Scotland. As usual, the lookouts were relaxed in the shears, facing forward. It was their habit to look ahead of the boat, watching for floating obstructions in their path, unlike wartime, when they had to also be concerned about anything that might come at them from any direction. Suddenly, with an awful roar, an airplane swooped down on them from behind, bellowing at them from out of nowhere. The plane was low enough to almost nip off the top-most parts of the submarine's shears. It was flying with no lights, obviously intent on doing something destructive.

As it passed directly over the boat from stern to bow, the airplane illuminated *Archerfish* and dropped what thankfully turned out to be two ten-pound practice bombs, one on each side of the submarine.

Mike Giambattista was the officer of the deck, and just about the time he yelled for everyone to hit the deck, the parachute flares opened and drifted down. The two objects exploded but seemed to be relatively weak, not like a real shell's blast would have been.

Captain Woods and his crew soon learned that they had surfaced right in the middle of a NATO exercise. The attacking plane had been from the Royal Air Force. *Archerfish* had been mistaken for *Nautilus*, which was participating in the exercise. The plane's crew thought they had caught her on the surface and "bombed" her.

For the *Archerfish* crew it was still a frightening experience.

The first order of the day upon their arrival in Bergen, Norway—in addition to liberty, of course—was taking care of refueling. This time they were scheduled to take on diesel, and it was supposed to have been pre-arranged. Mike Giambattista was in charge of making certain that bit of business went off without a hitch, just as it had in Hammerfest. The naval attaché's office in Oslo assured him all he had to do was contact the Esso bunker depot in Bergen and all would be taken care of.

The fueling went off without a hitch. While they were pumping the diesel fuel, Giambattista hurried to get his shoes spit-shined, his teeth brushed, and his dress blues on. He was in a hurry to get ashore for liberty.

He was almost ready to go when the topside watch called down to tell him there was a big Norwegian guy who spoke practically no English up there, demanding to see someone in charge about the 90,500 gallons of fuel that was now inside *Archerfish*'s tanks. It took lots of gesturing and pointing, but Giambattista finally deduced that the Norwegian was demanding payment for the fuel they had taken on. Giambattista tried to assure the man that it had been paid for already. He produced all the documentation he had, the same paperwork that had secured plenty of fuel without an argument several weeks before in Hammerfest.

No dice. The man wanted payment, and he wanted it immediately.

Giambattista checked the sky. Even in a place where the sun didn't set this time of year, it was still obvious to him that the hour was growing late. A new port of call awaited his inspection. He didn't have time to stand here and argue with this low-level bureaucrat.

In desperation, he reached into his pocket, pulled out his wallet, and took out his personal Esso gas credit card from back in the States. To his astonishment, the man smiled broadly as he took the card. He wrote all the information on his clipboard and pointed to the signature line. Giambattista signed without hesitation. He figured by the time the charge caught up with him, the mess would all be worked out anyway.

Giambattista maintains he never heard from Esso about the day he filled up a U.S. submarine and charged 90,500 gallons of diesel fuel on his personal gas credit card.

The crew's favorite spot in Bergen quickly became the Floyen Restaurant, atop Mount Floyen, which is still in business today. The only way to reach the place was by way of an inclined railway, called a funicular. The dining room offered a stunning panoramic view of the city, and the food was very good. Of course, it helped that there was also a bar, music, and dancing.

There were other sights to see as well. One highlight was a visit to the lakeside home of the famous composer Edvard Grieg. Ken Henry bought a book of postcards in the gift shop on the premises and mailed them to his old high school music teacher back in Maryland. Henry had been a reluctant student in the man's class. The teacher had made it a point to tell the youngster often, usually in front of the entire class, how lazy he was and that he would never amount to anything in life. That was humiliation Henry had never forgotten. He also remembered that the music teacher had idolized Grieg and even had a portrait of the composer in his classroom.

Henry inscribed a pointed note on the cards he sent the teacher. "I may never amount to anything, but at least I am here and you are there," he wrote, and signed his name. He never got a reply.

Three ex-German, World War II-vintage, Type VII-C U-boats were moored in Bergen at the time *Archerfish* was there. They were all operating in the Norwegian navy. Among them was KNM *Kaura* (S-309), which had originally been *U-995*. All three of the former U-boats have long since been decommissioned, but *U-995* was returned to Germany, the last remaining U-boat of its type in the world. It is open to the public and on display at the Submarine Memorial in Kiel, Germany. The other two boats in Bergen at this time were KNM *Kya* (S-307), originally *U-926*, and KNM *Kinn* (S-308), originally *U-1202*.

Everyone from *Archerfish* enjoyed his brief stay in Bergen. The food, beer, and scenery were all spectacular. However, there was still the cold attitude of the locals toward anyone from America. The fallout from the U-2 incident lingered. That's not to say, though, that at least one crew member didn't find himself a very friendly Norwegian.

When Pappy Bettis mustered the crew at quarters at 1730 on July 5, one man was missing. It was time to get under way, but Torpedoman First Class John Sullivan had failed to return from liberty. Everyone who could be spared was sent into town on Shore Patrol to look for him, but after two hours, no trace was found. Ken Woods waited as long as he could, but by 2140 he knew he couldn't postpone their departure any longer. The exec had cut a set of orders for Sullivan to report to the boat in Scotland. He sent Jim Moran, the yeoman, to the local chief of police with the orders and some money and hoped for the best. Finally, they were ready for sea, and Woods gave the okay to send the departure message, just minutes inside the two-hour window during which they were scheduled to get under way. Now everyone knew that *Archerfish* had had a sailor jump ship.

They later learned that Sullivan had fallen in love with a truly beautiful Norwegian girl and had gone home with her. Everything was fine until the boat had left port, then the girl's father informed Sullivan that if his intentions toward his daughter were serious, he would have to help herd the goats. The sailor quickly turned himself in to the American consul's office.

Meanwhile, *Archerfish* was back at work, running survey points. The biggest problem was the pack ice that prevented them from running about 360 miles of the planned track. Though the stuff could be a considerable nuisance and even dangerous at times, the floe ice, with its deep blue color, was beautiful to look at, like fine, rough-carved jewelry floating on the surface of the sea. It wasn't long before the lookouts began to spot bigger icebergs in addition to the growlers as they ran routes near Greenland and Iceland.

One day, David Dimmick decided he simply had to have his picture made standing on an iceberg. The captain was only too happy to oblige Dimmick and his whim. He ordered that they maneuver as close as they could get to a berg, near enough so the exec could hop off onto the thing. The captain had a plan, though. He was going to have the boat back away so nothing would be in the frame of the photo but Dimmick and his iceberg so the photo would be even more impressive. But once they pulled away, Ken Woods had every intention of backing away, turning, and steaming out of sight. Or at least driving far enough away that Dimmick would think they were actually going to abandon him on the berg. Unfortunately, they weren't able to get close enough to make the transfer, so Woods never got his chance to put a scare into Dimmick.

They did get close enough one day to another iceberg for the men to stand on the boat's bull nose and scoop snow off the thing and eat it. They also got plenty of pictures of the massive chunk of ice.

After leaving Bergen, Joe Cronin developed a raging case of hemor-rhoids. Rough seas made them unbearable. Doc Barboza told him that he could get rid of the pain if Joe would allow him. At that point, Cronin was willing to try anything.

Barboza gave him a shot of morphine and enlisted the help of several of the bigger enginemen to hold Cronin down on his bunk in the goat locker. The captain gave the order to dive the boat so Doc would have a sta-ble work area. Barboza didn't do surgery. After all, he was not an actual doctor. He merely made incisions to relieve the pressure. This same condi-tion had inflicted Cronin when he served on USS *Flying Fish* (SS-229) back in 1944. A real doctor on the tender had performed the same procedure, and the next day Cronin and his boat left the Gilberts on a war patrol.

Joe learned his lesson this time. When *Archerfish* got back to New Lon-don, he went to St. Albans Naval Hospital in New York city and had his problem taken care of properly.

When Operation Sea Scan was in its initial planning stages, it was agreed that *Archerfish* would operate outside the usual navy movement re-porting system. To ease the burden on the boat's crew, it was decided that she would only report her position once in each twenty-four-hour period. That would still give ComSubLant a general area in which to drop a me-morial wreath should anything tragic happen to her.

Archerfish was operating on the surface early one morning northeast of Iceland when all aboard heard the ominous sound of the boat's fire alarm and the announcement over the IMC: "Fire in the pump room!" The fire turned out to be minimal, but it involved the TBL motor-generator, which supplied power to the boat's most powerful radio transmitting system. It had shorted out when the radioman powered it up that morning. The same equipment had given trouble before, but now it looked as if it were down for the count. That meant that they would have problems getting their daily position report to ComSubLant because they were too far out to sea for any other transmitter aboard to reach that far.

Then, just as today, if a submarine fails to report on schedule, there is a four-hour grace period, then the navy issues a SUBMISS/SUBSUNK, immedi-ately mounting a massive search-and-rescue effort involving all available planes and vessels in the area. And considering the precarious international situation in those days, who knew what conclusions might have been drawn if a U.S. Navy submarine turned up missing?

Archerfish wanted to avoid setting all that in motion if there was any way to prevent it. Captain Woods gave the order to change course and head for Iceland as fast as they could go, hoping to get in range of one of that country's monitoring stations before the grace period was up. Meanwhile, Miles Graham asked for and received permission to violate watertight integrity in order to run wires through a hatch and a watertight door to get power to the transmitter. Graham figured with 250 tons of batteries, four 1,100-kilowatt generators and an auxiliary generator, they should be able to jury-rig the thing and somehow make the high-power transmitter operational. He assembled a group of leading petty officers in the wardroom: Rick Hardin, the leading radioman; George Hughes, the leading electronics technician; Ted Armstrong, the leading sonarman; Alvin Williams, the leading interior communications technician; and Frankie Stapleford, the leading electrician. They went right to work on the problem.

Not long after striking out for Iceland, the boat ran into a dense fog and had to slow to a crawl. It appeared now that they would never get close enough to transmit their message. Suddenly, out of the pea soup, they saw HMS *Unidie* (F-141) of the British Royal Navy. The Brits kindly agreed to relay their position report.

At about the same time, Miles Graham and his guys had found the various voltages and current the radio needed at sundry spots on the boat, from the control room to the conning tower to the battery well, and had run the cables needed to get it to the transmitter. They had it all working shortly after the contact with the British navy. On their first transmission, when George Hughes explained the problems they had been having, the reply from the ComSubLant operator was, "You have no problem. We do. You're blasting everything else off the air!"

Word soon came that the replacement motor-generator for the TBL would be waiting for them when they arrived in Faslane, Scotland. So, with that bit of a crisis under control, they continued on, taking their gravity readings. Now they were bound for Faslane, all the while making the best, as usual, of what they had to work with.

18

TO THE NORTHWEST PASSAGE

ARCHERFISH and her crew arrived at the Royal Navy submarine base at Faslane, Scotland, on July 24, 1960. The harbor pilot went ashore and the maneuvering watch was secured just before ten o'clock in the morning, local time. One of the first faces the crew saw was a familiar one. John Sullivan, whose love for his Norwegian sweetheart was exceeded only by his desire not to be a goat herder, was there, in the custody of local authorities. As soon as possible, Kenny Woods held captain's mass to get the whole incident over with once and for all. Sullivan was busted down from torpedoman's mate first class to second class. Most of the crew was surprised. A sailor could get himself kicked out of the navy for jumping ship and missing movement the way he had.

There was something else waiting for them on the pier at Faslane. The cable that Ted Armstrong had ordered many months before (while the boat was still in Key West) to install the JT sonar had finally caught up with the boat. So had the second order of cable, the one Armstrong placed while they were in Philadelphia when it appeared the first batch would not be delivered in time to install before they got under way from there. Both bundles were sent back to the States.

Keith Norlin had been working as a geologist aboard USNS *Bowditch* (T-AGS-62), an oceanographic vessel operating in the North Sea. He received word that he was to report to *Archerfish*, which was "lying at Faslane,

Scotland." Norlin had no idea the base would be so difficult to find. Even the fine Scottish citizens he asked had never heard of the place, but they sent him to Glasgow, which was, at least, somewhat closer than where he was. He was finally able to locate the base and got his first glimpse of what would be his new home for the next little while.

The geologist was a bit concerned. Norlin had only seen one submarine in his life, and that had been the *U-505*, a German Type-IX U-Boat from World War II at the Chicago Museum of Science and Industry. Now, here he was, about to climb aboard one of the odd-looking things and ride it away to sea.

"When I first came face to face with *Archerfish*, my initial thought was that she should have been in a museum, too," he says.

The first thing he noticed when he climbed down the ladder into the boat's control room was the smell. It was a fragrant mix of diesel fuel, fried food, and unwashed bodies. After a quick tour of the boat, he received instruction in perhaps his most important operation aboard *Archerfish:* how to operate a marine toilet. Flushing waste into the sanitary tank was a multi-step process that required sequential operation of several hand-turned valves and levers. It was important that the correct sequence be followed precisely, or the waste could be blown right back into the operator's face. Norlin admits he paid close attention to his guide and the instruction he gave him as he sensed it might greatly improve his quality of life aboard this vessel if he fully understood the procedure.

While they were moored at the Royal Naval Station at Faslane, the good liberty was in Glasgow, farther up the Firth of Clyde. In order to get there, though, the crew members had to walk to the main gate and take a bus about five miles up the loch to Helensburgh, and then catch a train at the railway station there for the trip over to Glasgow. Luckily for them, there was a spirits shop right in front of the bus stop. Some of the *Archerfish* crew stopped in the shop, stocked up, and were so drunk by the time the train got to Glasgow that they simply got right back on the next train for the return trip to Helensburgh.

Some of the officers made the sojourn up to the legendary Loch Ness and spent all afternoon in a restaurant overlooking the lake's dark waters, drinking and watching for an appearance by the famous monster that was supposed to live beneath its surface. Joe Cummings claimed that, after enough alcohol, they did see the beast, but it had two heads and a silly grin on its face.

There was one spectacular brawl in Glasgow involving the bunch from

Archerfish. A group of local ruffians, so-called teddy boys, were hanging around outside a club named Lacarno's, complaining loudly about the American sailors and the fact that they were getting all the local girls. It was actually Captain Kenny Woods who set the whole thing off. One of the toughs said, "I'm tired of it, mates. I'm gonna get meself a Yank." Woods happened to be passing by at the time and couldn't allow the challenge to go unanswered. He said, "Here! Get this Yank!"

The fight was on. Someone opened the front door of Lacarno's and yelled, "*Archerfish!*" All the crew members inside spilled out and joined the fray.

As usual in such brawls, no one was hurt seriously, and only one sailor ended up getting arrested. In the confusion, Red Dog Balthrop had thrown a punch or two at a local policeman who was trying to drag him off one of the teddy boys. Balthrop ended up before a woman judge. She heard the details and Balthrop's humble explanation, and then promptly dismissed the charges against the sailor. She also told him and his shipmates to stay out of Glasgow from then on.

The Derby Hotel (pronounced *Dar-by*) was *Archerfish's* unofficial headquarters in Glasgow. It became the crew's habit to rent several adjoining rooms at a hotel while in port, order up a staggering amount of booze, always have plenty of beer iced down in the bathtub, and keep the party going from arrival until under way.

Finally, after three weeks of "good liberty" in Faslane, it was time to get going again. On August 12, they headed back out to resume their continual stop-and-start survey runs. Before leaving the Scottish base, though, they had one last load of stores to secure aboard the boat. The shipment consisted of thirty cases of Tennent's Lager Beer. Navy ships were allowed to carry spirits to be used for recreational purposes while ashore, but the real reason for taking on this supply was that the next few ports of call were in Greenland. There was serious doubt they would be able to get a decent drink there at any time. There was also some conjecture as to where they would find room to store the brew. John Sullivan was the petty officer in charge of the forward torpedo room. He dutifully counted each case of beer as it was shoved into one of the torpedo tubes. Of course, the boat carried no torpedoes, and the tubes made wonderful beer coolers in the icy waters they would be traversing over the next few months.

Keith Norlin knew immediately that it would take some adjustment on his part to get accustomed to life on a submarine. With all hands back from liberty and everyone on board at the same time, the boat was downright crowded. He compared the sensation of being belowdecks while the boat was under way to riding in a fast-moving Pullman car. As he walked down the narrow aisle during their crossing of the Irish Sea, the boat swayed and clattered and seemed almost on the verge of coming apart. Also like the Pullman car, everything on *Archerfish* was built-in and compact, and there was no wasted space at all. In Norlin's closet-sized sleeping compartment, there was even a pull-down stainless-steel sink like those he had seen when traveling by rail.

He and the other hydros were housed in the forward battery compartment in what had been the chief petty officer's quarters in earlier *Archerfish* configurations. The compartment had five bunks and a closet crammed into it, in addition to the pull-down sink.

The next thing Norlin knew would take some time getting accustomed to was the showering facilities. Because of the shortage of freshwater aboard a submarine, showers were only allowed once a week. If a man missed the short period allotted for bathing, he had to wait another full week for his next chance for a shower. Anyone caught taking an unauthorized shower had to stand a four-hour watch on the distillation equipment where freshwater was made for the boat and its batteries.

Even when it finally came time for it, the weekly bath left a lot to be desired. Norlin was only able to have the water turned on long enough to get most of his body wet. Then he was required to turn it off while he soaped up and washed. Finally, he could turn the water on for another minute or so to rinse the suds away. That was it for another week.

Soon *Archerfish* was back in the North Atlantic, following the predetermined survey lines, steaming well off the normal sealanes. Except for the occasional lone fishing boat, they rarely saw another vessel.

In the North Atlantic, the roughest duty aboard the submarine was the two-man topside lookout watch. The weather was getting colder and wetter. Before going on watch, the men pulled on all the warm clothing they could find that was reasonably dry and then tugged on what rain gear was available. The farther north they went, the worse it got. Even on relatively good days, it was impossible for the watchstanders to stay warm and dry for four hours. When they came off watch, they hung their dripping clothes in the engine room to dry. For most of the time they spent in the northern waters, the engine rooms were filled with dripping clothes that never seemed to get completely dried out.

Though drier, it wasn't really all that comfortable belowdecks either. When they were running on the surface, the air temperature inside the boat often hovered near freezing. Everyone had to wear layers of clothing to try to keep warm. Then, when the weather and sea state forced them to have to dive to take readings, the temperature inside the submarine soared, and everyone had to strip down again to try to get comfortable.

Captain Kenny Woods initiated one very popular policy very early in their frigid mission. Whenever men came off watch after braving the bitter cold and wet, they each received a ration of booze to get the circulation going again.

Keith Norlin soon learned why a submarine had been chosen for this operation. They were southeast of Kap Farvel off the southern tip of Greenland when the seas became too rough to operate their instruments. After two blasts of the diving alarm, the bow tilted downward and he immediately felt the rolling and pitching of the boat subside. He found it hard to believe that 150 feet over his head, the waves on the Labrador Sea were being whipped to heights of forty-five feet by vicious wind gusts of between fifty and sixty knots. Soon the boat's rocking was minimized, and they were once again able to use their highly sensitive equipment as designed. The required data was recorded and then they could once again head back to the surface. At first, the thoughts of taking this old sub down a couple of hundred feet below the surface made Norlin a bit uncomfortable. Soon, though, the "hydro" began to look forward to those dives that took them to the far more peaceful waters found below.

They were encountering more and more icebergs by that time. At first, Captain Woods asked to be informed of each sighting. Shortly, he changed the orders to only report to him any iceberg that floated within two thousand yards of their course. Finally, he only wanted to hear of any bergs that required a course change.

On August 19 they passed two hundred icebergs in a single day before anchoring near Julianehaab, Greenland. *Archerfish* was the first American vessel to visit there since 1941 and the first-ever submarine. Their arrival caused quite a stir in the little Eskimo town. The boat had to anchor in the harbor since there was only room at the town dock for the merchant vessel that was tied up there off-loading essential supplies.

While they were anchored, Gus Emperador was awarded his silver dolphins, designating him as "qualified in submarines." That made him the first sub sailor ever to receive his dolphins in Greenland, an event that earned a nice mention in the New London Submarine Base newspaper, appropriately named *The Dolphin*.

When the crew finally got ashore for liberty, they had built up a powerful thirst. It took them no time to drink up the entire stock of beer at the only bar in Julianehaab.

"Where do your supplies come from," the chief of the boat, Vern Bettis, asked the bartender.

"Half the hold of that old freighter down at the dock is filled with my beer," the barman answered. "We're just waiting for them to get it unloaded."

"Well, let's go get it!" the COB declared.

They borrowed the barkeep's Jeep and headed for the wharf with the rest of the thirsty *Archerfish* crew members running along close behind. A bucket brigade was set up from the deep hold of the ship to the dock while the Jeep shuttled the brew back to the bar. The job was finished just in time to kick off a party that involved the whole town. All night long, pale, tattooed sailors swirled Eskimo ladies around the dance floor to the thumping beat of an old jukebox.

Archerfish was scheduled to depart Julianehaab early on August 20 but had to wait over four hours for a dense, cold fog to lift before she could get under way. Finally, with the mouth of the Hudson Bay to the west and the coast of Greenland to the east, they entered Davis Strait. John Davis had rediscovered Greenland three hundred years after the Norsemen, so the strait bore his name, not one of theirs. Davis Strait is the gateway to the arctic north of Canada and to the Northwest Passage. Every search for a shortcut around the Americas had followed this route, but it was not a typical sealane for submarines. Still *Archerfish* steamed on, plying waters in which icebergs were now visible in all directions. There was no doubt why this part of the world had been dubbed Iceberg Alley.

Rough seas and heavy fog delayed their scheduled arrival at the remote United States Air Force Base at Thule, Greenland. They were forced to dive to take their readings and were also having trouble with the increasingly cranky gravity meter. They had managed to get a replacement isolation transformer for the instrument, but it was the wrong voltage and tended to overheat if it was used for very long. While on the surface, they were constantly maneuvering, dodging the icebergs and pack ice. They spotted one berg that towered over six hundred feet above the water.

Then, to make matters worse, they encountered a storm that shoved them sideways almost as fast as they were steaming forward. One roll heeled them about seventy degrees to starboard, sending objects flying and crashing all over the inside of the boat despite their being rigged for heavy weather.

It was especially rough topside. A safety net had to be strung around the bridge railing to keep the watches from getting flushed overboard. The precaution paid off immediately when Miles Graham almost went into the frigid sea. After that, the watches were moved to the conning tower and the upper hatch was secured. The officer of the deck and one other lookout used the periscopes to keep an eye out for icebergs or other obstructions in their path.

The rolling seas caused one interesting but painful phenomenon. When the boat wallowed over, seawater momentarily covered the main air induction for the engine rooms. Since the upper hatch above the conning tower was now closed most of the time, this closure caused the engines to begin sucking air out of the boat and creating a considerable vacuum in the "people tank." This reminded the crew of time spent snorkeling while they were serving on Guppy boats, when the vacuum could at times be strong enough to pop the eardrums of some of the men on the boat.

Even the matter of frequent time-zone changes was causing discomfort and confusion. Since they were operating so near the north pole and following erratic courses to take their readings, the time zones changed often. There was a very short distance between each fifteen degrees of longitude. Executive Officer David Dimmick admitted he handled the shifting time in a way he thought would keep the crew off balance, all in an effort to make them more alert. He waited until they seemed to have adjusted to the schedule, then he would switch to whatever the true local time was. The truth was, the precise hour made no difference to anyone but the lookouts and the ODD, the crew members who had to enter notes in the log. For anyone else, even if they were topside for air, the sun was always shining, day and night, and the precise, correct time was little more than a curiosity.

As Davis Strait opened into Baffin Bay, the lookouts began to see many more fishing boats. This area had been prime summer fishing grounds for hundreds of years. Now *Archerfish* had to be careful to avoid colliding with those vessels or fouling their lines. On most of the fishing craft, the wheelhouses were empty. Every man aboard the boats was on deck, working, despite the congested traffic and the bitterly cold weather. Everyone on the sub agreed that fishing these waters was not an easy way to make a living.

They passed Melville Bay on the coast of Greenland, the site of numerous wrecks throughout history. There was so much ice scudding along on the sea's surface that the men belowdecks could hear its constant scraping against the boat's hide. The incessant banging and groaning even interfered with their sleep.

It was an unusually balmy forty-four degrees with clouds at three thousand feet when they carefully maneuvered around icebergs of all sizes and pulled into the little harbor at Thule on August 26. As the base came into sight, the place was not impressive at all. It was cold, desolate, and dirty and seemed to be sealed in a cloud of dust that was being whipped up by the wind from the base's maze of dirt roads. *Archerfish* moored starboard side to port side of USCG *Westwind* (WAGB-281) in what was another minor but notable first for the boat. It was reported to be the first time in U.S. Navy history that a submarine had ever moored alongside an icebreaker.

Thule was no more impressive up close than it had been from a distance. The base was made up of insulated buildings sitting on dirt. There were no trees or grass or any other vegetation to be seen anywhere, and the dust was billowing. The only other distinguishing sight that they could see was the great ice cap, visible in the distance as it hugged the Arctic ground.

As usual, though, the *Archerfish* crew soon found whatever entertainment might be available. There was a USO show in town, performing at the NCO Club. Someone found Irish whiskey on sale. And the club had a gambling facility. Rough and bleak as it was, Thule was a far sight better than hanging on to the makeshift net on the boat's bridge while she rolled and tumbled in rough, icy seas.

Archerfish was under way once more the morning of August 29, and by that evening she had reached the northernmost survey point in Baffin Bay. They were only a bit over eight hundred miles from the north pole when their assigned track finally took them back to the south. Everyone, including even the veteran submariners aboard, got their first look at two of the sea's oddest wonders while in Baffin Bay. They observed St. Elmo's fire and ice fog. St. Elmo's fire is a continuous electrical corona discharge that causes an eerie glow, usually seen in the masts of ships. Sometimes it is so bright the masts appear to be on fire. Submariners usually don't see such a sight, but conditions were right for it there in the far northern latitudes, and they could see the ghostly light in the boat's shears. Ice fog occurs when the air temperature reaches a point at which moisture in the air suddenly freezes, forming a fog so dense the lookouts on the bridge of *Archerfish* could not see her bow.

They were still having problems with the gravity meter, but the boat was on the verge of another much bigger casualty. On the evening of September 6, Ken Henry was sitting on a bench locker with his back against number-three main engine, reading a Perry Mason novel. Suddenly, the engine room was rocked with a deafening *kerboom!* The deck plates jumped from the force of the explosion, and the compartment immediately filled with smoke. It didn't take long to determine that the auxiliary engine, which had been lovingly named Leroy, had suffered a crankcase explosion. A Z-shaped piece of the lower crankshaft had broken at the number-six main bearing journal and at the number-six connecting rod bearing journal. The part was lying useless in the dry sump.

The engine was a goner. Nothing would do but to give their old "ship-mate" a proper funeral.

Robbie Roberts helped the enginemen make flowers out of Kleenex. Piedmont Davis laid out a visitors' book for all to sign when they came to pay their last respects. Thirty-nine sailors did. A wake was held in the after engine room with "Father" Davis conducting a very solemn service as they laid Leroy to rest. A headstone was fashioned out of cardboard. On it was his epitaph: "Seventeen years of sea duty, he never went ashore. Died of a broken crank, 6 September 1960."

The survey line they were scheduled to run in Cumberland Sound at the southeast corner of Baffin Island was never completed. The ice was simply too thick and much too dangerous.

During the midwatch on the night of September 11, Dale Ness and Martin Lafferty had the lookout. Suddenly Ness shouted out a warning of a huge iceberg dead ahead. The boat maneuvered to avoid the massive obstacle, but when they looked again, the thing was still directly in front of them. The boat turned again. The iceberg did, too. That's when someone realized the iceberg was actually the moon, coming up on the horizon. With the mist on the water at that time of day and the weird sunlight, the moon had looked exactly like a distant iceberg. Still, it was a while before the crew stopped goading the watch standers that night about trying to steer *Archerfish* around the moon.

Godthaab was the next stop. The capital of Greenland, the town is on the country's west coast, on Davis Strait. They anchored the boat in Skibshaun Bay because there would be no berth available in the tiny dock area until the next day. While they were at anchor, Eskimos paddled out and the crew members traded them fresh fruit for beer. The exchange rate was one orange or two apples for each bottle of brew.

Walter "Pine Tree" Casey and George Hughes completed their final test to become "qualified in submarines" and received their coveted silver dolphins while they were in Godthaab. Francis "Gunner Red" Gaughan reenlisted for six more years in the navy while they were there. He claims to be the first and only submariner in history to ever ship over while in Greenland.

Once ashore, the crew members managed to find the only bar in town, despite its not even having a sign out front to lead the way. The liberty party from the U.S. Coast Guard icebreaker *Westwind* soon joined them. One of the Eskimo girls, who knew nothing of the difference between the Coast Guard and the navy, took an interest in the Coast Guard shield that was sewn on the right cuff of the blues worn by the *Westwind* crew members. She asked why the *Archerfish* sailors didn't have one on their jumpers as well. Wayne "Dirty Hermie" Herman, with a completely straight face, explained to her that the shield was a navy symbol to identify venereal disease and anyone who had VD was required to wear one of those shields on his cuff until he was completely cured of his malady. That information spread through the bar like wildfire. From then on, the Coasties couldn't even convince any of the Eskimo ladies to dance with them.

The next day, Captain Woods hosted Greenland's governor, Finn Nielsen, for lunch aboard *Archerfish*. He proved to be a very fine gent and quite interesting to talk with. He explained that, as a result of the integration of Greenland into Denmark beginning in 1953, Greenland had been designated as a "suburb of Copenhagen" for political reasons. The governor requested that the submarine perform a demonstration dive in the old harbor before they departed. On September 19, with several hundred townspeople lining the shore to watch, Captain Woods and the crew took the boat out and made a trim dive, ran back and forth across the harbor with scopes up for about twenty minutes, then surfaced to cheers and applause from everyone watching.

What the fine citizens of Godthaab didn't know was that several of the boat's crew had brought their newly befriended local ladies aboard for a private tour and a genuine submarine ride. When they surfaced, there was no way to get the women off the sub and onto boats without everyone who was watching the demonstration dive seeing them. They casually slipped back up to the pier next to a Danish freighter, the *Lily Nielsen*, which was moored there, and got the women ashore.

On September 21, after passing through Hudson Strait and into Ungava Bay, they got word that a floatplane was going to attempt a sea landing near their position to bring them a crucial part needed for the gravity meter, a replacement for the overheating isolation transformer. The seas turned out to be too choppy for the plane to come down, and after trying to land for a half hour or more, the pilot radioed that he would land instead near the mouth of the Kiksoak River, near Fort Chimo. A small boat from the Hudson Bay Company met *Archerfish* farther out in the icy, shallow waters of the bay. It took Mike Giambattista aboard, and they were off to rendezvous with the plane and retrieve the part. It was a cold, wet trip for the SLJO, but at least they could now reliably use the delicate meter that was the primary reason for their mission to top of the world.

It soon got colder and wetter.

Two days after fixing the meter, *Archerfish* was running survey points in the Foxe Basin, south of Baffin Island and east of Canada's Northwest Territories. Again, they were swimming in waters where no submarine had ever ventured. The charts of the area were seriously outdated and not at all trustworthy. Those navigational charts had quite a history of their own. The English explorer Martin Frobisher had made the soundings on the Foxe Basin charts in the late 1500s while he and his party were searching for the Northwest Passage to the Orient.

Not only was the water shallow here, but also the weather had turned especially nasty. It was blowing, snowing, and cold. Air temperature inside the boat was twenty-eight degrees and the seas were so rough that men were literally being rocked out of their bunks onto the cold, damp deck. Midafternoon of the twenty-fifth, the ice seemed to close in around the boat, clutching at her hull. The decision was made to stop surveying at once and to try to find a clear passage into Hudson Bay before they got stuck there in that godforsaken place. After several more hours, though, they still couldn't see anything but wind-driven ice spray and the thick, seemingly impenetrable pack ice surrounding them. They even turned and tried to steam north, the opposite way they needed to go for the most direct route out of Foxe Basin, but there was no break in the thickening ice in that direction either. The situation was growing more and more treacherous.

The radio station at Frobisher Bay was happy to give them the latest ice report. Trouble was, the latest report was two weeks old. It said that the ice extended in varying concentrations from Seahorse Point to Salisbury Island, in the Foxe Channel. *Archerfish* decided to steer to the north and east of Salisbury Island, hoping the ice pack would be less dense near land and that they could get into Hudson Bay by that route.

On the way, they actually collided head-on with an iceberg. Fortunately, there was no damage. But things soon got worse.

The crew was already getting irritable. There was a chow shortage because they had been unable to take on many provisions while they were in Greenland and were overdue for restocking. The boat was also on the verge of getting critical on fuel.

As the evening wore on, the lookouts reported that what they had initially thought were whitecaps that they were watching through the sleet and snow were actually huge chunks of pack ice. Shortly after midnight on the twenty-sixth, the storm had turned into a full-fledged blizzard. Winds howled steadily at forty to fifty knots and dense, blowing snow had cut visibility to less than five hundred yards. The storm was sending chunks of ice skidding across the sea surface. The junky ice piled up around *Archerfish* as if she were a dam in the middle of a flooding river.

The stuff quickly became a real hazard for the boat's propellers as well. If the screws were damaged, the boat would lose propulsion. And if the sub could not move, she and her crew could be stuck out here in a very inhospitable place for a long, long time. It is one thing for a surface ship to become frozen in the ice, because the round curvature of the hull causes the ship to rise as the ice hardens. On a submarine, the hull curves in the opposite direction at the waterline. As the ice thickens, the boat is forced downward. Eventually it would be shoved below the surface—with the obvious consequences.

Finally, Captain Woods was called to the bridge. He took a quick look at the situation, listened to the reports from the watch standers, and then assumed the conn. For a while, he tediously tried to steer the boat around the massive chunks of ice, maneuvering *Archerfish* cautiously through miles of jagged ice floe, all the time looking hopefully for the edge of the stuff and some semblance of clear water.

Down in the maneuvering room, Robbie Roberts and Bill Suddy were admittedly concerned. They could clearly hear the chunks of ice crashing against and scraping along the hull. They could also tell from the continuous, rapid series of bells from the conn that it was a rough go out there. They would hear a solid crunch, then the order to back down on one or both shafts would be followed quickly by "Ahead, one-third," then "Ahead two-thirds." Then they would hear another jolting thud, and a calm "Backing order" once again. As the commands came quicker and quicker, the *thunks* against the hull became louder and more ominous.

"Gunner" Lewis had the watch in the after torpedo room. He stuck his head through the door to the maneuvering room to ask what was going on. Roberts and Suddy were rapidly working at the levers and rheostats to keep up with the ordered speed and direction changes. They were sweating even though the temperature in the compartment was near freezing. Roberts yelled for Lewis to come in and help them. He could keep the bell log. Roberts and Suddy simply couldn't keep up with the entries and work the "sticks" at the same time.

Everyone who saw him at the conn that night marveled at how cool and calm Kenny Woods remained in what was truly a precarious situation. Then, when it was obvious to him that they couldn't continue to chug along through the ice any longer without risking damage to the boat, the captain did not hesitate. He gave the boat a twist until he had a small pool of ice-free water, came to "All stop," and ordered a stationary dive, even though they were still in virtually uncharted waters. They would try to dive beneath the ice floe until they found clearer waters. That, the skipper decided, was their best way to keep from getting themselves stuck out there.

Of course, there were other problems to consider. They had no idea how long they would need to stay down before they found clearer water, and the batteries were not fully charged. If the batteries gave out and they had to come up to the surface too soon, they might well find themselves in the midst of an even worse situation than the one they had dived to get away from.

Finally, eight hours later, they surfaced at the edge of the pack ice without bottoming out. They had also managed to avoid striking an island or running into the bottom of an iceberg.

They were just in time. There was practically no battery left by then, and the air in the boat was so bad a match wouldn't light. But they had made it. The crew and their boat had been pushed to their limits and had apparently suffered no ill effects from their ordeal other than severe headaches all around from the lack of oxygen.

Duke Durgin had the midwatch as the officer of the deck. When he lifted the upper conning tower hatch and climbed onto the bridge, he could not believe what he saw.

There, riding piggyback on the after deck, was a chunk of ice the size of a large automobile.

19

A GOAT IN THE ENGINE ROOM

As *Archerfish* neared Fort Churchill on the west side of Hudson Bay, Robbie Roberts was visiting with radioman Rick Hardin in the radio shack. They were listening to the commercial broadcast station from Fort Churchill, recording on a tape machine some of the music the station was playing. As one of the songs faded out, the disk jockey announced, "Hey, is anyone from *Archerfish* listening? If you are, please come up on frequency for some official messages," and he gave the channel. Hardin and Roberts looked at each other in surprise. The radioman quickly dialed in the frequency the deejay had given between records and copied the messages that were waiting for them there.

When they got closer to Fort Churchill, the boat learned that the berths at the pier were all filled with grain ships. They were trying to get loaded and under way before getting iced in for the winter. The radio operator in Fort Churchill also casually informed them that their present position happened to be right in the impact zone of the atmospheric sounding rockets that some local scientists were about to begin test-firing. *Archerfish* might want to move. They did!

There was more complaining among the crew about the oft-changing time zones. The exec had finally relented in the face of all the grousing about continually shifting from one zone to another, sometimes several times a day. He told everyone to keep the boat on Greenwich mean time.

However, that raised another problem. In the western reaches of Hudson Bay, they were actually farther west than Galveston, Texas, or Chicago, Illinois, which were both on central standard time. Dimmick gave in again and had all the clocks on the boat set to CST.

After the cold, perilous trip through the ice coming out of Foxe Basin, everyone aboard had been looking forward to liberty in Fort Churchill. It was not to be. Prior to noon on September 29, the boat began lying to off Fort Churchill while waiting for information on the availability of a berth alongside a pier. That would be necessary to establish a land tie for the Hydrographic office.

After a four-hour wait at the entrance to the harbor, they were informed that it would be at least another thirty hours before they could get a mooring berth at the little frontier town's pier. The submarine simply could not wait that long. The order was given to turn away and return to their scheduled survey runs.

Kenny Woods knew how disappointed everyone was. So was he. The skipper made a command decision and instituted "liberty calls at sea." He began allowing a beer ration from the supply of Tennent's that they had stored in the torpedo tubes before they left Faslane. Each man was to get two cans daily. They received their first ration during the evening meal, which happened to be Italian night. The crew members had a grand old time, sitting in the mess hall, eating spaghetti and bread and washing it all down with the ice-cold beer. After that, they got their allowance of brew during the daily showing of the movie. Those men due to go on watch did not get theirs until after they finished their watch. No one would have abused the privilege and imbibed while on watch, but it was better to be safe than sorry.

The guys who lived in the after torpedo room had always kept an unauthorized stash of beer for their own private consumption. They developed an ingenious method of getting rid of their empties. They began covertly ejecting them from the after signal ejector, the device designed to launch smoke and signal flares from the boat while she was beneath the surface. The men found that the ejector held seven longneck beer bottles, ten beer cans, or a combination of the two.

Only one person on the boat decided not to take his share of beer each day: Captain Kenny Woods, whose idea it was in the first place, *never* took a drink while at sea.

Archerfish was running low on fuel and rations by now, but she still had important survey runs to make in James Bay at the southernmost end of

Hudson Bay before they could steam on to Halifax. They had planned to meet a Coast Guard icebreaker and take on fuel, mail, and rations, but the vessel was called to an emergency somewhere in the North Atlantic before they could meet up. The rendezvous never took place.

James Bay made David Dimmick nervous. The only chart available was dated 1915. Someone had scribbled across the bottom of the chart the clear warning: "This is a print of a canceled chart. The information shown should be treated with great caution." The Canadian version of *Sailing Directions* mentioned that, in these waters, "often an oar will touch bottom." Dimmick doubted anyone's oars were nineteen feet long, *Archerfish's* draft when she was on the surface. And what if they needed to dive to get good readings? It was a nerve-racking transit, but the lines had to be run.

Once more, the weather turned ugly. Everyone standing bridge watches wore a safety line to keep from getting washed overboard. A man could easily die in these frigid waters if he was not pulled back aboard in minutes. When his bridge watch was almost over each day, Miles Graham called the watch below, reminding them to wake his relief and to please turn his electric blanket on high. He wanted it to be ready for him when he got down there, stripped off his wet, ice-encrusted, clothes, and crawled beneath it.

During this time in her life, when *Archerfish* was on the surface, temperatures in the engine room were so glacial that everyone wore foul-weather gear and thermal underwear. When they submerged, the temperature soared and they had to strip to their skivvies.

Finally, *Archerfish* finished running the points in James Bay and headed north once again, making the frosty trip across Hudson Bay and around the northernmost reaches of Quebec, through Hudson Strait, into the Labrador Sea, and finally, back into the Atlantic. On October 9, 1960, the boat slipped into the Strait of Belle Isle, with Newfoundland a few miles to starboard and Labrador within sight to port. Once they were into the Gulf of Saint Lawrence, the seas became calm, and the temperature was an almost-pleasant forty-two degrees. Next, they passed through the Cabot Strait and once again into the Atlantic Ocean. On the twelfth, they moored port side to HMS *Auriga* (S-09), a British submarine, at Jetty 5, HMC Dockyard, Halifax, Nova Scotia, Canada.

Halifax was to be a major replenishment stop for *Archerfish*. The crew had been eating mostly Spam, peanut butter, and rice for the last few days before they reached port. Everything else was gone. Mike Giambattista and his troops had worked hard during the early part of the trip, even before they reached Julianehaab, Greenland, preparing a long list of requisitions for the food they would need. Captain Woods had pushed the list through channels to be sure it would all be waiting for them in Halifax. Not long after they left Thule, though, they learned that the Naval Supply Center in Bayonne, New Jersey, had somehow lost their lengthy requisition. *Archerfish* would have to resend the whole thing by Morse code over the radio. In the part of the world where they were operating during that time, communications could be sketchy. Since they were so near the north pole and the north magnetic pole, there was terrible electromagnetic interference to deal with. The size of the requisition message seemed to affect reception sometimes, too. The boat's radioman would raise someone on one of the communication channels and receive a report of a good, solid signal. But then, when he told them he had a message and that the "group count" (number of words in the message) was over ten thousand, the receiving operator would suddenly report a fading signal, too much static, or both. No one wanted to copy a message that size!

Someone was finally persuaded to take the radio traffic, and it was delivered to the supply depot. A fleet of trucks was loaded in Bayonne and sent to Halifax to meet *Archerfish*. There was, inevitably, one snafu, likely due to a garble in the transmitted requisition. One truck showed up at the pier filled completely with mayonnaise—enough mayonnaise to float a small navy. The *Archerfish* crew fell back on their old skills and promptly used the vast quantity of mayo to barter with the Canadian navy for other things they needed more.

When David Dimmick stepped ashore with two others from the wardroom, all three men noticed and commented on a truly odd sensation they felt. As they made their way side by side up the slight hill from the pier, the men had trouble walking and kept bumping into each other. It took them a minute to realize what was going on. Their equilibrium had not yet adjusted to being on solid land for the first time in almost a month. Their bodies actually missed the continual pitch and sway of the submarine due to the icy sea. Not having the deck moving constantly beneath them would take some getting used to.

Dimmick also noticed another strong feeling, a sensation that something was not quite right with this place. It took him a bit to realize what it was that seemed so different here. Then it hit him. Trees! It had been exactly two months since they had seen trees, the day they left Faslane. Here in Halifax there were big, glorious trees all over the place.

The tradition of renting most of a floor in a hotel as *Archerfish* party headquarters continued in Halifax. Here it was the Cornwallis Hotel, with one room dubbed the "party room" and the others reserved for sleeping off the celebration, showering, or for romantic interludes, should anyone be so fortunate. Beer was delivered to the party room ten cases at a time. The bathtub was filled with ice, beer, and mixers. The party began the first day of liberty and never stopped until the day of departure a week later. When one group returned to the boat for duty, those just going on liberty replaced them at the party.

The crew members were not the only ones who were thirsty when they pulled into Halifax. *Archerfish* took on 99,114 gallons of diesel fuel while in port. Since she only had a rated storage capacity of 94,000 gallons, it was clear the old girl was operating on little more than fumes when she first sidled up to Jetty 5.

The officers from *Archerfish* had ended up in their own party hotel while in Halifax. It happened that the World Series was underway while they were in port, and they were enjoying watching the games on television as they slaked their own enormous thirsts. The wardroom guys were having a wonderful time watching the seventh and final game between the Yankees and the Pirates when Captain Kenny Woods almost turned the course of sports history.

Bobby Shantz, a five-foot-six, 149-pound left-handed pitcher from Pottstown, Pennsylvania, was on the mound for the Yankees. The game was tied 9 to 9 in the bottom of the ninth inning, and the hometown Pirates were batting.

Captain Woods yelped in disbelief when Yankees manager Casey Stengel called time-out and walked out to the mound, obviously intent on removing Shantz from the game and replacing him with another relief pitcher. You see, Pottstown was just up the road from Philadelphia, the skipper's hometown. Woods was totally convinced that a former Philadelphian would have a better chance of getting the next batter out than some yahoo Stengel might bring in from the bullpen. The skipper was so convinced that he attempted to take command of the situation, just as he would have done on the bridge of *Archerfish* if a correct decision were required.

Woods grabbed the telephone in the hotel room and quickly placed a person-to-person call to a Mr. Casey Stengel, in the Yankee dugout in Pittsburgh.

Amazingly, the long-distance call went through, all the way from Halifax, Nova Scotia, to the visitor's dugout at Forbes Field in Pittsburgh.

Whoever answered the phone in the dugout said, "I'm sorry. Mr. Stengel is out on the field and can't come to the telephone right now. Would you like to talk with someone else?"

"No. If I can't talk to Casey, I don't want to talk with anybody," Woods answered. With that, he slammed down the phone. It was too late anyway. The Yankee manager had made his move, requesting someone from the bullpen.

The rest is baseball history. Stengel, without benefit of the counsel of the skipper of the *Archerfish*, went ahead and lifted Bobby Shantz. He brought in Ralph Terry to face Pittsburgh's Bill Mazeroski. Mazeroski promptly hit Terry's second pitch a mile. It was one of the most memorable home runs in World Series history, ending the game and giving the Pirates the 1960 World Championship.

On October 19, *Archerfish* pulled out of Halifax and headed back across the Atlantic to Belfast, Northern Ireland. They still had survey lines to run before the mission officially ended in Belfast, but the weather was not co-operating. Once they left the calm of Halifax Harbor, the seas became rougher and rougher, the water breaking brutally over the bridge and the boat floundering through the massive waves. On the twenty-fifth, they passed through the area known as the "Black Pit," that section of the Atlantic Ocean where German U-boats had been free to hunt Allied shipping during World War II without fear of reprisal. The area was too far from the aircraft that were based in Newfoundland to patrol, and it was not within range of Allied planes from Iceland or Britain. This was always the most dangerous point for any convoys steaming between America and Europe.

By October 27, the barometer had fallen to 29.3 inches as the wind increased to seventy-five knots. Wave heights reached forty-five feet.

As the rough weather continued, appetites disappeared, and many became seasick. Everyday functions like sleeping and working became torture. The mess cooks spread dampened towels on the tables to set dishes on so they would be less likely to slide off into the laps of diners. The meals that were served were mostly simple affairs, nothing fancy at all.

An antiseptic description of ocean storms belies their overwhelming power and might. These are survival conditions. All pretenses of useful work stop as the entire ship's company concentrates on the safety, and ultimately the survival, of the vessel. In the movies, captains typically order the crews to "batten down the hatches" in such furious weather. *Archerfish* did the same.

As they crossed the rocking ocean, John Gonzales could think of only one thing when he realized that they were scheduled to arrive in Belfast on

November 16. That was the first day of deer hunting season back home in Texas.

Everyone aboard got a serious scare on November 7. During battery charging, a ventilation line damper on the battery exhaust into the forward engine room was accidentally closed. That allowed the hydrogen level in the boat to suddenly shoot dangerously high.

"Bridge, maneuvering! There is five percent hydrogen in the boat," was the frightening message relayed via the 7MC speaker.

All submariners know how dangerous that condition is. *Archerfish* sailors were well aware of the near-tragic fire that had broken out on their own boat in 1952. Mike Casey maintains that those brief five minutes were the only time he was ever scared during his entire time in the navy. There was no place to run, nothing to do but "secure the charge," find the cause of the sudden rise in hydrogen buildup, and pray no stray spark set off a horrible inferno before the gas could be vented from the boat.

Bill Hiesley found the shut damper and opened it. After five minutes, the readings were back within the normal range, and everyone was allowed to go on about his business.

On November 13, the depth of water precluded *Archerfish* from diving and the sea state conditions were too rough for taking readings while they were on the surface. Captain Woods proclaimed that the Atlantic phase of Operation Sea Scan was completed.

When *Archerfish* moored in Herndon Quay, Pollack Basin, Belfast, Northern Ireland, just before ten in the morning on November 16, the engineers had their first opportunity to assess the extent of damage the heavy seas had done to the after superstructure. Somewhere between Halifax and Belfast, they had lost most of the decking between the after engine room hatch and the turtleback and both the mufflers off number-three and number-four engines. Some of the locals on the pier asked if the damage had been done by depth charges. It would have been a much better story if it had, but the crew admitted it had been nothing more than the rough weather they had encountered while crossing the angry North Atlantic.

The first act by a bunch of the crew upon arriving at the Emerald Isle was to tie down Richard "Red" Schlenker in the mess hall and dye him green from head to foot. They wanted to make him a true Irishman.

The local television station requested that several of the sailors appear on a popular program called *Around the Town with Tess*. Dale Ness was on restriction for some minor transgression but realized that volunteering to be on the show would get him off the boat and ashore, at least for a little while. He and Mike Lintner did appear on the TV show, and each man got paid two pounds, two shillings, two pence for his brief bit of stardom.

The crew was also asked to participate in a blood drive. Many did, and the event was played up in all the local papers and newscasts on the radio stations.

Belfast was cold, gray, and damp. The people were friendly and actually seemed to like Americans. Flunky Joe Forrest met a young lady and was invited to her home to meet her parents. He took his beloved Audi reel-to-reel tape recorder with him so he could play them some of the music he had recorded. When he plugged the recorder in and turned it on, it popped, crackled, smoked, and sizzled. Nobody had told him about the difference between electrical current in Europe and in the States.

The skipper and some of his officers were invited to a Sunday turkey dinner with the town's lord mayor. They were picked up in an Austin "Princess" automobile, similar to a Rolls-Royce, and driven through the streets of Belfast. They practiced their "royal waves" on all the poor residents they passed in the city's impoverished neighborhoods.

A Russian merchant ship, the *Priozierski*, was moored on the opposite side of the bight from *Archerfish*. The Russian sailors liked to stand at the rail, screaming in broken English, "Yankee, go home!" The *A-fish* crew didn't bother to yell back. They had been away from the States long enough that they agreed with the sentiment completely.

Not surprisingly, when the crew was mustered at 0915 on November 22, 1960, there were no unauthorized absences. Everyone was ready to head back to New London, Connecticut.

After the long trip westward across the Atlantic, Mike Giambattista brought them in for the last time on December 3. He was to be transferred to the *Tusk* before *Archerfish* left on her next phase, to be conducted in the Pacific.

Usually, when a boat returns to its home port after an extended deployment, the pier is lined with waving, welcoming wives and kids, a band is playing, and assembled brass and dignitaries await them. Not so with *Archerfish*. The only people waiting were the duty-section line handlers, a lone postal clerk with their mail, the commander, Submarine Development Group Two, and his aides, and the wife and son of Rick Hardin, one of the two married crew members.

The Shore Patrol had sent word that they would give *Archerfish* sailors one week to unwind. As long as nobody was killed and not too much damage was done, they would not write them up. They'd just bring them back to the boat when they passed out. The gesture was much appreciated. Many of the crew members took advantage of the generous gesture.

Mike Smalet was one of the hydrographic scientists onboard at the time. He was glad to have his feet back on solid ground again as well. He soon wandered into a bar near the base, a typical submariner's hangout. There he spotted a reasonably attractive barmaid and made his best pass.

"What time do you get off work?" he asked her. It had been a while, and he was admittedly out of practice.

"Never mind!" she answered icily. It was clear she was not interested.

Mike didn't give up. He used every line he could come up with, but the lady was still standoffish.

"Look," she finally said. "I don't ever have anything to do with sailors."

"Oh, I'm not a sailor," Smalet protested. "I'm not even in the navy."

"Don't lie to me," she responded, scrunching up her nose. "I know a submariner when I smell one!"

George Betts left for ten days' leave at home in Ohio. As was the usual practice, the crew pooled their money and bought flight insurance on him, naming themselves as beneficiaries, just as they did anytime one of their own was going somewhere by airplane. They figured if the worst happened, they could at least afford to throw one hell of a party in their shipmate's memory.

It was a Friday, ten days later, and Betts was due to return to the boat that day. A group of crewmen were listening to the radio when a bulletin interrupted normal programming. There had been a horrible air disaster. A United Airlines DC-8 had collided in midair with a Trans World Airlines Super Constellation over New York City. A total of 134 lives had been lost, all 128 of the passengers and crew aboard the two planes and 6 more people on the ground. As the *Archerfish* sailors listened to the details of the tragedy, someone realized that George Betts, their shipmate, was supposed to be on one of those airplanes, coming back from Ohio.

They were deeply saddened. George was a friend, a great shipmate. But they also were very rich! They quickly moved the wake to the Dolphin Bar, safe in the knowledge that the insurance company would be picking up what would become a considerable tab.

The memorial service was still going strong the next day when somebody looked up and spied a familiar face strolling into the Dolphin. It was George Betts! He innocently said, "Hi," and walked over to the bar to order himself a drink. From the condition of his buddies, it was obvious that he had quite a bit of catching up to do.

He noticed the place was eerily quiet. The only sound in the joint was the distorted boom of the jukebox.

Slowly, the sailors comprehended the unbelievable fact that their buddy was actually still alive, that he had not died in the horrible airline collision. They were ecstatic. Then reality set in.

If George wasn't dead, they weren't rich. And if they weren't rich, they were certainly in trouble with the bartender.

Then everyone was yelling angrily at George. He had no idea why his friends had suddenly turned on him. He was not even aware that one of the planes that had crashed the previous day was the flight he was supposed to be on, the flight that he had missed that morning back in Ohio. George had no idea that it was a miracle that he was still alive. All he knew was that his buddies were mad at him and accusing him of ruining one hell of a party by missing that airplane.

With the New Year, and as preparations continued for phase two of Operation Sea Scan, the boat lost another one of its characters. Vern "Pappy" Bettis, the chief of the boat, was transferred to shore duty. He was replaced by Lewis Gladwyn Holm, a World War II submarine torpedoman whose claim to fame was that he had been the inspiration for the character of O-Boat Holmes in Ed Beach's classic novel, *Run Silent, Run Deep*. The COB was, by position, the senior enlisted man on the boat and the person the commanding officer and executive officer depended on to execute policy. The general feeling in the wardroom was that *Archerfish* needed a COB who was tougher than Bettis had been, someone who could really keep the crew in line. Lee Walker had known Holm when they served together on USS *Trigger* (SS-564). When he heard the skipper and the exec were looking for a tough COB, he asked, "Do you want a real son of a bitch?" The answer was yes. Walker told them he knew just the man for the job. Holm was a tall, heavyset man, with a reputation for backing up his authority with brawn if necessary. Woods and Dimmick interviewed him and gave him the job. Holm's billing would prove to be accurate.

In early January, the commander of SubDevGru Two conducted a personnel inspection of the crew followed by an administrative and belowdecks inspection, just to make sure all was ready for the trip south, then into the Pacific. That afternoon, everyone lined up in the after battery and Doc Barboza gave each man his yellow fever inoculations, a precaution not necessary before they left to ply the North Atlantic.

The crew was in even higher spirits than usual on the eighteenth. It would be their last night in port, and everyone was ready to leave the cold of

New London behind in exchange for much warmer climes and new adventures. All that was left before they departed was a final night on the town, a chance to say goodbye to the barmaids, taxi drivers, police, and Shore Patrol.

That night, Speedy Gonzales and Galen Steck were wandering down Bank Street between watering holes when they met up with Nick Ross, an old buddy from another submarine. For some reason, Ross told them about a local farmer who was interested in selling a goat and a rooster. Owning a couple of barnyard animals sounded like a capital idea to Speedy and Turkey Neck.

"What prompted us to want a goat, God only knows," Gonzales says. "Maybe it was because we had struck out with every barmaid in New London already and that was all we had left for companionship."

No matter the reason, the three men hopped into Ross's truck, rode out to Groton, and paid the farmer $15 for his animals. When they got back to New London, they paraded up and down Bank Street, showing off their new friends, until the Shore Patrol stopped the odd contingent to see what was going on. The wagon driver radioed back to headquarters, trying to get a ruling on what to do with the sailors in their dress blues and their little menagerie.

"HQ, we've got some drunk sailors down here with a goat and a rooster. What do you want us to do with them?"

There was a long pause on the radio, then, "You've got what?"

"Some drunk sailors with a goat and a rooster."

"You mean they're together?"

"Best I can tell. One of the sailors claims they're all shipmates, and they refuse to be parted."

"How drunk are they?"

"The goat and the rooster appear to be sober. The others . . . well . . . they're under their own power as long as the goat holds them up. You want us to bring them in?"

"Hell, no! Just tell them to get off the street and stay off it!"

After a quick stop in the Dolphin, where they met up with another bunch of *Archerfish* sailors, they all decided they wanted something to eat, and that the goat and rooster seemed hungry as well. They ended up at the unfortunately named Hygienic Restaurant, where the sailors all ordered dinner for themselves and got a salad for the goat and a bowl of cereal for the rooster. David "Loony" Stevens broke some cigarettes up into the goat's salad and the critter seemed to really like the combination.

There is corroboration for this much of the goat story. Rick Hardin,

Archerfish's leading radioman, his wife, Candace, and their son happened to be in the Hygienic Restaurant that night, enjoying a late dinner. Mrs. Hardin could not believe what she was seeing. The loud, drunken sailors, "the mangiest group of people I have ever seen," she says, marched right into the restaurant, along with their goat and chicken, and took up most of the seats at the counter. The waitress served them and their barnyard animals as if such customers came in all the time. Once, Candace looked over and the goat was nibbling at the sleeve of her fur coat, which she had hung on a nearby rack. To make matters even worse, her husband actually went over and talked with these rowdy seamen, and he seemed to know them very well. She soon learned that this motley crew was her husband's shipmates. She couldn't believe it.

When it came time to go back to the boat, the sailors let the rooster run free but put the goat into the trunk of a taxi and headed toward home with the animal. When they got to the gate at the base, the marine guard leaned in to check IDs. The goat, meanwhile, was raising a ruckus, bleating and trying to escape from the trunk by kicking and banging his horns against the lid.

"What's that noise?" the guard asked, but by that time all the sailors in the car were bouncing, kicking, stomping, making goat noises, and hitting their heads on the headliner of the taxi, trying to muffle the sound of their bearded passenger in the back. The marine decided it wasn't worth the trouble. He waved them on through.

The topside watch on the boat merely shook his head when he saw his shipmates dragging the reluctant goat across the brow. A noisy battery charge was in progress below, and the goat had no intention of going down the after battery hatch toward whatever was making all that clamor. One of the men grabbed the animal by his horns, held him over the hole, and yelled, "Look out below!" With that, he dropped the goat down the hatch. The guys playing poker in the mess hall couldn't believe it when a full-grown goat landed on the deck near them.

Garrett Kelly was grabbing some rack time, getting ready for the four to eight topside watch, when he heard a cataclysmic noise. By the time he jumped from his bunk, pulled on some trousers, and went to check on it, the rowdy sailors had taken their pet to—where else?—the Goat Locker, the berthing space for the chief petty officers, and had awakened a CPO who had been sleeping off a night on the town. The resulting racket was what had awakened Kelly.

It didn't take long to figure out that they better find someplace else for their new best fiend. They decided to take him back to the after torpedo room, where there would be more space. Larry Dachenhausen had the battery charge in the engine room that night. When he felt the pressure difference that indicated the door between the after battery and the forward engine room had been opened, he looked up to see a wild-eyed goat, wearing a collar and a chain, jump through. On the other end of the chain was Jim Moran, followed by several more shipmates. The goat did not like all the noise from the charging engine, and when it went past the blower intake and felt its hair stand on end, the animal went berserk. Dachenhausen was afraid the critter might kick loose something vital and force him to stop the charge, so he grabbed the goat by the chain and dragged it into the after engine room. He chained it to the topside access ladder.

When Robbie Roberts, the charging electrician, peeked in from the maneuvering room to see what all the noise was, he saw the goat chained to the ladder, and it was obviously upset by all the noise and vibrations. It had long since lost control of its bowels.

Duke Durgin was the duty officer that night and was so far unaware of the visitor. On his way aft, he passed an off-duty engineman who was leaning against the sink in the mess hall and asked, "Who has the charge in the engine room?"

"The goat," the engine man replied.

Durgin assumed that was yet another nickname for one of the crew and headed on aft to the engine room. A few minutes later, he was back.

"There's a goat in the engine room!" he yelled, his eyes wide.

He quickly told everyone involved to get the animal out of there and off the boat. Some of the men tried to convince him that they should hang on to the goat as a mascot. The officer presented several sound reasons why a barnyard animal didn't belong on a U.S. Navy submarine.

"And what about the smell?" Durgin argued.

"We got used to it," someone shot back. "The goat will, too."

Finally, Durgin agreed that they could keep it in the after torpedo room for the rest of the night, but it had to go ashore first thing in the morning. When the time came, the men found it was much more difficult to get a goat out of a submarine than into one. They ultimately had to tie a line around its horns and pull from above while several other men tried to get beneath the animal and shove it up through the after torpedo room hatch. Joe Osier had the unpleasant task of climbing the ladder with the goat's butt on his shoulder and the animal's furiously kicking hind legs flailing away on the side of his face.

Well, the guys topside pulled on the line while Osier grunted and strained, pushing on the goat's rear end. The frightened animal bellowed and bleated pitifully, and then, without warning, shit spectacularly, the dung running down Osier's back. After a lot of pulling, pushing, and shitting, they finally got the goat topside, but had no idea of what to do with it next. Not knowing what else to do, they tied the goat to the dumpster at the head of Pier 9 and simply left it there.

A few minutes later, they watched as a pair of marines came by, checking parked cars. The two did a double take when they saw the goat tied to the dumpster. Nobody, including the topside watch on *Archerfish*, could tell them to whom the animal belonged or how it came to be tied up inside a U.S. Navy base. The marines left to go get instructions on how to handle such an unorthodox situation. While they were gone, some of the *Archerfish* crew decided their former shipmate was getting hungry and moved it, tying it to a fireplug in front of Building 1. It could graze on the shrubs that had been carefully planted there.

After a bit, the crew saw a navy truck pull up and haul the goat away. Later, the word was that the animal became a member of the Atlantic Submarine Medical Group staff and was accepted by Commander George Bond, one of the men who set the free ascent record from *Archerfish* off Key West in 1959. It was used in Bond's experimental work at the Submarine Escape Training Tank. Apparently the animal served its country long and well.

Years later, Garrett Kelly was assigned to another submarine, the USS *Corporal* (SS-346), operating out of New London. One day he was sitting in a bar on Bank Street and was retelling once again for a group of patrons the legendary story of the *Archerfish* goat. The other sailors in the bar were disbelieving, chalking it up as yet another overembellished sea story. But then an older gentleman farther down the bar broke in.

"That's no sea story, guys," he said. "This man is telling the truth. I was the driver of the cab that night when they brought back the goat!"

The ex-cabbie confirmed the whole story, even about everyone in his taxi making noise so the marine guard wouldn't hear the goat bleating and banging around in the trunk. The last thing the driver saw that night was the goat disappearing down the hatch of a submarine moored at the pier.

The day of their scheduled departure from New London, the officers of *Archerfish* watched President John Kennedy's inauguration on television at the officers' club and then walked through knee-deep snow to get back to the boat. An overnight blizzard had dumped a foot of the white stuff. The bridge between New London and Groton was closed, causing some of the sailors who were still at a party in New London to have to tip a cabby double fare to persuade him to risk the treacherous roads to get them back to the boat on time.

Archerfish sailed from New London just after two PM, en route to Curaçao, the largest of the Netherlands Antilles. From there they would pass through the Panama Canal and steam to Pearl Harbor, where the second phase of Operation Sea Scan would officially begin.

There were twenty new men aboard. That meant that twenty shipmates from phase one were now gone and would miss the next leg of the world cruise.

Within a few days, the weather was getting pleasantly warmer, warmer than most of them had seen in a long, long time. Of course, that meant it was getting downright hot below. By the time they were steaming south off Jacksonville, Florida, the air temperature in the pump room was 112 degrees.

On the other hand, they saw their first beautiful tropical sunsets and could even sunbathe during the day on the cigarette deck.

The warmth, the bright sun after so many months in the hooded sunlight of the high latitudes, the excitement of beginning a new adventure, had everyone in good spirits. Still, all those positives could not have accounted for the sudden joyous outburst one day from all the hydro people. The boat was about seventy-five miles north of Puerto Rico when the stylus on the scientists' gravity machine suddenly went wild. They poured out of their "hole" beneath the radio shack and requested that the boat make a few more passes over the same area so they could confirm their readings.

All they had done was record the deepest point in the Atlantic Ocean, a spot in the Puerto Rico Trench that was officially listed as 28,374 feet deep.

Once again, *Archerfish* had scribbled her name into the record books.

20

"IS THIS ALL THERE IS?"

THE crew of *Archerfish* had few thoughts of icebergs anymore. After all that time dodging bergs and growlers, trying to avoid getting frozen in place in the floe ice, they were now in the tropical southwestern Caribbean Sea. The boat eased into the harbor at Willemstad, Curaçao, in the early morning light of January 26, 1961. They ran in between the two old forts that had once guarded the town from pirates or those who were intent on conquest, then they moored port side to Nieuwe Haven Pier.

That night, the officers from *Archerfish* were the invited guests of Mr. and Mrs. Mervyn V. Pallister, the U.S. consul general and his wife. The consulate is a beautiful building, given to the United States by the Dutch before the Netherlands Antilles became an independent nation in 1954. The building sits on a hill overlooking the small bay and the picturesque town of Willemstad.

It was true that, while ashore, Captain Woods sometimes drank more like an enlisted man than like an officer, and that evening was a good example. That proclivity at times caused him to lose his sense of social obligation. But that is also one of the reasons the crew appreciated and respected their commander. This was his third command, and Woods fully understood the mission of his boat as well as the unusual nature of his crew. One of the new officers found out early on, before they left New London, that Woods was not the typical navy commanding officer. The officer found need to ask for a few hours off to take care of personal business. He was explaining to Woods all the reasons why when the CO raised his hand to stop him.

"You don't have to tell me, son," he said. "I'm not your mother." And he granted the man the time he needed.

As one of the crew members from that time says, "Woods's leadership style was one which respected the capabilities of the wardroom and crew. He allowed his people to exercise personal judgment and initiative, providing correction when he saw them tending toward real problems. It was very much an atmosphere that built confidence and permitted *Archerfish* to meet all her commitments on schedule over the two-year period that he was her skipper."

While the officers were wearing out their welcome at the U.S. consulate, the sailors made their way to the two primary hotels in town, the American and the Intercontinental. They could sit on the big second-floor open-air porch of the American Hotel, drink beer, and watch the ship traffic pass in and out of the tiny harbor, enjoying the fact that they were not in New London. And that's where one of the waiters told them about Campo Alegre—"the compound," or Camp Joy.

Campo Alegre was the island's only red-light district, and it was quite a place. The compound was located outside of town, across a floating bridge and near the Hato airfield. It was considered out of bounds for the Netherlands navy, *Archerfish*'s official hosts while they were in Curaçao, but there was no restriction on the American sailors. New girls arrived at the compound almost daily from all over the world. As long as the women followed the rules, they could rent a room from the island's government for ten guilders ($5 U.S.) per day for as long as they wanted. The government provided everything the women needed, including medical care and regular examinations. The only stipulation was that if they left the compound they had to leave the island.

The *Archerfish* sailors soon learned that Campo Alegre had better security than the sub base at New London. No booze or cameras were allowed through the gates. Lockers were provided just inside the heavily guarded entrance, and visitors were issued keys to the lockers by the guards. Patrons were then admitted through turnstiles that kept count of the number of visitors entering the compound to make sure the same number came out.

Once inside, the variety of offerings was astounding, both in the nationality of the women to be found there and the pleasures available. Some of the *Archerfish* sailors were surprised to see familiar faces in the compound, some of the girls they had met back in Havana before Castro ran them out of Cuba. They had a great time reminiscing about good times at the Ticky Bar, the Lido Hotel, the Miami Bar, New Chico's, The Pilot, and other legendary prerevolutionary waterfront joints.

The day after their arrival, the Dutch military threw a barbecue for the crew at their club. Everyone was having a great time, eating the wonderful food, swimming, and drinking, until word got around that the barbecue they were enjoying was actually goat meat. That broke up the party.

Two days later, the crew of *Archerfish* had to go to work. Six forty-five came awfully early after their good times with the hospitable islanders and the international smorgasbord of pleasures at Campo Alegre. They were scheduled to conduct exercises with the Dutch navy all day. A signal tower in one of the old forts regulated traffic into and out of the harbor and David Dimmick, as navigator, soon found out just how busy the little port was. Because a Shell Oil refinery, the third largest in the world, was located there, Willemstad handled an amazing amount of shipping tonnage, making her one of the busiest seaports on the planet.

Once they were out of the harbor, the exercises were relatively simple. *Archerfish* submerged so the Dutch navy's vessel, *Van Amstel*, could practice antisubmarine runs against a real submarine. Since they were running steady courses and depths during the exercises, Dimmick left the periscope up after diving so he could watch the ship pass above them in the wonderfully clear water.

"I could see every barnacle on her bottom," he says. "I was quite nervous during the episode and continually calculated what should be the clearance between the scope and their bottom. There was plenty of room, but when I'd look at them through the scope, it seemed as if they were going to crunch the thing."

The next day, they conducted exercises with airplanes as well as *Van Amstel* and ran over to the island of Bonaire, twenty miles east of Curaçao. Once again, they became the first submarine to visit a port when they moored to Jetty Pier in Kralendijk Harbor on Bonaire that afternoon. Townspeople gathered on the pier to see this strange critter ease up to their pier. Meanwhile, the crew took advantage of the clear water to swim and dive from the boat's deck. That night, the boat's officers were invited to the lieutenant governor's bungalow for a small party. The government official gave each of them a special gift, a small bottle of Curaçao liqueur shaped like a flamingo. Nearly a quarter of the world's flamingo population resides on Bonaire, so the gift was quite appropriate.

Lee Walker remembers that the party moved back to the Flamingo Hotel and the lieutenant governor ordered the bar to remain open until well past its normal closing time to accommodate their submariner visitors.

Walker had the bridge the next morning when they got under way, this time headed for the Panama Canal. They did tarry just off Curaçao for a bit to do a little shark fishing but had no luck.

The boat anchored in Limon Bay off Colón, Balboa, Canal Zone, the next morning, waiting their turn to enter the canal. This was the third such transit for *Archerfish* but a first for many of the crew members. They picked up their pilot, Captain Clayton, and proceeded through Gatun Locks and into Gatun Lake. Only one set of locks was open, so the going was slow, taking a total of eight hours, but that enabled many of those who had not been through the canal a chance to watch the process. They noticed that the tide on the Pacific end was sixteen feet, much more pronounced than the one-foot tide on the Atlantic end, the "other side of the continent." It was also surprising to discover that the Pacific end of the canal is actually east of the Atlantic end. Their transit had been from north-northwest to south-southeast, even though they were westward bound.

Once moored at the U.S. Naval Base at Rodman, Canal Zone, the crew members received their pay and headed for the limited opportunities to spend it in the nearby town. On February 7, now that they were floating in the Pacific Ocean, they officially reported to Submarine Squadron 1. On the first day in port, some of the crew spent the afternoon playing a softball game against the marines at the navy base.

Captain Howe, the chief of staff of the base, invited the sub's wardroom to a reception at his home on Fort Amador. In a much seedier part of town, over food and drinks, several members of the crew were discussing the idea of going in together once they were out of the navy and buying a Chinese junk. They could then sail the vessel around the South Pacific trade routes, leisurely exploring all the tiny islands in that part of the world. The next day, several of the sailors went to the disbursing officer and started allotments for a fifty-dollar savings bond each month, the money they would someday use to buy that boat. Of course, they never got around to doing it.

As usual, *Archerfish* got under way late in the day from the Canal Zone. This allowed them a full workday to take care of odds and ends and to steady up hands and heads after liberty. On February 11, *Archerfish* submerged in Pacific waters for the first time since June 1952, almost nine years earlier. Under a bright, warm sun and calm seas, they watched the mountains of Costa Rica slip away to starboard and sailfish leaping out of the azure waters, playing in their wake. John Gonzales rigged the topside showers when the captain authorized the OOD to lay to so the men could take a swim and then rinse the salt water off.

Later, they saw a large number of turtles in the sea and stopped to let Joe Cummings dive in and try to catch one. He couldn't. Then, when they tried to get him back aboard, they had a difficult time of it.

"Almost lost Joe" was Walker's cryptic comment on the incident.

They moored "in a nest of submarines" alongside USS *Sperry* (AS-12) in San Diego. Their new squadron commander came aboard with his party, spent a half hour, and left.

It was in San Diego that the replacement for *Archerfish*'s engineer, Miles Graham, reported aboard. He was a Naval Academy graduate named Frank Ford, and he remembers well his first glimpse of *Archerfish*.

"I remember the start of it all as I walked off the tender in San Diego," he says. "That was when I saw for the first time my future home nested amongst several spick-and-span, squared-away Guppies. Her rust-streaked, anachronistic lines looked like something out of a science fiction movie where she'd just surfaced from her last war patrol [in the midst of all those modern boats]."

Lieutenant Graham would remain aboard awhile longer, until the boat reached Pearl Harbor, to ensure that a complete turnover of the engineering department was accomplished. When they arrived in Pearl, he was transferred to shore duty in Houston, Texas.

Jack "Swede" Johnson was working in the conning tower on USS *Volador* (SS-490) when his exec climbed up the ladder from the control room and asked him if he was interested in volunteering for *Archerfish*. Johnson didn't hesitate. *Archerfish*'s reputation had preceded her. Johnson had gone from just hoping to get a glimpse of the storied boat while she was in San Diego to getting a chance to serve aboard her. When the exec told him the boat was looking for a single, rated, submarine-qualified fire-control technician, he said, "That's me! You betcha I want to go!" He had his orders cut while he packed his seabag then headed for his favorite watering hole to celebrate his good fortune. He soon met his new shipmates. A rowdy bunch of *Archerfish* sailors were at the Pirate's Den ahead of him.

It seemed that most of the *A-fish* gang had problems with the Shore Patrol while they were in San Diego. They soon learned an important fact, though. No matter what time they were picked up by the Shore Patrol, they were going to spend four hours in the drunk tank. If they behaved themselves during their incarceration, they were turned loose at the end of the four hours and were free to go. But if they made problems for the Shore Patrol, they were, instead, delivered back to the boat at the end of their jail time. As it turned out, how the men behaved while they were locked up in the drunk tank depended on the hour of the night at which they were picked up.

The bars on Broadway closed at 2:00 AM and last call was at 1:45. If the sailors were in the tank before 9:00 PM, they were on their best behavior the entire four hours. This insured that they would be released in time to get to a bar one more time before last call. Normally, they used the time in the tank to catch up on some much-needed sleep. In those instances when they were picked up late enough to miss last call at the end of their four-hour stay, they were certain to raise enough hell while in jail so they could get a free ride back to *Archerfish* in the paddy wagon and save the cab fare.

Bill Hiesley even went so far as to turn himself in early one night so he could be out in time for last call. Another night, he took a blanket and pillow ashore with him in the afternoon and went straight to Shore Patrol headquarters. He gave the blanket and pillow to the guy on the watch desk and asked him to give them back to him when he inevitably got brought in later in the evening. He said he was tired of sleeping on the cold stainless-steel deck of the drunk tank.

The "rag hats" (enlisted men) weren't the only ones having trouble with San Diego law enforcement. Lieutenant Duke Durgin fell asleep in a movie theater one night. When the cops tried to roust him, Durgin woke up with the thought that someone was attempting to rob him. He fought mightily against his attackers in the dark theater. A group of policemen finally subdued the officer, dragged him off to Balboa Park, beat him up, and eventually let him go.

On February 26, the duty section was charging the boat's batteries using number-two and number-four main engines while sitting alongside Broadway Pier. The exhaust from the engines was being discharged beneath the pier. The wind carried the smoke and fumes inside a nearby warehouse, where they soon set off the building's fire alarm system. In no time, fire trucks showed up at the head of the pier, sirens wailing, lights flashing. The *Archerfish* crew all came topside to watch the excitement, but they never let the firemen know the cause of the alarm.

It was also about this same time that Bob Athorp fired up the radar one day to run some equipment checks. It didn't take long to realize that the radar was not compatible with the neon in the signs for the bars along South Broadway. The neon tubes began popping like popcorn.

It was probably just as well that they soon got underway, bound for Pearl Harbor. They arrived in Pearl on March 7, spotting Diamond Head Light just before seven-thirty in the morning.

Once the old boat was back in Hawaii, there was a strong sense of déjà vu on several counts. Not only was she once again at the place where she had first entered the war but also her crew was soon busily scavenging for the equipment they needed, just as they had once done back on the East Coast. They found some old boats being cut up for scrap and absconded with an air-conditioning unit Mr. Ford wanted to install in the forward torpedo room. Some of the electricians went along on the raid, intent on locating controllers and other electrical equipment they needed for their part of the installation. They also spied the parts they needed to raise from the dead "Leroy," the auxiliary engine, for which they had already held a solemn funeral. The difference between these acquisitions and those in Philly was that they didn't have to hurriedly install them before anyone caught wind of their unorthodox requisition procedure. All the purloined parts were stowed in the forward torpedo room. The repair facility personnel would be the ones to install them once they arrived in Japan.

Soon they were under way again and were once more obediently taking their gravity readings and steaming along predetermined routes to get the proper data. The boat crossed the international date line on March 31, allowing them to skip April Fool's Day entirely. *Archerfish* had entered the "Domain of the Golden Dragon" for the first time since she returned to Pearl Harbor from Tokyo Bay following the Japanese surrender aboard *Missouri* on September 2, 1945.

A week later, *Archerfish* was in another familiar place, Yokosuka, Japan. She was moored port side to USS *Razorback* (SS-394) at Berth 1 in what was now a U.S. naval base. Everyone aboard was quite aware that they were berthed only a short distance from where *Shinano* had been constructed and launched on her ill-fated maiden voyage.

As they eased into place alongside *Razorback*, one of the men on the other submarine's deck yelled across to the *Archerfish* sailors. "Hey, does that cook that makes the Johnny Walker pancakes want to come over and make some for us?"

Dale Ness, whose experiment with whiskey pancakes had so pleased Captain Woods, just happened to be among the men on *Archerfish*'s deck that morning. He yelled back, "No thanks. I've already got a job and I like it."

The story of the unorthodox pancakes had already made it halfway around the world in about six months.

Captain Woods took most of the wardroom ashore and to the officers club. He was quite well known there from his previous days of shore duty in Yokosuka. There were also plenty of others at the club who had heard of *Archerfish* and her captain's exploits and wanted to meet him. Later, the officers went to the Kanko Hotel to catch the floor show there. Sitting in the back, they listened while a group of Japanese girls sang popular songs in English.

Suddenly, there was a familiar figure rising from the audience at the front of the club. Kenny Woods began to perform some kind of impromptu dance that gradually segued into a striptease. With a face that seemed to connote only boredom, he chewed his gum while dancing around the stage, bumping and grinding, removing his tie, his belt, and his shirt. Thankfully, he stopped stripping at that point and, to the delight of the audience, performed his "Muffin Man" routine, singing, bobbing up and down on one leg, then the other, all the while balancing a cup and saucer on his forehead.

"He was a lot more fun than anything else in the place," Lee Walker reports.

The officers finished up the night at the secret "submarine sanctuary," the pride of Pacific submariners and the envy of the surface fleet. Since the first days after the end of World War II, submariners in the western Pacific had donated money to keep the "sanctuary" in Yokosuka, but it was still a closely held secret fifteen years later. The place was an unofficial bachelor officers' quarters and consisted of several rooms on the top floor of one of the buildings in the shipyard. There was a dining room, a bar, and several bedrooms, all nicely furnished with rugs on the floors, soft couches in the bar, a television set, and curtains on the windows. The place was great for meeting fellow officers and swapping sea stories, and was perfect for catching up on sleep or getting oneself cleaned up while away from the boat.

About this time, the officers of *Archerfish* decided they needed some kind of distinctive civilian attire so they could be easily recognized at parties and other assorted entertainment events. The group all went to James S. Lee's tailoring establishment and got measured up for identical blue blazers. It would be several years later that they would learn that James S. Lee and several of his tailoring staff had been identified as part of a Soviet spy ring. While they were making suits for American sailors, they were also reporting on ship movements from their rather fortuitous position in Yokosuka.

Japan was a cultural change for most of the crew since they mostly came from the Atlantic Fleet. However, they easily adjusted to unisex toilets, taking a leak in the *benjo* (sewage) ditches, the fifty-yen cabs that scared the hell out of their passengers, and eating with sticks instead of forks. All the while they had a great time.

They did have to put up with the foolish rule about gabardine blues and Wellington boots not being allowed. And they suffered the ire of the senior petty officers from surface craft. The men from those vessels were required to be home by midnight while even the most junior petty officers on submarines had permanent overnight passes. The crew members were also exposed to military payment certificates for the first time. The scrip looked more like Monopoly money than real currency. No matter. The sailors spent the scrip with the same careless disregard they showed greenbacks.

A lengthy article about *Archerfish* appeared in the military newspaper *Stars and Stripes* while the boat was in Yokosuka. The story noted that she was already the world record holder for miles steamed in a single year by a conventional submarine, the 43,000 miles traveled in the Atlantic Ocean during Operation Sea Scan phase one. It also said she would add 80,000 to 90,000 more miles before the Pacific phase was completed in just over a year. A photo of Lieutenant Joe Cummings and one of the hydro scientists, Charles Selkirk, accompanied the article. They were shown positioned in front of a rack that held the oceanographic equipment that measured sea temperature, wave heights, and the other rather boring data.

It mentioned the rest of the hydros aboard at the time, Ken Fanning, Roger Bach, and William Fong, and quoted *Archerfish's* executive officer, Dave Dimmick, on why the boat carried a crew of all bachelors except one.

"Our deal with the hydrographic service keeps us at sea and away from the U.S. for months—even years—at a time. A guy with family problems— if the baby gets sick, the wife sends a 'Dear John' or the kids need new shoes—would be out of luck on our crew. He just couldn't get home in a hurry from, say, Hammerfest, Norway, the northernmost city in the world."

The reporter asked the boat's lone married crewman at that time how he felt. Yeoman Second Class Lucien Fraser answered, "It works out pretty well. My wife, Nancy, is getting her master's degree back home in Iowa, and she has plenty of time to study. I'll be home in a year. So this trip is no problem."

The article also revealed that the scientists would occasionally rely on an ancient method of scientific experimentation, the note in a bottle. The hydros were quoted as saying that they periodically dropped overboard a bottle with a note inside asking the finder to log the latitude and longitude where it was found and then mail it to the U.S. Navy in Washington. The story concluded with a recap of *Archerfish*'s war exploits.

It had become the custom in many of the ports they visited for *Archerfish* to hold open house for the public. They did so one day during this stay in Yokosuka. At least two thousand people, mostly Japanese civilians, climbed down the ladders and went through the boat, most of them carrying cameras and snapping away at everything they saw. They seemed especially interested in the Playboy Playmate pinups on the locker doors in the after torpedo room.

Finally, it was almost five PM and time to wrap up the tours. Mike Lintner, the leading torpedoman in the after torpedo room, was in the liberty section and was anxious to get ashore for a night of fun. He had closed all the tubes, already had his dress blues on, and was itching to go.

But then he got a phone call telling him there was one more group coming through. They were already headed his way. And this group was definitely different from the previous ones that had come through earlier that day.

Lintner rolled his eyes, but he had no choice. He would have to let the tourists look around for a minute and ask their dumb questions before he could head across the brow. He waited.

In a few minutes, an older Japanese gentleman poked his head through the watertight doorway and slowly worked his way into the compartment. Two younger men, two younger women, an older lady, and three kids followed him after he had carefully climbed through the door.

It was true. They were different. They stayed in line. There were no smiles. No pictures. The older man eased his way aft to where Lintner was standing in front of tubes number seven and nine.

"Is this all there is?" the man asked, his English relatively good and his voice clearly incredulous.

"Pardon me?"

"Is this all there is?"

Lintner immediately switched to his tour guide mode. He was accustomed to visitors being amazed at the boat's cramped quarters.

"Yes, sir, this is it. *Archerfish* is about 310 feet long and this is as far as you can go," he said.

The Japanese man snorted in disbelief and slowly shook his head side to side. There was a rueful smile on his face.

None of the other visitors said a word. They merely stood there, watching the older man's reaction.

"Were you on board this submarine during the war?" the Japanese man finally asked Lintner.

"No, sir."

"Is there anyone else on board who was on this submarine during the war?" the old man queried.

"No, sir," Lintner replied. "But there are three members of the current crew who served on other submarines during the war." Lintner was beginning to feel uneasy. The look in the old man's eyes and the demeanor of the rest of the party told him this was no ordinary visitor. "Were you in the war?" Lintner finally asked the old gentleman.

"Yes. In the navy," the Japanese man answered proudly.

"Oh. What rank?"

"Commander."

Lintner knew he had gone too far to quit asking questions there.

"Which ship were you on?"

Without hesitation, the Japanese visitor answered, "*Shinano*. I was her executive officer."

All the air seemed to leave the room. Lintner quickly got on the horn to the wardroom. The commander and exec had already gone ashore, but he told the duty officer that they had a very special visitor back aft and suggested he might want to come meet the guy. While he waited, Lintner said something to the effect that it was nice that former enemies could now meet like this and talk about times past without bitterness and rancor. The visitor, though, was still looking all about him, at the constricted quarters in the torpedo room, and still shaking his head.

"But you are so small!" he said with force. The old sailor was obviously unable to comprehend how such a small vessel could have somehow sent his massive new ship to the bottom of the sea that fateful, moonlit night off Honshu's southern coast.

When the duty officer showed up, he invited the former *Shinano* executive officer to the wardroom for coffee. The old man finally relaxed, smiled, and accepted the invitation. That seemed to be the cue for the others. The women visibly relaxed as well, the sons began snapping pictures of the pinups on the lockers, and the kids began climbing on the torpedo tubes, just as all the normal visitors had done that day.

Another afternoon, a group of Japanese yard workers came down to *Archerfish* to take a look at her. Some of this bunch had been on *Shinano* when she went down. Others had helped in the gargantuan carrier's construction. Almost all of them knew someone who had been lost when

Archerfish sank her. Once aboard the submarine, they were most interested in seeing the tubes where the fatal torpedoes had been launched. From the moment they dropped down the hatch, they became solemn, almost reverent.

When they were topside again, the crew in the duty section gave them coffee and snacks on the after deck. All of them hunkered down on the after deck and swapped stories for a couple of hours.

Ken Henry, who was there that day, says, "Many years after this, on July 4, 1992, I had the privilege of sitting one-on-one with Joe Enright as he described to me his periscope view as *Archerfish* chased and sank *Shinano*. There are probably not many of us who have heard firsthand both sides of this moment in history."

Archerfish and her crew had quite a scare a few days later. They were making their way to Hakodate, Japan, and had passed through the Shimonoseki Strait, the narrow body of water that divides the islands of Honshu and Kyushu, and then steamed into the Sea of Japan. It was harrowing going, dodging the tiny islands and hundreds of fishing boats in the area while trying to stay on their assigned runs. One afternoon, they were running on the surface when the seas became too rough to take readings. They were starting down when the chief of the watch, Joe Cronin, suddenly yelled, "Red board!"

They immediately backed down and emergency surfaced. That's when there was a very loud *pow!* in the maneuvering room, and a giant ball of fire jumped out of the cubicle. The compartment began filling with smoke, and the boat lost propulsion on the starboard side.

Robbie Roberts, the senior controllerman, quickly passed the word: "Fire in maneuvering!"

The men in the after torpedo room tossed in their CO_2 extinguisher and dogged the door shut to keep the smoke and fire out of their compartment. The emergency was over in minutes, with no casualties. The crew soon determined that a reverser contact in the cubicle had dropped off and shorted out the buss work. The starboard shaft was out of commission, and they had only limited use of the port side engines.

They were, for all practical purposes, dead in the water, adrift in the Sea of Japan.

Somehow, they rounded up enough spare parts and Chief Electrician O'Neill McKinney and the electrical gang began the long, hot, dirty task of fixing the damage. On the bridge, there was some concern that they might drift too close to the island of Obi Shiga, but the men got propulsion back before that became a serious problem.

By the third week in April there was more cause for concern, and it had nothing to do with the boat or fire. They were now conducting surveying operations off the coast of Russia and Korea, at times within sixty miles of the large Russian submarine base at Vladivostok. Speedy Gonzales remembers, "You could feel the tension in the boat."

They finally moored in Hakodate on May 3. The city lies behind a breakwater in the bight of a mountain-ringed bay and is the largest city of Hokkaido, the northernmost of the main Japanese islands. Despite its being a large port, Hakodate had not been visited often by U.S. vessels. *Archerfish*, as usual, caused quite a stir.

Most everything went smoothly as they took on fuel and fresh water. But then a glitch arose. The topside watch informed Lee Walker, the duty officer, that the man from the water barge was there, demanding to be paid. Walker headed up to see what the problem was. The man bowed deeply, smiled politely, but spoke no English whatsoever. Walker bowed in return but had no idea how he was going to explain U.S. Navy purchasing procedures to this fellow. It was hard enough to do when the language was the same.

But then Walker got a look at the invoice. It was for 360 yen. That figured out to be about one U.S. dollar. Walker pulled out his wallet and paid the man his money. Language barrier overcome.

The crew delivered several boxes of "Mercy Missiles" (bundles of clothing) to the Shirayuri Child Welfare Association of Hakodate. The Navy League of New London sponsored the association. A group of adults and children from the home came to tour the boat and pick up their packages. The clothing had traveled well over 14,000 miles since it had been placed aboard *Archerfish* in New London in mid-January.

The boat was back in Yokosuka by the middle of May 1961 for a two-week upkeep, which included a major overhaul of number-three main engine. That gave most of the crew time to go up the bay to Tokyo and do things that tourists do. Several of the sailors were in one of the area's notorious "kamikaze taxis" one day, headed for Tokyo, when their driver hit a man on a motor scooter at an intersection. The driver seemed to take it all in stride. He pulled over and stopped, jumped out, dragged the motor scooter out of the street, and leaned the injured, semiconscious man against a light pole. Then he yelled and waved his arms angrily at the gathering crowd, hopped back into his cab, and hurried away, his horn blowing menacingly, as if this sort of mayhem happened all the time.

After the close call with the fire in the Sea of Japan and the nerve-racking work accomplished in such close proximity to the Soviet Union, the crew was definitely ready for liberty again.

As usual, they made the most of the opportunity.

21

RICKSHAW RACES AND
SUZIE WONG

As if Thule and Curaçao weren't isolated or exotic enough places for *Archerfish*, the boat and her crew were about to make stops at some even more interesting places, taking in the sights and leaving their own unique mark wherever they paused. On June 18, they moored starboard side to USS *Charr* (SS-328) at North Arm, Victoria Basin, Hong Kong, British Crown Colony. As soon as the maneuvering watch was secured, one of the lead girls from Mary Sue's Side Cleaners worked out a deal with the chief of the boat to swap work in exchange for *Archerfish*'s garbage. During every meal, a young girl from one of Mary Sue's garbage barges was stationed by the trash cans in the crew's mess. She would take each sailor's plate from him once he had finished eating, then meticulously scrape the leftovers into the proper cans, based on food groups. In return for the men's garbage, the women chipped and painted topside, doing the chores that the seaman gang normally did while the boat was in port. Not to be left out, the engineman gave the girls some old main engine crankshaft bearings as payment for their chipping and painting the bilges in both engine rooms. The sailors supplied the paint and the tools. Mary Sue's girls supplied the labor. It was a wonderful deal for the girls (all but the crew leader were very young, still in their early teens) and for the liberty-bound sailors.

In addition to hitting the colorful local drinking spots that were scattered throughout the Wanchai district, many of the men toured the island on their first day there. They saw the fantastic statuary at the Tiger Balm Gardens, the blue waters and sandy beaches of Repulse Bay, the crowded harbor at Aberdeen with its much-photographed fleet of junks with their oddly tilted masts, the sampans scurrying about, the crowded dwellings of the colony's desperately poor, and the palatial homes of the fabulously wealthy.

A group of *Archerfish* crewmen ended up at Bar Neptune late that afternoon and were soon into some serious imbibing. Among them was the captain, Kenny Woods, who boldly and out of the blue announced to the group that he could outrun anyone in the bar in a footrace. Speedy Gonzales fancied himself as being fleet of foot and accepted the skipper's challenge. Most of the sailors spilled outside and watched as the two men raced along the sidewalk in front of the bar. When it was over, Gonzales had to buy the next round of drinks for the house.

Johnny Gentry told Woods that he didn't think the captain could do it again. Woods puffed out his chest and announced, "Not only can I do it again, but I can do it pulling one of those rickshaws."

That did it. This time, everyone in the bar, including the girls, emptied out into the street once again. The course was one block long and all traffic in one lane of exceedingly busy Lockhard Road would be blocked for the race. The sailors and bar girls lined up along the way to watch. Woods chose his rickshaw from the ones lined up along the curb and Gentry picked his out from the rest. They made a deal with the coolies that they could, for once, ride in their own rickshaws during the race.

It was no contest. Woods won easily.

Now everyone wanted in on the action, but the sailors were smart enough not to agree to pull the things themselves. That's what the coolies were for! Bets were made and rickshaws chosen. The sailors conferred with their coolies, promised big payoffs if their rickshaw should be the winner, and plotted their race strategy.

Once again, the main street in front of Bar Neptune was blocked off, this time taking two lanes, and the course was set. Not even the streetcars could get through. People crawled out of their cars and rickshaws to see what was going on, most of them yelling, either in the spirit of the contest or in anger at being held up in the quickly building, massive traffic jam.

Finally, the contestants were lined up and the start signaled. It was a close race for the first half of the block, each coolie valiantly straining to get out front with his rickshaw and the sub sailor who was riding in it. But suddenly all the drivers but one stopped abruptly, dropped their rickshaws, and fell to their knees, scrambling wildly for something in the middle of the street. Meanwhile, Mike Lintner's rickshaw puller kept running to the finish line. He was the only one to finish the race and was, of course, the winner.

It seems that Lintner had instructed his driver to keep running no matter what happened along the way and promised him a nice payoff at the end if he did. Halfway down the course, Lintner tossed out a big handful of Hong Kong dimes in front of the other runners, knowing they would instinctively stop to pick them up. The plan worked. He claimed the winner-take-all bounty. At the exchange rate of $5.75 Hong Kong for $1.00 American, Mike got quite a deal!

The William Holden–Nancy Kwan movie, *The World of Suzie Wong*, was still quite popular in the States at the time. Since it was most of the crew's first visit to Hong Kong, they wanted to see the locations that the movie had portrayed so vividly. They asked a cabbie to take them to the Wanchai district, to the same bar where "Suzie" worked. When they asked for Suzie, they were told, "She no work tonight!"

Instead of talking with Suzie, they haggled with the famous sampan girls who worked across the street from the bar, but no one took the girls up on their rather graphic offers. The women were simply too dirty, too decrepit, even for a group of adventurous submarine sailors on liberty.

The Wanchai district as portrayed in *The World of Suzie Wong* and as it was when the men of *Archerfish* experienced it is no more. At that time, an overflow of rickshaws, bars, sidewalk industry, and bordellos blended into a colorful potpourri of seething humanity. It was an exciting place to be. Nowadays, sterile and cold office buildings rise shoulder to shoulder in every direction. A visitor might just as well be in the financial district of any of the world's major cities.

Some of the men did other tourist-type things, like taking the Star Ferry that ran between Hong Kong and Kowloon. It played a part in the movie as well and turned out to be a good way to see the sights of the harbor for only a twenty-five-cent fare each way.

Hong Kong was also a good place to shop. Both Mike Lintner and Galen Steck bought new Rolex watches for $125 each. Steck maintains his watch still runs today, but Lintner had a problem with his. Not with the works. It kept time perfectly. Two years after his visit to Hong Kong, he was assigned to the USS *Haddo* (SSN-604), a nuclear submarine under construction at the New York Shipbuilding Yard in Camden, New Jersey, across the Delaware River from Philadelphia. When he stepped aboard the nuclear boat, he immediately set off all the radiation alarms he passed. The problem turned out to be his Hong Kong Rolex. The dial must have been painted with a generous dollop of the purest radium imaginable. It pegged the meter on a Geiger counter. The engineering officer on *Haddo* offered to encase Lintner's prize watch in a lead box for him until he got transferred or went home. Since *Haddo was* his home, he refused. He was just glad to have found the probable cause for why his left wrist had been aching horribly for the past several months. He tossed the watch over the side, into the water, and it's likely still there, in the silt and mud at the bottom of the Delaware River.

Bill Fong, one of the hydros, became the crew's "party chief" in Hong Kong by default, but he readily accepted the responsibility. A second-generation Chinese American from California, his parents came directly to the States from China. The rumor was that his father had been a member of General Chiang Kai-shek's Nationalist government when it fled the country ahead of the Communists. Fong spoke the language and was only too happy to play the "local" when they were out on the town. When a waiter brought them a menu in English, he sent it back, insisting on the Chinese version. It inevitably had the better nontourist choices, not to mention more favorable prices.

Archerfish had only five days in Hong Kong, but the crew had made the most of the stopover. On June 23, they finally got everyone rounded up, including Ted Armstrong and Fred Yentz, who were an hour and a half late, and were underway at 1730, bound for more survey routes and, eventually, Subic Bay, in the Philippines. As David Dimmick said, "Hong Kong gave us the most problems with the crew ashore. Troubles. People not aboard for scheduled sailing. Sending men back over to check the local whorehouses to find the missing. The crew was a real pain in the ass for this visit. So what happened? The local equivalent of the USO presented us with a plaque for our exemplary conduct while we were ashore!"

Another one of the hydrographic scientists, Keith Norlin, had been aboard *Archerfish* for phase one when she traversed the chilly North Atlantic waters, then left while she was moored in Thule, Greenland. He rejoined her while she was in Hong Kong. Norlin checked out of the hotel where he had been staying until the day the submarine sailed for Subic Bay. He noticed the difference on the boat the instant he dropped down into the hydro hole below the radio shack.

"It was 93 degrees, and that was under the small air-conditioning duct we were fortunate to have down there. Other parts of the boat were over

100, and it seldom dropped below 110 in the engine rooms. The boat smelled like a combination of a greasy diner, an oil refinery, and a men's gym. Except for the smell, which was still the same, it was quite a change from my last tour on *Archerfish*."

All the men enjoyed being topside, though. The temperature was usually in the mideighties, and there was often a gentle breeze blowing. Many of them spent what time they could up there, smoking, talking, working on their tans, airing out their armpits. When they stripped off their shirts, many of them sported brand-new tattoos after their most recent stop. It is said that Hong Kong has some of the world's best tattoo artists, and some of the *Archerfish* crew had taken advantage of their talents. Of course, there is little privacy on a submarine, and the crew's quarters in the after battery and in the berthing areas in the forward and after torpedo rooms were a kind of moving, breathing art gallery. Simple but intricate designs vied with near-full-body masterpieces, representing the work of tattoo artists from ports all over the world.

Most people have seen the simpler or less obnoxious types, the wrist bracelets, the hearts enclosing the name of some long-forgotten sweetheart-for-life. Clothing usually covers the more rude ones. Even sailors visit their mothers sometime. Some are simply funny. One torpedoman aboard *Archerfish* had the words HOT and COLD tattooed above his nipples. Another chose "SWEET" and "SOUR" for the same locations.

One of the more spectacular pieces of art belonged to an engineman who had a devil needled on each cheek of his bum. The devils were using shovels to throw coal up the sailor's anus, from which spewed flames and smoke, all in vivid color.

July 2 was a significant day in *Archerfish*'s history. She made her three thousandth dive at 1507 that afternoon, slipping routinely beneath the rough waters of the South China Sea to make her gravity readings at a calmer depth. The good news was that she successfully surfaced forty-one minutes later to complete the dive. Chief Torpedoman Lewis G. Holm, the chief of the boat, was the conning officer for the submergence. Chief Engineman Joseph J. Cronin, the senior enlisted man on board, was the diving officer. Torpedoman First Class Michael Lintner, Electronics Technician Third Class Joe D. Forrest, and Commander Kenneth Woods, the commander, served as members of the diving team. According to a navy press release that detailed the event, "An appropriately decorated cake was prepared for the occasion."

The press release went on to mention some of the highlights of the boat's history, then said, "Three thousand dives is significant not for the number but as a mark of continuing service to the country. *Archerfish*, now demilitarized, her torpedo handling equipment removed and oceanographic equipment installed, is engaged in a two-year, two-ocean oceanographic survey called 'Operation Sea Scan,' which has taken her 72,000 miles since May of 1960, just two thousand miles less than she steamed in her wartime service. She is continuing her life as a useful and unique member of the Submarine Force, U. S. Pacific Fleet, and aiding the seagoing nations of the world by adding to man's knowledge of the world's oceans. *Archerfish* is currently a unit of the Seventh Fleet."

Over the next two weeks, *Archerfish* crisscrossed the South China Sea between the Philippine island of Luzon and a little known southeast Asian country that would soon be on the lips of all Americans. Vietnam. Maybe it was symbolic that poisonous sea snakes were said to be swimming in the murky waters around the submarine. There was always speculation about what might happen if one of the venomous critters got caught in the shears or fairwater during an ascent. Would it pounce on the first person to come through the hatch? Luckily it never happened, but in the near future many Americans would lose their lives in this literal and figurative quagmire of a region. Those men would be doing the same thing as USS *Shark 2* (SS-314) and USS *Snook* (SS-279) were doing when they sailed in those same waters during World War II—fighting for freedom.

The U.S. naval facility at Subic Bay in the Phillipines—returned to the Filipino government in 1992—was a huge military installation in 1961. As with most such facilities down through history, a town had grown up outside the base's gates, made up primarily of establishments and people who were there to serve the various needs of the personnel who spent time on the base. In this case, the town was Olongapo, and the *Archerfish* crew found it to be quite hospitable—with a few exceptions.

At the same time the crew was sampling the fare in Olongapo, the boat's corpsman and exec wanted them to try a bit of self-improvement. At that time, President Kennedy was pushing physical fitness for the country and mandating a workout regimen for all military personnel. There wasn't much opportunity for jogging or doing calisthenics on a cramped diesel boat, but once they were moored at Riviera Wharf in Subic Bay, Doc Barboza and Dave Dimmick wanted to make sure the crew of *Archerfish* got their daily "JFKs."

Barboza herded the sailors onto the wharf each morning for their workout, which was especially difficult for those who had just come in from the previous night's liberty. The boat was moored astern of USS *Alamo* (LSD-33). That vessel's marine detachment fell in on the wharf early each morning for their daily run. Dimmick thought it would be a good idea for the *Archerfish* crew to join the jarheads in their jog. There were several near-death experiences the first day, including the exec himself. Mike Lintner remembers giving it a try, but he only made it as far as the end of the pier. He and some of the others had hidden a stash of San Miguel beer in a wire-enclosed equipment bin there for hangover treatment; therefore, there was an incentive to run at least that far anyway. The entire physical fitness program was abandoned after a few days.

One bunch of sailors from *A-fish* found four rooms to rent in a shack over the top of a grocery store in Olongapo. It was down a long dirt road behind the cockfighting arena and not exactly in the best part of town. However, the place had a lot going for it. There were eleven barmaids living in the same joint. The girls had a full dinner on the table for them by five o'clock each day, and they all enjoyed the meal together. Then, when the girls went to work at the bars at six PM, the sailors cleaned up the mess and washed the dishes before going to join their new friends until they all came back home together in the wee hours. The girls were also kind enough to wake the guys at six AM so they could get breakfast and head back to the boat for quarters.

It was a perfect home away from home. The sailors bummed a soda pop cooler from the old lady who owned the grocery store and carried it upstairs to the common area. Each morning, the old lady filled the cooler with beer, and the iceman came by each day to make sure the contents stayed cold. The sailors bought food for everyone in the place—fish and rice three meals a day. On the weekend, they loaded all the girls into a fleet of cabs and went to the beach. The consensus was that this was the next best thing to having a harem.

When they were ready to sail on July 24th, it came time to settle up with the old lady from whom they were renting. It cost them a grand total of thirty-five pesos per man for the rooms. For their thirteen days there, counting rent, food, transportation, and booze, the cost per man was about $75. The girls even threw in laundry service and a few other fringe benefits for free since the guys bought food and cleaned up the rooms for them.

There were a few complaints about the Philippines, though. It was the rainy season while they were there, and the tropical precipitation was near constant. When it did stop for a few minutes, the mosquitoes were almost unbearable.

It could also be a dangerous place.

It was not uncommon at all for groups of locals to gang up on U.S. personnel and rob them. One *Archerfish* sailor, Buck Bevill, was taking a jeepney (jeep converted into an open-air taxicab) along Magsaysay Street in the heart of Olongapo. He was the only American aboard among a group of Filipino locals. The local gang jumped him and tried to rob him, but Bevill proceeded to whip all four of the guys and then took care of the driver, who was obviously in on the ambush. Once he had them down for the count, he proceeded to lay all five of them out in the middle of the street and tipped the jeepney over on top of them.

Then the sailor passed out. During the fight, one of the robbers had managed to cut a gash from Bevill's shoulder all the way to the elbow with a *ballsong*, a butterfly knife. The driver had also whacked him over the head a time or two with a lug wrench.

Bevill was obviously a tough bird. He was another of the seasoned World War II sailors who had found a comfortable home in the navy, particularly in the pump room of old diesel boats like *Archerfish*. With the coming of the nuclear navy, he and his type would become more and more anachronistic, but they were certainly in their element on fleet boats like the *A-fish*.

It doesn't take long to realize that the Submarine Force, which is an all-volunteer service, consists of a unique, select group of men. Those who are selected for this most unusual duty quickly form a special esprit de corp. On long patrols, there is no place for personalities that find it difficult to operate within close-knit groups. The cramped quarters and lack of privacy do not allow for those who might have volatile temperaments, either.

To this day, a special bond, based on shared experience, exists among submariners. That bond pointedly excludes the surface navy, marines, and, especially, the flyboys. This may be partly due to the fact that, in wartime, the principal threat to a submarine comes from aircraft and surface ships, and destroyers in particular.

Often, while ashore, a good way to blow off steam and prove the commitment to this unique and exclusive bond is for submariners to challenge those who represent, however indirectly, their nemeses. *Archerfish* guys were seasoned hands at this form of recreation. It mattered not that they were all in the same navy.

The boat's next stop was Bangkok, Thailand. Along the way, they had to tread softly through uncharted waters, where the depth could go from four or five thousand fathoms to only ten feet in seconds. In those days, the charts for the southeastern part of the South China Sea, the very area where the boat was running survey points, had large, ominous areas on them noted only as "Dangerous Ground." The location was not only poorly surveyed but also littered with uncharted rocks, reefs, and shoals where the bottom rose up with heart-stopping swiftness. Most of the reefs and shoals that were charted bore the names of British vessels that had located them by decidedly disastrous means: Barque Canada Reef, Stag Shoal, Owen Shoal.

Archerfish even attempted to have one of these uncharted shoals named after her navigator. They wanted to call it Dimmick Desperation Shoals after an incident that required frantic emergency backing once the water began rapidly disappearing beneath the boat.

There were ample opportunities for swim call in the warm waters. The major precaution, though, was making certain a man with a M-l rifle was stationed in the shears to watch for sharks. Once the lookout assured them the waters were clear, the men could dive in.

Archerfish steamed due west, around the great delta at the southern tip of Vietnam, into what was then known as the Gulf of Siam and is now called the Gulf of Thailand. Everyone aboard was aware they were sailing over the final resting places for many of the fifty-two submarines lost during World War II. And that some of them looked just like their own boat. *Growler, Flier, Robalo, Barbel, Logarto*—boats and crews still on eternal patrol beneath the very waves through which they were plowing. There were no worries of being strafed by Japanese Zeroes or being bombarded by thudding depth charges. Their dangers were mostly limited to hydrogen, rust, old age, and tired equipment.

Bangkok is located about thirty-five miles upriver from the gulf, on a winding, jungle-lined stream whose name, Chao Dhraya, means "Father of Waters." There were no channel markers in those days, so once a vessel crossed the entrance bar, the boat had to stay in the middle of the river and dodge fishing nets as best she could. The banks would occasionally have its thick green foliage broken by houses held high on stilts, small villages, or a *wat*, a Buddhist temple, with a full contingent of saffron-robed monks outside watching them as they made their deliberate way upstream.

The American sailors who met the boat at the quay wall at New Harbor, Bangkok, didn't look at all comfortable in their ill-fitting uniforms. They were part of the controversial military-advisor group that had been stationed in that part of the world prior to the United States' full-scale involvement in Vietnam. They had come down to handle the sub's lines and to pay the crew. For most of them, the occasion was the first time since their arrival in Southeast Asia that they had been required to put on a uniform.

Lieutenant Subin was *Archerfish*'s Thai liaison officer. He was an eager and friendly young man, totally willing to please. He proudly read off a long list of receptions, parties, tours, and soccer games that the crew was expected to be a part of while they were there.

On the other hand, just up the dock, its paint peeling and looking seedy and neglected, was the Mosquito Bar. That looked like a much better place for a sailor to begin his tour of Bangkok.

The wardroom and hydros didn't have much choice. There was a huge buffet dinner that first evening in port at the U.S. naval attaché's home, followed by a reception at the Arawan Hotel that included about a hundred invited guests. Half the admirals in the Thai navy and most of the people from the U.S. embassy were there. A native band in traditional costumes played Thai folk music.

One morning David Dimmick got a call informing him that the country's crown prince would arrive at the boat in a half hour for a tour. *Archerfish* was a mess and hungover sailors were bunked out everywhere. Dimmick hit the general alarm, and all hands turned to in order to help tidy up. The exec jumped into the shower and then pulled on his dress whites.

The prince was only nine years old and had decided to stop by to take a look at the American sub while he was on his way to his riding lesson. He was accompanied by a huge contingent of military brass, and every time the kid climbed anywhere, there was a general or an admiral to catch him should he slip and fall.

The boat got lots of press coverage, especially after the prince's visit. *Archerfish* was soon overwhelmed with visitors. At the same time, the wardroom had arranged for a sightseeing bus for the crew so they could visit some of the places of interest. When the bus showed up to pick up the liberty sections for the tour, everyone not on watch had already escaped. There was no one left to go on the arranged tour. The next day, the exec made sure liberty did not commence until the bus arrived, then escorted all the crew members aboard it. Even then, at the first stop, everyone got off to take pictures and see the attractions, but very few were around to climb back on the bus when it came time to leave again.

On their third day in Bangkok, a group of *Archerfish* sailors decided to find themselves a party headquarters for the rest of their time in port. A cab driver told them he knew just the place. They piled into two cabs and raced off into the city's suburbs, to Klong Toei, a marshy area near a bend in the Mae Klong River. They stopped in front of a high-walled property on a tree-lined street. The sign on the huge, ornate, wood-and-iron, double-door gate indicated they had arrived at Green House No. 41.

One of the cab drivers entered the gate while the sailors waited outside, then came back and motioned for them to follow. They made their way along a curving walk through beautiful flower gardens to the porch of a large house. An elderly lady beckoned them into a front room that was filled with wooden tables and chairs that looked as if they belonged in an old western saloon. The windows were open, and ceiling fans made the room quite comfortable, despite the humid heat outside. Music came from somewhere in the house, and there was the unmistakable aroma of pork roasting on an open fire.

They were seated and cold beers were brought to them from a bar in the corner. Soon, a few at a time, the girls started to casually step into the room, some from the front of the house, others from the back. They were all quite attractive.

After a short conference between the cabbie, the old lady, and the sailors, a deal was struck. They would have rooms, meals, and cold beer for the entire time they were in port. The girls would double-bunk with the sailors, and the submariners would provide the beer, food for the entire household, and $5 U.S. per day per person. The two cabbies would be on call at the gate as long as they stayed there and would take them anywhere they wanted to go for $5 U.S. per cabful.

It was perfect!

There were three bedrooms inside the main house, the large room with the bar, and the owner's private quarters. There was also a large room for bathing just inside the back door. A stream with a small footbridge ran through the backyard, and on the other side was an open-air kitchen and a long, narrow building that was divided into four additional bedrooms. It had a covered porch running its entire length. A similar building ran off to the side of the main house. It was all nestled beneath large shade trees and surrounded by well-kept gardens and lawns.

There were cobra baskets placed near certain doors for protection, a legacy from the time when the Japanese occupied the area during the war. The old lady told the sailors, "Don't bother the snakes, and they will not bother you." The sub sailors took her at her word.

Dale Ness ended up with an interesting but quite utilitarian souvenir of Thailand. The girl he hooked up with was quite well endowed, and when he left, he stole one of her bras. Back on the boat, he hooked the lingerie into the springs on the rack just above his. It was perfect for storing cigarettes, loose change, his wallet, books, and anything else he didn't know what to do with. Of course, he was told to take it down and hide it whenever visitors were on the boat.

Archerfish left Bangkok on August 20, headed for more gravity readings and eventually Singapore. Apparently, due to some civil unrest there, they were not able to stop. That was a disappointment for all. They lay in the offing and received the naval attaché and his disbursing clerk so they could be briefed on their next port of call and take care of business.

The submarine made the first part of the two-day run up the Malaka Strait at night, all the time watching out for the seemingly endless procession of freighters and tankers coming from the other direction. Still, despite the traffic, there was a full moon, and the sweet smell of the jungle made for pleasant sailing.

On the first of September, they anchored in Penang, Malaya, at Georgetown Harbor. Locally hired water taxis were necessary to ferry personnel back and forth between the boat and the beach.

Penang was Britain's first colony in the region. It lies at the head of the Strait of Malaka and has been an important trading post and strategic port down through history. During World War II, both the Germans and Japanese used it as a submarine base. USS *Grenadier* (SS-210) was lost in the Lem Voalan Strait northwest of Penang during the war. All hands got off but were captured and spent the rest of the war as slave labor in Japanese prison camps. Four of her crew died in the camps.

Still, most of those aboard *Archerfish* had never heard of the place before they dropped anchor there in September 1961. They did enjoy their brief stay but were soon back at work again, steaming through the Andaman Sea and Bay of Bengal, working their way toward the tea island of Ceylon.

The weather turned nasty in the Bay of Bengal, but they were able to dive and continue their mission. At one point, they were within 200 miles of Burma and drew as close as 350 miles to the east coast of India.

By the time *Archerfish* moved into the harbor at Colombo, Ceylon, the old girl was showing the rigors of being at sea for so long. The formerly gleaming black hull was streaked by jagged rust, and what paint was left had long since faded. The crew looked just as seedy as their boat did after a lack of fresh water for bathing and laundry. While she was still in Penang,

ComSubPac had recommended to BuShips that *Archerfish* be scheduled for regular overhaul at Pearl Harbor the next spring and summer. Still, somehow, she seemed at home in this latest port.

"*Archerfish* fit right into the down-in-the-mouth appearance of the Colombo waterfront," Keith Norlin remembers. "A tramp submarine!"

Ken Henry and Dale Ness made a local tattoo parlor one of their first stops. After quenching their thirst, of course. The two sailors had taken a liking to Singhalese writing and asked the artist to write something in the distinctive script on their skin. Anything. They didn't care what it said.

The parlor's proprietor refused at first. He told the men to come back when they were sober, but they finally persuaded him to tattoo a message on their arms. Having no idea what he had written on them, they paid the smiling guy eight rupees, a little over one U.S. dollar each, and left the shop, heading for the bars so they could proudly show everyone they met their new tattoos. The only problem was, every Ceylonese native who saw the inked message on the sub sailors' forearms thought it was hysterically funny.

Finally, one of the bar girls translated the words for them: "Yankee go home!"

As in every other port they visited, the local population took great interest in the submarine's arrival. Usually the newspaper and other local media covered the event, and there soon were plenty of sightseers anxious to see a real American submarine. The first tour group in Colombo was a contingent of Boy Scouts. Most of them arrived on the pier on their bicycles.

While the Scouts were visiting on board, the USS *Greenwich Bay* (AVP-41), the flagship of a notorious by-the-book admiral, steamed into harbor. The vessel was painted a brilliant white and was manned by "textbook" sailors, all wearing starched white shorts and perfectly pleated shirts. As was the custom, the admiral's ship docked in the preferred position in the harbor and immediately invited *Archerfish* to "Tie up outboard of me." It was an invitation that could not be refused, even if the sub's skipper, most of the officers, and two-thirds of the crew were ashore on liberty and the boat was crawling with visiting Boy Scouts. And that the crew would have to cross the deck of the admiral's ship when they returned each night.

Still, the duty officer stationed the section maneuvering watch and prepared to shift berths from North Pier to Delfy Pier. The Scouts were elated that they were to actually get a ride on a sub, but that joy turned to panic when they realized they would leave their bikes behind on the pier. It was a long hike back from where they would end up.

No problem. The duty officer told them to bring their bikes along.

They did just that. Soon, lines were taken in and belching black smoke signaled that *Archerfish* and her slim crew of dirty, sweating sailors and a gaggle of wide-eyed Boy Scouts and their bikes were crossing the harbor as ordered by the newly arrived admiral.

One can only imagine the thoughts in the admiral's mind as he watched the dirty, rusting pig boat ease alongside his nice, clean, virginal-white vessel. As he observed his line handlers, each man recruiting-poster perfect in his spick-and-span uniform, while the sub's topside crew was a collection of half-dressed greasy enginemen who were about as far from regulation as they could get. And for some reason, the ragged bunch on *Archerfish* was surrounded on her deck by an odd assortment of kids and their bicycles. What navy were those guys in?

There would be other problems with the *Greenwich Bay* before the stay was over. The *A-fish* crew had overnight liberty and civilian clothing privileges. The flagship's crew had only Cinderella liberty (back on board by midnight) and uniform-only restrictions. There was thus no way to tell *Archerfish's* officers from her enlisted men. The *Greenwich Bay's* quarterdeck crew eventually got tired of saluting every *Archerfish* crewman who crossed the officers' brow in the wee hours of the morning and of trying to direct nonofficers to the enlisted men's brow. Since they couldn't tell an officer from a sailor, they saluted every drunken submariner who came aboard and allowed him to pass, officer or not.

Somewhere along the way, Captain Woods got mad at some slight or insult from the admiral and ordered a battery charge on number-one and number-three main engines while they were alongside, starboard side to the admiral's pristine white vessel. With no exhaust deflectors, they smoked up the entire side of the ship beautifully.

Besides the usual port entertainment, some of the crew went on a tiger hunt. They never saw a tiger but spent the entire day riding around through the jungle on elephants.

On October 1, Doc Barboza gave everyone aboard his cholera inoculation. More than one sailor remarked that he was several ports of call too late with that precaution.

After leaving Ceylon, the boat was soon approaching the equator. The Shellbacks aboard (those who had already crossed the equator and had been duly initiated) began preparing for a visit by King Neptune and the proper ceremony for the Pollywogs aboard (those who had never been across the equator). Apparently the roughhousing got a bit out of hand. One of the boat's cooks, Romeo Neri, was tossed out of his bunk and injured his neck and back. The skipper (a Pollywog himself and none too excited about the traditional hazing) promptly ordered the festivities ended, put four engines on line, and steered a course directly for Fremantle, Australia, to get medical help for Neri. It turned out he was not seriously hurt but it was frightening for all involved.

As they steamed ahead steadily through the Indian Ocean, the topside watches could gaze upward at night and see the unfamiliar constellations that filled the moonless sky of the southern hemisphere. For those sailors aboard who were accustomed to Polaris, the North Star, it was quite a thrill to now watch the Southern Cross instead. So was listening to the beautiful purr of the diesels, watching the plankton shining in their wake and the sea rolling up the saddle tanks.

Even now, after all these miles and all the experiences they had shared, every man aboard knew there was plenty more to come. And it was all straight ahead, out there beyond the bulbous nose of *Archerfish*.

"LAND OF A THOUSAND WIVES"

THE hot, desolate coast of Western Australia has been a graveyard for hundreds of ships down through history. Strong southwesterly winds are common, but the occasional northwest gale can spring up without warning, shoving an unwary vessel into shoals, reefs, or one of the many islets nearby. The entrance to the harbor at Fremantle was well marked by a 120-foot-tall lighthouse by the time of *Archerfish*'s arrival.

Rottnest Island, ten miles northwest of the entrance to Fremantle Harbor, is the landfall for entry into the chief commercial port in that part of Australia. The island is occupied by small, nocturnal marsupials that the early Dutch explorers mistook for rats, thus the name of the island: "rat's nest." The town of Fremantle was established in 1829 as the port for the fledgling Swan River Colony, but nearby Perth later outgrew it.

Archerfish tied up just down the quay from the main dockside that was, at the time, the passenger terminal for the big P&O ocean liners that sailed in and out of the port. Word was spread that if the sub sailors wore their uniforms, they could ride the train the seven miles from Fremantle to Perth for free. Everyone was anxious to get ashore and begin enjoying this friendly land.

A representative of the Bank of New South Wales met the boat and converted the crew's money into local currency. Soon after the banker returned to his office, he realized he had made a major mistake in changing the money, a several-hundred-dollar mistake that would come from his own pocket if he did not rectify the situation. The banker assumed there was little chance of that happening. No sailor was going to willingly return that much money with liberty looming directly ahead and with there being little chance of him getting caught with the unearned cash.

Still, the banker returned to the boat and explained his predicament to the exec. The word was passed over the IMC announcing system. Within minutes, one of the *Archerfish* sailors appeared and counted out enough cash to make up the entire amount of the error. The sailor had not realized there had been a mistake until the announcement was made and he checked his stash.

American vessels have been enjoying liberty, rest, and recreation in Australian ports for centuries. American whalers were the first in a long succession of Yankee ships to enjoy Aussie hospitality. U.S. soldiers from World War II and Vietnam still tell of leave time spent in King's Cross in Sydney and other hot spots in the country. That friendliness has quite naturally resulted in thousands of marriages between American servicemen and the "sheilas" of Australia, thus making it the "land of a thousand wives." The fact that *Archerfish*'s crew consisted of almost all bachelors only added to the interest the Aussies had in her.

During World War II, the United States maintained submarine bases in Australia at Brisbane, Darwin, Albany, and Fremantle. Many war patrols originated from those ports. The crews spent their time between patrols in those towns, and many submariners ended up marrying local women they met there. Quite a few of them returned to Australia after the war and are still living there.

The newspaper in Perth acknowledged *Archerfish*'s arrival with a delightful cartoon. It depicted the boat's skipper looking through binoculars from the bridge at a boatload of women who were rowing out to greet the Americans. As was typical, the captain wore ribbons and medals covering most of his uniform and had dollar bills erupting from his pockets. Americans, and especially submarine sailors, were often assumed to be wealthy by local standards, and in many foreign ports Yankee sailors were considered a free ticket to the land of plenty that is the United States. Providing the girls could get one of the guys to fall in love with them and marry them, of course.

Many did. At least four men from *Archerfish* married girls they met in Australia. Roy Glasco found his wife in New Zealand. Clyde Mack and Robert Millspaugh returned to Australia and made their lives there.

There was also an article in the local newspaper by a female reporter,

Roberta West, who met the boat at the pier. She talked with crewman Fred Yentz, identifying him as the youngest man aboard, at nineteen, and asked him if she could go below for a tour of the sub. He told her she would have to wait until everyone was finished changing clothes, getting ready for liberty. She did visit below decks, and completed her article by writing, "After climbing up, bumping my head several times, I got out into the open air again, and, though it was raining, I was very glad."

The officers and scientists aboard *Archerfish* were invited to a cocktail party thrown by the Australian-American Association, a group ostensibly formed to promote understanding and mutual admiration between the two countries. For its younger female members, though, it was a perfect venue for getting first dibs on potential mates-for-life who visited their port.

There was one problem from the association's perspective. They were accustomed to welcoming vessels with much bigger contingents of officers. This submarine had a grand total of eight able-bodied men among its wardroom and hydro personnel, and one of those had to remain back on the boat as duty officer. The eventual odds at the cocktail party turned out to be fifty girls for the seven *A-fish* representatives. It was an enjoyable evening for the gang from *Archerfish!*

Several of the men spent their time in Australia journeying into the outback at the invitation of various friendly folks they met when they went ashore. The boat's phone rang constantly as people called to invite sailors to join families for dinner, for picnics, or for trips. Often the callers had to be told that there was no one left to send. Many of the men commented on how novel it was to have liberty in an English-speaking port where an American accent was a cue for friendly attention.

"Let me buy you another beer, Yank!" they would say. "You saved us from the Japs after all!"

Though it had been almost twenty years, the Australians still held plenty of memories of World War II. The city of Darwin in the Northern Territory had been bombed by Japan in preparation for an invasion. Much of the territory was evacuated when that invasion appeared to be imminent. Most Australian soldiers were far away at the time, fighting in North Africa, and the Japanese could have easily conquered a good portion of the island continent if they had been able to launch the planned invasion. It was the U.S. Navy and Marines, though, who stood strong in the South Pacific and blocked the empire's expansion. The folks in Australia had not forgotten, and were more than willing to express their appreciation to any Yanks who stopped by.

In its edition of October 11, 1961, the Perth *Daily News* featured an article with the headline, "Giant-Killer Spells Here," a reference to *Archerfish* and her sinking of *Shinano*. It was accompanied by photos of the boat and three of her crew members with the subhead "The Ship Is New Here . . . but Not All the Crew." The picture showed Lewis Holm, Marvin Bevill, and Richard Bishop, the three *Archerfish* crew members who had spent time in Fremantle during World War II.

There was trouble during the visit, but it didn't involve the locals. It happened at a dance hall called Sunrise L'Aurora. The place was full of *Archerfish* sailors and hydros, friendly Aussie ladies, and half-drunk British sailors who were also on liberty. Bill Fong was dancing with a girl when one of the Brits decided he would have a turn with her and rather rudely cut in. Fong took offense and told the Limey what he thought of him. It was clear the two were about to tussle. Joe Osier jumped up to give Fong a hand. A group of the Limeys did the same for their mate. The rest of the *Archerfish* gang joined in. Soon the place had exploded into a full-scale bar brawl.

In the midst of the fracas, Osier spotted a big hunk of a man headed his way. He knew his only chance was to land the first blow, but when he gave the giant his best shot squarely to the jaw, the guy didn't even blink. Greasy Joe was sure he was dead, but then the guy announced, "I'm with the Royal Navy Shore Police and I need help breaking this thing up." Before long, the fight was stopped with no major damage to people or property.

"I'm sure glad we always had such nice, short, orderly fights," Osier later said.

The boat was scheduled to get underway again at 1800 on October 30. Bill Hiesley had been on restriction for the previous six days for some transgression but was allowed to go ashore for the final day in Fremantle, provided he was back to the boat in time for movement. He didn't waste a second looking for a pub. "Bacco Bill" did make it back, just in time to stumble through the huge, friendly crowd that had gathered on the pier to say their goodbyes. In fact, his momentum took him across the brow, over the deck, and right into the harbor. Johnny Gentry hopped down onto the tank top and fished Hiesley out of the water before he drowned.

There had been an impromptu farewell party in the hotel bar nearest to where the boat was moored most of the day, and none of the *Archerfish* crew was really anxious to go just yet. The people there were so warm and friendly and seemed to genuinely like spending time with the submarine crew.

Duty called, though, and they were underway at 1801, waving to the crowd on the pier as long as they could still see them.

Archerfish steamed northward, paralleling the Australian west coast, standing well to seaward of Point Moore Light and avoiding the four-fathom shoals it guarded. They also skirted the Abrolhos Islands, a danger-ous group of coral islets and rocks surrounded by barrier reefs, a navigation hazard that is well littered with wrecks of vessels that have crashed there, some as early as the 1600s. The area was marked on nautical charts as Wreck Point. As they crossed the Tropic of Capricorn, those still topside got a last glimpse of the Australian continent as the 450-foot-high North West Cape Light slipped off the starboard beam.

While *Archerfish* was in this area, daily swim calls in the warm, clear waters were the norm. Men stood in the shears and waited for the boat to roll over enough so they could dive and still clear the tank tops. The visibil-ity in the water was so good that they could swim deep beneath the keel and look up and clearly see the boat riding on the surface above them. They paid little attention to the fact that the waters in which they swam covered the Sunda Trench, one of the deepest points in the world's oceans at over 24,000 feet. When the swim call was concluded, the refreshed sailors washed off the salt at the topside showers.

Bali was scheduled to be the next stop, but the boat received word that they would not be able to anchor there after all. Word was that the Russians were anchored there already, and no one wanted both countries' represen-tatives in the port at the same time. There was also speculation about Gen-eral Sukarno, the Indonesian leader, who had been getting cozy with the Soviets, importing weapons and seeking aid from the Communists to use against rebels in his country who were threatening a full-scale takeover. It was not a good time for an American submarine to drop anchor anywhere in Indonesia, even if it meant having to pass up the promised pleasures of Kuda Beach on Bali. By the time they got the official word that the visit was to be scrubbed, they were close enough to Bali to smell the land and see the palm trees waving gently to them from the shore.

The trek from Western Australia toward the next scheduled stop, Oki-nawa, led them through the Strait of Lombok, a passage that had once been a perilous one for the submarine's sister boats. Three members of the *Archerfish* crew, Buck Bevill, Richard Bishop, and Lewis Holm, had passed this way many times during the war. They could have told many stories of the hazards they faced in these constricted waters if they had been willing to talk about them. For the most part, they weren't.

The strait was narrow, the currents unpredictable, and the Japanese had been everywhere. For U.S. submarines that worked out of Fremantle, almost every patrol meant two trips through these confined waters. Two trips if they were lucky, one if the odds caught up with them and they were sunk. That's what happened to *Bullhead* on August 6, 1945, just days before the war ended. She was sunk with all hands as she cleared Lombok on the way to the area of her third war patrol. *Bullhead* was the final American submarine lost during World War II.

The runs were usually made on the surface and in the middle of the night, but it was rare for a boat to make it all the way through without being detected by the enemy. Then the crews had to use all the guile and bravery they could muster to escape the noose that was drawn tight about them.

It was certainly a different passage through the strait for *Archerfish* in the fall of 1961. She sailed through on a bright, beautiful, clear day with the vivid mountains of Bali, their tops shrouded in clouds, visible off the port side, and the island of Lombok and its majestic Mount Rinjan drifting past to starboard. The water was a sparkling blue as she ran along on the surface then stopped for swim call just as she entered the Java Sea.

Lee Walker recalls sitting on the bow planes and snapping a photograph of the boat as she lay gently rolling in the blue swells, her flag fluttering in a light breeze, the island mountains rising off in the background. It was as close to paradise as many men ever get.

The boat entered the Celebes Sea the first week in November. *Archerfish* would spend the next two weeks crisscrossing this area. They were doing their first survey work since the beginning of October. The crew had enjoyed close to a month's vacation.

Even though they were back at work, the job was easy. There was no need for them to dive to make their measurements. The waters were glassy smooth, and, for anybody belowdecks, it was hard to tell when the boat was moving.

It was about this time that the *Archerfish* crew experienced a prime example of naval "intelligence." The hydro guys' gravity equipment in the old dry storeroom ceased to function one day. The civilians who were on board at the time were operators, not technicians. They willingly admitted that much of their technical competence consisted primarily of being able to use the on and off switch on the gizmo.

They were in luck. At that time, Torpedoman First Class Mike Lintner was working on an electronics correspondence course from the Cleveland Institute of Electronics. Mike, along with Electronics Technician Second Class Bob Athorp and Radioman Second Class Rex Maynard, decided to try to figure out where the problem was with the gravity machine. They started at the beginning and, just as in a submarine qualification program, sketched out their own schematics of the equipment to get a better picture of how it operated. When they finished, they were able to locate the problem and repair it. The equipment was working again, and they now had over twenty pages of drawings they could refer to should the thing go on the fritz again.

Much to their chagrin, the electronics officer collected all of their notes and drawings and immediately burned them. He explained that they were not cleared for the level of information that was in the drawings they had made of the equipment they had just repaired.

On one run, *Archerfish* passed close by to the port of Balikpapan, once the crown jewel of Royal Dutch Shell. When the Japanese threatened to capture the refineries and oil fields that were located there during the war, the facilities were destroyed to keep them from falling into the hands of the enemy invaders. However, the Japanese moved in anyway and quickly got them back on line, producing oil. The tanker traffic between Balikpapan and the Japanese homeland soon became primary targets for *Archerfish* and her sister submarines.

On November 10, in the Sulu Sea, Lee Walker reported spotting the North Star again for the first time since they had crossed the equator headed south. At that time of the morning, the four-to eight watch, the Southern Cross was still visible as well. It was another reminder of how remote their location was, how far they had come, and how far they still had to go before they would touch American soil.

"The 'old girl' is getting tired," Walker wrote. "We've had two engines and one of our main motors break down since we left Fremantle. Thank heaven the weather has been calm or we would be well behind schedule. As it is, repairing an engine while at sea is no easy task. They have most of the parts of an automobile engine but are much larger. Space in which to work is at a premium, and removing the upper crankshaft in a moving ship can be quite dangerous."

The boat's newspaper, the *A-Fish-L-Blast*, noted that since the beginning of Operation Sea Scan in May of 1960, the enginemen had been called on to perform major repairs on an engine a total of twenty-six times. The paper also determined that in the eighteen years since *Archerfish* was first commissioned, fully one-third of the total hours put on the engines had occurred in the last eighteen months.

The engine trouble persisted. Engineer Frank Ford proclaimed, "I will not take time to shave until we have four main engines and four main motors on the line!" He didn't know it at the time, but he was destined to be the only man aboard with a full beard.

The mechanical problems would only get worse. They were still steaming back and forth between the Sulu and Celebes Seas, still en route circuitously to Okinawa, when major difficulties developed with the main motor brush rigging. Repairs were necessary, the kind that could not be done at sea and that were likely beyond the capabilities of the yard at Okinawa. The most logical course of action would be to go back to Subic Bay, which was closer, but some of those aboard (those in the wardroom, the officers) preferred Yokosuka. Most of the sailors were only too happy to return to Subic Bay. As one crewmember said, "Subic was a great port for those with meager needs and not much money."

Despite their preferences, the decision was eventually made for them. They were informed that the yard at Yokosuka was already filled with ships needing repair. There was no room for *Archerfish*. She would have to return to Subic Bay in the Philippines.

On November 20, the log indicated that only half the main motors were working, one on each shaft. Though they were still ahead of schedule, the detour to Subic Bay put into jeopardy upcoming scheduled stops in Samoa and Tahiti. There were other worries. Some aboard the boat were concerned about old girlfriends back in Subic Bay, whether or not *Archerfish* had left the port in good graces, and whether such a quick turnaround had possibly not allowed enough time for things to cool off since their last visit. After all, they had not expected to return to the port anytime soon.

There was another complication. Stewards aboard U.S. submarines at that time were most typically Filipino or black. *Archerfish*'s stewards were Filipino. One of them had a pregnant girlfriend and an indignant uncle. It was an explosive situation that the steward had hoped to postpone resolving for a while longer. Now he would have to face the music in only two days' time.

Probably the biggest disappointment was simply that the crew didn't necessarily want to do any backtracking. They had grown accustomed to almost always pointing toward new, colorful, never-visited ports of call.

"Depart your present position and proceed most direct route to Ship Repair Facility, Subic Bay" came the order. So backtrack they did.

Repairs began immediately upon their arrival at Subic Bay. They also received word that they would get two new ensigns who would catch up with them later in the cruise. Ensigns are the most junior officers in the navy, and in this case, straight from college by way of submarine school. They had never been to sea before, and their first real taste of the Silent Service was to be *Archerfish*. There was general concern about how they would fit into the unique brotherhood that existed aboard the boat.

"We didn't know what we were going to do with them," Lee Walker wrote. "If there was anything we didn't need, it was more officers."

There were to be other crew changes in the coming months. Some of the original members of Kenny Woods's Sixty Thieves were drifting away already. Engineman Second Class John "Speedy" Gonzales, an excellent auxiliaryman and editor of the *A-Fish-L-Blast*, was transferred to shore duty in Long Beach, California. Ken Henry remembers the first time he met Speedy, well before they ended up as shipmates on *Archerfish*. They were standing next to each other in a most ominous position, among a group of other sub sailors with their backs against the wall and their hands on top of their heads. They were in Henry's Bar (no relation to Ken Henry) in Havana, Cuba, trying to convince a Thompson-submachine-gun-toting contingent of Castro's rebels that they really weren't supporters of Fulgencio Batista (see chapter 11). Now, for the last two years, they had been an integral part of the adventures enjoyed by crew members of *Archerfish*.

There was an impromptu farewell party for Gonzales at the enlisted men's club on the naval base. It was an uncharacteristically subdued affair.

There were two incidents that occurred during the return visit to Subic Bay that showed the true nature of *Archerfish*'s skipper, Ken Woods. Larry Dachenhausen, one of the auxiliarymen, was stranded in a little bar along the strip in Olongapo. None of the rest of the crew was around, it was after curfew, and he didn't have enough money with him to pay the going rate to spend a night with the girl he was talking to. He didn't even have enough money to sit there and drink all night. Dachenhausen had no place to go.

Just then, in walked Kenny Woods. The skipper sat down at the bar, a few stools away from Dachenhausen. There was no place for the sailor to hide.

When he spied Dachenhausen sitting there, though, the skipper didn't yell. Instead he bought the sailor a beer, even before he checked his watch.

"What are you still doing here?" he finally asked.

Doc told him his sad story, and then added, "By the way, I don't have enough money to get through the night." Oh, well, Dachenhausen decided, nothing ventured, nothing gained. "How about loaning me some?" he boldly asked his captain.

Woods thought for a moment then reached into his pocket and handed the sailor $20. He looked Dachenhausen directly in the eye and said, "You don't know me and I don't know you. Understand?"

"Okay!" the sailor assured him, then grabbed his girl by the arm and went off to hide for the rest of the night.

The next day, the belowdecks watch informed Dachenhausen that the captain was sitting alone in the wardroom with the curtains drawn across the entrance. Doc took a twenty from his pocket, reached around the curtain without showing his face, and held out the bill in front of the surprised skipper.

"Who is that?" Woods asked.

"You don't know me and I don't know you," Dachenhausen answered through the curtain. The captain chuckled as he took the bill, and that was the end of the matter. No one ever mentioned it again.

Dale Ness had once again received a promotion to commissaryman third class two weeks before their turn back toward Subic Bay. At that point, everyone still assumed *Archerfish* would be going to the yard at Yokosuka for repairs. Captain Woods looked at the cook sideways and said, "Ness, I'll bet you a bottle of booze that you'll find some way to get into enough trouble to lose third class before we get to Yokosuka."

Ness thought for a moment. Because of the needed repairs, they were now supposed to be at sea continually, steaming toward Yokosuka. How much trouble could he get into in the middle of the South China Sea? He took the captain's bet.

Then, of course, they got redirected to Subic Bay. Ness had his usual fun in Olongapo but managed to stay out of any kind of real trouble that might cost him his promotion. The bet still looked like a good one.

Then one night he was leaving a bar with a case of beer on his shoulder, headed back to the boat. One of the bar girls ran after him and stopped him. She had overheard several of the locals plotting to come after him, hit him over the head, and steal his beer and Rolex watch. She offered to take him to her place for safekeeping. Well, this particular bar girl was an especially attractive lady, the night was still young, and Ness didn't especially want to get mugged. The sailor took the bar girl up on her offer of sanctuary for the night.

Later, when he awoke, it was almost midnight. Oh, no! As he hopped out of bed, cold reality washed over him. The gates back at the base would soon be locked for the night. He would really have to hustle if he was going to avoid getting into big trouble. He knew that if he were caught in town after curfew, he would have to go to captain's mast. That would give the skipper the excuse he was looking for to take away his recent promotion. Ness knew the captain would throw the book at him in order to win the bet.

Then he looked down at his lovely companion, at her dark hair shining in the moonlight as it fell across the white pillowcase. Next he considered the fact that most of a case of beer was still sitting there on the table.

He promptly hopped back into bed.

There was no rush the next morning. Ness knew that he was already "over the hill," so he went back to the bar before heading back to the boat to face the inevitable. He had only been in the place a few minutes when Ness spotted a familiar face coming through the door. When the newcomer spotted Ness sitting there at the bar, the man burst into laughter.

"I told you I'd get that rate before we got to Japan!" he crowed. It was Ken Woods. "You better not miss movement." And out the door he went.

Later, on Pearl Harbor Day, they were already under way for Japan when Woods held captain's mast for Ness. True to his word, he busted the sailor back to seaman. Ness says, "I never did pay off the bet. It was bad enough I had to give him a stripe. I wasn't about to give him a bottle of booze, too."

The boat held sea trials as they were leaving Subic Bay and after saying goodbye to everyone with whom they had been spending time on this rebound visit. There were still problems with the boat, though, so they came right back in and said hello again. Finally, late that afternoon, they were able to get under way. In a few days, they were dodging a typhoon. Despite more engine trouble that cropped up along the way, they would make it to their next port, Yokosuka, on schedule. They even had to slow down a bit on their final survey leg to keep from arriving too early.

On December 20, the lookouts sighted Nagata Misaki Light at the entrance to Tokyo Bay. Everyone was aware that they were once again in the same waters where *Archerfish* stalked and sank *Shinano* in 1944. They sailed up Sagami Bay with Mount Fuji in the distance, the sun bright and reflecting off its cap of snow.

Yokosuka seemed more like a home port to *Archerfish* than Pearl Harbor ever did. That was because she and her crew had spent so much time there lately. It was a beautiful, clear day when the boat arrived at the navy base. A gentle haze gave the landscape a watercolor look. All the radios around the base were playing Christmas carols. While at sea, it had been easy to forget that the holidays were so near. Now the signs were everywhere.

As soon as liberty went down, a couple of *Archerfish* sailors grabbed clean clothes and headed for the Grand Palace Bath House, one of the nicest places in the area. The sailors still wore the same clothes they had on when they left Subic Bay two weeks before. They had not had a shower since then, either. The plan was to get a good steam bath, a scrub, and a massage and to toss the old clothes into the trash. Then, once they were all sparkling clean, they could head for Submarine Alley.

The staff at the bathhouse had other ideas. They took one look at the filthy sailors and told them, "You no come in here! You too dirty! You wash first then come back for bath."

Neither man was interested in taking a bath so they could take a bath. They grabbed a taxi and went instead to a much more sleazy (and less discriminating) bathhouse.

Since the cruise was now almost completed, the crew invested the boat's considerable slush fund in a big blowout at a hotel, a party that would last seventy-two hours straight so all three duty sections could participate. Booze was procurred from the base PX. A band was hired and told to play anytime anyone was present in the ballroom, day or night, dawn or dusk. The hotel management was required to maintain a never-ending supply of fresh hostesses at all times. At three in the morning, the party tended to wane just a bit, what with everyone in a stupor or having wandered off to an upstairs room. But then a new group would wander in, and the merrymaking would kick off again. By day two, the whole community of bar owners, bar girls, and other submarine sailors in town on liberty had managed to crash the whirlwind affair. It metamorphosed into a legendary submarine-community block party.

Christmas dinner, 1961, aboard *Archerfish* included lobster cocktail, roast tom turkey, sage dressing and giblet gravy, Hawaiian baked ham, whipped potatoes, buttered peas, pumpkin pie with whipped cream, fruitcake, and more.

Since any night in port for *Archerfish* usually resembled New Year's Eve, regardless of what the calendar claimed, midnight on January 1, 1962, was nothing special. Lee Walker was the duty officer, and at midnight he mustered the duty section topside. The youngest man aboard rang twelve bells (ships' bells usually don't go past eight). All the other ships in the harbor sounded their whistles and sirens and flashed searchlights in the air. Since it was a bit cool topside, Walker authorized the medical corpsman to issue whiskey to all hands as "protection against exposure." His last chore for the watch was to make his notes in the first log of the new year but, in an old nautical tradition, he did it in rhyme:

Amidst the crowded harbor, filled with ships of gray,
Archerfish is lying this chilly New Year's Day.
Yokosuka is the port o' call on the island of Japan
And Berth One in the Naval Base is where we're moored to land.
We're not alone as tied here; we're in a nest of three,
With *Coucal* to our port side and *Greenfish* to the sea.
Units of the Pac Fleet, yard and harbor craft
Comprise the ships here present, down to the smallest raft.
The Commander of Seventh Fleet is senior here afloat
In *Oklahoma City*, a cruiser of some note.
We've seen the old year vanish; now we'll do what we can do
To make the world a better place all the New Year through.

It had long been the policy of the boat's yeoman, Jim Moran during phase one, and then Luke Fraser in phase two, to "file" all records of disciplinary action, leave, or other personnel paperwork in a most unusual way. Instead of putting them away neatly in filing cabinets, they instead shoved them into the nearest locker, where they were immediately forgotten. One afternoon while the boat was still in Yokosuka, Fraser came back to the galley to see Dale Ness.

"Nasty, do you realize you're eligible for a good conduct medal," he asked.

Ness looked at the yeoman as if Fraser was deranged.

"How in hell can that be?" he sputtered. "I've been to captain's mast at least four times in the past two years alone."

Fraser shrugged.

"I don't know, but there's no mention of any captain's mast in your records. In fact, according to your record, you've never been in any trouble at all the whole time you've been on *Archerfish*."

Ness knew Fraser must have had a short memory. The yeoman had been present at two of Ness's sessions with the captain, including the latest one, at which he had been busted to seaman for his antics in Olongapo.

"All right, then," Ness said. "If my records show I deserve a good conduct medal, then I want it."

Fraser shrugged, turned, and went forward to fill out the paperwork.

The area around the Yokosuka Naval Base was then a virtual sea of bars catering to sailors. Based on the well-proven economic theory that "closer to liberty-bound sailors must be better," the drinking establishments seemed to jostle with one another as they crowded close to the gate, seeking space and exposure. Competition for Yankee dollars was intense.

One entrepreneurial bar owner sought to single out a hard-drinking core of the fleet by naming his bar the Dolphin White Hat Club. This dive quickly became the on-shore home-away-from-home for submariners in the western Pacific.

Some sailors took a week's leave and spent the whole time at the Dolphin Club. Sailors taxied from their boat to the PX for a case of cheap liquid supplies and then headed straight to the Dolphin for the duration. There was little reason to go anyplace else. The bar provided booze, girls, and a place to crash, all the basic services that shore-bound sailors required.

The submarine sailors did tend to be fiercely territorial over "their" place. If anyone with the wrong affiliation attempted to enter, he met stiff—even forcible—resistance.

On the afternoon of January 7, Ned Reilly and Larry Dachenhausen were in the Dolphin, sitting at a table just inside the door. Three marines came strolling in and took seats at the next table. Ned wasted no time in telling them to get the hell out of the place, and he was not polite in his suggestion. The marines took offense, gave him some mouth, and Reilly proceeded to toss all three of them out the door. They promised that they would be back.

About 2030 that night, the door to the Dolphin opened and marines started filing into the place in columns of two, as if they were taking positions on a parade ground. There were "gunnies," "bucks," a couple of first sergeants, a bunch of corporals, and some just plain "grunts." There were enough marines that they filled the place from the front door to the back wall.

They turned so they were standing back-to-back and a huge, black first sergeant announced, "This *used* to be a *sub*-mo-reen bar, but now it's a mo-reen—"

He never finished his pronouncement. Ned Reilly had already stuffed his fist into the marine's mouth. It was a great fight. There were sailors from *Archerfish*, *Greenfish*, *Ronquil*, and *Rock* in the Dolphin that night. To a man, they answered the call to defend their territory.

It wasn't long before the Shore Patrol, Military Police, Armed Forces Police, and the local cops all showed up to quell the riot. They had the paddy wagons backed up to the front of the place and were herding sailors in one direction and the jarheads in the other. It was obvious that the authorities had a plenty of experience with these types of disturbances. They had things under control in no time.

But when the dust had settled, the Dolphin remained a submariners' bar.

Even though the cruise was quickly drawing to an end and *Archerfish* would soon be pointed toward San Francisco for a desperately needed overhaul, there was still more work to be done. They were underway on January 9, en route eventually to Sasebo, Japan. Their route took them northeast, then north along the east coast of Honshu, before eventually turning west and entering the Sea of Japan through the Strait of Tsugaru.

Soon they were headed directly for the Soviet Union. At one point, *Archerfish* was within fifty miles of the coastline. Even though she ran parallel to the coast for about eighty-five nautical miles, *Archerfish* was never once challenged or shadowed by the Soviets. Someone remarked he hoped that it would be a different story if a Russian submarine was caught operating so close to the States. Surely the Russians would at least be buzzed from the air.

The two new ensigns, Jon Bryan and Dave Thompson, joined the boat in Sasebo. Bryan had been forewarned. His dad, an old navy man, had gone aboard *Archerfish* in Yokosuka a month before, checked it out, and even went drinking with some of the crew. The elder Bryan had lived all over the Pacific and was well aware of the legendary boat to which his son had been assigned. From the crew's perspective, it was the consensus that both young newcomers seemed like okay guys and had the potential to be good officers. Maybe they would work out after all.

There were eight girls on the quay in Sasebo to see them off the day they got under way for Guam. That was the most people they had seen anywhere waving goodbye recently except for Fremantle. The short visit had been a success.

Except for a time during World War II when it fell to the Japanese, Guam has been under American control since it was ceded to the United States after the Spanish-American War. It was to be another relatively short stop, mostly to pick up mail, take on provisions, and allow some of the crew to depart for new assignments. A big bag of missing mail caught up with *Archerfish* there. Jon Bryan opened up a fruitcake to find it was covered with thick, green mold. It had obviously been chasing him around the Pacific Ocean. It had been in transit since at least Christmas of 1960.

Will Berger, Duke Durgin, Ken Henry, Bill Hiesley, and Jack Johnson found orders waiting for them at Guam. They were to depart the next day for their new assignments. Their replacements were waiting on the pier when the boat arrived. The old crew was breaking up.

There was a serious crisis not long after leaving Guam. It involved the chill box. The temperature inside the freezer was varying, sometimes getting warm enough that all the provisions stored in it were in danger of going bad. Luckily, they managed to fix it so it stayed safely cold. Otherwise it would have required a diversion to Guam or a return to Subic Bay. Had that been the case, they would have almost certainly missed their stop in Samoa.

Also along the way, new ensign Jon Bryan had his birthday. A cake was baked, candles lit, and everyone sang "Happy Birthday." The newly arrived officer was twenty-three years old.

On February 25, someone realized that even though it had been twelve days since they left Guam and that they had steamed over four thousand miles during that time, steering in circles while taking their surveys, they were, on that day, only about 150 miles from Guam.

On March 3, after a run through the Mindanao Sea, they made their way up the channel to Cebu City in the Philippines and headed to the Mactan Island fuel pier. Mactan was the spot where the local natives killed explorer Ferdinand Magellan on April 27, 1521, after the explorer foolishly became involved in island politics. The locals had not been impressed with that particular sailor.

The navy sent a P5M seaplane down from Cubi Point with mail and new movies for *Archerfish*. There was talk of moving the boat out into the main harbor so they could meet the plane. The pilot had other ideas. He set his plane down in the channel between Cebu and Mactan Island and proceeded to taxi right up next to the sub with his cargo.

As everyone now expected, *Archerfish*'s stop in Tahiti was canceled. As they steamed past the island one morning, the men on watch could smell the freshwater and *tiari*, a fragrant Tahitian gardenia, from forty miles at sea.

The last required survey work for phase two of Operation Sea Scan was completed on March 17, 1962. In celebration, a cache of beer that the boat was conveniently carrying was broken out and every man received two cans. Again, not very "navy," but, as one sailor noted, "The captain is still king."

Pago Pago, American Samoa, was the next stop, and it proved to be a beautiful port. Lush vegetation covered the towering mountains, and the harbor was deep and quiet, with dark bluish-green water. The crew later learned that the harbor was actually the crater of an old volcano that was open to the sea on one side. There was a club not far from where they berthed adjacent to the fuel pier. The place was usually closed on Tuesday nights, but the management agreed to open up that night for *Archerfish* and her thirsty crew.

Back in *Archerfish*'s Key West days, there had been a quartermaster aboard who loved the sea but hated the navy. He especially disliked submarines. He told anyone who would listen that when he got off *Archerfish*, he never wanted to see another submarine again. When his enlistment was up, he took his discharge and, without looking back, moved to the West Coast. The man eventually took a job as the skipper of an oceangoing yacht. His job was to take the vessel anywhere in the world its wealthy owner wanted to go, then the owner and his entourage would fly in and sail around the area.

As luck would have it, on the morning *Archerfish* steamed into Pago Pago, that yacht was anchored in the harbor waiting for its owner and his party to fly in. The old quartermaster from the Key West days was passed out topside, sleeping off the previous night's bout of hard drinking.

That's when a deep-throated ship's whistle awakened him. A vessel of some kind was entering his quiet, secluded harbor. When he pried open his eyes, he could just make out through the morning mist the low profile of what could only be a submarine.

But that couldn't be! Submarines didn't come to Pago Pago!

Then, in disbelief, he spied the numbers on the boat's side: 311! No! Any boat but *Archerfish!*

That bad dream was enough to either make a man swear off liquor or want to drink even more. Later that night at a bar, the old quartermaster was slurring his words when he told Garrett Kelley and others about his rude awakening that morning. It appeared that he had chosen the latter.

Another vessel in the harbor at the same time as *Archerfish* was a beautiful old wooden sailboat out of San Francisco, a schooner named *Wanderer*. Built in 1893, she had quite a history of her own. She had once belonged to the actor Sterling Hayden and the story was that he had kidnapped his children from his former wife in defiance of a court order and brought them to Tahiti on the *Wanderer*. She was running charters out of Tahiti at the time she shared the harbor with *Archerfish*.

The chief of the boat was insistent that *Archerfish* get herself a new coat of paint while she was in Samoa. The reluctant deck gang began dragging the gear and cans of paint out of the topside locker, then started chipping and scraping to prepare the hull for primer and paint. It was hot work, and the guys were soon very thirsty. Not for iced tea, either. There appeared no way for them to get any cold beer and still get the job done, since the COB was keeping a close eye on their progress.

But as they worked, a few Samoans approached them with a wonderful proposition. It seemed that the Samoans wanted to trade the *Archerfish* crew a case of cold beer for a five-gallon can of the navy-gray paint they were using. Done!

The case of beer didn't last long, it being so hot and all. But the Samoans agreed to another trade, paint for beer, then another, until the sailors were finally down to their last can of paint. No problem. They used paint thinner to dilute the single can that remained until it was plentiful enough to cover the rest of the boat. Amazingly, the job looked pretty good. There was no way anyone could tell the greatly adulterated coating from a regular, full-strength application. Everybody was happy. The COB got his boat painted. The sailors had plenty to drink while they performed the hot chore. The Samoans got all the paint they could use.

Later, two days out of Samoa, the section that had the watch included Ted Noakes, one of the deck gang who had stretched the paint thin so they could barter for beer. The boat made a trim dive during the watch, and Noakes went topside as one of the two lookouts after they surfaced. When the sailor looked down, he was shocked to see that during the dive, every speck of the thinned paint they had applied in Pago Pago had washed off. Every bit of it. All that remained was the dull, faded, old paint and the bright streaks of rust.

Just then, Captain Woods came up to the bridge. He stood there and stared at the rust spots on the superstructure and hull where the new paint should have been covering it. He turned to Lieutenant Frank Ford, who was the officer of the deck.

"That's odd. I've never seen anything like it," Woods said, loud enough for the lookout to overhear. Noakes almost fell out of the shears. They were caught! KW was going to be livid when he realized what had happened. But then the captain shrugged his shoulders and thoughtfully concluded, "It must be the salt content of the ocean in this part of the world."

While they were docked in Pago Pago, the boat was overrun by visitors. A submarine was a novelty the locals could not pass up. First to show were the members of the local legislature, which was composed of all the local chiefs. They each wore the traditional lavalavas, a type of sarong, with leis of flowers and stone or shell necklaces around their necks. Most of them sported elaborate tattoos. They looked like something out of a *National Geographic* photo. The men were big, too, all over 225 pounds. In Polynesian culture, the bigger the man, the more important he was, and it was clear that some of these guys were very important.

Next came hundreds of schoolchildren. A group of junior-high-aged boys sang and danced on the pier. Then it seemed as if everyone else on the island was lining up to take a tour of the boat. Still, they were a friendly and cordial bunch, anxious to meet the sailors and to invite them to visit.

Archerfish returned the favor by showing the locals some of the new movies the seaplane delivered back in Cebu. They set the projector up at the country club in town in the evenings as well as in a nearby leprosarium in the afternoons. The films were a big hit.

There were several parties thrown for the crew, official as well as unofficial. One get-together turned ugly. A group of sailors had been invited to a party one night that was being given by one of the island's most important chiefs. During the festivities, a huge Samoan man cracked Quartermaster First Class Harry Wall over the head. Either the initial blow, the impact of his head hitting the ground when he went down, or the Samoan's kick to Wall's noggin once he was down fractured the *Archerfish* sailor's skull. Wall ended up at the local hospital and was later flown up to Pearl Harbor. No one ever knew what started the fracas, but it was not typical of the hospitable nature of the Samoans they met.

The boat was under way for Pearl on the last day of March. The only reading taken during the trip was wave heights. Gravity measurements had been completed, and none of the other oceanographic equipment was functioning by then anyway.

It was hard to believe *Archerfish* had been out of its home port of Pearl Harbor for so long. Ships that have been out of the country for over a year are authorized to fly a homeward-bound pennant one foot long for each man aboard who has been out for that period of time. As she sailed into Pearl Harbor on the morning of April 7, 1962, a good breeze kept *Archerfish's* sixty-five-foot pennant impressively unfurled and gloriously streaming away from the boat. She made quite a sight. Even Admiral Roy S. Benson, who was standing among the palms on the shore, was overheard to remark to his chief of staff how sharp she looked.

Prior to mooring at Sail 7, Lieutenant Commander David Dimmick, felt the need to enlighten the crew on what they could expect to find once they went ashore. He passed the tongue-in-cheek information over the IMC, the ship's announcing system.

"We are entering a U.S. port. The primary language is English. The rate of exchange is one dollar for 360 yen. Make sure to see Doc Barboza before going ashore in order to get some protection. The book tells us there is a high VD rate here."

Eleven days later, the boat began what turned out to be an uneventful crossing of the Pacific from Hawaii to the U.S. Naval Shipyard at Hunters Point in San Francisco. Their stay in the yard there didn't look promising for generating much excitement, but it turned out not to be quite so humdrum as they expected.

While they waited for the overhaul to begin, *Archerfish* was assigned to work with USS *Permit* (SSN-594). The new *Thresher*-class nuclear submarine was conducting her precommissioning sea trials. *Archerfish* would act as safety observer.

On a clear night with calm seas, *Permit* was submerged and *Archerfish* was running on the surface. Suddenly, Captain Woods noticed on the radar that the swift-running nuclear sub was on a collision course with a cargo ship, the *Hawaiian Citizen*. He quickly notified *Permit* of the imminent danger, but it was too late for her to avert. Fortunately, no one was hurt in the collision, and damage was minimal to both vessels. The new sub was able to surface safely. *Permit* went on to a long service record, mostly operating from the West Coast.

Kenny Woods had saved his money during his two years on *Archerfish* and was determined to buy himself a new white Cadillac convertible now that he was back in the States. He traipsed all over the San Francisco area until he found a dealer willing to sell him the car he wanted for fifty dollars over dealer cost. It was immediately his pride and joy.

Another of the *A-fish* crew got a good deal on a car as well. Bill "Dinky" Earl heard that one of the guys in the yard had a car for sale, a 1939 Pontiac that was supposed to run all right but was in dire need of a paint job. Earl went to look at it and promptly bought it for $250. When he got back, he pulled his new purchase down to the pier between the service barge and dry dock where *Archerfish* was being worked on. He enlisted the aid of some of his shipmates, and a couple of them set up the spray equipment while others taped newspapers over the windows and chrome. Then they went to work, painting the vehicle with navy-issue black enamel paint. As soon as they were finished, they carefully tore off the newspaper, climbed in, and drove the car to the Horse and Cow Bar to show it off. The old car made many round trips between Hunters Point and San Francisco over the next few months. When Earl eventually left the shipyard, he sold the car to someone off another boat for $500, doubling his money.

During her time in the yard, *Archerfish* had considerable turnover in ship's company. The most noteworthy was her captain. On September 2, Lieutenant Commander Jack N. Lyman reported aboard for duty as prospective commanding officer. Lyman was an experienced submariner from Cedar Bluffs, Nebraska, who had spent four years as an enlisted man in the navy in subs before he attended and graduated from the Naval Academy. During World War II he made four war patrols as an enlisted man, on the submarines USS *Plunger* (SS-179) and USS *Parche* (SS-384). The academy yearbook said about him, "When there was a hop, he always seemed to have a date . . . when Jack leaves the academy he plans to go back into submarines, where he won his famous chest full of ribbons." The crew quickly dubbed him "Whiskey Jack" or "Captain Jack."

Lyman relieved Kenny Woods in a change-of-command ceremony at ten AM on September 8. Woods had been ordered to report to Senior Member, Navy Sub Board of Inspection and Survey, Pearl Harbor, Hawaii. The ceremony was surprisingly emotional for all who were there. Though he could be stubborn and rude at times, Woods still had an obvious need for friendship. He found it on this old diesel boat. *Archerfish* had been his home and family for the past two-and-a-half years, and he was clearly very attached to her. He was unable to finish his speech at the ceremony, claiming his throat was sore, but it was obvious he was choking back a sob. Those who had served with him, including some who had been there for the entire period, unashamedly shed tears that morning.

Afterward, the old-timers in the crew presented him with a beautiful desk set of Parker 51s on a marble base with a gold plate. Engraved on the plate was the simple, straightforward message: "To Ken Woods, U.S. Navy, from the crew of the *Archerfish*." The wardroom gave him a silver napkin ring that was also suitably inscribed.

Later Woods said, "I went directly from change of command to the chief's quarters. I stayed there for two or three hours and then went to the Horse and Cow. I still had on my full dress blue uniform. I put my sword behind the bar as a donation to their collection of memorabilia. Fortunately, they were kind enough to give it back to me several days later. I was dating an airline stewardess at the time, and she picked me up from the bar and had her way with me."

Kenny Woods had finally been separated from his Sixty Thieves.

23

TSUNAMIS AND SEASICKNESS

I was where a sailor was supposed to be and nowhere else can I remember such serenity. I have never seen such beauty as I saw with a sunrise or a sunset at sea. I still feel a calmness when I recall sitting on the cigarette deck after a watch; a flat sea with a full moon and being very comfortable in just a pair of cut-off dungarees, and sitting there until my next watch. I can still hear that beautiful purr of the diesels, the plankton shining in our wake, the sea rolling up the saddle tanks. I used to love watching how the porpoise would suddenly appear and play alongside, and then just as quickly disappear. I think it was just the whole atmosphere aboard Archerfish that made it so special.

"She was a great boat and we had a great crew."

That's the way Quartermaster John Foley rather poetically remembers his days aboard *Archerfish.* His thoughts are typical of those who served aboard the boat as she plied the waters of the Pacific, the South China Sea, and the Indian Ocean during Operation Sea Scan, but his final sentence could just as easily apply to any other incarnations of the boat.

For the better part of the next six years, *Archerfish* crisscrossed the Pacific Ocean a number of times, steaming through dead calm seas and storm-tossed maelstroms, diving and surfacing as need be, with the hydros in their "hole" taking gravitational readings. During that time they completed Operation Sea Scan phase three and a much shorter phase four as well. All along the way, the submarine and her crew continued to maintain their rowdy reputation even as they did a world of good with their recurrent public relations efforts in every port they visited. And those ports of call ranged from the mundane to the usual to the truly exotic. San Diego, San Francisco, Portland, Seattle, and Vancouver, British Columbia. Pearl Harbor, Hong Kong, Kwajalein, Midway, Guam, and Yokosuka. Mazatlán and Acapulco in Mexico. Newcastle and Sydney in Australia, Auckland and Wellington in New Zealand, and Sǔva in the Fiji Islands. Of course, there were plenty more stories about wild nights on liberty, broken hearts, and sprawling fights in which nobody seemed to ever get seriously hurt. Although this was mostly a new crew, they seemed doggedly determined to maintain the reputation of their forbears and of their legendary boat during the rest of her days.

When her period in the yard was completed in the fall of 1962, *Archerfish* left the West Coast of the United States en route once more for Pearl Harbor. It was a truly precarious time, and there would soon be a dark cloud over the entire nation. That especially included the military. Soviet missiles were discovered already deployed in Cuba, aimed at American targets. The world was about to come as close to nuclear war as it ever had. *Archerfish* didn't know about all this when she sailed away for her next portion of Operation Sea Scan, but she was about to find herself right in the middle of the preparations for World War III.

With "Whiskey Jack" Lyman in command, they pointed for Pearl and final preparations before going back to work. There was no doubt about how Lyman got that moniker, by the way. While he was in command, *Archerfish* always made sure when she left port that she carried on board two cases of Jack Daniels whiskey, one for the wardroom and one for the crew. Every Sunday while they were at sea, crew members would line up for a shot of the whiskey. There were rules that had to be followed. The whiskey could not be saved, sold, or given away to a buddy. Each man was required to either stand there and drink it or throw it away. No one remembers anyone throwing any of it away.

Not long after they arrived in Pearl Harbor, the crew got its first hint of how exceedingly taut international tensions had become during their passage across the Pacific from California. Once they were moored, Larry Dachenhausen, one of the few old crew members remaining from the Atlantic phase of Operation Sea Scan, went over to another sub, the USS *Wahoo* (SS-565), to place a phone call to the power plant. He needed someone to come down to the pier and unlock the freshwater valves so *Archerfish* could hook up. He got past the other boat's topside watch, but when he dropped down the after battery hatch, he found himself staring into the business end of a .45-caliber pistol. The belowdecks watch was demanding to know who the hell he was and what his business was aboard the boat.

Over the next few days, the crew watched all the boats around them take on war shots and ninety days' worth of stores and full loads of fuel, all in preparation for heading out to sea and God-knows-what after that. The base was soon almost empty of vessels. *Archerfish* had to remain behind. The "noncombatants" couldn't be placed in harm's way should all-out nuclear war break out. One good thing about the whole mess became readily apparent: there was little competition at liberty.

The crew set up a TV on the cigarette deck and watched the news coverage of the stare-down that was going on between President Kennedy and Chairman Khrushchev. To be truthful, some of the *311* crew sat on the deck, smoking and joking and making rude remarks to the sailors on the other boats. Jokes about how *Archerfish* was remaining in port so her men could repopulate the world after the nuclear war was over. About how the departing crews would find their wives and girlfriends just as they had left them, "freshly loved."

On October 22, everyone in the duty section gathered to watch President Kennedy speak to the nation about the missile situation and the blockade he was ordering around Cuba. The crisis had reached a truly dangerous point. Everyone realized that if war came, the crew would likely be disbanded and sent to the "fighting navy." Most were gung ho, ready to go fight if their country needed them. Still, there was sadness that their anticipated cruise might be postponed or even canceled altogether. Jerry Oliver remembers, "My thoughts at that time were that it must be time to go to war, and what might happen to the *Archerfish* crew if we did."

Such preparations for imminent hostilities were eerily similar to those that had taken place right there in Pearl Harbor less than two decades before.

On October 28, word came that President Kennedy and Chairman Khrushchev had reached an agreement on a way to end the crisis. Now the crew could worry about the more usual things. About having to stand for inspection in their dress whites on a hot deck. About making certain they had enough provisions to last the trip to their next port of call.

Most everyone agreed on one point: they were tired of liberty in their home port. They were more than ready to steam out of Pearl and head off again for new places.

Before they left Pearl Harbor, the boat's "recreation committee" invested in a handtrap, some clay pigeons, and a shotgun. The plan was to be able to shoot skeet from the cigarette deck. They held their first shoot on Sunday, November 4, and it became a regular recreational event. The weather was beautiful that day, the sea calm, and everyone who partook in the trapshooting had a good time. Later in the cruise, after leaving Yokosuka, it was another Sunday, just after the noon meal, when someone invented a new variation on traditional trapshooting. The biscuits served in the mess hall that day were especially dense, so a tray of them was brought up to the cigarette deck. It turned out they made decent substitutes for clay pigeons. They sailed out over the ocean quite well, but according to Norman C. Gilmore, "It was difficult to determine when you had made a direct hit since they just wouldn't come apart."

Contrary to popular belief, sailors are not immune to seasickness. Certainly some never experience it, but most who go to sea have fallen victim to the malady at least once, especially in storms while aboard small vessels. It even happens occasionally to those who serve on the mammoth nuclear submarines. Keith Norlin, one of the hydro scientists aboard *Archerfish*, remembers a particularly rough time for him. The boat was between San Diego and Pearl Harbor when rough seas clobbered them. They were in the middle of a gale, a thousand miles from the nearest land, when they surfaced. The lookouts were hardly in the shears before they spotted a Japanese fishing vessel, one of the small longline boats that venture far from shore, and it was bobbing around like a piece of driftwood. It was so close that everyone on *Archerfish* realized that they had almost surfaced beneath the vessel. Even so, the swells were so high it took them a while to verify the ship. The sub would drop into a trough, and the fishing boat would be lost in the next deep trough. Then they would bob high again and spot it once more through the rain and wind-driven spray.

Norlin was on the bridge, trying to get some fresh air in hopes it might settle his already queasy stomach. He could see a couple of the fishermen working on the other boat's deck while hanging on for dear life. He watched in fascination, unable to take his eyes off the vessel as it rose and fell, up and down, on the towering waves. He got sicker and sicker and finally vomited over the side. Three days would pass before he would be able to eat again.

Naturally, according to Murphy's law, the middle of a rough storm was the perfect time for the scientific instrumentation to break down. Robert Christensen and Wally Scoggins joined Keith Norlin in the hydro hole to try to fix it, but between their violent bouts with seasickness and the constant lurching of the boat, they had no luck. Captain Lyman ran the boat in circles while they tried to fix the gear. He didn't want them to miss any of their survey points. Finally Norlin sent word up to the skipper that they would have to return to California to repair the equipment, that it couldn't be fixed at sea.

When that word spread quickly throughout the boat, a loud cheer went up. Everyone was ready to leave the stormy waters and seasickness behind and head for sunny California to get their feet—and their stomachs—back.

Norlin, still weak and sick, headed for his bunk and was soon asleep. Two hours later, one of the other hydros excitedly shook him awake.

"Keith! Keith! Wake up. I've fixed the meter."

It was Robert Christensen.

"What do you mean? It can't be fixed," Norlin responded drowsily.

"Well, I kept working on it, even when we turned for San Diego. Finally something just clicked and away she went. Now we don't have to return to port."

When the pitch of the engines signaled a change in course, back to the survey line in the midst of a storm-tossed ocean, a loud groan ran the length of the boat. Norlin knew anyone associated with the hydro crew was now a prime candidate for being thrown overboard or keelhauled. But there was nothing he could do. The gravity meter worked now, and they would have to tough it out. Norlin, though, stayed in his bunk, still too seasick to move.

When *Archerfish* was in port during the latter two Sea Scan phases, she typically was able to get the parts, supplies, and other items that were needed to keep the boat going. It still wasn't easy, because of limited funding, but they usually managed. However, on one of their visits to Pearl Harbor, the crew had a chance to hone their old scavenging skills. When they pulled in, there on the pier, as if left especially for them by a fairy godmother, were ten fifty five-gallon drums of 9250 lube oil and ten Fairbanks-Morse cylinder liners. Apparently, another diesel boat was planning an overhaul, but no one could possibly need this stuff as much as *Archerfish* did. Paul Hammack was among the duty enginemen that day who quickly got the lube oil struck below before anyone noticed. They also "requisitioned" nine of the cylinder liners—all they needed for the boat's nine-cylinder engines—and politely left the tenth liner on the pier with the empty oil drums.

One problem: there was only one nine-cylinder Fairbanks-Morse diesel boat stationed in Pearl at that time. Inevitably, the trail would lead to the *311*-boat.

The night before they were scheduled to get under way, the chief engineman on the boat that was supposed to have gotten the liners got drunk and decided he would come aboard *Archerfish* to reclaim his parts. When he reached the after engine room hatch, he fell down the ladder, broke his shoulder, and had to be taken to the base hospital. He never did get his liners back. *A-fish* made good use of them, though.

There is inevitably a feeling-out period when new officers, and especially a new commanding officer, come aboard. The *Archerfish* crew quickly found out what kind of guy their new captain was. Loren Eggleston remembers that soon after they arrived in Yokosuka in March 1963, word came down that Captain Lyman had received instructions from up the line to hold a personnel inspection. The COB collected every crewmember's dress blue uniform and sent them out to be cleaned and mended, at the boat's expense, so they would be ready. Everyone certainly appreciated the boat picking up the tab.

When the uniforms came back, the crew was told to lay them out on their bunks, then to fall in topside for quarters. They did. Captain Lyman was notified, and when he came around the fairwater, Carl Masters, the executive officer, called out, "Ready for inspection!" All the crew members still wore their dungarees and were hardly clothed for inspection. Their newly cleaned and mended uniforms were still below, laid out neatly on their bunks.

Despite their attire, the captain told the executive officer to have the crew stand at ease, and then he went below to check their uniforms. He came back topside and said, "I'm pleased to announce you have all passed inspection. You are granted early liberty."

Later that day, one of the men ran into "Whiskey Jack" in town. He asked him point-blank why he had not required the crew to put on their uniforms prior to holding inspection.

"You don't think I would have you put your filthy bodies in those nice, clean uniforms, do you?" he replied with a wink.

Three months later, the boat was heading up the Columbia and Willamette Rivers in a cold, hard rain, making the ten-hour transit to Portland, Oregon. William H. "Benny" Bennett pulled on a rain slicker and asked the officer of the deck for permission to come up. Captain Lyman, who had the conn, was on the bridge, along with the navigator and one of the quartermasters. When he spotted him, the skipper asked Bennett, "What in hell is a snipe doing up here in this freezing rain?"

"I'm just interested in learning how you manage to keep the submarine lined up in the channel," he replied.

"Are you really interested?" Lyman asked.

"Yes, I am."

Taking a chart from beneath his raincoat, Lyman showed Bennett a mark on the map and then pointed to the features along the beach that the mark indicated. As they talked, the skipper was continually calling course and speed down to the helmsman. The river was swift and the boat had to use plenty of power to keep on course, so the captain was busy. Even so, for over two hours, Lyman continued to patiently explain to Bennett what he was doing and why and to answer the sailor's questions. Bennett says, "It was quite an education. I always thought that it was pretty neat for the captain of a ship to take the time to share his decisions with 'Joe Sailor.'"

One other sailor got an insight into what made this particular skipper tick. Norman E. "Skip" Julian says, "I found out from Captain Jack just before he was transferred that he had a son who was killed in a car wreck. He had blond hair and blue eyes and was about my size. Jack told me, 'Every time I look at you, I see him.' I guess that's why the skipper kind of took a shine to me and kept me out of a little bit of trouble."

Jon Bryan left *Archerfish* in June of 1963, just before the boat arrived in Portland, Oregon, for the city's annual Rose Festival. Bryan still has a copy of a message he sent from the boat while at sea, asking his fiancée, Jan, to begin plans for their wedding.

```
DEFERRED
FROM: USS ARCHERFISH
TO: NAVCOMMSTA SFRAN
-T-M 291006Z            COST        $1.90
-FM NYUG                TAX          .19
-TO AMQD                TOTAL       $2.09
BT
UNCLAS
MSG CK10 COMLE P A WESTLUND 1015 SYLVAN CIRCLE
NAPERVILLE ILL
PLAN WEDDING TWO TWO OR TWO THREE JUNE
            JON BRYAN      USS ARCHERFISH
BT
```

The wedding took place on June 22.

Years later, Bryan was operating out of Guam aboard the USS *Tecumseh* (SSBN-628)(Blue). There he actually had an opportunity to use the gravitational anomaly overlay charts that were created from the data *Archerfish* dutifully gathered in the various phases of Operation Sea Scan.

On the morning of July 25, after returning to Yokosuka, the commanding officer awarded Silver Dolphins to Ron Reddick, Ben Vinca, Gary Davis, Fred Firks, Charlie Dietrick, Martin Davis, Tom Mucker, and Ferminico Gallardo during personnel inspection. Liberty was granted as soon as inspection secured, and all hands not in the duty section proceeded to the Hatsone Hotel for yet another three-day ship's party.

"Whiskey Jack" Lyman was good friends with the commanding officer at Midway. He brought his friend some "things" on one of their trips over from Pearl, and, in return, the friend agreed to turn one of the old barracks on the island into a party hut for the crew while they were there. They quickly made themselves at home. A collection was taken up, and a group went to the chief's club to acquire beverages. The party was soon in full swing.

Two days later the revelry was rather rudely interrupted. Just after midnight, sirens began blaring all across the base. Everyone ran out of the barracks to see what was going on. People were running in all directions in what looked like panic. Some of the *Archerfish* sailors stopped someone who was stationed on the base and asked him what the sirens were for.

"Tidal wave warning!" he shouted and bolted away. "Head for high ground!" he called back over his shoulder.

Well, they had visited Midway often enough to know there was no such thing as high ground on the island. It was little more than a sandbar in the middle of the Pacific Ocean. They headed for *Archerfish* instead. After all, they reasoned, their boat was accustomed to being under water.

When they got to the pier, the sailors found the sub was already breasted out, with only the bowline holding. They scrambled aboard, the line was tossed off, and they started backing down. All the topside hatches had already been secured, so they had to go below through the conning tower hatch. The object was to get the boat out of the port and away from land before the tsunami hit. Their chances were much better if they were some distance from the island.

The boat's deck log says they anchored that night for four minutes as they maneuvered through the tricky channel. The truth is, in their haste to get as far from the island as possible, they ran aground. They were hightailing it for the open sea when the boat suddenly jolted to a halt. Captain Jack grabbed the microphone and called for help.

"Harbor Control, Harbor Control, this is Aground, this is Aground. We *are* aground."

In an ironic twist, *Archerfish*'s radio call sign at the time was "Aground."

"Ship that is aground, identify yourself," the operator on watch in Harbor Control responded. "Where are you aground?"

"Harbor Control, this *is* 'Aground.' *We* are aground," Lyman answered.

The confusion continued, and it never got cleared up. William "Dinky" Earl reports that after a few minutes of blowing bow buoyancy and the forward group, the ballast tanks forward of the mid-point of the boat, all the while answering bells for "All back full," they finally broke free and proceeded to sea without any help.

The tsunami never materialized.

24

THE PRAISE OF AN ADMIRAL

THE navy base at Yokosuka had become a regular stop for *Archerfish*, and there always seemed to be little reminders of the submarine's previous history with the place. When they arrived there in November of 1963, they found a huge Mosler safe waiting for them on the pier. The problem was how to get the massive thing below. It was too big to fit through any of the boat's hatches. A master welder soon arrived from the ship repair facility. He took one look at the safe and another at the size of *Archerfish*'s hatches and then sent his helper back to fetch his "special torch."

While they waited, the welder shared a bit of history with Benny Bennett. The man recounted that he had been a young apprentice welder working on *Shinano* in 1944. He was aboard the ill-fated carrier the night she made her maiden run out of Tokyo Harbor, seeking the shelter of the Inland Sea. He was in his bunk when the first *Archerfish* torpedo struck the massive ship. The explosion blew him out of the rack and onto the deck. Then, each time he tried to stand up, another concussion would send him sprawling again. The welder told Bennett that there was no way he could have ever imagined that someday he would be working on the very vessel that had almost claimed his life that fateful night.

Bennett would have liked to have heard more, but the helper showed up just then with the "special torch." The welder proceeded to cut the edges off the "indestructible" safe and rounded off its corners as if he were cutting through butter with a warm knife. They soon had the safe lowered below and rigged from compartment to compartment until it was at its new home in the control room. It was secured in place and, after a quick coat of paint, looked as if it had been factory-installed.

On November 19, 1963, Lieutenant Commander Thomas R. Eagye II relieved Jack Lyman as captain of *Archerfish*. Eagye was a native of Charleroi, Pennsylvania. The *Lucky Bag* at Annapolis noted his satirical sense of humor and talent for photography, two skills that would stand him in good stead on the slightly off-kilter and well-traveled *Archerfish*. The yearbook went on to say, "That warm smile and ability to make and hold friends presage success whatever his chosen field."

Roderick H. "The Hook" Potter was the boat's public information officer (among other duties), while Tom Eagye was skipper. He says, "Tom, a former flag aide to ComSubPac, was a great mentor. He played every angle possible to enhance our reputation as goodwill ambassadors, and he gave me lots of pointers on ensuring that we would receive a warm welcome when we hit the next port. We had a press kit that we would send ahead whenever possible, announcing the arrival of the famous World War II–veteran submarine and her all-bachelor crew. Tom had about a three handicap in golf and he would always challenge the SOPA as soon as we arrived in port."

The SOPA is the "senior officer present afloat," which equates to the senior commanding officer among all the COs of all the ships that might be in port at any given time. This could change daily as ships came and went from the port.

Potter continues, "In foreign ports especially, [Eagye's golf skill] was always an entrée into whatever could be done to make sure that the crew was properly welcomed."

Of course, the crew had its own way to assure they had a good time wherever they moored. William G. "Doc" Shinn, the first class hospital corpsman, was legendary when it came to arranging parties, including what had by then become an *Archerfish* tradition any time there was enough money left in the slush fund: the three-day affairs that were held at the Hatsone Hotel in Yokosuka's Honcho District.

"Doc never did anything halfway," Larry D. "Loganberry" Meyer remembers. "On one occasion he spent days at one of the mess tables designing the gift certificates for the top three door prizes that were to be awarded at the party. The certificates were really ornate, their unique design and hand lettering making them suitable for framing."

The third-prize certificate was redeemable for one "Routine jump—missionary position." Second prize was for an "Around the world—without ever leaving Yokosuka." And the top prize was a certificate good for "An all-nighter—name your poison!" Doc had prepaid for the prizes at a local house of prostitution. All the winners had to do was show up and redeem the certificates.

"I was not one of the winners," Meyer says. "But I probably would have kept one of the certificates as a souvenir."

November 23, 1963 (November 22 in the United States), was a dark day. Word of President Kennedy's assassination was received that morning. A conversation that took place in the mess hall is indicative of how out of touch the boat and her crew were with politics back home.

"Who's president now?"

"The vice president, dummy."

"I know that, but what's his name?"

There were blank looks everywhere. No one could remember the name of the vice president of the United States.

A representative of SUBFLOT Seven came down to the boat and addressed the crew at quarters. The entire armed forces were immediately placed on alert because of the situation. Bill Gumert, one of the hydros, recalls that some of the Japanese yard workers were concerned that there would be a revolution in America now that the president had been assassinated. No one knew what might happen.

Being noncombatant, *Archerfish* was allowed to go ahead and leave on schedule for her cruise to Australia, despite the alert.

The trip to Australia required another crossing of the equator and, of course, the initiation of the Pollywogs. Lloyd W. "Max" Maxwell had been to Australia as a member of the crew of USS *Sterlet* (SS-392), but the yeoman on that boat had failed to note it in his service record. To his dismay, Maxwell had to go through the initiation all over again when *Archerfish* crossed the line.

The first order of business when they arrived in Newcastle, as was becoming the routine by now, was a four-hour "international relations cruise." Members of the media and a flock of local dignitaries were herded aboard. Then the boat went out and made dives, showing them how it was done. When they arrived in Sydney around the New Year, they made two guest cruises, each one lasting about three-and-a-half hours, with two demonstration dives for each group. Everyone aboard was duly impressed with the skill of the crew but remarked most about the claustrophobic quarters in which the men lived.

Navigator Richard Meaux remembers the cruises as being "tedious, giving them all time on the scope when harbor traffic was running around everywhere, but it was time well spent." He recalls they would "dive, bottom, and feed them some good submarine chow, then cruise around submerged to give them periscope time. In the afternoon, we would surface and return them to the beach. It took one day of liberty time but the returns were great—lots of press coverage with the subsequent opening of many doors to all of us on board."

Lin "Mac" McCollum remembers one international relations cruise from Auckland, New Zealand, that almost gave their guests more excitement than they bargained for. McCollum had wandered back to the maneuvering room to talk with Larry "Light Lunch" Meyer, the senior controllerman working the port side of the cubical. They were discussing the previous night's adventures when the klaxon sounded, signaling they were making a dive for their esteemed guests. Meyer continued with his story while he did his thing, working his levers and rheostats without even having to think about what he was doing. Then both sailors noticed that the down angle was increasing to far greater than what they usually took. Items began falling off shelves and skittering along the deck, and both men had to grab hold of something solid to keep on their feet.

Suddenly the motor telegraphs rang "All back full." Meyer went to work again, slamming the chrome levers. So did the junior controllerman on the other side. Soon the stern broached, and some serious blowing forward finally allowed the boat to level out on the surface. Meyer calmly started putting everything back where it belonged and said, "So, after we left that bar—" He picked up his story where he had left off, as if nothing out of the ordinary had happened.

They later learned that the officer of the deck was showing off for the visitors and accidentally caused the sudden steep, dangerous descent. The passengers thought the whole thing was normal. The crew knew better. It could have been disastrous.

There had always been conjecture about who decided which ports *Archerfish* visited in the vicinity of her assigned survey lines. The squadron commander in Pearl was under the impression that the Naval Oceanographic Office (formerly the Naval Hydrographic Office) told them which ports to go to. The Oceanographic Office assumed the folks in Pearl decided that. Captain Eagye admits it was usually his decision.

"In reality, we went wherever I decided to go," he says. "When Rear Admiral Bernard A. Clarey was being relieved by Rear Admiral Eugene B. Fluckey as Commander Submarine Force Pacific Fleet, the two men were looking at a map of the Pacific Ocean that covered one wall in the operations center. The map was speckled with pins to indicate the location of all the U.S. submarines throughout the Pacific. Admiral Fluckey commented, 'I notice all of the boats are represented by black pins with the exception of *Archerfish*. Why is their pin white?' Admiral Clarey told him, 'You watch it for a while and you'll think it's a damn yacht!' "

Richard Meaux remembers, "The ship did range all over the ocean and much of my time as navigator was spent in the South Pacific, using blank charts based on British Admiralty work from the 1850s. No electronic or satellite aids down there at all in those days, so classic celestial navigation was what we used at times. It was a great experience to have had."

As long as there have been navy exchanges, there have been complaints from single sailors about the checkout lines. One morning while they were still in Pearl Harbor, Mac McCollum stood in line at the register for what, to him, seemed an interminably long time. In front of him were about five or six navy wives, and none of them seemed to be in any particular hurry. The woman at the cash register was arguing with the cashier about something insignificant. The wife directly in front of Mac had a little boy with her who was crying and raising quite a ruckus. Still, McCollum waited patiently to pay for the few goodies he had selected.

Soon after *Archerfish* returned to sea, McCollum sat down with Jerry Bowman and put together a letter to the editor of *Navy Times* complaining about the women and kids who always seemed to be in the way of sailors at the exchanges. They wrote that sailors were tired of having to stand in line waiting while some "brown bagger's" old lady with a pair of unruly, snot-nosed kids dug through her purse looking for the correct change.

McCollum's and Bowman's letter was published in *Navy Times* in the fall of 1964.

They had signed the missive, "All-Bachelor Submarine Crew." Needless to say, the answers came flying back to the boat. Who else in the navy was there with an all-bachelor crew but *Archerfish?* Someone suggested that they send an apology, but they never did. Finally, the *Navy Times* editor wrote in his column that he, too, had been flooded with replies to the "Bachelor Submarine Crew" letter and that he was calling a halt to the entire controversy.

It must have done some good, though. Not long after the *Archerfish* sailors' letter appeared, the Navy Exchange System initiated special registers that authorized head-of-the-line privileges for personnel in uniform during certain time periods.

While the boat was under way, the uniform of the day was usually swimming trunks, shorts, sandals, and T-shirts. When they went on liberty, the crew members wore civilian clothes. When inspections were held, everyone had to scramble to find uniforms to wear.

"What a great navy!" Cy Getts recalls.

Robert E. "Deacon" Davis remembers how, when it rained, the crew would grab their swimsuits and bars of soap and hurry topside to stand on the forward deck, enjoying a shower without having to worry about conserving water. One day, they had about a dozen sailors all lathered up when they ran out from beneath the rainstorm. The officer of the deck requested that they stop, turn around, and drive back into the squall so they could rinse off.

Permission was granted.

Another day, a group was topside getting ready for swim call when one man, Ernie Goin, jumped over the side before the boat was completely stopped. Before he knew it, he was over a hundred yards behind, bobbing in the boat's wake, waving and yelling, "Come back! Come back!" Martin D. "Bilge Valve" Davis grabbed a heaving line and went in after him and managed to bring him back.

One night in Suva, a contingent from *Archerfish* returned to the boat after a night of imbibing. It was a warm night and they were all hot, so they decided on a whim to go skinny-dipping off the side of the boat. Walt Bumbarger, Pete Gunn, John Barabas, and several others had a wonderful time, splashing around in the water. The next morning, while they were all topside, the chief of the boat, Harmon B. "Gunner" Lewis made a special point of showing them something in the water next to the boat. There, in the exact spot where the men had been cavorting a few hours before, swam two of the biggest sharks any of them had ever seen.

Archerfish submerged and surfaced for the four thousandth time at 0830 on September 24, 1964, just prior to entering the port of Auckland, New Zealand. Lieutenant Rod Potter was the diving officer.

The boat got her fourteenth commanding officer on November 24, 1964, when Lieutenant Commander Gordon W. Engquist assumed command from Lieutenant Commander Tom Eagye while the boat was moored in Yokosuka, Japan, for upkeep. Captain Eagye presented the new skipper with a brass "Playboys of the Pacific" plaque as a welcome-aboard.

The crew of *Archerfish* had devised and adopted the well-deserved nickname, "Playboys of the Pacific," during Tom Eagye's time as commanding officer. They wore the moniker proudly. An article in the *Seattle Times* on Saturday, July 4, 1964, described the rubber stamp with the "Playboys of the Pacific" logo on it that was used aboard the boat to decorate outgoing mail. It also told of the practice of "branding" new men with the stamp when they reported aboard. A photo accompanying the article shows Rod Potter and Jim Kendrigan branding their new shipmate, George Eliason, on the bridge of *Archerfish* while Ron Reddick and Charlie Dietrick look on.

Archerfish made a two-day fueling stop in Guam in December 1964. By then, staff personnel for the squadron of fleet ballistic missile submarines that would soon be in Guam had arrived aboard the tender *Proteus*. No "boomer boat" had yet visited Guam, but the first one assigned to Submarine Squadron 15 was already on patrol by then.

Just that little bit of activity had already attracted attention. A Soviet spy trawler had taken up station just outside the three-mile limit, keeping an eye on the comings and goings of vessels at Guam. On the spur of the moment, *Archerfish* decided to have a little fun with the snooping Russians.

As *Archerfish* approached the outer harbor entrance one day, they dialed in an arbitrary VHF radio frequency and transmitted just two words: "Toilet bowl." Then they proceeded into port. Captain Engquist was curious as to whether the trawler would even pick up such a short transmission on a nonassigned frequency. They must have heard it, though, because in three later encounters, the Soviets dogged *Archerfish*, coming to meet the boat on entry and going to flank to keep pace as long as she could on exit. The trawler gradually fell below the horizon since four-engine standard speed gave *Archerfish* some advantage.

Of course, the radioman chose a different arbitrary frequency with each encounter and made properly elegant transmissions each time, such as "Douche bag" or, "Finger wave." Even today there is speculation about the possibility that dusty files on these encounters might exist, buried in some cobwebbed Russian OGPU office—files that detail the mysterious diesel boat *Archerfish* and the secret radio code she was using. The crew took great delight in conjecturing about all the man-years of wasted Soviet "spook" time, all because of *Archerfish*'s little practical joke.

New Year's Eve of 1964 proved to be quite memorable and nearly tragic. *Archerfish* was running several hundred miles from the Marianas when a young sailor, George J. Smith, a fireman apprentice, came down with acute appendicitis. It was soon clear that his condition was serious, likely life threatening, and he needed to get to a hospital at all due speed. Such medical emergencies were not uncommon, and the corpsman on board could typically handle it until they could get to a medical facility. This time, though, they were steaming in an especially remote section of the ocean, far from doctors or hospitals.

When they checked the sailing directions for the area, they found that there was a French atoll not far from their position that was supposed to have a hospital and doctor. Guam was the next closest medical facility, and it was five hundred miles away. The radioman tried to raise someone on the atoll to verify they would be able to get help for Smith there. He was unable to raise anyone on any of the usual frequencies.

Captain Engquist made a command decision. Sailing directions weren't always right. Guam was a known quantity. Doc Shinn kept Smith as comfortable as he could while the crew went to work. They blew the fuel ballast tanks and cranked on four-engine flank speed. The engines never hiccupped the whole way across the Pacific. They averaged 21 knots on a light following sea on the speed run all the way to Guam at the tail end of the Marianas.

Everyone aboard *Archerfish* was exhausted when they got there, but they still came topside to watch their young shipmate be lifted ashore and placed into an ambulance. He was operated on within the hour. Smith went on to a complete recovery and eventually returned to duty on *Archerfish*.

Things could have turned out differently. Engquist later learned that the French hospital was nothing more than a dispensary and the doctor was a medical assistant, less qualified than Doc Shinn to deal with a serious emergency like appendicitis.

Captain Engquist later said, "There is no doubt in my mind that Smith survived only through Doc Shinn's expert care during the longest twenty-four hours of my tour in *Archerfish*, our speed run to Guam."

The next morning, New Year's Day, it was back to sea and to work.

By mid-January, the boat was back in Subic Bay for upkeep. The British submarine HMS *Amphion* (S43), which was home-ported in Singapore, made a port call there while en route to England for decommissioning. She moored alongside *Archerfish* to starboard, with the *311* assigned as host boat. It was a great week with a convivial group of fellow submariners.

Also while in Subic Bay, *Archerfish* performed a very unusual operation that may not sound like much to the uninformed, but any submariner can appreciate its uniqueness. USS *Perch* (APSS-313) was home-ported at Subic and was in the floating dry dock for a partial overhaul. Before she left port, *Archerfish* was asked by ComSubFlot Seven to go alongside the dry dock and charge *Perch*'s batteries. The other submarine had been in the dry dock longer than planned and needed a refresher charge. Cables were run from *Archerfish*'s cubicle, up and across the floating dry dock, into *Perch*'s cubicle, and for almost six hours she charged the other boat's batteries. As soon as the charge was complete, *Archerfish* got under way for a speed run to Hong Kong for a week's worth of R&R prior to surveying all the way back to Pearl Harbor.

When they got to Hong Kong, Bruce Teasdale bought a camera and all the stuff that goes with it so he could photograph various attractions in the city. One of the pictures he most wanted was of himself crossing the street with one particular building in the background. He carefully set his camera up on the tripod and got the scene framed and focused just the way he wanted. He set the timer on the camera and hurried out into the street so he could turn and walk back toward the camera for the shot. About the time he turned around, a car hit him. He was thrown up over the hood and landed in the middle of the street. The Hong Kong Police Department took him back to the ship. From there he was taken to the USS *Henrico* (APA-45) where he was X-rayed. No serious injuries were found, so he was returned to duty.

Teasdale would never tell anyone whether he captured the magic moment on film.

Also each day while they were in Hong Kong, the garbage barge tied up outboard and its all-girl crew picked up the ship's refuse. One afternoon Ken Sanderlin did some smooth talking and persuaded the girls to take him, Archie Moore, and Phil Splan on a tour of Victoria Basin. The tour took place on the garbage barge, of course.

Even as late as the 1960s, boats like *Archerfish* were still not equipped with online teletype or other ways for the crew to receive news reports. Instead, the navy transmitted news updates, sports scores, and other information on regular nets, using CW (Morse code) that had to be copied by the boat's radio operators. A fading signal, a static crash, or a quick bit of interference could blank out bits or even whole sections of the transmission, sometimes leaving puzzling gaps. Still, everyone on the boat eagerly awaited the "daily press" as soon as the radioman had copied it, typed it up, and, if one was available, run off copies on the mimeograph machine. If there was no duplication equipment, he just made as many carbon copies as he could. When at sea, this rough "newspaper" was the crew's only link to what was happening back in the States or with the rest of the world.

The "daily press" was usually quite succinct. "Johnson elected in a land-slide." "Red Sox hammer Yanks." Sometimes there were only abbreviated box scores with some of the crucial numbers erased by the static crashes that are so common when using AM radio in the South Pacific. When details were missing or garbled, the radio operator simply X-ed out the blanks or muddled characters and went on. The headline might just say, "XXXXX elected in a landslide."

To spice up the daily news, Radioman Second Class Ken "das Goat" Sanderlin began adding scores and standings to each day's sports updates for a totally fictional group of teams, all members of the nonexistent West Coast Hockey League. He created the league in his head, patterned after the old Pacific Coast baseball league. He made up teams, invented star players, and kept day-to-day standings based on totally imaginary games. By his own admission, Sanderlin knew nothing at all about hockey. How-ever, he had read a fictional story about a hockey team in a book from the ship's library. In the book, Seattle had a team, so he added a Seattle team to his league. Sanderlin dubbed them the "Seahawks" years before the Na-tional Football League team adopted the name. He also granted teams to Portland, San Francisco, Oakland, and Los Angeles. He put another team in San Diego and made them the league's underdogs. They were the Con-dors, and their hero was a young man named Angel Gomez-Gomez, a Mex-ican native who had never even been on skates until he was nineteen years old, but now he dominated the "league."

Gomez-Gomez routinely performed "hat tricks" and other gallant feats that were mentioned in the book Sanderlin had read. But at one point the young star was knocked out of the lineup by what the "daily press" du-tifully reported was a particularly nasty social disease. The crew aboard *Archerfish* began avidly following the teams, most of them rooting for Gomez-Gomez and the team from San Diego since they could most closely identify with the underdogs. Of course, the "season" ended with the Con-dors claiming the title in a thrilling playoff series, in spite of the fact that their star player had been tragically killed before the final game. It all con-veniently culminated just as they arrived in Pearl Harbor.

Not long after arriving in Pearl Harbor for the first time after assuming command of the boat, Gordon Engquist got a taste of the anti-*Archerfish* prejudice that existed in some circles of the navy's upper staff. Whether it was jealousy or a distaste for anything and anybody as far from "spit-and-polish" as the 311-boat, there was a great deal of open animosity toward her and her crew. That was especially true in her nominal home port, Pearl Harbor. That's one reason many in the crew disliked going "home."

"The [rowdy] reputation [of *Archerfish* throughout the Submarine Force] provided good fun for us," Engquist later wrote. "But Tom Eagye had warned me about its downside when I relieved him. In fact, Tom had conducted a public awareness program during his tenure to diminish its negativity. His lengthy correspondence with the division commander, "Bones" Thomas, and others was informative, filled with positive facts, and underlaid with the crew's professionalism while not downplaying their fun-loving spirits."

Eagye's constant lobbying must have done some good. There had been a row while they were in Pearl for submarine refresher training. Engineman First Class Bob Heaning and his forward engine room crew had started stripping about fifteen layers of paint off the inside of their pressure hull before they ever reached port. Several days after their arrival, a dirty, disheveled Heaning, sporting a three-day growth of beard, took a break from the grimy work and was spotted across the street from the pier by some ComSubPac staffer. Word quickly spread about this prime chance to see a typical *Archerfish* sailor. All that one needed to do was to look out the window. A filthy, disgusting crewman was, at that very moment, fetching a Coke and smoking a cigarette just outside the ComSubPac headquarters building.

In a bit of poor timing, all the *Archerfish* officers except for the duty officer were away from the boat at the time, in the submarine base attack trainer. The division commander heard about the "slovenly *Archerfish* sailor" and placed a call to the boat's skipper. Lieutenant Junior Grade Jim Kendrigan was the *Archerfish* duty officer. He reported that the commander was not on board. How about the exec? No. Any of the other officers? No.

The division commander didn't give Kendrigan a chance to explain where they were. Almost instantly, word reached all the way to ComSubPac Rear Admiral Gene Fluckey that all the *Archerfish* officers were ashore, goofing off or worse, during working hours. The report also maintained that the boat's crew made the characters from the television show *Hogan's Heroes* look like the Buckingham Palace guard.

Meanwhile, in the attack trainer, the *Archerfish* wardroom was in the middle of a problem when a messenger from the duty officer burst in shouting, "Get back to the boat on the double! Admiral Fluckey's on his way for a walk-through!"

Not knowing the reason for the sudden unexpected visit, the officers weren't concerned at all as they returned to *Archerfish*. But when the admiral strode across the brow, the skipper knew from the look on his face and the fire in his eyes that they were in trouble for something.

"Where has the wardroom been?" Fluckey demanded to know.

"Attack trainer, Admiral."

"All right, let's take a look belowdecks," he ordered. If there was a softening of his tone, it wasn't evident.

So they proceeded to walk through the entire boat. Bob Heaning and his forward engine room gang didn't look any better than before, but in the context of their air-hammer environment, they presented a totally different picture. Heaning looked the admiral right in the eye and said, "When we get out of Puget Sound Shipyard, Admiral, come back down here and take a look at a classy engine room."

By the end of the ordeal, Admiral Fluckey, if not fully convinced, was at least coming around. It takes more than one positive impression to overcome years of prejudice, but it was obvious that points had been scored.

The crew would get the last laugh. Admiral Fluckey did visit the boat once again after the overhaul was completed. He walked through and, when he finished his tour, declared *Archerfish* the prettiest boat in the Submarine Force. That was high praise indeed, and especially when directed at *Archerfish*.

The truth was that throughout the life of their boat and despite their grousing about all the hard work, *Archerfish*'s crew took pride in her appearance and safety. It was, after all, their home, and they tried to make it as comfortable as they could.

"It was a rare and memorable moment for the old *Archerfish* hands to savor," Captain Engquist says of the admiral's comment. "I never heard any of them crow about it. They bragged and laughed a lot about liberty adventures, but the admiral's praise was something to hold close. We were lucky to have caught him instead of some other guy who might not have had a fair mind and an even hand."

The bias against *Archerfish* didn't go away, though. Not even with the admiral's endorsement. Engquist would encounter it even after he left the boat.

"Three years later, as a ComSubPac staffer, I observed that the old prejudice against my old boat, though more subtle, was still very much around," he wrote. "Somehow I'm glad the word 'conventional' always applied to *Archerfish*'s power plant, not to its crew, even to the end."

And to the crew of *Archerfish*, those words from one of her skippers probably meant even more than the praise of Admiral Fluckey.

25

EARTHQUAKES AND WAR ZONES

T HE old girl got a hysterectomy in March 1965. *Archerfish* settled into the shipyard at Bremerton, Washington, and the workers immediately got busy, removing her torpedo tubes. This was to provide more room for berthing and storage for personal gear and more space in which to install electronic equipment as needed for special operations. At the preoverhaul conference in Subic Bay, the original shipyard estimate to do the work was submitted. They figured it would take $10,000 to $15,000 to accomplish the rather major surgery required to take out all ten of the submarine's torpedo tubes. The squadron engineer looked over the estimate and approved the work list. Not long after that meeting, *Archerfish* was in Bremerton, ready for radical surgery. Had the cost been higher, the job would have never been approved.

Problem was, there had been a misplaced decimal point in the shipyard's estimate. It should have been for $100,000 to $150,000! Once the work was started, though, with huge holes cut into the boat's pressure hull and the torpedo tubes already being removed, it was too late to stop.

The tubes were removed one at a time, and intact. Once out of the boat, all the ready-to-fire levers were chromed and made into paperweights. Admiral Fluckey received one of them the day he declared *Archerfish* the prettiest boat in the force. Another paperweight was set aside for

Captain Joe Enright, the *Shinano* stalker, but he apparently never received it. No one admits to knowing where the other eight ended up.

Archerfish lost all her distinctive-sounding klaxons while she was in Bremerton as well. An electronic tweeter that was sounded over the IMC replaced them as the diving alarm. Frank Ely remembers, "The damn thing sounded like a turkey call!"

To some, it seemed that their boat was being dismantled piece by piece, slowly being decommissioned a part at a time. Still, as long as the navy kept working on her, that meant she had some life left, some useful purpose to serve.

Archerfish had been in Bremerton for about six weeks when disaster struck the area. On April 29, an earthquake measuring 7.3 on the Richter scale rocked the Pacific Northwest just after eight o'clock in the morning.

Captain Engquist was just putting on his pants in his room at the bachelor officers' quarters when the floor began rocking and rolling beneath him like the deck of his boat in a storm. He had to grab the bed and hold on to keep from being thrown to the floor. His first thoughts were of his boat, which, at that moment, was sitting on blocks in the drydock. He could imagine her being tossed off the blocks by the quake, lying there on her side in the bottom of the dry dock.

When he managed to get to the yard through all the panicky confusion, he found his charge still sitting upright, unharmed. The men working on the boat were all fine as well. Steve Hahne and Mike Royle were topside at the time of the tremor, and Ben Vinca was working inside the forward trim tank when the earthquake happened. All three of them made it to the top of the dock in record time. An inspection found *Archerfish* to be structurally okay as well, but she had shifted a quarter of an inch on the blocks.

The next day's edition of the *Bremerton Sun* reported: "Puget Sound Naval Shipyard reported all dry docks to be all right and watched with some apprehension as the tide dropped rapidly after the earthquake—twenty-nine inches in an hour. Shipyard tugs were manned and sent away from the pier to stand by in Sinclair Inlet in case needed. Special watches were set on the mooring lines. A possible tidal wave alert was issued by the 13th Naval District."

Maybe the part of the newspaper story that most distressed the *Archerfish* crew was the one that said, "At the Ranier Brewing Co. plant in Seattle, two 2,000-barrel aging tanks were knocked off their foundations. One tank split and enough beer for 15,000 cases spewed out."

In the early hours of the morning of May 23, Wayne Tollefson, a young

Archerfish sailor from the Polish section of Detroit, lost control of a rented motorcycle while on liberty at Milton, near Tacoma, Washington. He was thrown from the 'cycle and struck a tree. His liver was lacerated, and he died shortly after he was taken to a local hospital.

It was the duty of the executive officer, Glenn D. Bates, to inform Tollefson's father of his adopted son's death. Benny Bennett had an even more difficult task. After being briefed by a navy corpsman at a military hospital on the duties of an "escort," he rode with the young sailor's body on the train all the way across the country, from Tacoma to Detroit. The Naval Reserve unit in Detroit provided a military honor guard for the funeral. Many of the two hundred or so persons who attended the ceremony commented on the huge floral bouquet sent by Tollefson's shipmates, the crew of *Archerfish*.

There are many instances that exemplify the strong brotherhood of submarine sailors in general and *Archerfish* crew members in particular. Robert Davis experienced some of it when the Bremerton yard period ended in August 1965. On the day they were to get under way, he received a telegram informing him that his father had suffered a serious heart attack and he was needed at home immediately. Unfortunately, it was several days before payday, and the young seaman was flat broke. The Red Cross managed to get him a ticket home, but he had no travel money.

As he was finishing packing, one of his shipmates came to his rack, told him that the crew had heard about his predicament and wanted to help. He handed Davis an envelope. There was almost $200 cash in it. Considering everyone else was counting the days to payday as well and likely as tapped out as Davis was, that was quite an impressive sum of money.

"I can't accept this," Davis told his shipmate. "I'd never be able to pay everyone back."

"It ain't a loan," the other sailor responded without hesitation. "Consider it a gift to a friend in a time of need."

Davis later wrote, "That was when I found out that we weren't just crew members, but in an odd sense, we were family. Thanks, fellows, for the help . . . and for the memories."

On their return to Pearl Harbor, *Archerfish* was greeted with the news that they were to undergo an operational readiness inspection (ORI). One of the drills that is typically held during the ORI is called "Man Battle Stations Torpedo." That, of course, seemed very strange to the *Archerfish* crew, considering the fact that all the torpedo tubes had been removed while they were in the shipyard.

Archerfish got another new skipper on November 20, 1965. Gordon Engquist was relieved by Lieutenant Commander Robert B. "Scotty" Mc-Comb. The commander of Submarine Squadron One and the Commander Submarines Pacific were both aboard for the inspection and change of command ceremony.

Even so far along in her life, *Archerfish* still caused a commotion everywhere she went. She spent Christmas 1965 in Sydney, Australia, and the local papers still made much of the "wealthy" and unmarried American sailors. The headline in one of the papers, just above a big photo of the boat, was "Bachelor Yanks—Dollars Galore." There were a couple of telling quotes in the accompanying story. Captain McComb told the reporter that any Sydney girl would be "very, very welcome" on the sub. But at the end of the story, the skipper was also quoted as saying, "We would be delighted to have any underprivileged children visit us."

A female reporter noted that the submarine had taken sixty-six visitors on a twenty-mile goodwill cruise the previous day. And that Captain Mc-Comb "was a bit bewildered by the number of guests. 'We invited forty-five. Now there are sixty-six. They can't all be stowaways.'" But then McComb told the reporter; "I went below a day or two ago and discovered two girls peeling potatoes in the galley. They said they'd been there for ten days peeling onions and crying. I don't know where they came from. Some of the crew are pretty cagey. You've got to watch them."

The same reporter also had anxious moments during a demonstration dive. "Peering up the periscope was interesting, but the trickle of saltwater on my head was unnerving," she wrote.

It was the midsixties, a time of turmoil back home. *Archerfish* and her crew got a taste of it all as well. "Akadama" Joe Miller and Ken Sanderlin had been on liberty in Yokosuka. They fell asleep in their taxi on the way back to the base and woke up in front of the gate right in the middle of one of the biggest antiwar/antisubmarine/antiAmerican rallies anyone had ever seen. There they were, in their U.S. Navy uniforms, their submarine dolphins prominently displayed, and all around them were several thousand mad, radical locals, protesting America's presence in their country, in Vietnam, on the planet. The Japanese police were swinging clubs, busting heads, but were hopelessly outnumbered. The two sailors suggested to the driver that he get them the hell out of there. Somehow he managed to do so without anyone in the mob noticing the two American sailors he carried in his cab.

In August 1966, *Archerfish* made one of her several forays into the territorial waters of Vietnam. That meant that they were technically in a war zone. The word was passed over the IMC, "Anyone wanting to fire a gun while we are in the war zone, lay topside." Many of the crew did. Larry Meyer recalls, "We almost had a couple people become eligible for Purple Hearts. That'll teach them to give a loaded gun to a submarine sailor."

One afternoon, while they were steaming through Vietnamese waters, radar picked up five contacts. They turned out to be a group of American tin cans (destroyers). One of them pulled away from the formation and came to challenge *Archerfish*, blinking "AA AA AA" with his light. As the vessel drew within a couple of hundred yards, quartermaster-of-the-watch John Foley began sending the message, "United States Submarine *Archerfish* AGSS-311." They were close enough by then that Foley could see the other ship's signalman, standing on the bridge, all decked out in his starched and pressed dungarees, his white hat squared away, just like all the other sailors standing on the vessel's bridge next to him.

That's when Foley realized that on his own boat, Frank and Jack Ely (*Archerfish*'s only brother combination) were serving as lookouts in the shears, and they likely presented an interesting sight to the regulation-navy crew on the tin can. One brother wore his favorite orange Bermuda shorts, the other his special plaid shorts. For his part, Foley was decked out in his usual "uniform," cut-off dungarees and little else. Most everyone lounging on the *311*-boat's cigarette deck was in his customary casual attire as well. He could only imagine the thoughts of the tin can's crew as they approached this particular U.S. Navy vessel.

It was sometime during the first week of September that Mark Christopherson, Kenny Crocker, Sam Harris, and "Hack" Hansberry boarded a DC-3 at Hickam Air Force Base in Hawaii and headed for Midway Island and a rendezvous with their new boat, *Archerfish*. There were a few other passengers on the plane, as well as medical and food supplies bound for the island.

After an uneventful flight, they landed on Midway at about 1030 local time. *Archerfish* was due to arrive in port at about 1430, so the new crewmen only had about four hours to kill until they could get settled into their new home. Or so they thought!

That four-hour wait turned into forty-three long days. And they were spent on a very small piece of real estate with little to do to pass the time. *Archerfish* had received an unexpected change of operational orders, diverting them to carry out a special operation. The nature of that mission remains classified to this day.

The inescapable truth was that time was growing short for the old girl by the end of 1966. She spent Christmas of 1966 in Mazatlán, Mexico. Just before the New Year, she eased down Mexico's southwestern coast to Acapulco, which was already a booming resort town.

It was in Acapulco one day that some of the crew got an angry upbraiding from an unlikely member of the navy brass. An old torpedo retriever that had been refitted as a yacht zoomed past where *Archerfish* was anchored. The vessel's CO was a full commander in the Naval Reserve, but the crew took little notice of its passing. Besides, there weren't many other U.S. Navy types in Acapulco, Mexico, so they were hardly looking for anybody to pass that required a salute.

A few minutes later, the yacht turned and came back to where *Archerfish* lay. The vessel eased up close enough for its skipper to give everyone on the sub's deck a good tongue-lashing for not rendering honors when he passed.

The crew members who were topside merely explained that they were busy at the time, trying to chase away the local kids who were stealing lightbulbs and anything else from the submarine that they could get their hands on. That seemed to satisfy the miffed commander. He signed autographs and invited the crew to be his guests at a cocktail party that night at the luxurious Las Brisas Hotel.

The irate skipper was the actor John Wayne.

Bill Dana, a comedian whose character, Jose Jiminez, was very popular on television at the time, was also in Acapulco while the sub was there. He came alongside *Archerfish* in his speedboat and graciously offered water-ski rides to anyone who wanted to give it a try.

The guys who had the watch that evening set off several grocery bags full of fireworks at midnight on New Year's Eve, going into 1967 with a bang. For a while, it sounded as if a war had broken out in Acapulco.

On February 1, the boat submerged for the five thousandth time. Captain McComb had the conn, and Lieutenant Bob Jenner was the diving officer. They went to 150 feet before successfully surfacing again without incident. An optimistic Glenn Christensen made and decorated a large sheet cake with the proclamation "5000th Dive" to honor the occasion. He was confident the old girl would complete the dive by surfacing successfully and without incident. The year before, in early 1966, USS *Bashaw* (AGSS-241) had also made her five thousandth dive. Their cook had been a bit less optimistic. Commissaryman Second Class Larry Clark baked and decorated their cake to commemorate their "5000th Surface." The *Bashaw* wouldn't celebrate until the boat was actually back on the surface.

When the boat eased into Pearl Harbor on February 8, 1967, she made quite an entrance. The topside personnel, including the lookouts in the shears, wore sombreros and colorful serapes, souvenirs of their visit to Mexico.

On the morning of May 24, following captain's inspection of personnel, Rear Admiral J. H. Maurer, Commander Submarine Force, U.S. Pacific Fleet, broke his flag on *Archerfish* for the presentation of the ComSubPac Unit Commendation. The citation reads, in part: "For exceptionally meritorious service as a member of the Submarine Force during the period 10 May 1960 to 7 February 1967. . . . Throughout this period, ARCHERFISH, manned by a bachelor crew, has not only performed in a thoroughly professional manner but has also acted as an outstanding representative of the United States, the Navy, and the Submarine Force in many ports not frequented by submarines. The impressions and image established on these visits have been of great credit to the Force. The superlative, sustained performance of ARCHERFISH in all aspects of operations, administration, and public affairs reflects glowingly on her commanding officer, officers and men, and is in keeping with the highest traditions of the United States Navy Submarine Force."

The citation came at a time when the boat and her crew were popularly referred to as "Scotty McComb's Traveling Animal Act."

When they left Pearl this time, headed back for their new home port at San Diego, they had a last goodbye ready for the island. During the final upkeep there, Torpedoman Second Class Terry Hageman had his seaman gang paint ALOHA in huge, white letters on the side of the superstructure behind the port bow plane. Jerry "Corny" Cornelison remembers that the word wasn't visible when the bow planes were rigged in, but as *Archerfish* departed the pier for the final time, they rigged out the planes in a way that allowed all to see their unique farewell to the place.

Operation Sea Scan phase three officially ended on July 24, 1967, with the sighting of the U.S. coastline. The trip from Pearl Harbor to San Diego, the boat's new home port, was a roundabout journey. It took one hundred days to complete the transit since they were running survey lines along the way. These lines were the first part of phase four, which began on July 25. It was her final Sea Scan assignment, and it kept her close to land, taking her mostly up and down the Pacific Coast, still doing her vital surveying work but within sight of the mainland most of the time. She would no longer head off to far-flung points of the globe, steaming thousands of miles at a time through the world's great oceans, visiting mysterious ports where no submarine had ever moored and where no submariners had ever enjoyed liberty. Even so, she found a few more nearby but interesting ports to visit, experienced a few more encounters to add to her file of stories.

It was still tedious work. The northern coast was often shrouded in fog and the waters were filled with fishing boats and cargo vessels.

After a foggy ten-hour transit through the Strait of Juan de Fuca, *Archerfish* visited Victoria, British Columbia, mooring at the Royal Canadian Navy's western base at Esquimalt, across the harbor from the city. The local radio and newspapers made a great deal of favorable noise about the visit, and a large number of locals toured the boat during general visiting hours.

The base at Esquimalt was the home port of another elderly diesel submarine, the HMCS *Grilse* (SS-71), which was at sea at the time of the *311*-boat's visit. *Grilse* had begun life in Portsmouth Naval Shipyard, just up the way from the *311*-boat, as *Burrfish* (USS-312). She was *Archerfish*'s sister!

At the time, she was on loan to the Royal Canadian Navy, and, though she would eventually meet the same fate as *Archerfish*, she would outlive her by a year and a month. *Burrfish*'s life had not been nearly as colorful as her sister, but she still earned five battle stars for her service in World War II, completed three tours with the Sixth Fleet in the Mediterranean, and served as a radar picket boat off the East Coast of the United States.

When *Archerfish* made another visit to Portland, Oregon, on September 1, there was another change of command. Commander John Perry Wood relieved Lieutenant Commander Robert B. McComb in a ceremony attended by a number of guests, including the mayor of Portland, Terry Schrunk, and Commander Submarine Division Fifty-three, Commander R. L. Murrill. Also in attendance was a bunch of winos who were sitting on the nearby seawall drinking out of brown paper bags. Commander Wood was a native of Columbus, Ohio, and a Naval Academy graduate. He held a master's degree in electrical engineering, and in addition to holding other positions and serving on various other vessels, he had previously been executive officer of *Archerfish*.

The old boat had lost none of her popularity. What with the publicity about the boat and the change of command ceremony, hundreds of visitors lined up to see the legendary vessel over Labor Day weekend.

Prior to departure from Portland, Archie Moore decided it would be a good idea to let the gang at the boat's favorite bar in San Francisco, the Horse & Cow, know they were on the way. Moore went to the pay phone and called the bar's owner, Bill Looby.

"We're heading your way," Moore told him. "Get us a fifty-five-gallon drum of wine and have it ready for our arrival!"

When *Archerfish* got to San Francisco in September 1967, Mike Burkholder, "Pigger" Johnston, and Archie Moore headed immediately for the Horse & Cow. The first thing they saw when they walked in was a large wooden cask resting on sawhorses. It was the fifty-five gallons of wine that Archie had ordered from Portland.

Looby told them that after he spoke with Moore, he checked around with several of the wineries in the Napa Valley to see if he could get a barrel of wine at a good price. One of the wineries told him, "We'll do better than that. We'll donate the wine to you if you'll allow us to take pictures of them drinking it for use in our *Wine Country Magazine*."

Naturally, Looby agreed. The winery got its pictures, and the *Archerfish* crew got their barrel of wine.

While *Archerfish* was in San Francisco, the exec, Sam Adams, arranged for eight Bunnies from the local Playboy Club to visit and tour the boat. They arrived in two limousines, all wearing skintight white slacks and snug, black, sleeveless tops. The crew was waiting topside to greet them. The women presented the crew with the official Playboy Flag. The skipper and crew gave the ladies a ship's plaque to commemorate their visit.

In all, the Bunnies spent about three hours aboard the submarine. When they departed, the manager of the club extended membership privileges to the crew for the remainder of their stay in San Francisco. "The Playboys of the Pacific" had a new and very appropriate home-away-from-home.

By the end of 1967, *Archerfish* had become a regular fixture in San Diego. When they received word that they were going to get R&R in Mexico, the crew was ecstatic. Acapulco for Christmas and Mazatlán over New Year's! Many of the crew had come aboard within the past twelve months and had not yet had a "great adventure" on *Archerfish*.

John Hyatt remembers that he couldn't wait to get started. Little did he know that this would be his first and last foreign liberty port. The crew didn't know it at the time, but *Archerfish* had only a little more than four months remaining in commission, and only ten more months of life left in her.

There had been continuing problems with the bow planes's rigging system. They simply would not rig in all the way to the hull the way they were supposed to. While the boat was in Mazatlán, the electricians adjusted the limit switch to try to make the planes work correctly. Unfortunately, they gave the switch a little too much oomph, and the planes turned into a giant vice that tried to compress the forward superstructure. The bull gear in the gearbox could not handle the extra load and made a loud, unsettling boom when it folded up. It was necessary to put a steel cable from one plane to the other, awkwardly stretched across the walking deck to hold them up against the superstructure until the gearbox could be replaced.

John Hyatt, who was one of the cooks, remembers, "We continued diving on schedule, but without the use of the bow planes, it was almost impossible to maintain depth. I could hear discussions between the diving officer and the poor guy on the stern planes all the way back in the galley. 'Keep your bubble!' he'd yell. 'If this was a real patrol you'd have to be able to handle it!' And so it went all the way back to San Diego. No matter how hard the planesman tried, he couldn't keep the boat level."

It was obvious by now that the old girl was getting very tired. It seemed like everyday it was something else that needed attention. Everyone aboard figured that if they could just hold on for a couple more months, they would be in the shipyard for another much-needed overhaul. That would give *Archerfish* a new lease on life.

On January 19, 1968, the crew received the disappointing word that the fateful decision had already been made. The overhaul had been canceled. The boat was to be decommissioned. The word came for most of the crew in the "Plan of the Day," a one-sheet schedule that was posted each day in the control room by the exec. Along with the mentions for "soup call" at 1515 and "movie call" at 2030 was a note that said, "Due to recent budget decision, a decision has been made to cancel the *Archerfish* overhaul and decommission the ship not later than 1 June 1968. Even though we will be decommissioned, we will still have to operate until that time, so with the exception of the overhaul plan, all routines will be conducted as normal."

Archerfish submerged late in the afternoon of February 21 for what would be the final operational dive of her commission. No more can be requested of a submarine than that the number of surfaces equal the total number of dives. Thankfully, fourteen minutes after disappearing below the surface of the Pacific Ocean, *Archerfish* surfaced for the 5,388th and final time. Lieutenant Eugene Kudla was the diving officer at the time.

Two hours later, he made the landing as *Archerfish* moored port side to USS *Cusk* (SS-348) at the Submarine Support Facility Pier, San Diego, California.

A team from the Board of Inspection and Survey conducted a material inspection of *Archerfish* on February 27 and 28. During this inspection, divers were sent over the side to inspect the rudder, screws, and stern planes. That's when they discovered that the starboard stern plane was missing entirely. It had been severed at the yoke. There was a good deal of rust on the severed shaft end so it appeared it had been missing for a while. A search of the immediate area by the divers failed to yield the missing stern plane.

There were still some options as far as the crew was concerned. The navy could send the boat to Mare Island Naval Shipyard, install a new stern plane, and resume surface and submerged operations. That would cost about a half million dollars. They could also simply continue operations with only one stern plane and restrict the boat to surface operations only. Or they could resume normal surface and submerged operations with only one stern plane.

There were problems with all the options. First, no one was willing to pay the half million to replace the plane. The Sub Safe program was just getting under way at that time, so no one wanted to take the responsibility for authorizing further operations of any kind by a boat having only one stern plane. Nobody knew of any other submarines in the navy that were operating with missing stern planes, either.

Decommissioning was the only option left.

The board found *Archerfish* unfit for further service. They estimated that the cost of the repairs and alterations that would be required to restore *Archerfish* to minimum fleet standards would be almost $4 million. In view of these findings, the board recommended that *Archerfish* be stricken from the naval vessel register and disposed of.

On April 15, 1968, the secretary of the navy instructed the chief of naval operations to "take necessary action incident to disposal of *Archerfish*."

Finally, her duty done and worn down by all her travels, the old diesel boat was on the verge of making the ultimate sacrifice for her country.

26

WHAT THE JAPANESE
COULD NOT DO

T HE crew was mustered at quarters at 11:30 AM and *Archerfish* was decommissioned for the final time at 2:32 PM on May Day, May 1, 1968, in a formal ceremony at the Navy Undersea Warfare Center pier at Ballast Point, off Rosecrans Street in San Diego. Lieutenant Junior Grade Randall B. Christison was the duty officer for the final day *Archerfish* was in commission. The ComCruDesPac band played the National Anthem. Chaplain R. W. Aldrich gave the invocation. The Commander Submarine Development Group One, Captain Albert Beutler, was the principal speaker. Former skipper Robert B. "Scotty" McComb, by then a representative of the Navy Oceanographic Office, was also a speaker. In his remarks, he said something that many former members of the boat's crew had also mentioned. *Archerfish*, at times, seemed to them to be a real person.

"You know, if any of us in the military, or anyone in these United States, could look back on a quarter century of service to our country as this ship can, we could certainly be most proud, and perhaps even content to rest on our laurels. They say that a ship's soul is her crew, and without them, there is no ship. I wouldn't dispute this, but I remember once as we sailed down Tokyo Bay with the homeward-bound pennant flying, I involuntarily patted her on the side, and I swear she responded with a shudder from within. *Archerfish*, as I know her—and I know her well—is a fine woman. Like a good woman, if she was treated well, the returns were more than ample. She was feminine all right—expensive to take out and always putting on more paint. Perhaps I'm allowing myself to get a trifle sentimental now. Perhaps in the next hour we shall all become a bit maudlin. But I know her to be a great and gallant lady, and I shall always remember her just that way, the way she was."

At least one other former captain chimed in on the boat's humanity. Captain Joseph Enright, the skipper at the conn when *Shinano* was sunk, had been invited but was unable to attend. He sent a telegram that was read aloud. It said, in part: "Best of luck to you, officers and crew on decommissioning *Archerfish*. I assume you bachelors are properly preparing the fine ship for the long delayed rest she deserves. Regret I cannot be with you for the ceremony."

Seated among the guests on the pier were past crew members, their families, and many longtime friends. One of them was "Snorkel Patty," a well-known barmaid who held a special place in the hearts of *Archerfish* and her crew.

Published accounts of the event mention her all-bachelor crew, of course, and the vital work they had been doing (or at least the part of it that was not still classified) as part of Operation Sea Scan. The stories noted that the boat had, on average, steamed over five thousand miles per month during that eight-year period and that she had visited areas so remote that the only navigational charts available were from the cruises of Magellan and Captain Cook.

The reports also recalled her seven war patrols in enemy waters during World War II, and, of course, her sinking of the largest ship ever built up to that time.

Commander John P. Wood closed his remarks by issuing his final order as commanding officer to the executive officer, Lieutenant Milan Moncilovich: "Haul down the colors." Quartermaster Third Class Wes Atchison and Quartermaster Third Class Ken Crocker slowly lowered the Stars and Stripes while a bugler from the Commander Cruiser-Destroyer Force Pacific band sounded taps. Chaplain Aldrich offered a benediction, and it was over.

At decommissioning, there was still about $5,000 left in the boat's slush fund. Darby's, a bar on Rosecrans Street just down the road from the Ballast Point Submarine Base, donated a keg of beer. The money was spent on more booze and food for the party, which lasted two days. Sam Adams took a tape recorder to both nights of the decommissioning party and recorded the thoughts of the crew and their guests.

The oceanographer of the navy, Odale "Muddy" Waters, attempted to spare *Archerfish* from the ignominious fate that had been planned for her. He requested that the Commander First Fleet turn the former *Archerfish* over to the Naval Undersea Warfare Center in Pasadena. The plan would be to sink her by controlled flooding on the San Clemente Island Range in 650 to 800 feet of water. The sunken hulk would be used by Submarine Development Group One for search, location, and salvage operation drills. He felt this would be a useful task as well as "a meaningful end to a gallant lady."

ComSubPac and CinCPacFlt thought it was a fine idea as well. However, the sunken hulk would not be *Archerfish*. By the time the decision was made, she had already been prepared as a mobile target, and it was not cost effective to use *Archerfish* when an alternative nonmobile hull was available. The former *Moray* (AGSS-300) would be turned over to the development group and sunk off San Clemente. *Archerfish* would be used by ComSubPac as a torpedo test target as originally planned.

Five and a half months after the emotional decommissioning ceremony, on October 17, the USS *Florikan* (ASR-9), tied lines to what was left of *Archerfish* and towed her out of the navy base at San Diego to a predetermined point in the Pacific Ocean. Nearby, the USS *Tulare* (AKA-112) served as a helicopter platform for choppers from Support Squadron 5 at Ream Field.

According to the November 15, 1968, edition of *Periscope*, a publication of Submarine Flotilla One, the officer in charge of the target control team was Lieutenant James C. Thomas. The last men to ride aboard *Archerfish* as she was towed out of San Diego that day were EN1 William A. Freeman, EM2 Louis Deniz, MM1 Glen Noel, and OM3 Dale Robinson. Lieutenant Marty Paul, the exec of *Florikan*, supervised the towing.

Once they reached the area and the men were taken off the boat, the legendary submarine was left steaming on her own power, making between seven and twelve knots on one engine as she moved in a broad circle through the calm Pacific waters. Meanwhile, the USS *Snook* (SSN-592) stalked, sighted, and ultimately fired three torpedoes in her direction. The first, a Mark-37-2, did not acquire or attack the target. A second Mark-37-2 torpedo hit the stern and exploded but did not sink the target. The third deadly weapon, a Mark-14-5, hit *Archerfish* broadside, almost perfectly in her midsection.

She split in half near the after battery hatch and sank almost immediately. She ultimately came to rest in 2,000 fathoms of water at latitude 32 degrees, 23.0 minutes north and longitude 122 degrees, 58.1 minutes west.

The operation was a routine service weapons test, a drill for *Snook* to keep her offensive weapons skills sharp and at the ready. It is one of the means that is employed by the navy to make sure its active warships are ready should they be called upon to fire a torpedo in anger. It is not unusual at all for decommissioned vessels to be used for such practice sinking. Only the history and the character of this particular target made its otherwise routine destruction noteworthy.

Archerfish had served her purpose one final time.

Polaris, a publication of the Submarine Veterans of World War II organization, gave an account of the event in its November 1968 issue. It noted, "The exercise accomplished what the Japanese failed to do November 28, 1944, after *Archerfish* sank their . . . carrier *Shinano*, only seventeen hours out on her maiden voyage."

Those aboard *Snook* that day certainly knew the record of the old, rusty, used-up diesel boat they sent to the bottom of the ocean. They may not have known, though, how many times she and her crew made history as her Fairbanks-Morse engines took them around the globe. Or the unique character of the hundreds of men who called her their home in her twenty-five years of life.

It would not have made any difference, of course. The old boat had done her duty well, and it was time for her to be put to rest. There was some consolation in the fact that she was still serving her country when she died that day.

Still, it's sad that no one can visit her now, touch her hull, or drop down the same hatches that passed so many colorful, dedicated sailors. That no one can stand in her conning tower, peer through her scope, or man her bridge and imagine what it must have been like to be in that spot, stalking an enemy vessel in the distant moonlight or overlooking an ice floe in Foxe Basin or smelling the fragrant mountains of Bali while the crew enjoyed swim call. That no one can ever again experience the cramped heat of her pump room, the camaraderie of her mess hall, or the deafening throb of her powerful engines.

But the dwindling numbers of shipmates still have their memories. Not even her death can take those away. Thank goodness they have been wise enough to pass along those recollections for the rest of us to share.

The memories. They are just one more thing for which we need to be forever grateful to *Archerfish* and her crew.

"And this is all that is left of it! Only a moment: a moment of strength, of romance, of glamour—of youth! A flick of sunshine upon a strange shore, the time to remember, the time for a sigh and—goodbye!"

—From *Youth*, Joseph Conrad

In memory of our shipmates who made the supreme sacrifice
to ensure our freedom.

James S. Clark, LCDR
USS *Golet* (SS-361)
Lost with "All Hands"
June 14, 1944

Fred "A" Tarbox, EM3(SS)
USS *Swordfish* (SS-193)
Lost with "All Hands"
January 12, 1945

Edward A. Johnson, ENC(SS)
USS *Thresher* (SSN-593)
Lost with "All Hands"
April 10, 1963

Rodney J. Kipp, ETR3(SS)
USS *Scorpion* (SSN-589)
Lost with "All Hands"
May 22, 1968

There is a port of no return, where ships

May ride at anchor for a little space

And then, some starless night, the cable slips,

Leaving an eddy at the mooring space . . .

Gulls, veer no longer. Sailor, rest your oar.

No tangled wreckage will be washed ashore.

—From *Lost Harbor* by Leslie N. Jennings

AUTHORS' NOTES

COMPLETING the biography of this remarkable submarine and her crew has been much more than a two-man effort. Wherever possible, we have relied on the accounts and recollections of the men who served aboard *Archerfish*—sailors, officers, and hydrographic scientists. We all owe a big debt of gratitude to the hundreds of shipmates who so willingly and openly shared their stories and memories with us, and our appreciation to them for allowing us to use them. The really difficult part of writing this book was deciding which stories had to be left out. We apologize for not being able to include every one of them. Perhaps there will be another book someday.

Many of the stories and details have appeared in various forms on the excellent Web site dedicated to *Archerfish*, www.ussarcherfish.com, and in the revived continuation of the boat's bimonthly newsletter, the *A-Fish-L-Blast*. Ken Henry, Leo "Doc" Carter, and Jerry Cornelison have lovingly compiled these contributions down through the years for both outlets.

A second major source of information in this book is actual and official navy documentation, from deck logs to patrol reports to copies of correspondence. Gathering that information required several trips to the National Archives II in College Park, Maryland, and to the Naval Historical Center Operational Archives in Washington, D.C., where Ken and his wife, Colleen, spent countless hours, poring over documents, copying them, and boxing and loading them so they could be hauled back home for collating and filing. In some cases, it was necessary to petition for declassification of some of the material. More often than not, the requests were regretfully denied, as even forty years later some parts of Operation Sea Scan are too sensitive to release.

Additional thanks go to:

Deborah Edge, researcher at the National Archives II in College Park. She has been Ken's key contact over the years, both by phone and in person. She even became so involved that she took a pile of request forms home and got her mother to help her fill them out over a weekend. She wanted to make sure everything would be ready when Ken and Colleen showed up on Monday morning. Without her invaluable help, we would still be trying to figure out where to start.

Mike Walker, researcher at the Operational Archives Branch of the Naval Historical Center in Washington, D.C., who gave excellent help over the phone and always returned calls.

Archerfish shipmate Robbie Roberts, who made the trip up from Charleston to the National Archives Washington National Records Center in Suitland, Maryland, and spent an entire day copying deck logs.

Archerfish shipmate Dick Aubin, who spent a day at the Northeast Region Branch of the National Archives in Waltham, Massachusetts, locating and copying much of the information we have about the boat's construction, commissioning ceremony, and sea trials . . . almost everything prior to the first war patrol.

Stephen Kehl for information on his father, Commander George Kehl, *Archerfish*'s first skipper, and his memories about the day the boat left Portsmouth for the Pacific Theater.

Still more material was gleaned from various newspapers and navy publications. Wherever that exclusive information was used in the book, the publication has been credited.

In addition to the deck logs and patrol reports, some of the information in the chapter on the sinking of the *Shinano* was taken directly from Captain Joseph Enright's personal notes that he prepared while writing his own excellent book on the subject. The authors are most appreciative to Kristine Enright King, Captain Enright's granddaughter, for saving and sharing the information following his death. The book, cowritten with James W. Ryan, was originally published in 1987 by St. Martin's Press under the title, *Shinano!* It was reissued by St. Martin's Press as a mass-market paperback in 2000 under the title *Sea Assault*. We highly recommend the book to anyone with further interest in *Archerfish*, or, for that matter, in naval history in general. It's a wonderful story and Mr. Ryan and Captain Enright did a magnificent job telling it.

The authors also appreciate the sharp eye and shared knowledge of Commander (Retired) George Wallace, former skipper of USS *Houston* (SSN-713), who not only helped with proofreading the manuscript but also offered information on some technical points as well as information on more recent submarine technology that we used in the book. While commanding *Houston*, Commander Wallace invented the swimmer lockout procedure used by Navy SEALs. He is Don's cowriter on a novel, *Final Bearing*, published in 2003 by Forge Books.

Special thanks go to Bill Tunnell, the executive director of the USS *Alabama* Battleship Memorial Park in Mobile, Alabama, and to his staff. They were kind enough to allow us an all-access tour of the wonderfully restored USS *Drum* (SS-228) to give Don a better idea of how the boats were laid out and equipped and bring back for Ken a million renewed memories. We especially appreciate the time and efforts of the boat's caretaker, Leslie Waters, who took time from her pressing chores on a hot day to show us around the boat. Thanks to Leslie as well for answering our questions. She also had some for Ken that have been asked by visitors to the boat over the years. Bill, we hope you've located propellers for the old girl by the time this book is out.

Finally, we have to thank all the men who shipped out on an old diesel boat named *Archerfish*, those still with us and those on eternal patrol. You see, if you had not lived it, there would have been no story to tell.

Ken Henry
Rainbow Springs, Florida

Don Keith
Indian Springs Village, Alabama

Index